IMPORTANT VOICES

North Dakota's Women Elected State Officials Share Their Stories 1893–2013

To Sophie,

I hope you are inspired by these stories,

Susan Wefald

IMPORTANT VOICES

North Dakota's Women Elected State Officials Share Their Stories 1893–2013

By

Susan E. Wefald

FEATURING

Heidi Heitkamp, Rosemarie Myrdal, Kathi Gilmore, Kelly Schmidt, Sarah Vogel, Kirsten Baesler, Beryl Levine, Mary Maring, Carol Kapsner, Laura Eisenhuth, Emma Bates, Minnie Nielson, Bertha Palmer, Berta Baker, Bernice Asbridge, and Ruth Meiers

With a Foreword and Conclusion by

Dr. Kjersten Nelson

Published by the Institute for Regional Studies Press
North Dakota State University
Dept. 2360, P.O. Box 6050, Fargo, ND 58108-6050.
www.ndsu.edu/ahss/ndirs

Important Voices: North Dakota's Women Elected State Officials
Share Their Stories, 1893-2013

By Susan Wefald

Book design by Deb Tanner.
International Standard Book Number: 978-0-911042-79-5
Library of Congress Control Number: 2014957334
Printed in the United States.

THIS BOOK IS DEDICATED TO MY SON
Thomas Olav Wefald (1977-2013)

Tom and I talked together on the phone as I was writing *Important Voices.* He could sense my enthusiasm as I researched the stories of the North Dakota women who had first served as elected state officials. As always, he was encouraging and supportive of my new "project." At age 17, he was so excited when I won my first election to the Public Service Commission. I remember him bringing a friend up to the 12th floor of the Capitol building, where they sat in the commissioners' chairs in the hearing room and took pictures of themselves pretending to be commissioners. When I attended a commissioners conference in San Francisco, Tom, his sister Kate and his friend Derrick accompanied me and skateboarded their way through the city. He died in a vehicle accident in Kings Canyon National Park in late August 2013. Tom was a terrific son and man who also loved to write. He kept a journal for over 20 years, which is a wonderful keepsake for our family.

This book is also dedicated to all of the women who ran for statewide office in North Dakota but did not win.

THANK YOU TO THE FOLLOWING FOR THEIR HELP IN WRITING THIS BOOK

Thank you to my husband, Bob, who served as North Dakota attorney general (1981-84), and demonstrates daily the meaning of "public service." Thank you to my daughter Sarah, a computer engineer, who is always willing to offer her mom "tips" on working with her computer. Thank you to my daughter Kate, a talented writer, who read through my drafts and offered suggestions.

Thank you to Marty Boeckel, who helped me with important contacts at the start of this project. Thank you to Kathy Davison for her guidance and advice on Laura Eisenhuth.

Thank you to Jim Davis and the other staff at the State Archives of the State Historical Society of North Dakota for helping me locate all of the reports, books, photos and letters that I wanted to use as I wrote Important Voices. Any proceeds I receive from the publication of this book as author and editor will be donated to the State Archives of the State Historical Society of North Dakota.

Thank you to the Bismarck Tribune for access to its files and photographs.

CONTENTS

INTRODUCTION

The women in this book are fabulous. Each one, from Laura Eisenhuth to Kirsten Baesler, is a pioneer. Many of them were the first woman to be elected to their particular office in North Dakota. Among the hundreds of men who have served as our statewide elected officials, only 17 women have been chosen by North Dakotans for this service from 1889 to 2013.

State Superintendent of Public Instruction Laura Eisenhuth is notable because she was the first woman in the nation to be elected to statewide office.

These women state officials knew how to overcome challenges. Berta Baker only went to school until she was 14, but as state treasurer and then auditor, she was an expert on the state's finances during the Great Depression. Superintendent of Public Instruction Minnie Nielson had to get an order from the Supreme Court before she could occupy her office. Beryl Levine was 35 years old with five children when she decided to go to law school and eventually become our first woman Supreme Court justice. Each woman who has served has been an important voice in government. They influenced and made important decisions.

As of summer 2014, the score card of women serving as *elected* officials in North Dakota state government is: U.S. Senator – one; U. S. House – none; Governor – none; Lieutenant Governor – two; Attorney General – one; Secretary of State – none; Treasurer – four; Auditor – one; Tax Commissioner – one; Agriculture Commissioner – one; Public Service Commissioner – one; Insurance Commissioner – none; Superintendent of Public Instruction – five; Supreme Court Justice – three. (Two women have held more than one elected office.)

Important Voices focuses on the time period when each woman held statewide office. Many of the women held legislative, local or county office before running for statewide office, but these stories are for another book. They are mentioned in passing so that readers know how the women gained knowledge and skills before running for statewide office.

The emphasis in this book is to use *the words of each woman state official* to tell her story. Each living state official, except Beryl Levine, has written her own chapter, telling her story in her own way, choosing what she wanted to share about her time in office.

It is almost impossible to find this type of information when researching the deceased women elected state officials. News articles are helpful but rarely tell how the woman feels about what is happening. People didn't save private journals or letters they wrote about their experiences. Perhaps, like most people today, the women were just too busy to record their thoughts. Maybe readers of this book will know of, and share, lost correspondence with archives in our state.

Important Voices shares the experiences of these fascinating women. People who contributed to this book wrote their stories with the hope of inspiring more women to serve as elected state officials in North Dakota. Hopefully, this book will serve this purpose. Our state needs the "important voices" of many women leaders as it meets the challenges of the 21st century.

Also, perhaps this book will encourage more public scholarship on each of these special women.

All proceeds that I receive from this book as author and editor will be donated to the State Archives of the State Historical Society of North Dakota to further their important work.

Susan Wefald

THE NORTH DAKOTA LIST

Women Elected to Statewide Office as of Summer 2014

Laura J. Eisenhuth, Superintendent of Public Instruction, 1893-1894*

Emma F. Bates, Superintendent of Public Instruction, 1895-1896

Minnie J. Nielson, Superintendent of Public Instruction, 1919-1926

Bertha R. Palmer, Superintendent of Public Instruction, 1927-1932

Berta E. Baker, State Treasurer, 1929-1932

Berta E. Baker, State Auditor, 1933-1956

Bernice Asbridge, State Treasurer, 1969-1972

Ruth Meiers, Lieutenant Governor, 1985-1987

Heidi Heitkamp, Tax Commissioner, 1986-1992

Sarah Vogel, Agriculture Commissioner, 1989-1996

Rosemarie Myrdal, Lieutenant Governor, 1993-2000

Heidi Heitkamp, Attorney General, 1993-2000

Kathi Gilmore, State Treasurer, 1993-2004

Susan E. Wefald, Public Service Commissioner, 1993-2008

Kelly Schmidt, State Treasurer, 2005 to -

Kirsten Baesler, Superintendent of Public Instruction, 2013 to -

Heidi Heitkamp, U.S. Senator, 2013 to -

Women Elected to the North Dakota Supreme Court

Beryl Levine, Supreme Court Justice, 1985-1996

Mary Maring, Supreme Court Justice, 1996-2013

Carol Kapsner, Supreme Court Justice, 1998 to –

*First woman in the nation to be elected to statewide office

FOREWORD

By
Kjersten Nelson

At one time, North Dakota was a path-breaker when it came to women in politics. In 1893, the state's first statewide elected official – Superintendent of Public Instruction Laura Eisenhuth (Chapter 11) – was also the nation's first woman elected to statewide office. Two years later, North Dakotans elected the nation's first female Republican to statewide office when Emma Bates became the Superintendent of Public Instruction (Chapter 12). In 1933, less than two decades after American women earned the right to vote, state Representative Minnie Craig became the nation's first female speaker of the House. During her tenure 50 years later, state Representative Tish Kelly served as the country's only female speaker of the House. Later that decade, Sarah Vogel was elected state Commissioner of Agriculture, the first woman in this position in the U.S. (Chapter 5).

Paired with these incredible firsts, however, is an underlying trend of female underrepresentation in state elected offices. North Dakota has never had a female governor. While it elected its first woman to the U.S. Congress in 2012 (Senator Heidi Heitkamp, Chapter 1), it was the 44th state to do so.[1]

The state ranks 41st in the percentage of the state Legislature that is female. With 17 percent of its Legislature female in 2014, it falls beneath the national average of 24.2 percent. Perhaps most notable is how unfavorably this legislative percentage stacks up to the state's neighbors. Minnesota ranks fourth in the nation (33.8 percent female); Montana is 17th, with 27.3 percent; and South Dakota, with 22.9 percent, is ranked 28th in the nation.[2] At the same time, this places North Dakota amongst states that are not typically seen as culturally similar. It shares the 41st rank with Arkansas; Virginia is ranked 40th (with 17.1 percent), while Tennessee and Wyoming are tied for 42nd (16.7 percent). In fact, North Dakota, Wyoming and Utah are the only states in the bottom 10 which are not considered part of "the South."[3]

It's more difficult to compare states based on statewide elected positions because the total number of these varies so much by state, but a quick comparison of North Dakota to its neighbors reveals a similar, though not identical, situation. As of 2014, 25 percent of North Dakota's statewide elected offices were occupied by women, compared with 15 percent of South Dakota's, 36 percent of Montana's and 57 percent of Minnesota's.[4]

Into this context comes the current volume, which gives the reader an in-depth view of the women who have succeeded in statewide elected office in North Dakota – when possible, in the official's own words. In this area – i.e., the study of women in North Dakota politics – we encounter what social scientists like to call a "small 'n' problem." In other words, the universe of women who fit this description (that is, women who have been elected to statewide office in North Dakota) is too small to analyze with statistical methods strictly for technical reasons. Instead, here the reader gets a qualitative investigation of the exceptions to the rule. These narratives may highlight several things: how are these women, who "made it," different from the average North Dakota woman? What set them on this path to a specific, but rare, type of public service? Ultimately, how could these findings be translated into practical ideas for increasing North Dakota women's ambition for elected office and making these positions more open to – even welcoming of – female candidates?

Capturing these stories is important for several reasons. First, from the perspective of history, it is vital to have these stories accessibly entered in the public record. Those too immersed in their modern perspective may lose sight of the specific obstacles pioneers faced: I hope that none of us reading this will have to endure being referred to, publicly, as "little woman," as Berta Baker did (Chapter 15), or need to develop a unique strategy for winning the office of Superintendent of Public Instruction because it is the only election women are allowed to vote in (as candidates for this position had to do before 1917.)[5]

These stories tie into a larger question, though, of why it is important to study women in politics – or to advocate for more women in politics – in the first place. After all, one of the main tenets of at least one wave of feminism is that few, if any, fundamental differences exist between the sexes. At least, no differences that should matter when it comes to running for office or governing. However, scholars have found some empirical differences in the types of policies that elected women focus on, as well as the way that they conduct business. Female Democratic and moderate female Republican members of Congress, for example, were found to be more likely to sponsor bills associated with stereotypical "women's issues" – issues like domestic violence, women's health and childcare.[6] Female members of Congress were also more likely to use floor time to talk about these issues.[7]

Lieutenant Governor Ruth Meiers (Chapter 17) provides an excellent example of an elected official who focused on these policy areas and acknowledged women's general tendency to prioritize these types of issues. Lieutenant Governor Rosemarie Myrdal also devoted a significant portion of her time in office to children's and education issues

(Chapter 2). Supreme Court Justice Beryl Levine wrote many key decisions, oftentimes in dissent, that urged the state Supreme Court to take new approaches to family and divorce law, approaches that often emphasized the interests of children and women. Moreover, she spearheaded efforts to address issues of gender discrimination and imbalance in the state's legal system (Chapter 8). Attorney General Heidi Heitkamp highlighted domestic violence during her time in that office, well before it was widely discussed. Since entering the Senate, she has focused on protections for Native children(Chapter 1), as well as measures to crack down on human trafficking, including sex trafficking.[8]

Studies of state legislatures have found similar things.[9] The issue agenda may change as women achieve a certain "critical mass" of representation.[10] More female representation could mean a real difference in a state where women earn, on average, 78 cents for every dollar the average man earns.[11]

Moreover, once women achieve success in elected office, leadership styles tend to change. In Chapter 7, Superintendent of Public Instruction Kirsten Baesler emphasizes her approach to leadership as being a "servant leader." This comports with studies of female leadership in state legislatures. Again, this change is dependent upon women's representation reaching a "critical mass" – but when it does, leadership styles tend to become less hierarchical and more inclusive.[12] It seems it can only be a good thing if our democratic institutions become more open to a diversity of leadership styles; these studies suggest that gender diversity may be one means of achieving this goal.

Finally, the study of women in politics, and the advocacy to break down barriers that keep more women from these offices, is vital from the perspective of future leaders. From a very young age, many individuals strongly identify with one gender or the other. The distinct lack of gender representation from one major group – women – puts limits on the aspirations and dreams of the next generation of leaders. The lack of representation also sends a distinct message, one that is undergirded throughout the culture: Important positions are reserved for men.[13] Even if there were *no* observable differences in the issue focus or leadership style of elected female leaders, the lack of role models and the reinforcement of this second-class status is reason enough to label this shortage a problem.

I hope you enjoy reading about these inspiring women. This volume is long overdue; but the proud – if limited – history of women in statewide elected office in North Dakota is, finally, all in one place for us to ponder.

Making an Impact on North Dakota

1986-2013

ONE

Standing Up for Every North Dakotan

By

Mary Kathryn "Heidi" Heitkamp

State Tax Commissioner
1986-92

Attorney General
1993-2000

U.S. Senator
2013 - Present

"Making tough decisions and taking sides is an essential part of leadership. You have an opportunity to make the 'right' decisions. If your goal is 90 percent of the vote, to be loved by 90 percent of the people, then you may have a tough time making the hard decisions that have to be made as a state official."

U.S. Senator Heidi Heitkamp

Mary Kathryn "Heidi" Heitkamp*

1955-Present

Tax Commissioner 1986-92
Attorney General 1993-2000"
U.S. Senator 2013-present

Senator Heidi Heitkamp - 2013
(Senator Heitkamp's office)

First Woman in North Dakota to Serve as Tax Commission, Attorney General and U.S. Senator

First Woman to hold Three Elected Statewide Offices in North Dakota

Personal Information
Born 1955 in Breckenridge, Minnesota, and raised in Mantador, North Dakota. Married to Darwin Lange, two children. In "spare time," enjoys grabbing a cup of coffee with friends.

Party Affiliation
Democratic - Nonpartisan League

Education
Hankinson High School; received B.A., University of North Dakota; awarded J.D. Lewis and Clark Law School, Portland, Oregon.

Professional Experience Through Time in Office
Environmental Protection Agency Attorney, Washington, D.C., 1980-81; Office of North Dakota State Tax Commissioner, Assistant Attorney General, 1981-85; Administrative Counsel, 1985-86. North Dakota Tax Commissioner, 1986-92. North Dakota Attorney General, 1993-2000. Director, Dakota Gasification Company's Great Plains Synfuels Plant, 2001-12.

Memberships Include
As Tax Commissioner: Multistate Tax Commission, vice chair, 1987; Federation of Tax Administrators, board of trustees.

As Attorney General: Presidential Appointment to Trade and Environmental Policy Advisory Committee, Office of the U.S. Trade Representative; National Association of Attorney Generals (International Trade Issues Task Force, vice chair; Bankruptcy and Tax Working Group, chair; Supreme Court Committee, vice chair); Juvenile Justice Task Force, chair.[14]

*Bio contains information through 2013

On November 8, 2012, I stepped up to the microphone in Fargo to talk to my supporters. I was probably still in shock after my narrow 3,000-vote win in the U.S. Senate race against Congressman Rick Berg. I had carried Fargo and Cass County by 9,900 votes, which was remarkable since Fargo was my opponent's home town. I was so excited and thrilled to be going to the U.S. Senate that it didn't matter that my voice was hoarse after months of campaigning. "To the extent people are calling this historic, to the extent people are calling this an upset," I announced, "pat yourself on the back!"

Drawn to Public Policy Issues

In 1972, when I was 17 years old, I worked on Byron Dorgan's first campaign for Tax Commissioner. Although my family, with seven children, did not discuss politics much at home, my maternal grandmother always loved party politics, and was a strong and verbal "Roosevelt" Democrat. I must take after her with my interest in politics and public service.

So it was not surprising when I attended the University of North Dakota from 1973 to 1977 that I decided to major in history and political science. I was interested in issue-oriented politics. I became involved with a letter-writing campaign to support the Equal Rights Amendment (ERA) and was delighted in 1975, when ERA passed in the North Dakota Legislature. I was also interested in surface mining and other environmental issues, and so I decided to attend Lewis and Clark Law School in Oregon, which specialized in environmental law.

After law school, I moved to Washington, D.C., and worked for the U.S. Environmental Protection Agency (EPA) for a year and a half in 1980-81.

It was while I was working at the EPA that I met Democrat Kent Conrad, who had just been elected North Dakota Tax Commissioner. One of his attorneys had left to go to work for Senator Quentin Burdick. Kent met with me in Washington, D.C., and we had a great visit. He wanted me to work on his staff as an attorney. I wasn't really convinced I wanted to do tax law but decided it was a good place to start in North Dakota.

I had decided to get involved in public policy issues in my home state, having just seen the impact a presidential election was having on public policy. It reinforced that it matters who you elect.

My First Run for State Office

In 1984, when I was 28 years old, I ran for state auditor. I had no idea I would be running for office until I got to the Democrat state convention in Minot. It was one of those campaign years when the party had a difficult time finding a candidate for state auditor. My boss, Tax Commissioner Kent Conrad, without telling me, put up huge posters on the walls that read "Heitkamp, Heitkamp, Heitkamp" and people at the convention began to encourage me to run. Geraldine Farraro was running for Vice President of the U.S., and I was part of the Democratic NPL Woman's Caucus. The caucus was working to get a woman on the ticket as lieutenant governor. We were not bold enough yet to set our sights on a woman candidate for governor.

It became pretty important to the people at that Minot convention to have a "gender balanced ticket." Bud Sinner promised to select a woman to run as lieutenant governor, and that is one of the reasons he received the nomination for governor at the convention. He chose Ruth Meiers and Ruth wanted another woman on the ticket.

When I received the party endorsement, many people came up to me and promised to help in whatever way they could, and they followed through on their promises, which doesn't always happen. And most of those people were women.

My opponent in that race was Republican Bob Peterson, a 12-year incumbent. Lieutenant Governor candidate Ruth Meiers and I campaigned together. We would pick a town and go visit the cafes, the radio station, the newspaper, go to a political event and raise $20 or $30, stay overnight with a friend, and start the whole process over again the next day.

I campaigned hard around the state and raised the issue that Bob Peterson, incumbent state auditor, was behind on state audits – although it was 1984, he was working on audits from 1976. I lost the election by only a few percentage points. However, by the time Bob Peterson ran again, he was up to date with his audits. It's important to remember, even losers can have an impact on how state officials perform.

This was a terrific first campaign experience. I loved driving around North Dakota and meeting North Dakotans. I lost the election, but the race was fairly close. It was probably my favorite campaign.

Appointment by Sinner for Tax Commissioner in December 1986

When Kent Conrad was elected U.S. Senator in November 1986, Governor George "Bud" Sinner had a chance to appoint the new Tax Commissioner.

I knew Sinner from the 1984 campaign when I had run for state auditor, and I had four things going for me to get the appointment: I knew Sinner. I had campaign experience in 1984. I had come close to winning the election against Bob Peterson. I knew the issues in the tax department because I had been an attorney in the Tax Department since

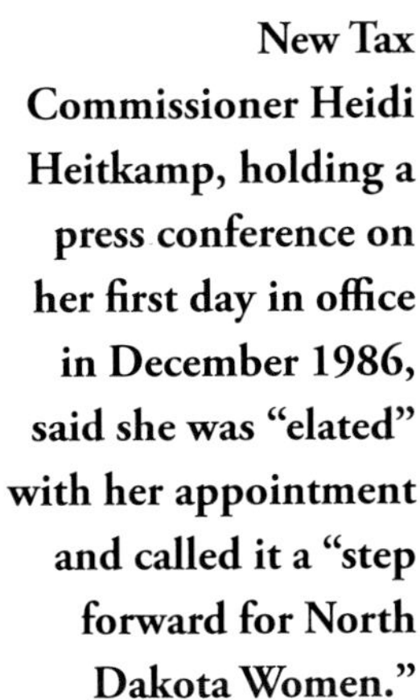

New Tax Commissioner Heidi Heitkamp, holding a press conference on her first day in office in December 1986, said she was "elated" with her appointment and called it a "step forward for North Dakota Women."

(*Bismarck Tribune* photo file - Casey Lake photo)

1982 and chief attorney since 1985.

Sinner was under some pressure to appoint a woman. This appointment was considered a plum appointment because former Tax Commissioner Byron Dorgan had been elected to Congress and his successor Kent Conrad to the U.S. Senate. Tax Commissioner was seen as a stepping stone to higher office.

Sinner announced my appointment on December 1, 1986, and on December 2, 1986, I became the first woman to serve as the state's Tax Commissioner. In my first remarks to the press as Tax Commissioner, I announced, "I will be a very visible female in a very important position, and I welcome that challenge."

My Six Years as Tax Commissioner

Early Days in Office

As soon as I took office in December 1986, I was involved with addressing important state tax issues. Because of the need to avert a negative ending balance for the 1985-87 biennium (there was a $27.7 million projected deficit), Governor Sinner called a special session of the Legislature in December 1986. Along with other measures enacted to beef up state revenue, the special session passed a bill which included the provision to withhold state income tax from all employees who had federal income tax withheld.

This became a big political issue. When referral petitions on this matter were filed with the Secretary of State at the end of December, Governor Sinner called a special election for March 1987. The voters approved withholding the state tax, and the measure went into effect at the conclusion of the 1987 legislative session.

On May 13, 1987, I made my first appearance before the U.S. House of Representatives Ways and Means Committee. Here I was 31 years old, state Tax Commissioner for six months, and I was testifying in front of a U.S. House Committee. Pretty heady stuff. I testified on a bill Congressman Dorgan had sponsored, the "Interstate Sales Tax Collection Act of 1987." The bill would have closed a tax loophole which benefited out-of-state businesses and denied states tax revenues. It is interesting to note that as a U.S. Senator, 25 years later, I have been working on a bill which would achieve the same goal – which the Senate passed for the first time when I helped lead it in the chamber.

Description of Official Duties as Tax Commissioner

Four-year term. Supervises the state's property tax system, assessors and assessments of real property, including the public utilities and railroads; administers and collects income tax, sales and use tax, cigarette tax, oil and gas gross production tax, oil extraction tax, coal severance tax, motor fuel tax, privilege tax on coal conversion facilities, estate tax, and tax on banks and savings and loan companies; administers other laws under which taxes are paid to county treasurers, such as the bank and savings and loan taxes, taxes on rural electric cooperatives and mutual telephone companies; represents North Dakota on the Multistate Tax Commission; offers expert testimony to the legislative assembly on tax legislation.

Member: Board of Tax Equalization, secretary.[15]

Spiegel and Quill Litigation

Forcing interstate retail firms to collect and remit state sales tax to North Dakota was an important issue for the Tax Department and involved millions of dollars of potential revenue for the state. In 1987, right after I took office, the Legislature passed a bill which expanded the state's sales and use tax jurisdiction to include direct marketers.

In July 1988, the Tax Department filed an action in district court requesting the court to declare that Spiegel Inc. must obtain a North Dakota sales and use tax permit, and collect and remit state use taxes on sales made into North Dakota.

I was proud to announce in April 1989 that Spiegel Inc. had agreed to an out-of-court settlement of the lawsuit. Subsequent to that settlement, Spiegel agreed to collect use taxes in all states.

In July 1989, the Tax Department filed a suit against Quill Corporation, which marketed office supplies, equipment and furniture from out of state. Quill Corporation also did not want to collect or pay sales and use tax on sales made in North Dakota. I kept close watch on this important case for the rest of my career at the Tax Department as it progressed through the North Dakota court system and was heard by the U.S. Supreme Court in 1992. However, in 1992, the Supreme Court ruled that Quill did not need to collect or pay use taxes because the corporation did not have a physical presence in the state.

The Fair Share Program

My staff and I worked hard to use tax payer money wisely. Starting in 1983, the Legislature had agreed to appropriate $960,000 for additional audit staff and travel money if the Tax Department could generate $10 million a biennium in additional tax collections.

Each biennium, the Tax Department made the goal and funding contingent. During the 1987-89 biennium, the Fair Share program resulted in more than $12.1 million additional tax collections – $2 million over the biennial goal.

The 1988 Election

My friend Joe Satrom went out to lunch with me in 1988, when I was running for my first four-year term as Tax Commissioner. During lunch Joe asked me, "What are we going to do to convince the public that you are competent?" Well, I was quite taken aback when he said this. Here I had been on the job for two years, doing a very good job as Tax Commissioner, and he seemed to think people still needed convincing. However, I decided to confront that question during the 1988 election, and this is still an important question when women run for any position in government.

My opponent in 1988 was Republican Marshall Moore. When the November votes were tallied, I won the election by 90,000 votes.

Drought and Tough Economic Times

A severe drought in 1988 and 1989 compounded the economic problems facing North Dakota individuals, businesses and government. 1990 brought adequate moisture to the state for the first time in three years. While 1991 was a year of recession nationally, North Dakota continued on a path of slow recovery, and that year the legislative assembly was able to enact a budget without the need for a tax increase.

Litigation – True Family

One part of the job of Tax Commissioner is making decisions on disputes regarding tax law. One important piece of litigation during my 11 years at the Tax Department was the True family dispute. The True family, who owned many businesses involved with the oil industry, had filed state taxes from 1973 to 1982. Then the True family sought a major refund, and as an attorney with the Tax Department, I was involved with the Tax Commissioner's decisions in 1984 and 1986 to deny their claims.

By October 1989, the True family claimed the state owed them $4 million in refunds and interest. In 1989 as Tax Commissioner, I denied their claim after an administrative hearing, and the case, known as *True v. Heitkamp* went on appeal to district court and the North Dakota Supreme Court. The Supreme Court upheld my decision in May 1991.

Personal Computers

It is difficult to imagine now, but it was a big step in the 1987-89 biennium when I decided that each auditor would have access to a portable personal computer! You must remember in 1987, most personal computers were quite large and bulky. However, I wanted to increase the productivity of the audit staff, and wanted each auditor to be able to transfer, at the audit site, information from the databases to their portable computers. The Tax Department tried to use the latest technology available through state government.

A Working Woman's Guide to Living in the Real World – Juggling Family and Work

Of course, my other life as a mom and wife went on while I was holding state office. Ali, my daughter, was born in 1985, and my son, Nathan, was born in 1990. Sometimes I wonder how I managed. My husband, Darwin, and I didn't do a lot besides go to work and go home and take care of our kids, home and yard. I soon realized that there were closets in my home that had not been cleaned in five years. I knew that some mornings we struggled to get the kids to school on time. I soon found that I did not have perfect children because I was not the "perfect" mother or the "perfect" wife. And many days I went to work dog tired.

Combining a full-time career with being a wife and raising kids is not easy. I used to think, if only I was more organized, if only I was smarter, if only I had not gained those pounds since high school, life would surely be better. And the days passed, and the wrinkles came, and I thought, I really cannot take much more of "having it all."

But after a while I realized:

1. There are only 24 hours in a day.
2. Our time is just as important as our bank account.
3. Not one of us, no matter how outwardly successful, is perfect.
4. The challenges that our mothers faced are not our challenges, and the challenges that we face are not our mother's challenges. Our daughter's challenges will be different from ours.

I knew I had to redefine "having it all." It took me awhile, but I could see that I could not keep a perfect house, be a superwoman at the office, raise two children involved in every extra activity they expressed interest in, and take on other volunteer positions as well. But I found I could be an excellent state official, keep a healthy house and raise great kids without putting them in every activity known to mankind. I also asked for help when I needed it from my husband and extended family.

So when people ask me, "Can I have it all?" The answer is "No, you cannot." All is too much to ask. When our focus is on the "all," the game is rigged and failure is not only possible, it is certain.

In Greek mythology, there is a character named Sisyphus who angered Zeus, and so Zeus condemned Sisyphus to rolling a rock up the hill, only to have the rock fall before it reaches the top. Even though Sisyphus knows that he will never get to the top, he keeps rolling the rock. Some philosophers have argued that Sisyphus is a heroic figure because, even though he will never succeed, he keeps trying.

I think Sisyphus is a tragic figure. Just think about what he could have accomplished if he had joined the real world and lived in the land of the possible.

I learned to dream big, but realistic dreams. The dreams must be my own, and they must not involve a life of rolling a rock up a hill only to fail to reach the top.

The 1992 Election Year – Musical Chairs in the Democrat Party

In 1992, I decided to run for Attorney General. It was a very interesting campaign year due to the interest in the congressional races, the race for governor and my own campaign. Bill Clinton was running for President against incumbent George H.W. Bush.

By 1992, Byron Dorgan had already been the state's lone congressman for 12 years. Kent Conrad, who had won the race for the Senate against Mark Andrews in 1986, had served in the U.S. Senate for six years. In 1986, Kent had made a campaign promise that he would not run for his seat in the U.S. Senate in 1992 if Congress hadn't balanced the budget. Congress did not balance the budget, and Kent announced that he would not be a candidate for the U.S. Senate.

Kent Conrad actually acting on his promise surprised people. But they were not surprised when Byron Dorgan decided to run for Kent Conrad's U.S. Senate seat. This allowed North Dakota Insurance Commissioner Earl Pomeroy to announce that he would run for the U.S. House seat previously held by Byron Dorgan.

After 11 years in the Tax Commissioner's office, I was ready to move on. I had assumed that Earl Pomeroy would run for Attorney General in 1992, but he backed out and ran for Congress, and it gave me an opportunity to become involved in issues that I wanted to be involved in. I think like a lawyer, and it made sense to take a lawyer's job and run for Attorney General.

Then in September 1992, Senator Quentin Burdick died. Governor Sinner appointed Mrs. Quentin (Jocelyn) Burdick to serve as U.S. senator until December 14, 1992. Jocelyn Burdick was the first woman to serve in the U.S. Senate from North Dakota. Kent Conrad announced he would be running for the U.S. Senate seat previously held by Quentin Burdick, and Kent was elected to the U.S. Senate in a special election in early December.

Meanwhile, Republican Ed Schafer was running for Governor against former Attorney General Nick Spaeth. Spaeth had not received the nomination for governor at the spring Democratic convention, but he decided to put his name on the primary ballot. When the votes were counted after the June primary election, Spaeth became the Democrat candidate for governor.

I was running for Attorney General against Republican Warren "Duke" Albrecht. During my campaign, I visited towns all across the state and discussed many issues, including domestic violence and defending state financing for public schools. I won the election by over 70,000 votes. I was 37 years old.

Working as North Dakota Attorney General from 1993-2000

As North Dakota Attorney General, I had one of the most interesting jobs in the country. I was the chief legal officer of the state with a staff of 149 people organized into 10 divisions. Below are just a few of the important issues in which I became involved as Attorney General.

Domestic Violence

Before I ran for Attorney General, I had a friend whose cousin was in a domestic violence situation. I asked if she needed help getting an attorney, and I was told that the

Description of Official Duties as Attorney General

Four-year term. The Attorney General is the legal adviser for all state departments, officials and agencies; renders legal opinions to state officials, the legislative assembly, state's attorneys and city attorneys upon request; functions as the state's chief law enforcement officer, supervising the Bureau of Criminal Investigation, the Criminal Regulatory Division, the Drug Enforcement Unit, the Fire Marshall Division, the Natural Resources and Indian Affairs Division, the Gaming Division and the Consumer Fraud and Antitrust Division; issues licenses for retail alcohol beverage establishments, Class A and Class B gambling organizations, detectives and detective agencies, hearing aid dealers, polygraph (lie detector) operators, and amusement games and devices.

Member: Board of Pardons, Board of University and School Lands, Industrial Commission, Judicial Conference, Interstate Oil Compact Commission, North Dakota Federal Practice Committee.[16]

cousin had found an attorney.

A few months later, I read in the paper that both the cousin and her child had been shot and killed by her husband. She was running to her car, carrying her child to safety, and was shot in the back and killed, and then he killed the child.

What I could not understand was that the paper described the husband as a nice guy. "How could any man who killed his wife and child be described as a 'nice guy'?"

Therefore, one of my first initiatives as Attorney General was to create and develop a five-year plan to address the domestic violence problem in North Dakota. Before I came to office, domestic violence had mainly been a public health issue. Now I advocated that the state criminalize it. Intervention made a difference. Bonnie Palecek, director of the North Dakota Council on Abused Women's Services, provided great support for my work in this area.

Local task forces were established to coordinate and create the most effective violence prevention efforts and to provide training to local law enforcement agencies, prosecutors, judges and domestic violence prevention program participants.

By 1997, there were 13 local domestic violence task forces in North Dakota, and training had been offered in 28 locations to over 700 peace officers, prosecutors and domestic violence prevention advocates.

The Minnesota Externalities Law

In the 1990s, 70 percent of the electricity generated in the state of North Dakota was exported to other states – mainly to the state of Minnesota. Most of the electricity was generated from burning lignite coal in our huge power plants in the center of our state. Although Minnesota needed electricity, wind power advocates in Minnesota wanted to develop more renewable energy in their own state. They advocated putting in place a

Minnesota tax (externalities cost) on lignite-generated electricity, which would increase the cost of North Dakota-produced electrical power in Minnesota and reduce purchases of that power by Minnesota energy companies. Although I could understand their desire for more renewable energy, the tax was unconstitutional and bad news for an important industry in our state.

Throughout the 1990s, I worked closely with the lignite industry on this case as the state of North Dakota challenged the constitutionality of the Minnesota tax. I was a frequent speaker at the Lignite Energy Council annual meetings, where I would give updates on this case and other legal cases affecting the lignite industry.

Tobacco Settlement

In the mid-1990s, more than 40 states sued tobacco companies for serious issues such as violating antitrust and consumer protection laws and withholding information about the adverse health effects of tobacco. I was chosen to be one of the leaders in the negotiations that led to the historic tobacco settlement in November 1998. The settlement resulted in the award of about $336 million to North Dakota taxpayers to date and required tobacco companies to tell the truth about smoking and health. It was one of the largest civil settlements in U.S. history. I am very happy that I could be a part of reducing tobacco-related deaths in our state.

Our state, along with 45 other states and a number of territories, negotiated the settlement over six months in 1998. The settlement contained provisions prohibiting the tobacco companies from targeting advertising toward children, for monetary payments to the state, for restrictions on the tobacco companies' participation in lobbying efforts and the establishment of the American Legacy Foundation, a national foundation established to reduce tobacco usage in the U.S. through a public education campaign.

My work in this area did not end when I chose not to run for another term as Attorney General in 2000. In 2008, I worked with others in a campaign to pass Initiated Measure No. 3. This initiated measure would require the state Legislature to use the tobacco settlement funds to fund a comprehensive tobacco prevention and control program at the recommended U.S. Centers for Disease Control and Prevention spending level. This level of support required only 16 percent of the money coming into the state from the lawsuit.

I provided a great deal of public information as a spokesperson for Initiated Measure No. 3 and was very pleased when 54 percent of the voters approved the measure.

Shutting Down Meth Labs

As prices fell and police pressure increased on the West Coast, methamphetamine (meth) dealers spread their operations to rural North Dakota. Our sparsely populated prairies offered isolated, private places to produce meth. From 1995 to 1997, the narcotics section of the Attorney General's office helped close down nine meth labs that were capable of producing large quantities of meth. All of these labs were in western North Dakota except for one in Fargo. Also, extensive training was provided to both local law enforcement and fire department personnel because of the dangers posed by meth labs to public safety personnel.

The 1997 Grand Forks Flood

Although our state had many disasters in the 1990s, the 1997 Grand Forks flood was a disaster of historic proportions. The water in the Red River had been rising for days, after a very snowy winter with high amounts of precipitation. Grand Forks residents worked tirelessly to build the river dikes to 49 feet, the projected crest of the river.

However, on Saturday morning, April 19, Mayor Pat Owens announced that Grand Forks residents should evacuate the city within a few hours. Over 50,000 people needed to seek shelter in public spaces or with friends and relatives around the state. The Red River, which crested at 54 feet, went over the top of the levy and spread quickly throughout the city. Then major fires broke out downtown. All utilities were affected, and it was weeks before people were allowed to return home and start rebuilding their homes and lives.

One important aspect of the work of the Attorney General's office during the aftermath of the flood was to require background checks on all contractors coming into the city to perform clean-up work. Working with the National Guard and other state agencies, the Consumer Protection and Antitrust Section of the Attorney General's office set up "one stop shops" in Grand Forks to ensure that contractors met state requirements in order to do business in the state. Picture identification cards were issued to provide residents an assurance that businesses doing renovation work in their area were properly licensed.

I visited Grand Forks after the flood and could not believe the devastation and work that would be required to restore living conditions in this beautiful city. Having lived in Grand Forks as a college student, I had a personal relationship to the city and its people. As a state official, I did everything I could to help the city recover.

Consumer Protection

Furniture stores were running suspect "sale" ads in the newspapers, on TV and radio, and there were a number of complaints about their practices. So while I was Attorney General, the Consumer Protection and Antitrust Section drafted deceptive acts or practices rules. However, the furniture store retailers were adamant that they didn't want the new rules.

I decided to attend one of the proposed rule-making meetings to share some thoughts with these retailers. "I have an idea," I said. "Let's eliminate all regulation on this. And then every week, I will run an ad saying, 'Don't believe anything you read in the furniture advertisements.'" Well, they didn't think that was a good idea, but they got the point and were willing to talk about proposed rules. *Deceptive Acts or Practices Rules* went into effect in 1994.

My Favorite Attorney General Opinions

As Attorney General, I issued many "opinions" on questions that were posed to me by legislators, state officials and other officials identified in state statute. One of my favorite opinions was in response to a question from Mr. Charlie Whitman, the Bismarck City Attorney, regarding improvements to the intersection of Avenue C and Washington Street in Bismarck. In my response, I determined that the boulevard trees in the Bismarck Cathedral Area Historic District were an integral part of the historic district (2000 L-36). This opinion may very well have saved the beautiful, huge trees that still line the streets and avenues near the intersection in question.

Another favorite opinion (2000-F-05) was requested by Dennis Johnson, McKenzie County State's Attorney. The question presented was whether federal land in North Dakota can be burdened by public roads established by prescription under state law and by the state's section line law. My opinion was that federal land in North Dakota can be

Attorney General Heidi Heitkamp and Agriculture Commissioner Sarah Vogel riding in a horse and carriage in a 1994 Minot Parade. (SHSND 11078-41)

burdened by public roads established by prescription under state law and by the state's section line law. In the opinion, I noted that the right to use such roads has "existed for over 100 years and it is a 'vested' and 'absolute right.' This right, until recently, has never been questioned by the federal government."

Fun Moments as Attorney General

One day when I was working with the Land Board, I had strong opinions about one of the issues and I said, "Now this is the deal," and I went on to lay out my ideas about how to take care of one matter on the agenda. After the meeting, a farmer in the audience came up to me and said, "So you kind of run things around here!"

Another time, I had to run to the store and just ran out in a very casual outfit, hair a mess, and was hoping I would not run into anyone I knew. However, as I was leaving the store, a man spotted me, and said, "Hey, aren't you that Heidi Heitkamp?" "Yes," I said, as I stopped, waiting for a tirade on something the man didn't like about my work. Instead, he smiled at me and announced, "I like your stuff."

Working With the Legislature

When working with the Legislature, I saw my role as an advocate. And, to be effective, I knew that I could not be the only voice advocating an issue. For example, if I was advocating legislation regarding crime issues, I would recruit sheriffs, chiefs of police and other law enforcement personnel to testify to legislative committees on the issue.

Although many people had a hard time working with House Majority Leader John Dorso, he and I worked well together. I tried to find common ground on issues. Also, the Legislature respected my assessment of the legality of legislation and the need for information. One of my duties was to tell the Legislature if a proposed law was unconstitutional.

However, as a Democrat, I did have my problems working with Republican-dominated legislatures. The Legislature was not generous with my budget and it removed attorneys from my office. For example, in 1995, five Workers Compensation Bureau attorneys were transferred from the Attorney General's office and put under workforce safety.

Then, in 1999, the Legislature attempted to take me off the Industrial Commission, where I served with Republican Governor Ed Schafer and Democrat Agriculture Commissioner Roger Johnson. The Legislature passed a study resolution, which stated, "Whereas, because the Attorney General serves the dual roles of member of the Industrial Commission and legal counsel for the commission, the responsibilities of these roles may conflict at time … ." Of course, this was not a new situation since the Attorney General had been a member of the Industrial Commission since it had been established in 1919.

I worked with others to provide helpful information to the interim committee studying this issue and other aspects of the work of the Industrial Commission. In the end, the committee did not make any recommendations for changes.

Serving on the Industrial Commission

I found I spent about one-third of my time addressing the legal issues of the state, one-third on administration of all the other sections within the Attorney General's office (Bureau of Criminal Investigation, etc.) and one-third on Industrial Commission business.

The Industrial Commission is the public board which provides leadership and makes policy decisions for several agencies and programs, including the Bank of North Dakota; the North Dakota Department of Mineral Resources, which includes the Oil and Gas Division; the North Dakota Housing and Finance Agency; and the North Dakota State Mill and Elevator.

During my first four years on the Industrial Commission (1993-96), I served with Republican Governor Ed Schafer and Democrat Agriculture Commissioner Sarah Vogel. It was the first time in the history of the state that women held two of the three seats on the North Dakota Industrial Commission. Sarah was the first woman to serve on the Industrial Commission, and I was the second to hold this position.

I enjoyed the work of the Industrial Commission and I enjoyed working with Ed and Sarah on the issues before us. For example, as part of our work in the Department of Mineral Resources, I loved learning the important research work which was being done by the North Dakota Geological Survey, headed by John Blumley, in the mid-1990s.

Lessons I Have Learned

Politics

Politics gives me an opportunity to do the job and the public policy work I do. My least favorite part of politics is raising money – my favorite part is meeting people. It is always interesting to see how other people view you, which is probably different than how you view yourself.

Leadership

Making tough decisions and taking sides is an essential part of leadership. You have an opportunity to make the "right" decisions. If your goal is 90 percent of the vote, to be loved by 90 percent of the people, then you may have a tough time making the hard decisions that have to be made as a state official.

Speaking Out on Important Issues

I am known for speaking my mind on important public policy issues. Early in my career, sometimes people would try to clarify my remarks or soften them, or say things that I felt undermined what I had to say. I would just say to them, "No, that is not what I said. I said what I wanted to say."

Advice for young women

Be confident that you can do the job.

Running for Governor in 2000

Some years are unforgettable. The year 2000 was such a year for me – the excitement at the spring Democratic convention when I was nominated for governor, executing the campaign plan, travelling around the state and talking with people about jobs, wages and education. I was running against John Hoeven, the President of the Bank of North Dakota.

My husband, Darwin Lange, was my biggest asset during my campaign for governor. When I give talks about politics, I always say "choose your partner wisely." I am not sure he has great patience for the political process, but he believes in what I do. Throughout the 2000 campaign, he did his work as a family medicine physician *and* he helped raise our kids, who were 14 and 9 at the time. The public didn't see him – he's very shy, but I couldn't have run the campaign for governor without him.

By September, Hoeven and I were running very close in the polls. Then on September 20, I held a press conference announcing I had breast cancer and that I would need to have surgery and chemotherapy. So, in the final weeks of the campaign, I was a wife and mother, Attorney General, on the campaign trail as a candidate for governor, and recovering from surgery to remove my right breast and surrounding lymph nodes. I had also started receiving chemotherapy.

I could have resigned from the race for governor. But my daughter, Ali, a competitive swimmer, looked at me one day and said, "Mom, you aren't going to quit running for governor, are you? You've worked so hard, it would be like getting out of the pool before the last leg of the 100 meter. You've got to finish!"

I finished the race for governor, participating in debates, holding news conferences and attending rallies. However, in November, I lost the election to John Hoeven. I didn't realize until I lost the race for governor how invested my husband was in my political climb. Losing the race was hard for me, but it was really hard on him. And, of course, we were both very emotionally involved in my battle with cancer.

After the campaign was over, I needed time to regroup, spend time with my family and work on new projects. I did not realize when I finished the governor's race in 2000 that it would be 12 years until I sought another political office.

My 2012 Campaign for the U.S. Senate

When Senator Kent Conrad announced in 2011 his planned retirement from the U.S. Senate, I decided to run for his Senate seat. I knew that it wouldn't be an easy race, but I didn't shy away from something that would take hard work. And my fellow Democrats were thrilled that I was interested in running for Kent's seat. So in mid-March 2012, I found myself at the Democratic-Nonpartisan League convention in Grand Forks, accepting my party's nomination to run for the U.S. Senate.

Former President Bill Clinton was the guest speaker at the convention, and he gave me a great send-off as I started the campaign. Everywhere I went, I talked about the need for our country to have a balanced budget, the importance of energy and agriculture to our state, and how innovative North Dakotans were in creating new ways of doing things.

My opponent was Republican Rick Berg from Fargo, who had been elected to the U.S. House of Representatives in 2010.

I knew I would need to raise a great deal of money for this U.S. Senate race since my opponent was also raising a great deal of money. Between the two of us, we raised and spent a total of $11.8 million on the Senate campaign, which was more money than had ever been spent on a U.S. Senate race in North Dakota. One of my favorite fund-raising events during the campaign was a "hot dish" fundraiser in Fargo attended by Public Radio's Garrison Keillor and Minnesota's first woman U.S. Senator, Amy Klobuchar.

Senator Kent Conrad and former Senator Byron Dorgan were extremely helpful during my campaign, but as the candidate, I had to make the decisions each day and live with those decisions. I participated in TV debates, hired staff, recruited volunteers, created a great website, walked in parades, made commercials, attended picnics and gave people plenty of opportunities to shake my hand. Although the campaign kept me very busy, this time around, my children were grown, and I was able to campaign and not also be responsible for a state agency at the same time.

I knew the race was close. It really didn't sink in that I had won until I gave my mother a hug at 2 a.m. the morning after the election, when I came out to greet the public in Bismarck. I was tired from all the activity of the final days of the campaign. But there is nothing like a "win" to give you all the energy you need to keep on going.

U.S. Senator

Description of Official Duties as U.S. Senator

Six-year term. Represents the people of North Dakota as one of two U.S. Senators in the 100 member U.S. Senate.

113th Congress Committee Assignments: U.S. Senate Committees on Agriculture, Nutrition and Forestry; Banking, Housing and Urban Affairs; Homeland Security and Governmental Affairs; Indian Affairs; Small Business and Entrepreneurship.

The U.S. Senate Swearing-in Ceremony

As I entered the Senate chamber to the take the oath of office on January 3, 2013, it was a true honor to have both Senator Conrad, my friend and mentor, and Senator Dorgan walk me in. They are giants in my mind – and giant advocates for North Dakota. It was a symbolic passing of the torch. Just like they were, I want to be someone who is not just fighting for North Dakota, but also getting things done. My goal is to try to live up to the high standard they set for our state and the Senate. It is not an easy task.

After the swearing-in, there was a reception held in my honor where so many of my friends from North Dakota hugged and congratulated me. Vice President Joe Biden came through to welcome me to the Senate, as did many other Senators. Also present were Senators Conrad and Dorgan, and Congressman Earl Pomeroy beaming with pride. Throughout the day, most of my siblings and my dear friends, Rosey Sand, who was Deputy Attorney General when I was Attorney General for North Dakota, Deb Klein and Donna Rockstead joined the festivities. That's how my family does it – we surround each other with support.

On Presiding Over the Senate

As a freshman Senator, I preside over the Senate chamber for about three hours per week. While some may consider this a tedious task, I enjoy it. It's been a great way to learn about how the Senate functions, including the many arcane procedures, as I get to see it in action. I've been there presiding for some of the biggest debates on the Senate floor over the past year – from immigration reform to the Marketplace Fairness Act to the government shutdown, and so much more. From that chair, I have seen partisanship at its worst. But I have also seen Republican and Democratic Senators work together to support important legislation to help their constituents.

My favorite part is when I'm the first Senator presiding for the day. Before the Senate begins its business, everyone in the chamber stands and we recite the Pledge of Allegiance. The first time I led the Senate in the Pledge of Allegiance, I became quite emotional. It was this "ah-ha" moment and a powerful reminder that I'm just a kid from Mantador, North Dakota, who is now serving as a U.S. Senator for the state and people I love so much. Each time I lead the Senate in the Pledge of Allegiance, I think about where I am, how far I've come and what I'm here to do. I always am reminded that we live in a great country.

Tackling Important Issues

Over the course of my first year in the Senate, there are many policies that I've been proud to fight for on behalf of North Dakotans. But one stands out. On October 30, 2013, I introduced my first bill in the Senate to create a Commission on Native Children. The commission would conduct an intensive study into the issues facing Native children – such as high rates of poverty, staggering unemployment, child abuse, domestic violence, crime, substance abuse and few economic opportunities – and make recommendations on how to make sure Native children are better taken care of and given the opportunities they deserve.

Since working as Attorney General in the 1990s, I have spent a great deal of time in Indian Country, seeing firsthand the obstacles tribal governments confront in responding to the needs of Native children. I pledged that once I was in a position to do something to help these children, I would. It's only appropriate that my first bill in the U.S. Senate would take a serious look at the challenges facing Native children and offer real solutions to fix them.

I also pledged to work across the aisle to find real solutions for North Dakotans. Republican Senator Lisa Murkowski of Alaska helped me introduce this bill. We bonded early on, talking about the need to stand up for Native children, and we united over the need for legislation to address this issue head on. When I eventually leave the Senate, if I haven't done anything to help Native families, I'll consider that a failure.

I came to the Senate because I want to get Congress working again and I want to stand up for every North Dakotan. Every day that I'm in the Senate, I'm working to do just that – and that will not waver.

TWO

My Experiences as Lieutenant Governor

By

Rosemarie Myrdal

North Dakota Lieutenant Governor
1993-2001

Capital for a Day –
"I visited the schools, nursing home, hospitals, museums and participated in special events like bed racing in Garrison … . As we returned to Bismarck, we had a better understanding of the citizens that we served and what they thought about state government."

Rosemarie Myrdal

Rosemarie Myrdal nee Lohse*

1929-Present

Lieutenant Governor 1993-2000

Lieutenant Governor Rosemarie Myrdal - 1996
(*Bismarck Tribune* photo file)

Personal Information

Born 1929 in Minot and lived on a farm near Mohall until she was 10 and then moved to Fargo. Married to John (died in 2000), five children. In "spare time," enjoyed going back to their farm in Pembina County.

Party Affiliation

Republican

Education

Fargo Central High School; received B.S. from North Dakota State University.

Professional Experience Before Taking Office

Teacher, Business Manager for Edinburg Public School District; Member Edinburg School Board; served four terms in the North Dakota House of Representatives, 1985-91.

Memberships and Committees include

As Lieutenant Governor: State Investment Board, chair; Children's Services Coordinating Committee, chair; Governor's Americans with Disabilities Act Consortium, chair; Yellowstone-Missouri Fort Union Commission, chair; Capitol Grounds Planning Commission, chair; Red River Trade Corridor, board member; Governor's Centers of Excellence in Rural American (CERA), coordinator; National Conference of Lieutenant Governors.

Other: Volunteer for Camp Sioux for Diabetic Children; North Dakota Diabetes Association, board member; Pembina and Red River Valley historic and cultural preservation activities.

*Bio contains information through 2000

From a Pembina County Farm to Bismarck

John and I were sitting at the kitchen table with our three sons the morning after a July hailstorm in 1984. There were going to be no crops to harvest and we needed to change our plans for the summer and fall. As we talked among ourselves, John said, "We have the cattle and there will be plenty of hay to cut." The sons, in anticipation of a good harvest, had bought a new combine. They would look for custom combining. The best idea I had was to promise to take the first job offer.

The next morning, J. Oliver Johnson, our Republican precinct committeeman for District 11, called with a question: "Would I consider putting my name in for endorsement to run for the House to replace the candidate who was moving to New Mexico?" I said, "Yes." At the meeting of the District Committee, I was endorsed to run for the House with Representative Alice Olson and Senator Kent Vosper. We campaigned together and I was elected to serve in the 1985 legislative session with Alice and Kent. I served four terms in the House, and in the 1991 session, I served on the Appropriations Committee. During that session, I was part of an informal group of House members who searched for candidates who would seek endorsement for state office. As part of that effort, I attended a Republican candidate recruitment retreat at the Rivery south of Bismarck.

After the day's discussion and meetings were over in the late evening, I headed to the kitchen to hunt for a bedtime snack. I found Ed Schafer in the kitchen, and we shared a visit over milk and toast, talking about the candidates seeking endorsement at the 1992 state convention. In April in Grand Forks, Ed Schafer, Bismarck, was one of the three candidates seeking endorsement for Governor. The other two were Gary Nelson, Casselton, and Gary Porter, Minot. Ed Schafer won the endorsement, and a messenger from Ed came asking me to a meeting with him. Would I consider running with him for the office of Lieutenant Governor? I said "Yes, but first let me talk to John." John agreed that it was a good idea. So within a very short time, I was giving my acceptance speech to the delegates.

The next step was to develop a campaign strategy. The Democrats, in the primary election, chose Nick Spaeth, Attorney General, to run for Governor, and his running mate was Julie Hill, a House member. Now we had to convince the North Dakota voters to vote for the Schafer-Myrdal ticket.

The 1992 Statewide Campaign

As the campaign plans developed, it became obvious that Ed and I came to the campaign with diverse experiences and from different North Dakota communities. We built a campaign using some of that potential to relate to voters. I was the first Republican woman to run for the office of Lieutenant Governor. I came to the campaign with legislative experience. I had worked as a teacher, school business manager and school board member. I had a degree from North Dakota State University and had grown up in Fargo. I was married to a northeastern North Dakota farmer, John Myrdal, and we had three farmer sons and two California daughters.

Ed had a very different North Dakota background. We knew different people and places, but we shared common values and beliefs. We campaigned separately and together. I had a campaign assistant, my niece Melanie Smith. I have memories of Melanie carrying a big black bag containing a very early version of the cell phone. We were supposed to use this to keep in touch with the office, but cell phone towers were few and far between, and few calls were completed.

On a cold and snowy day in November 1992, North Dakota voters elected Republican candidates, and Ed and I were chosen to serve as Governor and Lieutenant Governor for four years. I was the first Republican woman elected Lieutenant Governor. After watching election returns that snowing evening, I realized that I would be living and working in Bismarck for the next four years, and I was anxious to get started.

Description of Official Duties as Lieutenant Governor

Four-year term (elected with the Governor). The Lieutenant Governor acts as chief executive in case of the Governor's death, resignation or on other occasions when the Governor is unable to fulfill his responsibilities; serves as President of the Senate and in the event of a tie may cast the decisive vote; assumes other board chairmanships and functions as prescribed by the Governor.[17]

A New Home and a New Office

The first thing I did was rent an Arikara apartment next to the Arrowhead Shopping Center. This was within walking distance of the Capitol. The shopping center was like a small town main street where I could walk to do my shopping, I could walk to church and to the YMCA, and even fill my car with gas for the trip home to the farm.

The 1993 Inaugural Ball was a festive occasion, and I very much enjoyed sharing the celebration with my family, friends, the campaign staff, and Ed and Nancy. The next thing was settling into the beautiful front office just off

Lieutenant Governor Rosemarie Myrdal is escorted by Sen. Bill Devlin and Sen. Lyle Hanson into the 1999 joint session of the Legislature. (Rosemarie Myrdal photo collection)

the Great Hall. Ed had chosen to have the large office down the hall, with the conference table for staff meetings. Ed and I agreed to combine our reception and support staff, and I attended the early morning staff meetings, listening and participating in the discussions. I enjoyed these meetings and Ed's leadership style.

The Legislature went into session the first week in January and I was the presiding officer for the Senate. Carol Siegert, Secretary of the Senate, met with me to go over the agenda for the day and to prepare me for my duties. I was new to the Senate and I had a lot to learn, and I was grateful for Carol's guidance.

As we organized for our executive branch work, I found that many of the committee chairmanships for the Lieutenant Governor came from legislation. Other committee assignments were to be made by the Governor.

One of the Schafer campaign promises was to carefully reduce the size of state government. This meant reducing the number of state employees. Ed created a committee to do this, with the Lieutenant Governor as the chair. I worked with Rod Backman, Ed's appointee to the Office of Management and Budget. The committee was to meet with agency heads who wanted to fill openings created when state employees resigned or retired. Department heads were to explain to the committee why they had to fill the position and could not assign duties to other employees. Sometimes after thoughtful discussion, they agreed that they could manage with one less employee. This was part of the effort to use tax money wisely.

Moving From the Legislative to the Executive Branch

As I accepted my assignments in the executive branch, I began to think about the differences between these two branches of government. During the eight years as a member of the House of Representatives, I voted on a multitude of laws. When a law is passed, it often instructs the executive branch to do something. Elected state officials, including the Governor and Lieutenant Governor, can set up committees and assign duties, but they have to follow the laws. For instance, state law says that the Lieutenant Governor is the president of the Senate and shall preside over meetings of the Senate.

Voters elect a number of state officials: for instance Attorney General, Secretary of State, State Treasurer, Agriculture Commissioner. The Governor does not tell these officials what to do. But the Governor does appoint a number of state officials: for example, Director of the Office of Management and Budget, Highway Patrol, Director of the Department of Human Services, Department of Tourism, Department of Transportation.

These people in the executive branch work with the Governor to serve citizens honestly and efficiently and to use tax money to provide high-quality public services, as directed by the Legislature.

My committee assignments made by the Legislature included the Children's Services Coordinating Committee and the Centennial Trees Committee. Governor Schafer made the appointment for me to chair the State Investment Board. I am not sure how I came to be appointed to the School to Work Committee. That federal program would be part of the Department of Public Instruction working with the Clinton administration.

I found myself chairing many committee meetings and found that to include working with state employees. The committee chair works on the preparation of the meeting agenda, needs to understand the goals of the committee and then use Roberts Rules of Order to move forward with decisions on how to accomplish the goals. It helps to understand the issues and the people on the committee and the legislative intent. There was always plenty to learn in my capacity as the chairman.

The Children's Services Coordinating Committee (CSCC)

As newly elected Lieutenant Governor, I held my first meeting with the CSCC in December 1992. The committee was to meet four times a year and it had a long history. In 1985, Governor George Sinner appointed a Commission on Children and Adolescents at Risk (CAAR). The purpose was to plan for the effective delivery of services to children and adolescents at risk.

In 1987, the Legislature adopted the CAAR recommendations creating the CSCC, with Lieutenant Governor Lloyd Omdahl as chair. In 1988, the Annie E. Casey Foundation funded a pilot project in Region 8 (Grand Forks) called Families First. I participated in the Families First project as a legislator from Pembina County.

By 1989, the state CSCC committee (agency heads dealing with children and families) came up with a plan to create CSCC committees in each of the eight regions of the state and the four tribal nations. After seven years of planning beginning with the work of Lieutenant Governor Ruth Meiers, the Legislature voted to provide $2 million for the statewide organization of the CSCC committees. I must have voted to do this in the 1991 session.

So there I was in December 1992, chairing the committee with a plan and an appropriation. The 1993 Legislature again provided funds for these newly established regional CSCC boards. I remember that not all of my Republican legislator friends favored this idea. And we talked about it in my office. The Families First Region 8 was the model for the other regions.

Now the project became unique to North Dakota. Federal funds for Children and Families were available but required matching state funds provided by legislative appropriation. But there was another option: (the Families First idea). This was to fund the federal match by doing time studies of state and local money being spent to provide services for foster care children and families. Don Schmid, Director of Children and Family Services from the Department of Human Services, was instrumental in setting up and guiding the project.

The first regional time study reports prepared by the local participants resulted in federal refinancing claim of $3.75 million. The Families First project was working.

Meanwhile, the tribal CSCC committees were organized so that they could do time studies and submit claims, too. But there was one problem. The tribes don't collect local taxes and were funding their local programs for children and families with U.S. federal treaty money. The rule was you can't fund federal match with federal money. As a person interested in history, I had often thought of treaty money as land rent to the tribes so that homesteaders could live on and farm the land that had been formerly used by the Indians. Maybe that "land rent" money could be used as federal match.

Working with Don Schmid, we came up with a plan to talk to the Bureau of Indian Affairs in Washington, D.C. I went to Washington and found my way to the office of Hilda A. Manuel from Wisconsin, Acting Deputy of Indian Affairs, and explained to her what we were doing for children and families in North Dakota and our match idea. She promised to see if she could make it happen. A little while later, she sent a letter to Don and the tribal CSCCs could also participate in time study refinancing.

The total federal match funds received from five claims (1994-2001) was $28.1 million. This money was allocated to the tribes and regional CSCCs to be used for locally identified needs for children and families. During this period, the national Kids Count report gave North Dakota top rankings in the years 1993-2001 for the well-being of children and families.

After 1997, no more state general funds had been appropriated to meet federal foster match requirements. The match funds were state and local funds identified with CSCC regional and tribal time studies. Other states and tribes began to take notice of this unique North Dakota project and finally Washington began to realize the financial impact if this idea spread to other states. The time study match was no longer accepted and the state Legislature did not appropriate money for the match. Only in Region 5 and Region 2 did the local match continue, funded by foundation grants. It was the end of the CSCC era.

Fetal Alcohol Syndrome (FAS) and the Four State Consortium

As I worked with issues relating to services for children and families as part of my involvement with the CSCC, I became part of a committee of human service providers concerned with FAS. By attending those meeting, I began to understand the relationship of FAS to many problems with foster care and children and families. FAS is a condition of lifetime brain damage created by prenatal exposure to alcohol, with a higher incidence among Native American tribal members. As chairman of CSCC, I could see it affecting foster care, adoption, special education, the juvenile justice system and the Department of Corrections.

This condition is preventable if mothers do not drink alcohol during pregnancy, preventing lifetime brain damage. Dr. Larry Burd of the University of North Dakota conducts research into ways of preventing FAS. I was impressed with his project.

The Four State Consortium

I attended a national conference in Maryland of Lieutenant Governors in 1995 representing North Dakota. The conference program was about issues relating to the well-being of children and families, especially African American families. After one of the sessions, I was sitting with the Lieutenant Governors from Montana, South Dakota and Minnesota, and I talked about FAS prevention research. We all shared Native American Indian populations and a concern about FAS. The discussion resulted in an agreement to explore the idea of a Four State Consortium to share research and prevention program ideas.

The first meeting of the state representatives was in North Dakota, and each state adopted a special prevention study initiative: Montana, prison population with FAS; South

Dakota, restricting access to alcohol for pregnant women; Minnesota, special prevention programs; and North Dakota, special education services for children with FAS. Each state agreed to share research on its issue and participate in symposiums. Funding for the consortium was obtained from the federal Department of Health with help from Senator Byron Dorgan. Dr. Larry Burd, UND School of Medicine Fetal Alcohol Syndrome Research Center, became the program coordinator. The work goes on with research and prevention projects. Dr. Burd is working with the North Dakota Department of Health to improve prenatal care with an emphasis of preventing FAS.

State Investment Board

The State Investment Board chairman was the Governor's appointment, and Ed gave me this assignment. Perhaps he thought my work on the House Appropriations Committee made me qualified. It was a great opportunity for me to work with the state investment officer, Steve Cochrane, and the board in making investment decisions at board meetings. This was serious work because these funds needed to grow at an 8 percent rate to cover the retirement payments to public employees and teachers. The board hired professionals to give advice, and I learned about the process of investing funds to earn maximum returns while being very serious about managing risk. During the years I served as chairman, it was a reasonably stable investment climate.

The Centennial Trees Committee

In 1989, North Dakota was celebrating 100 years of statehood, and the Centennial Committee decided that a statewide goal to plant a million trees was a great idea. When I took office and inherited the chairmanship, there were still some trees left to plant. The State Forester, Larry Kotchman, was anxious to achieve this goal by encouraging tree planting across the state. I have always been enthusiastic about planting trees and I looked forward to the annual Arbor Day celebrations, where we participated in a community's tree planting efforts.

I have Arbor Day memories of standing outdoors in cold, windy weather giving short speeches to shivering audiences. One Arbor Day, we participated in the planting a Family Forest in Bismarck south of the Game and Fish Department headquarters. Nancy Schafer and I helped parents and children pick up their trees and put them in the ground. Those trees are growing taller each year in the Family Forest.

Another tree memory is of a trip to Regina, Saskatchewan, to thank the Canadians for a gift of prairie-hardy tree seedlings. The Canadians are good at ceremonies, and I was invited to review red-clad Royal Canadian Mounted Police cadets at their academy. It was a memorable moment.

Just recently, I read about tree planting in Adams County. One of the Centennial Trees Committee ideas was to work with the Department of Transportation to plant living snow fences. According to Larry Kotchman, Adams County planted 400 miles of trees between 1999 and 2008.

School to Work

Bill Clinton was elected president in 1991, and Ed and I served in North Dakota during his presidency. School to Work was a program designed to improve the workforce by encouraging schools and students to prepare for participation in the job market.

This was a federal program, and in North Dakota, it was under Wayne Sanstead, Superintendent of Public Instruction. My qualifications for this assignment were the years I had spent in the K-12 education as a teacher, school business manager and school board member. I chaired this committee, with Dean Monteith as the executive assistant. Local school districts could choose to participate in this program and receive federal money. Schools were encouraged and supported in setting up programs for curriculum changes, counseling, and college and career planning. Dean and I represented North Dakota at national meetings and participated in discussions with state representatives from across the country.

Centers of Excellence in Rural America (CERA)

As Governor of North Dakota, Ed Schafer was committed to working with the Legislature and elected state officials to diversify the North Dakota economy and encourage private economic development. During his first term, Ed became very interested in the potential that information technology (IT) represented for economic development. In conversations with a Bismarck High School classmate retired U.S. Navy Admiral Bill Owens, he saw an opportunity for rural North Dakota communities. Admiral Owens offered to arrange for technical support from Science Applications International Corporation (SAIC), which was a San Diego-based defense contractor.

CERA was to be a pilot project seeking to promote the use of IT to create jobs in a rural community. The early oil boom in western North Dakota was over and Watford City, McKenzie County, was one of those cities seeking a new economic strategy. Gene Veeder, Economic Director for McKenzie County, was enthused about the CERA idea and Watford City became the pilot community.

I was assigned to work with SAIC and Watford City to explore and model the use of IT to create jobs. SAIC provided a consultant to work with Gene and the community and to educate the Governor's office about the developing IT world. I traveled with this consultant to view a model city in Orlando, Florida, and to Camden, Maine, to a conference featuring IT pioneer professors.

Gene worked in Watford City with issues relating to infrastructure, job training and call center development. Gene found that it was hard to get US West interested in connecting a small town to the Web. McKenzie County Electric, a rural electric co-op, accepted the challenge to make Watford City a wired community. As I look back on those meeting and plans, I can appreciate Ed's vision and business experience.

Capitol for a Day

Governor Schafer really liked people, and he was happy to spend time listening and talking with his fellow North Dakotans. Capitol for a Day was the Governor's idea and became that kind of event. Communities were encouraged to invite Governor Schafer and his staff and agency heads to spend a day in their town and to plan a full day of activities and meetings. Law enforcement, transportation, county social services, senior centers, schools, local businessmen and local legislators had a chance talk with their counterparts at the state level.

I visited the schools, nursing home, hospitals and museums, and participated in special events like bed racing in Garrison. The four of us driving home in the Highway Patrol

Lt. Governor Myrdal (third from left) standing next to Governor Ed Schafer with the Schafer-Myrdal 1996 Campaign Team. The picture is inscribed, "Hi Rosemarie! Remembering a great campaign team! Ed." (Rosemarie Myrdal photo collection)

car with Colonel Jim Hughes talked about what we had learned at Capitol for a Day. As we returned to Bismarck, we had a better understanding of the citizens that we served and what they thought about state government. The morning briefing papers were good preparation, but talking to the citizens was very good.

The National Prayer Breakfast

I attended the National Prayer Breakfast in Washington in February of 1994. I was part of an audience of 3,000 that included President Clinton and his wife, Vice President Gore and his wife, and congressional leaders.

Mother Teresa, an 83-year-old nun, was the main speaker. I will never forget her words about the social ills of America, including abortion. She said America has become selfish and that abortion is one expression of that selfishness.

The next few years, Governor Schafer sponsored a Governor's Prayer Breakfast in Bismarck, and I was always privileged to be part of that expression of Christian faith in a non-governmental setting sponsored and organized by a local group.

Speeches and Travel

As Lieutenant Governor, I was often invited to local events to give a speech or represent the Governor. I usually drove a state car if the distance was less than 100 miles. Sometimes Colonel Jim Hughes provided travel and security arrangements. For trips over 100 miles, I often went by plane, sometimes catching a ride with Department of Transportation engineers. I remember trips to Williston to meetings with state and local historic site people. I was with the state historical people flying off to the northwest on dark winter evenings. The rich history of the region made the trips so worthwhile.

Another kind of travel experience was driving south toward the South Dakota border with Bertha Gipp from the Health Department to visit the Standing Rock reservation. We had good conversations about life on the reservation and Bertha's experiences there as a nurse. Deb Painte, Indian Affairs Commissioner, was another Native American friend, and one year, I was her guest riding in the car with star quilts on the hood in the Bismarck Pow Wow parade.

For national Lieutenant Governor meetings, I would fly from Bismarck to the meeting site, often Washington, D.C. I usually traveled without security. But one memorable time when I arrived for a Lieutenant Governor national meeting in Rhode Island, I was met by a state Highway Patrol officer who was assigned to provide security throughout the three-day conference. I was happy to go on a long walk with him one evening to explore the Capitol grounds and Portuguese neighborhoods.

Going Home to the Farm December 2000

As I prepared to leave the beautiful front office, people came from the State Heritage Center to pack up boxes of papers and collectibles with historic significance. I watched those boxes go off to the Heritage Center, and I was thinking about what I was taking home with me, especially a multitude of memories and friendships and a great appreciation and affection for North Dakota. I also knew that I would be getting organized and be learning to live in my familiar northeastern world without John.[18]

Now in 2013 as I have written about those eight years as Lieutenant Governor, I realize that people in government today are still dealing with many of the same issues. The list includes the well-being of children and families, problems with drug and alcohol abuse and addiction, investment of retirement funds to provide enough money to pay retirement benefits and, of course, development of a skilled workforce to serve the growing economy. There are no permanent solutions.

One more thing: I am glad I accepted the offer to put my name in to run for the District 11 House seat after that July hailstorm in 1984.

A Thank You Note

These are the people who helped me research and remember my work as Lieutenant Governor: Don Schmid and Karla Mittleider, CSCC; Larry Burd, FAS and the Four State Consortium; Naomi Myrdal, names and titles; and especially Susan Wefald, who gave me an assignment and a deadline.

THREE

Baptism by Fire

By

Kathi Gilmore

North Dakota Treasurer
1993-2004

"It is a fact of life that if you are of one party and the majority of the legislative branch is of the other, the majority party cuts your budget, cuts your staff, literally cuts the size of your office, and then attempts to eliminate it altogether. All of this happened during my 12 years in the office."

Kathi Gilmore

Treasurer Kathi Gilmore - 1992
(*Bismarck Tribune* photo file)

Kathi Gilmore nee Simpson*

1944–Present

State Treasurer 1993-2004

Personal Information

Born 1944 and raised in Modale, Iowa. Married to Richard, four children. In "spare time," is a voracious reader, family entertainer and sports enthusiast.

Party Affiliation

Democratic Nonpartisan League

Education

West Harrison High School, Mondamin, Iowa; attended North Dakota State University, Bottineau Branch.

Professional Experience Before Taking Office

Partner in a family-owned business for 10 years; served two terms in the North Dakota House of Representatives, 1989-92.

Memberships and Committees

As Treasurer: National Association of State Treasurers, president of Midwest division and also a member of the Pensions Committee; National Council of State Treasurers; College Savings Plan Network; National Conference of State Liquor Administrators; Retirement and Investment Office Internal Audit Committee; State Employee Incentive Committee; Council of State Governments Strategic Planning Committee.[19]

*Bio contains information through 2004

I was born in 1944 in a small town in Iowa. My parents were people who believed strongly in participatory government. My father served on the town council for our small community and he served as secretary/treasurer for the school district. Mother was involved in a very substantive way in the community also. For many years, she served in a variety of positions within the church at a local, district and regional level. She was a 4-H leader for 25 years and judged 4-H fair entries at a local, county and state level. She also served for 30 years on the election board at the local and county level. You can see that as a young girl, I was exposed to the idea of public service – they planted the seed and it grew.

Getting Started in North Dakota Politics

We first arrived in North Dakota in 1966 when my husband accepted a job. Dick served in several locations, and our last move and longest stay was in Bottineau in 1973. The District 6 Democrats asked me, in 1975, to sit on the election board as a Democrat. I wasn't politically active but liked the neighbors who approached me to serve in that capacity, so I said yes. I began attending the district meetings and was asked to run for Vice Chair Woman for District 6. I was delighted! I attended policy level meetings in Bismarck and had a bird's-eye view of women at work in politics. Women I admired – Senators Corliss Mushik, Tish Kelly, Bonnie Heinrich, Sarah Vogel and a young Heidi Heitkamp. I was impressed!

When I first got involved in the party, we held the Senate seat and both House seats. Within a few years, Senator Erdman moved from the district and Representative Larry Herslip was defeated. Dave O'Connell moved into the Senate race and we struggled through several election cycles to win back the House seats. I ran for a House seat in 1988 on the Democrat ticket. The campaign was a learning experience centered around meeting the public and listening to their concerns. I was pleased to win a very competitive race. I served that session with Senator O'Connell (D) and Beth Smette (R). Beth was a fine legislator and I found her to be genuine and lovely. I enjoyed serving with her! Other women from both sides of the aisle that I admired were Corliss Mushik, Tish Kelly, Bonnie Heinrich, Janet Wentz and my very favorite - Brynhild Haugland. I had a particular admiration for Brynhild. She was honest, fair and cared deeply about North Dakota.

In the 1988 race, I was paired with Brian Skaar and we both won! In 1992, because of redistricting, we found ourselves potentially running Democrat against Democrat. In other words, the redistricting committee placed three Democrat Representatives from two gerrymandered districts in a race for two positions. The question became: Did I want to run against friends in a district race or did I want to move to a statewide race? The years of service in the North Dakota House had been positive. I had worked hard and formed strong opinions about the difference between fairness and cheap political maneuvers. Had my baptism by fire equipped me for a statewide race? I hoped so. I began to explore the possibilities.

Running for State Treasurer in 1992

There were two races I was interested in – Public Service Commission and State Treasurer. I sought advice from party officials, elected Democrat officials and family. They all pointed me to the State Treasurer's race. Leo Reinbold was an incumbent on the PSC with a long record of service, a sense of humor, and was known statewide. He was a hard campaigner, loved being a Commissioner, and was, in my mind, virtually unbeatable. The Treasurer's office, on the other hand, was an open seat. The office was term-limited and the incumbent, Bob Hanson, couldn't run for another term. My decision was made. In the summer of 1991, I threw my hat in the ring.

Campaigning on a statewide level is a grueling job. Every day during the election, I was up and on the road to somewhere, speaking to groups on the issues they were concerned about, shaking hands, riding in parades, sometimes several in a day – and always listening to the people, learning about the state and the needs of the people. To

Kathi Gilmore's three grandchildren joined her on the campaign trail when she ran for state treasurer in 1992. (Kathi Gilmore photo collection)

Description of Official Duties as State Treasurer

Four-year term. The state Treasurer's office is organized into four main divisions: Administration, Controller, Collection and Alcoholic Beverages. The office receives, manages and disburses state funds; renders accounts to the Office of Management and Budget, reports on activities and status of the treasury; maintains custody of state securities and copyrights, records all transactions relative to securities held or owned by the state; collects beer and liquor taxes; acts as state liquor administrator and licenses liquor and beer wholesalers; maintains the Permanent Fund; distributes money to political subdivisions from the highway tax, coal severance tax, estate tax, coal conversion facilities tax, cigarette tax, oil and gas gross production tax, homestead tax credit, personal property replacement tax and the state revenue sharing distribution.

Member: State Investment Board, Teachers Fund for Retirement Board, State Canvassing Board, State Board of Equalization, State Historical Board, Board of University and School Lands.[20]

run a good pre-state convention campaign, you must hit all the district conventions to meet delegates and convince them you're the person to vote for. I hit every district convention and many times returned for their fund raisers.

With the preconvention travel over, I went into high gear for the convention. I had no doubt I would win the nomination – don't know why, but defeat never entered my mind. When the convention was over, I indeed had won the nomination and went to bed that night thinking: I'm going to be the next Treasurer for the state of North Dakota! The fact that I would have a Republican opponent never entered my mind!

The race for State Treasurer was nothing remarkable – very rarely do voters home in on the lower ballot races. I repeated my pre-convention strategy and added staff both in a Bottineau office and also joined forces with Bob Hanson (candidate for Tax Commissioner and former State Treasurer) and hired Carol Siegert, long-time and talented Democrat politico to act as our campaign manager. We all worked hard right up to the day of election, which we were gratified to have won. After the election, I was told by a Republican friend that my opponent, Claus Lembke, was overheard saying, "How did that woman beat me?!?" My response to that is: How, indeed. I worked for it!

Serving as State Treasurer

We moved to Bismarck and I began to serve my first of three terms. I had a small staff of seven. They were fine people who did their jobs with no complaints over lack of decent equipment. It is a fact of life that if you are of one party and the majority of the legislative branch is of the other, the majority party cuts your budget, cuts your staff, literally cuts the size of your office, and then attempts to eliminate it altogether. All of this happened during my 12 years in the office. Legislators on the other side of the aisle are fickle friends. Many of the same Republican legislators who attempted to raise havoc with my office are still in power in the Legislature today. You can bet that the present Treasurer, also a Republican, is not suffering as I did. That's how partisan politics are played. My Democrat friends in the House and Senate always protected me as best they could and never let me down. I remember them all with fondness.

During my time in office, I was president of the Midwest division of the National State Treasurers Association, and sat on the National Council of State Treasurers. I brought the NAST Midwest convention to Bismarck and was proud to show off our state. As State Treasurer, I sat on numerous boards: State Land Board, State Historical Board, State Investment Board, TFFR Board, State Canvassing Board and the State Equalization Board. The work on all was interesting and varied in degree of importance.

Working for the people was a pleasure, but my tolerance for cheap political maneuvers was gone. Hence my decision not to run for another term. I was never defeated in a political race. I left because it was time.

A Few Final Thoughts

I am pleased that North Dakota has entered a time of wealth due to oil exploration. The increased revenue has built a rainy-day fund that is envied by the majority of states in the nation. I applaud the frugality that keeps the state in good shape. I believe, however, that is the duty of state officials to remember government and government revenue belongs to the citizens. Oil revenue is no exception. Proper consideration should be given to the needs of vulnerable citizens, increases to state retirees who live on the margin and to proper workloads for people working in social service areas – the list goes on. The lives of many can be improved if the legislative body cares for the citizens, as they care for themselves every two years with a salary and per-diem increase.

To my great dismay, the number of women at the state and national level hasn't grown as I had hoped. Men are in the majority in government and continue to pass inappropriate and dubious laws concerning women and their rights. I look forward to the day we have a woman in the Governor's Office in North Dakota and most important of all - in the White House.

I still talk about North Dakota as "my" state. It always will be – I miss much of it. The harvest of wheat in the fall will always be a special memory for me. I also miss the Badlands and their striking vistas. I love the history of the state. I will always remember the many powwows I was privileged to dance in. I will miss the people – always the people. And yes, I miss the parades!!! I was honored to be elected, privileged to be the first person to serve three terms as State Treasurer, and I'm happy to have survived with my health intact. I look back now and I remember more of the positive things than the negative. It was truly the experience of a lifetime. Thank you North Dakota – I'll always love you!

FOUR

Passionate About Change

By

Kelly Schmidt

North Dakota Treasurer
2005 – Present

"The Treasurer's Office had always dealt with dollars; now we were working on change."

Treasurer Kelly Schmidt

Kelly L. Schmidt nee Miller*

1962-Present

State Treasurer 2005-present

Treasurer Kelly Schmidt - 2013
(North Dakota Treasurer's Office)

Personal Information

Born 1962 in Elmhurst, Illinois. Married to Charles (Chuck), four children. In "spare time," enjoys using power tools on cabin/home improvements and gardening.

Party Affiliation

Republican

Education

Moorhead High School, Moorhead, Minnesota; attended Moorhead State University; attended North Dakota State University, majoring in Behavioral Sciences.

Professional Experience Before Taking Office

Insurance Investment Brokerage Manager (1985-92); Self-employed, worked on advocacy issues such as Bush Clear Skies Initiative; Mandan Planning and Zoning Commission (2001-05); North Dakota House of Representatives Appropriations Committee, Clerk (2003).

Memberships Include

As Treasurer: National Association of State Treasurers, president (2011); National Association of State Treasurer's Foundation, past chair; National Jump$tart Coalition, board member; American Savings Education Council, board member.

Other: Morton-Sioux Counties Special Education, volunteer as surrogate parent; North Dakota Board of Podiatric Medicine, board member; Mandan American Legion Auxiliary, past vice president; Mandan Kiwanis, past president; North Dakota Republican Party, secretary.[21]

*Bio contains information through 2013

Running for public office was never on my list of things to accomplish. It had crossed my mind only once, when it showed up on the list of career choices after taking an aptitude test in high school. I had a need to be of service, but public service wasn't on the list.

I have always been willing to roll up my sleeves in an effort to help others. Fundraising began in grade school: hosting carnivals to raise money for the Rapid City flood victims in 1972 or helping "Jerry's kids." Selling raffle tickets for the church bazaar or planning a breakfast for a young mom gravely ill; it was something that came naturally to me.

Talking came naturally, too. I can still hear my Dad say, "Tell them what you think, Kek." And I did. I grew up in a male-filled world - brothers, cousins, sons and the financial world of male colleagues. I didn't think like they did. I was the girl; I had an opinion of my own.

My journey into public service started with a gravel road, a poorly maintained road on the edge of town. It was that road which pushed me to a run for the Mandan City Commission. I ran without much direction, knocking on doors until sundown. I lost to the power of incumbency.

My final attempt was different; I had a plan, I raised some money and knocked on more doors. I lost that race by 76 votes. The quote from Samuel Smiles, "We learn wisdom from failure much more than from success" could not have been more fitting. That final loss was the best thing that ever happened to me. I connected with the people, heard their concerns and their priorities. I had developed a foundation.

I became actively involved in party politics first in my legislative district of Mandan and then with the state Republican Party. I was elected State Party Secretary. In 2003, I was hired as a clerk for the House Appropriations Committee for the regular and special legislative sessions. Little did I know the value of those lessons and how they would serve me in the years ahead.

The Opportunity

Studies show, in most cases, women who run for office need to be asked. I was no exception. It was North Dakota Republican Party Executive Director Jason Stverak who did the asking. I was at State Party Headquarters assisting with a project when he pulled me aside and asked if I would consider running for State Treasurer. I was surprised and flattered. I had so many questions relating to the convention process, elections and the Office of State Treasurer. With my first questions answered, I headed home to give the idea some thought and have a conversation with my husband, Chuck. More questions, more conversations and then finally, the family meeting.

Chuck and I gathered our family, Michael (16), Connor (10) and Evan (8). Our eldest son, Justin (20) had joined the Navy in 2002 and was no longer living at home. This would disrupt their lives and the routine they had come to know. Chuck worked shift work at the Mandan Refinery and had for 22 years, so when we married in 1992, we agreed I would leave my career and stay home to raise our family. This would provide some stability to our busy lives as our family grew. I contracted work to meet the financial demands of our growing family, which was now six. It worked well for us. We were content and happy.

We discussed the many changes, challenges and opportunities this race would bring to our family and to our state. Finally, it was decided: "Mom, it's your turn…" "Let's do it…" "We'll make it fun." We jumped in with both feet and never looked back.

So it Begins

As with most campaigns, we began with the announcement circuit starting in Grand Forks, Fargo and Bismarck on day one, followed by Minot, Williston and Dickinson on day two.

Chuck and I, along with the three boys, made the trip to Grand Forks the night before my early morning press event: my first, in front of the cameras and on my own. I didn't know what to expect.

I woke early that morning, and not wanting to wake the rest of the family in our shared hotel room, I slipped out to the pool area. There in the early morning hours of the day, I rehearsed my speech, again and again.

The Grand Forks and Fargo announcements went off without a hitch, and as each passed, I became more comfortable and relaxed. But nothing could have prepared me for the overwhelming support I received in Bismarck. We arrived at Republican Headquarters to a room filled with supporters, and standing among them stood every Republican statewide elected official. That support and that moment is something I will never forget.

Mikey Hoeven had graciously agreed to introduce me. I did a quick once-over on my family: hair in place, check; collars down, check; smiles ready, check. They were ready. I was ready. I was ready for everything except for, perhaps, Dale Wetzel, the reporter for the Associated Press. I had been told Dale could be tough. I have great respect for Dale and his knowledge of government. He knew more about state government than most in the room. He was, and for many years, remained my barometer of the people. His test was the next test I had to pass. He asked many questions relating to the state of the Treasurer's Office, my plans for addressing the prior audit issues and then he asked, "Why Treasurer?" I responded, "Look around" as I gestured to the statewide office holders in the room, "What's left?" "Why not Agriculture Commissioner?" Dale asked. To which I quickly responded, "Dale, until I married my husband, I didn't know the difference between a cow and a heifer." The room erupted in laughter and that concluded the interview. It was the truth.

2004 State Convention

Nominating speeches, floor demonstrations, candidate booths and hospitality rooms are just a few things which make up the preparations for a state convention. Throw in Evan's 9th birthday and you've really got a weekend!

I've been blessed to have one or more of our sons, along with a friend or colleague, give my convention nominating speeches. Our sons have written their own speeches. I have suggested they share an item that most wouldn't know about me and perhaps something I have taught them. I have reserved the right to edit. I believe the only edit I made was to Michael in 2008 when I changed the word "cheap" to "frugal." It just sounded better and I'm not cheap, I am frugal. I have insisted on reading them prior to the convention to avoid "eye leaks" at an inappropriate time.

In 2004, good friend and longtime Republican, Diane Lillis, gave my nomination. Eldest son, Justin, offered the second. He made note during his speech, "My mom may not be the best cook in the world, but she'll make a great State Treasurer." Just thinking about it gets my dander up. I'm a great cook, when I cook.

The Campaign Trail

With the help of my friend and Campaign Treasurer, Theresa Tokach, and many others, the details came together. My days were spent raising money, looking over audit reports, attending state meetings, and learning the roles and responsibilities of the job I hoped to earn.

Under the wing of Attorney General Wayne Stenehjem, Insurance Commissioner Jim Poolman and the other incumbent elected officials, I learned the ropes of campaigning. Lincoln Day dinners, local festivals and parades filled my time. The car became my classroom on campaigning, the value of a good stump speech and "how things worked."

That first campaign, I carried a step stool with me as a prop. I was "stepping up to the plate." What many didn't know was I needed that stool to reach the microphone and see over the podium. I am 5 foot 4 inches, a sharp contrast in comparison to the likes of Wayne Stenehjem, Al Jaeger and Jim Poolman. I still have that stool.

Parades, Festivals and Food

We've done many parades over the years. Aneta became a family favorite, fondly referred to as "parade followed by food." I worked the line of attendees at the annual Turkey Days while my family filled up on BBQ turkey and fixings. Food and boys go hand in hand and this day fit the bill.

The Mandan Fourth of July parade, the largest in the state, is one of the more difficult for which to find parade walkers; there are so many politicians participating, and as a resident of Mandan, many of our friends were volunteering in other ways. I recall one year I challenged Michael, "You find 20 walkers and I'll continue to do your laundry, 19 and you're on your own." He found 20; I continued to wash his clothes. We still chuckle about that.

An invite to a family barbecue after the Oakes parade became a regular event and no one will forget the LONG state fair parade, and the year Evan came down with heat exhaustion. We remember them all; they were the highlight and the agenda of our summers.

I have a long-standing date with my husband, Chuck, on the second Wednesday in October. It is on this day that we head to the sauerkraut capital of the U.S, Wishek, N.D., for Sauerkraut Days. It is there where we meet new friends, reconnect with others and are reminded of what makes North Dakota special - it's people. Something we can never take for granted.

My first opponent was a "former state Senator, a cattle rancher and newspaper humor columnist." He was a big guy, kind-hearted and boisterous. He had run out of candy while participating in the Dickinson Fourth of July parade and casually helped himself to handful from our son, Evan, who was 9 at the time. Evan was terrified he would attempt a second handful and spent the remainder of the parade in the backseat of the car. Little did my opponent know, Evan was fully prepared for the next parade in Mandan. He was armed with a Super Soaker and stood waiting in the back of our pickup for an opportunity should that "big guy" attempt to "borrow" more candy. He was ready.

My 2004 opponent also wrote a weekly column in several statewide newspapers. In an effort to compete with exposure, the state GOP sent a letter to newspapers across the state. The letter asked them to either stop printing the columns until after the election or to allow me to also run accompanying columns. It made national news. Now, I was running for office AND writing a weekly column. I don't recall how many weeklies picked it up, but something was submitted every week. Those articles have been placed in the "Schmidt archives" for generations to come.

Election Night 2004

That first campaign I added over 19,000 campaign miles on my car and thousands more while riding with others. I had made my case to the voters. With no regrets, Chuck, Michael, Connor, Evan and I headed to the election night gathering in hopes we would be celebrating the fruits of our labor. I anticipated a late night as the race was expected to be close. It was the last race called. It was after 11 p.m., while doing a live interview with Scott Hennen, the Associated Press called my race. We had won with 56 percent of the vote! We had something to celebrate, and I couldn't wait to get home and share the news with our son, Justin, who was stationed in Spain.

That moment was short-lived when an established longtime member of my party came to me and said, "Now, you can get in there and shut that office down!" You see, I was inheriting an office that had been on the ballot twice, by my own party, to be eliminated. Twice, the people had voted to retain it and now they had elected me to be their Treasurer. It was now my job to assess the situation and give them something to be proud of.

Description of Official Duties as State Treasurer

Four-year term. Processes deposits and receipts for all state agencies and reconciliation of their accounts; custodian of all state funds and fiduciary of many; collection and distribution of various revenues to more than 500 political subdivisions, including indigent defense, coal severance, domestic violence prevention fund, highway tax distribution, estate tax, coal conversion tax, cigarette tax, oil and gas production tax.

Member: State Investment Board, Teachers Fund for Retirement Board, State Canvassing Board, State Board of Tax Equalization, State Historical Society Board, Board of University and School Lands.[22]

The Work Begins

My background in investments, insurance and tax prepared me for the position, but nothing prepared me for the antiquated office I was walking into. The tax distribution system was written in COBOL, a computer language developed in 1968. Reporting was being completed on printers needing green bar paper and ribbons that were no longer available, except for the backup supply in the storage room. Audit findings, the implementation of the new state accounting system, PeopleSoft, and the need for policies and procedures were among the challenges. The list was long. The question: Where do we start? The Treasurer's Office had always dealt with dollars; now we were working on change. That became our motto.

I appointed Lawrence Hopkins as my Deputy. Lawrence was a CPA. He had experience with PeopleSoft, the legislative process and management in the private sector. His skills were exactly what I needed.

Because we were not given the opportunity of a transition period from the previous administration, members of the treasury staff invited us to off-site meetings in an effort to lay the ground work for our first week. This proved to be extremely valuable. It was their efforts that enabled us to hit the ground running.

As the legislative session began, so did we. Working with State Auditor Bob Peterson and his team, we began to move down the list, one audit finding at a time.

The state checkbook had been reconciled to the bank on a daily basis, but it had not been reconciled to the accounting system, PeopleSoft, in months; nor was there a process in place to do so because the Treasurer's Office had not participated in the implementation of PeopleSoft. One process, one procedure and one day at a time through the legislative session, we worked our way through with the help of Lawrence, our team and so many others.

I remember my first Legislative Committee meeting as Treasurer. I had assumed the legislative bills submitted relating to our office were being tracked. This is a standard in all state agencies, and in our office, a role of the Executive Assistant, who I had inherited. I soon found I couldn't assume anything. On one of those first mornings in office, she came in and said, "The clerk from House Industry, Business and Labor committee just called, they are waiting for you, something about a bill we submitted." "Print me a copy of that bill!" I said, to which she responded, "I don't know how." I quickly printed a copy of the bill, read it while in the elevator and swiftly made my way to the committee room. Without missing a beat, I entered the room, identified myself for the record and introduced the bill. It passed unanimously in committee. I was thankful for my time spent in the legislative process.

She's Just My Mom

My kids have never been too impressed with my title. To them, "I'm just Mom or now, Gramma." This couldn't have been truer than one summer afternoon in 2005.

I was in the Minneapolis airport waiting to catch my connection to Washington, D.C., for a State Treasurer's meeting when Evan called. "Mom, can I have a pop?"... "Where's your Dad?"...."He's in the back mowing the lawn"..."Evan, do you know where I am?"...."Where?"...."I'm in the Minneapolis airport on my way to Washington, D.C., for work"...."Oh, can I have a pop?" Need I say more?!

A True Test

In the spring of 2006, I received a call from our son Justin that would rock our world. Justin, who was stationed in Washington State, was heading to Iraq in less than three weeks. There he would replace his Navy uniform for an Army uniform and carry on his duties as a member of a joint composite squadron. I was now among the ranks of so many North Dakotans who had sent their sons and daughters off to war.

I was at the Fargodome, participating in an event, when I received his first call since arriving in Iraq. I was overwhelmed and so very thankful to hear his voice. We chatted, I brushed myself off and it was back to business.

It was my staff, with their support and encouragement, that I was able to accomplish what we did during those six months. It was difficult to stay focused.

I have been reminded, time and time again: You are only as good as those who walk with you. I and the people of North Dakota have been blessed to have so many talented and good people in the Office of the State Treasurer. A special thank you to my assistant of seven years, Lisa MacPherson.

In the 2007 legislative session, we secured funding necessary to begin our new Tax Distribution Outstanding Check system (TDOC). The system we inherited required manual entry. If any error was made, even a transposed number, the entire distribution would have to be wiped clean by ITD and begun again. This new system gathered information from systems throughout state government, allowed a process of checks and balances and an opportunity to make a correction. It brought "transparency to the treasury" as we now had the tools to post distributions made by our office to the political subdivisions.

TDOC is "THE" system of the Office of State Treasurer. As funding becomes available, we continue to add more distributions and make the updates required due to legislative changes. The complexity and the amount of detail have changed dramatically during my tenure. The timing of TDOC and the challenges of our oil and gas distribution was no coincidence.

A Second Run

The more things change, the more they stay the same.

We had accomplished much during my first term as Treasurer. For the most part, the idea we no longer needed a Treasurer's Office had dimmed. There were those who just couldn't see past it, but I didn't allow them to slow me down. There was still work to be done and I hoped to be part of it in a second term.

I announced my intentions to seek a second term in January of 2008 and so the

On the campaign trail at Kindred in 2012, Treasurer Kelly Schmidt follows the adage that a candidate connects better with voters by walking in a parade. (Handing out candy doesn't hurt either!) (Kelly Schmidt photo collection)

circuit of announcement speeches, Lincoln Day dinners and district conventions began again. I enjoy attending these functions in and off the election cycle and do so regularly, but during an election year, especially when you are on the ballot, the pace and the expectations are much higher.

This election cycle, the pace and the expectations both personally and professionally would put me to the test.

In an effort to shorten the drive and share in the expense, we often coordinate resources when attending political events. Prior to the 2008 State GOP convention in March, those of us on the ballot or seeking the nomination are busy attending district conventions. State Senator Bob Stenehjem was seeking the nomination for Public Service Commissioner. Both of us being from Bismarck-Mandan, we shared many of those late, cold trips. The conversation was never the same and once again, I learned a lot.

March 5, 2008 – Bob and I were in Minot attending their district convention. We took our turns in the lineup of presentations, and when all was done, Bob, his brother, Alan, and I began to make our way to the door. I had noticed several missed calls on my phone and planned to address them when we hit the road. That's when my husband, Chuck, called. My Dad, 68, who lived in Florida, had experienced a heart attack and was in surgery. I was numb. We were still grieving the loss of Chuck's dad, Paul, four weeks earlier.

We didn't say much that night; Bob and Alan knew my heart. They had lost their father way too soon. The battery on my personal cell phone went dead, so I began to use my official state phone to get any information I could. Alan and Bob made every effort to drive me home that night instead of dropping me at the headquarters parking lot. I assured them I was fine.

Bob, knowing I am an early riser, called at 5:30 that next morning. He gently asked, "How's your dad doing?" To which I replied, "My dad died last night, Bob. I'm leaving for Florida shortly." "I'm sorry to hear that." We were now members of the same "club."

Two weeks after my dad's funeral, with the help of my family and friends, I stood in front of the state GOP convention seeking my second nomination with everything in order.

I was honored to have Attorney General Wayne Stenehjem deliver my nomination that year.

Excerpt from Wayne's speech:

> "Four years ago, a wind swept into the third floor of the Capitol in Bismarck. A wind like the breeze that brings the spring rains to the farms and ranches of North Dakota. A wind that blew out the mustiness and the mold that had permeated the previous two decades in the State Treasurer's office.
>
> That force, that refreshing breeze was Kelly Schmidt.
>
> 20 years of moribund, status quo operations in the Capitol were swept clean with a breath of fresh, pure North Dakota air when Kelly Schmidt took her place at the helm.
>
> I watched as the first wisps of air in Kelly's campaign intensified into a whirlwind that swept across the state, and at long last, the GOP re-captured the Treasurer's office in 2004. And from the moment Kelly took the oath of office, she was about change."

In carrying on with tradition, sons Michael and Connor offered their second.

Excerpt from Connor's speech:

> "Hi, my name is Connor Schmidt, and I am a son of Kelly Schmidt. I am in the eighth grade and going to school in Mandan.
>
> We are the type of family that supports and aids one another. It's like a big football team at my house; my mom is the coach. She calls the plays,

tells us what we need to work on and what needs to be done. She calls us Team Schmidt!

My mom, Kelly Schmidt, is pretty cool. She will even wake me up in the morning if I hit the snooze on my alarm clock. She likes to play video games like Guitar Hero PS2 and Bowling on the Wii.

A few things my mom has taught me are trustworthiness, honesty and to be yourself in any situation.

The reason I think she should be re-elected is because I think she is really good at her job. She has made a lot of new friends in the last four years. She works really hard and even though I don't always understand what she is talking about, I know she really loves her job.

The point being, I think she's the right person for the job because she always does her best. She is a wonderful Treasurer for North Dakota, a loving mother to me and my brothers, and a great friend to many. That's my mom, Kelly Schmidt!"

Back to Business

Several weeks later, Deputy Lawrence came to me and gently asked for my check of $2 and some cents to cover the costs of my personal calls, made on my state-issued phone, the night my dad passed away. It served as a quick reminder of the many compartments there are in this business of government, politics and life. How they must remain separate and always in balance.

Once again my days were filled with my duties as State Treasurer, while my evenings and weekends were filled with parades, festivals, political events and whatever sporting season was on the calendar. We were a busy household and I didn't miss much.

I didn't see my opponent much that summer. He was described by the press as "A retired newspaper editor, teacher, writer and photographer who's active in Democrat politics."

Labor Day is traditionally when the issues of a campaign take off, and so they did. His attempt was to discredit me and my investments made to the Veteran's Postwar Trust Fund. The fund had been audited, reconciled regularly and was invested responsibly.

I had recently received an award from the AMVETS Department of North Dakota. "Your efforts on behalf of veterans programs in our state have resulted in significant improvements. Thank you for your hard work and dedication."

I was disappointed that this fund and our veterans were being used for political gain. I was reminded: There are few rules in politics.

This fund was personal to me. I come from a family rich in military service: My grandfather, father, uncle and husband have served; at this writing, my brother, Mike (30 years); sons Justin (12 years) and Michael (three years), and daughter-in-law Katie (three years). All four serve our great nation as members of the U.S. Navy.

Most of the campaign was spent setting the record straight. I was continually reminded: Numbers are difficult to communicate and reporters don't find it easy to report. The voters valued my work and rewarded me with a victory. I won that election with 61 percent of the vote.

Term Two – Oh, the Places You Will Go

It was during my first term that the exploration of drilling for oil increased; in 2008, it really took off and has since become an international event. North Dakota is now the second largest oil-producing state in the nation. This has not only changed the landscape of North Dakota, but this has changed the landscape of my office, in what we do and how we do it.

The Legacy Fund, which diverts 30 percent of oil revenue, was approved by the voters in 2010. The Office of State Treasurer made the first deposit to the Legacy Fund in September 2011. It has exceeded all expectations.

We have seen changes every legislative session since I have been in office to the oil and gas distribution formula. This is now the most complex and challenging of all our state distributions.

We continue to address the low interest rate environment and our federal government's attempt to fix it and the economy as we manage the general fund. The record amount of revenue flowing into our state brings with it challenges and opportunities.

The introduction of a constitutional measure to eliminate property tax failed on the 2012 ballot. I learned North Dakotans are looking for and want to see how their money is being used. We saw an average of 10,000 hits a month to our website during this time.

It was during my second term I was recognized by my peers and was elected and served as President of the National Association of State Treasurers. I also served as Chair of the National Association of State Treasurers Foundation, which oversees the educational activities of the organization, which include the New Treasurers Symposium, the International Project assisting Mexican Public Finance Officials, as well as initiatives to promote financial literacy across the nation. I had the opportunity to serve on the Board of Directors for the National Jump$tart Coalition and the American Savings Education Council.

In 2009, I was named a "Toll Fellow" by the Council of State Governments for my achievements and service to state government.

Term Three

The decision to run again was easy. I continued to love what I do and the changes in North Dakota brought the challenge.

At the state convention in 2012, Senator Rich Wardner honored me with his nomination, followed by speeches from sons Connor and Evan.

> "Hey, everyone, I am Connor Schmidt. I am 18 years young, third of four in the lineup, and enjoy long walks on the beach and watching the sunset. But that doesn't matter right now.
>
> I'm here to talk about my mother and your current State Treasurer, Kelly Schmidt. Since I was in fourth grade, my mother has been blessed to serve the people of North Dakota to the best of her abilities. Eight years later, I am college-bound and my mom is still working her tail off and giving it all she's got, and I still have no idea what she's talking about when she gets home. However, it's plain to see that her job is something she is passionate about, so I nod my head and smile while trying to make sense of what on earth she is saying.
>
> My mom, Kelly Schmidt, is an amazing woman. No one has ever made me so happy, angry, embarrassed, proud, grateful, crazy, confused, calm or inspired the way my mom can. For some, she can be a knight in shining armor, for others a walking nightmare. However, nothing stops my mother from getting the job done. Give her 50 cents and she'll get you a dollar by the end of the day. That's just the kind of woman my momma is.
>
> Mr. Chairman, I second the nomination of my mom for her third term as State Treasurer. I don't believe anyone can fill the

Treasurer Kelly Schmidt was a delegate to the 2012 National Republican Convention.

(Kelly Schmidt photo collection)

shoes she'd leave in the Capitol. I also ask you to consider this before deciding the nomination: If momma ain't happy, ain't nobody happy."

Evan continued:

"Hello, I'm Evan Schmidt. I'll be 17 next week and the youngest of Team Schmidt, unless you are my mom who calls me, "The Baby." My mother has taught and inspired me to do several things, things such as: playing the piano, helping me become a more organized person, learning how to treat others with respect and becoming more independent. Heck, I learned how to do my own laundry over the summer!

My mother is usually the one that asks me every single morning, right before I walk out the door, "Evan did you brush your teeth? Did you do your homework? Are you going to this place after school? Even though it can get rather annoying at times, you just stop and think for a second and react in a nice way. That's another thing my mother has taught me.

Being the youngest and the smallest in the family, Mom has had to come to my rescue on a few occasions. Big brothers can be mean … and remember, I'm the baby. We may be taller that her, but she can still take all four of us at the same time. She is a very intimidating character; one look in the eye and it's a quick look away from the four of us. My mother has always put her family before herself, and we do the same back for her. She has confidence in what she does; that's when you learn to respect her the most.

Honestly, I don't know what my mom does in her job, but she loves it. And although I'm the last son to have the privilege of saying this … Mr. Chairman, I second the nomination for my mom seeking a third term as State Treasurer. Thank you."

And We Were Off

Some would think the third time around you can let you hair down and relax a bit. I've always had the mindset, "Don't take anything for granted." I didn't, but this campaign was a bit different. There was more to balance. Family and the increasing responsibilities of my position came first, then the campaign.

Intertwined with the summer of parades and festivals was the marriage of Michael and Katie. This marriage brought with it our first grandson, Brayden, who was 6.

My opponent, described by the press as a Mandan resident and former state employee, did his best to bring up issues, none of which the public took notice. Once again,

I was rewarded for my efforts and was re-elected by the largest margin of the statewide candidates – 66 percent of the vote. I was overwhelmed.

My roles and responsibility as a board member have changed and brought many challenges over the years. A few examples:

The State Investment Board

This board is now responsible for nearly $7.5 billion. The 2008 stock crash, which hit all state funds with vengeance, challenged me to new heights. I have served on the Search Committee as we sought to hire not one, but two Chief Investment Officers. The introduction of the Legacy Fund: We completed the asset allocation study, policy committee discussion and its implementation and the challenges of a low-interest rate environment as a long term investor.

Teachers Fund for Retirement

These challenges relate to the funding status of our pensions; benefit changes affecting our current and future teachers; and the impact of oil and the expansion of education, new teachers, and how it will change the status of our pension fund.

Board of University and School Lands

The Common Schools Trust Fund has nearly tripled in the past four years to $2.6 billion; we have completed the asset allocation study and are now in the process of implementing funds to new asset classes. In many ways, the Legislature has redefined the role of this board. We are now tasked with the approval of Energy Impact Grants to counties, cities, school districts and law enforcement. Who would have thought we would be discussing day cares and dust on the Land Board?

State Historical Board

To participate in the designing, planning and building of our new Heritage Center, along with its exhibits, has been a once-in-a-lifetime opportunity.

We Continue on in the Treasurer's Office

With the assistance of the Information Technology Department (ITD) and its team, we have maximized our use of technology. New projects are in the works which will bring additional efficiencies and transparency. We provide analysis, data and explanation relating to our duties to legislators, state agencies, political subdivisions and the general public. Our role is now defined. With technology and hard work, we have the foundation to address whatever lies ahead. These are changing, challenging times, and similar to other state agencies, we are extremely busy. But it is not about how busy we are; it is about the accomplishments we bring to the process. I am proud of those accomplishments and look forward to the future.

In Closing

It takes great personal strength for a woman to succeed in politics. Woman must balance family responsibilities, internal doubts and challenges to authority. I am thankful to God and the citizens of North Dakota for the privilege and honor you have given me to serve as your State Treasurer. To my husband, Chuck, my greatest blessing and my "biased" critic: I could not do this without you at my side. Thank you for sharing this journey. To my children, Justin and Amy (Jack and Callen), Michael and Katie (Brayden and Tanner), Connor and Evan: Thank you for keeping me grounded and forever reminding me of what is really important.

FIVE

Advocate for Agriculture

By

Sarah Vogel

North Dakota Agriculture Commissioner
1989-96

"I used to say that because more than half of the farm land in North Dakota is owned by women, and women are equal partners in all farms owned by married couples, and women have to sign all the mortgages and promissory notes, women should be better represented in the leadership of agriculture organizations. This is still true today."

Sarah Vogel

Sarah Vogel

1946-Present

State Agriculture Commissioner 1989-96

First Woman in the U.S. Elected to be Agriculture Commissioner

Agriculture Commissioner Sarah Vogel - 1988
(*Bismarck Tribune* photo file)

Personal Information

Born 1946 in Bismarck and raised in Garrison and Fargo, North Dakota. One son. In "spare time," trains for triathlons (running, swimming and biking) and reads.

Education

Mandan High School; received B.A. from the University of North Dakota; awarded J.D. from New York University Law School.

Party Affiliation

Democratic - Nonpartisan League

Professional Experience Before Taking Office

New York City Department of Consumer Affairs, corporate attorney; Federal Trade Commission legal staff; U.S. Secretary of Treasury, Special Assistant for Consumer Affairs; private law practice in Bismarck and Grand Forks; North Dakota Attorney General's Office, Assistant North Dakota Attorney General specializing in farm issues.

Memberships and Committees include

As State Agriculture Commissioner: Midwest Association of State Departments of Agriculture, past president; Mid America International Agri Trade Association.[23]

*Bio contains information through 1996

Growing Up in the League: The Origins of My Involvement in Politics

Ordinarily, a person invited to summarize his or her political career would start with the first campaign. However, I have to go back almost 100 years since I can't write about my involvement in politics without first discussing the Nonpartisan League.

As is known by most native North Dakotans, the League, or "NPL," was a grassroots political party that originated in North Dakota to alleviate the suffering of North Dakota farmers caused by exploitation by out-of-state economic forces.[24] What is less known is that the League also achieved notable benefits for workers, women, children and Native Americans. It believed that government existed to serve the people and adopted a number of sound laws and regulations, many of which survive today. For example, the League established a number of sensible debtor protection laws that inoculated North Dakota homeowners, nearly 100 years later, from the housing mortgage meltdown in 2008.

The League was started in 1915 and grew rapidly. It gained virtually complete control of North Dakota state government from 1917 to 1921. The League remained active and rose up again to thoroughly control state government during the "Great Depression" of the 1930s. For many years, it had an uneasy alliance with the Republican Party, but it shifted to the Democratic column in 1956.

While the League is no longer an independent entity, the League's populist and agrarian philosophy still survives in North Dakota. Its principal legacies today are the state-owned Bank of North Dakota and the state-owned Mill and Elevator, which were created by the League in 1919, and the Industrial Commission, the most powerful agency in North Dakota, which is composed of the Governor, the Attorney General and the Commissioner of Agriculture.

I was born and raised as a "Leaguer" (not as a Democrat or a Republican) and the influence of the League played an enormous role in my political career. Both my father, Robert L. Vogel, and grandfather, Frank A. Vogel, were very active in the League.

Growing up, I was immersed in stories of the League: about the role of government in bettering the lives of people; about the virtues of the family farm system; how government could help people during tough times; how the farmer could always be trusted; and about how law and the legal system could be an instrument of justice for regular people or could be abused, depending on who was in power.

At the kitchen table and in the family car on interminable drives across the prairie, I learned from my father about the heroic leaders of the League: William Langer and his foreclosure moratorium in 1933 and the grain embargo the same year; my grandfather, Frank Vogel, and his policies as manager of the Bank of North Dakota that allowed impoverished farmers to stay on the land; Judge Charles Amidon, who upheld NPL laws;

Edwin F. Ladd, a scientist who proved North Dakota was being cheated by the Minneapolis millers and was later elected to the U.S. Senate; Lynn Frazier and William Lemke, who together authored the famous federal law that helped refinance farmers all across the country (the Frazier/Lemke Farm Bankruptcy Act); Usher Burdick, who stopped farm foreclosures with the Farmers Holiday Association and was elected to Congress; John Baer, a wickedly good cartoonist who was also elected to Congress; and others.[25]

Being a third-generation Vogel in the small world of North Dakota politics was both an honor and a burden. I was taken to innumerable political meetings along with my siblings. In high school, I was a driver for my dad's 1962 congressional campaign. When I attended the University of North Dakota from 1964 to 1967, I would ask my father for topics for research papers and he always suggested League-oriented subjects. As a result, I did research on German/Russian immigrant voting patterns in favor of Senator Langer (they voted for Senator Langer, even after he had died!), and the Farmers' Holiday movement, which stopped many foreclosures in the 1930s.[26]

When I moved to New York City to attend New York University School of Law from 1967 to 1970, I focused my legal studies (as far as I could do so) on themes that resonated with my League upbringing: economic justice and equality for the little guy, consumer protection, the rights of women and minorities, the role of government to restrain corporate power, and use of cooperatives by Native Americans. The closest "fit" to my NPL upbringing for a legal career was work in consumer protection and that is where I began to work.

By the time President Reagan was elected in November 1980, my East Coast legal career in consumer protection had lasted 10 years and culminated in appointment as the Consumer Affairs Adviser to President Carter's Secretary of Treasury. Before President Ronald Reagan's inauguration, I decided to move back home and raise my 3-year-old son in North Dakota (by then I'd become divorced). I hoped I would be able to represent "real people" (not big government or big corporations).

Returning to North Dakota in the fall of 1981, I was quickly caught up in the cataclysmic economic debacle now known as the "1980s Farm Crisis."[27]

Prompted by my NPL upbringing and by my sympathy for the farmers being buffeted by financial currents that were similar to those of the Great Depression, I began to represent family farmers in North Dakota who were threatened with foreclosure, repossession and "starve-out" tactics by Farmers Home Administration, an agency of U.S. Department of Agriculture. Armed with an NPL sense of mission, the legal skills I had developed in law school and applied during a decade of consumer protection work on the East Coast, and – most importantly – a lot of naivete, I began to develop a legal strategy to stop FmHA's abusive collection tactics.

After more than a year of preparation, co-counsel and I filed a class action case, *Coleman v. Block*, against the Farmers Home Administration on March 11, 1983. U.S. District Court Judge Bruce Van Sickle issued a preliminary injunction on May 5, 1983, that halted all FmHA foreclosures in North Dakota. Judge Van Sickle later expanded the protections of the case to a national class[28] in decisions issued in October and November 1983. He then issued a final permanent injunction on February 17, 1984. The early 1980s were busy, intense, difficult, painful and joyful times: I would never want to repeat them.

How does this tie in to politics? My farm crisis work came to the attention of Democratic- NPL candidate Nick Spaeth during his successful campaign for Attorney General in 1984. Shortly after Nick took office in January 1985, he offered me a position as an Assistant Attorney General, asking me to work primarily on farm crisis issues. I happily accepted the offer (in part because it would have a salary!), and moved to Bismarck from Grand Forks, where I had been employed by my father's law firm. I started work at the Capitol in March 1985. The farm crisis had not abated in 1985: indeed, problems experienced primarily by Farmers Home borrowers in 1983 had spread to borrowers from the Production Credit Associations, the Federal Land Banks and private banks.

As an Assistant Attorney General, I had the opportunity to continue the same type of farm crisis work I had done in private practice, but now I could speak for the state of North Dakota. While I was doing this work, I could not help but compare the broad array of activities being undertaken by the Attorney General's office to the relative passivity and inactivity of the Department of Agriculture.

While the sitting Commissioner of Agriculture was doing some very good work, it wasn't enough. I believed the farm financial crisis was huge, and getting worse, and much more had to be done by the Department of Agriculture. I often shared this view with my friend Heidi Heitkamp, who was then the Tax Commissioner.[29] Heidi eventually said that if I didn't like how the Agriculture Department was run, I should run for the job of Commissioner of Agriculture myself. It was like a light bulb going off and I started to dream about becoming the Commissioner of Agriculture.

How I Turned a Dream of Becoming Agriculture Commissioner Into Reality

The First Step is to Start!

I knew I'd need someone who was a good administrator and could deal with budgets (I was still traumatized by my solo practice financial difficulties in 1982 to 1983 before I'd joined my father's firm). So I went across the hall to the Governor's office to visit with Jeff Weispfenning, Governor Sinner's chief policy analyst on agriculture and natural resources issues. I'd worked with Jeff on a host of issues and I believed that he would be a great Deputy of Agriculture, as he knew a lot about state government and had previously been a policy analyst at the department. I told Jeff I wanted to run for Commissioner and would become a candidate, but *only if* he would agree to become Deputy Commissioner of Agriculture in the event that I'd ever get elected. He thought about it for what seemed like a nano-second, and said "sure."[30]

Even though I had lined up a deputy, I didn't understand the process to get the Democratic NPL's endorsement for that office and how to get on the statewide ballot. Though I wanted the job, I didn't take the proper steps to become a candidate. Time went by and two other strong candidates announced – both of them were state senators: Jerry Kelsh, a farmer, and Dean Meyer, a rancher. I needed to act quickly if I wanted to become Commissioner. Luckily for me, a group of Democratic-NPL women with experience in working on and running campaigns (led by the inestimable Carole Jean Larsen) came to my house one weekend. They said if I would run, they would tell me what to do and would help me, but if I wasn't going to run, they would move on to other candidates. I had to decide. I immediately said I did want to run and so they agreed to help.

Many more people came forward as the months went by and because there were so many, I will not try to name them all. They know who they are, and I am deeply grateful. I learned that many people come forward to help a candidate who is a political neophyte. These supporters may care about the issues that are involved with the office, or may be friends and family, or they may dislike your opponent, or, very often, they simply want a person of their political persuasion to be in that office.

The wonderful experience of having so much support from so many people convinced me that in politics, if one "leaps" into a political race, the "net" of support will appear. Of course, you have to work hard and do your best to line up support, but you shouldn't worry if you don't have all the support you need when you start the process of running for office. It will be there when you need it.

I learned from Carole Jean and the others that my first big task was to get commitments of support from state delegates at the upcoming 1988 state Democratic-NPL convention so that I could become endorsed by the state party, and thereby appear on the general election ballot. I learned that the Democratic-NPL Party's office had lists of persons who had been delegates to state conventions in 1986, 1984 and earlier years, and that a large percentage of these delegates would again be delegates at the 1988 convention. Accordingly, I got those lists. My first campaign letter was sent to all the people who had been Democratic-NPL delegates in several recent election cycles. A few days later, I formally announced my candidacy to the public. This all happened in December 1987, 11 months before the November 1988 general election.

That winter, I made many campaign appearances, including at every district convention (where the delegates to the state convention were selected). But in addition, I or my campaign manager called every delegate (there were hundreds of delegates), and if a person was undecided about whom to support or inclined to be favorable to me, I talked to every one of them about the issues and explicitly asked for their support. All this work leading up to the convention paid off. To the surprise of the statewide press and the public at large (who were unaware of all our preparatory work leading up to the convention), I received more than 50 percent of the votes on the first ballot and was endorsed.

This process taught me that intra-party competition for a political position can be extraordinarily beneficial. I am convinced that but for the process where Jerry, Dean and I presented our qualifications and reasons for running to scores of Democratic-NPL meetings, farm organizations and community groups over many months, I would not have won the general election that fall. As years have gone by, I remain convinced that party leaders should not dictate who would make a good candidate or seek to deter any person from running for a position. Instead, I believe the best practice is to encourage everybody who would like to run to do so and let the district and state conventions decide who should be the candidate after an open and competitive process. Competition is good in intra-party politics and helps the candidate who is eventually endorsed run a better race in the general election.

I Pretended That the Election was a Statewide Job Interview

I had had many job interviews over the years and found it was helpful to think that an election was a job interview with thousands of people weighing in on the decision to hire. Just as a person is unlikely to do well at a job interview by simply saying "I want a job," a candidate for office is unlikely to do well at an election by saying that "I want to be a politician."

As I approached the Agriculture Commissioner race, I tried to identify my strengths and why I was running. I was already well known from my work on the *Coleman v. Block* case and I had often been in the news while I'd been Assistant Attorney General. I had a strong background in state and federal government. I knew how state and federal programs worked, and I had the skills to fight for the farmers if those programs were not run properly. I said I'd be an advocate for agriculture and argued that being a lawyer was a strength, not a weakness.

With regard to being a woman, I said it was a desk job that didn't require any heavy lifting. With regard to not being a farmer, I said farmers already knew how to farm; they didn't need farming lessons from a Commissioner of Agriculture. I also argued that my legal background gave me necessary skills to combat unfair practices by businesses such as grain and cattle buyers and sellers of farm supplies like seed, feed, fertilizer and pesticides.

As a non-farmer with an understanding of the powers of the Commissioner of Agriculture, I also knew that the job affected everybody in North Dakota, not just farmers.

I developed specific campaign themes on non-agricultural issues, from economic development programs for struggling small towns to bringing back the 5-pound flour sack at the State Mill. As I went around the state debating with my two principle general election opponents (Kent Jones, the incumbent Republican Commissioner, and Keith Bjerke, the candidate endorsed by the Republican convention), I tried to show that I would be an advocate for the family farms and farm families of North Dakota and also serve all citizens of the state.

I knew it would be a difficult campaign, and it was more difficult than I'd imagined in terms of travel and stress. I've lost track of the numbers of debates that were held during 1988 after the convention, but there were more than a dozen. The race attracted a lot of press attention, and many polls were taken. (The polls were tight.) None of the candidates ever relaxed. It was tough on all of us, but I think it was tougher on me. I was a single parent and tried to be home as much as I could be, thus drove home many nights – even when it was dangerous – to relieve the baby sitter and to see my son in the morning.

Also, I had to be at work all day, every day. To pay the bills, I needed to remain as an Assistant Attorney General, and I was scrupulous about never doing campaign tasks from the job. If someone called me on a political issue while I was at work, I would refuse to talk and would call back on my lunch break from a phone booth in the Capitol's lobby or from home. As the demands of campaigning increased, I took unpaid leave from Labor Day to the election, which provided much needed relief from the pressure of trying to fit the campaign into evenings and weekends. Despite all the challenges, there were many fun and interesting moments, too.

The best campaign advice I received came from Lucy Calauti (Lucy was very instrumental in many campaigns, including Kent Conrad's first campaign for the U.S. Senate.) Lucy said that I should have a weekly press conference from the convention to the election in various locations throughout the state, and at each one, I should deal with a discrete subject that reinforced my theme of being an advocate for family farmers. If I did that, she predicted people would know me when they voted at the general election, even if I didn't have a lot of money for campaign ads. I followed that advice, and I think it worked.

Just before the election, I called a press conference in Fargo on the theme of why I was the candidate for family farmers, but the candidate endorsed by the Republicans was for big business. The room was empty. About 20 minutes after the press conference was to start, Mikkel Pates (then a reporter for the Fargo Forum) came and was quite disinterested. When I asked Mikkel why no other press members had come, he flatly said that

Description of Official Duties as Commissioner of Agriculture

Four-year term. The Commissioner of Agriculture determines and coordinates operations of the Department of Agriculture and represents the agricultural community in formulating public policy. Many state government functions related to agriculture are the responsibility of other executive agencies. The Commissioner of Agriculture supervises the North Dakota Agriculture Mediation Service, the Agriculture in the Classroom Program, the Animal Damage Control Division, the Apiary Division, the Dairy Division, the Livestock Division, the Marketing Division, the Noxious Weeds Division, the Pesticide Division, the Pesticide Control Board, the Plant Protection Division, the Poultry Division and the State Waterbank Program.

Member: Industrial Commission; State Board of Equalization; State Water Commission; State Seed Commission; Pesticide Control Board; Interstate Compact on Pest Control; U.S. Department of Agriculture: Food and Agriculture Council, State Emergency Board; Northern Crops Council; Waterbank Advisors Board; Wetlands Mediation Advisory Board; State Intermodal Transportation Team; State Soil Conservation Committee; Agriculture in the Classroom Council and several agricultural product councils.[34]

my press conference topic wasn't newsworthy: everyone already knew that I was for family farmers and my opponent was for big business. I took that as a compliment, even if it wasn't meant as such.

After more than a year of extraordinarily hard effort, I woke up on Election Day, November 8, 1988, feeling confident that I would win. The election returns that night confirmed my gut feeling: I had been "hired" by the voters of North Dakota to be the Commissioner of Agriculture of North Dakota.[31]

The election was historic in a number of ways. I was the first woman Commissioner of Agriculture in North Dakota. Indeed, I was the first woman to be elected as a Commissioner or Director of Agriculture in U.S. history. (When I went to my first seven years of National Association of Agriculture Department meetings, I was the only woman at the table.)[32] I was also the first woman to serve on the Industrial Commission, the most powerful board in North Dakota.

The next election in 1992 was less stressful and much easier than the first. I was handily re-elected for a second term by a wide margin.[33]

Significant Achievements During My Two Terms In Office

Helping Farmers Deal With Lenders During the Continuing Financial Crisis

The very first challenge I dealt with was deeply connected to my work on farm foreclosures. Not only FmHA, but also Federal Land Banks and Production Credit Associations and private banks were leaning heavily on farmers who were simply unable to pay. During 1988, many USDA, Federal Land Bank and PCA collection actions were slowed down until regulations were written to implement a farmer-friendly new law: the Agriculture Credit Act of 1987 (ACA). The implementing regulations of the ACA took many months to write, and during this period, the backlog of collection actions built up and were added to the existing backlog created by USDA's refusal to comply with the terms of the *Coleman v. Block* injunction.

Because I had been deeply involved in the passage of the ACA and the implementation of the regulations, I knew that thousands of North Dakota farmers were facing the threat of foreclosure in the very near future if they did not properly complete FmHA "packets" (very complex documents showing their assets, cash flows and other financial information) that would permit them to have their debts restructured and to stay on their land. In addition, we had a chance to help borrowers with the Federal Land Banks and PCA resolve their problems if we could work with them in mediation.

On Election Day of 1988, I knew that the Agriculture Department was not at all ready to do this work. We immediately started to prepare, even though I wouldn't take office for two months. With extraordinary effort by Roger Johnson (whom I appointed to be head of the Farm Credit Counseling/Agriculture Mediation Service and his able assistant Jet Collins) the unreadiness of the department was soon converted to readiness. Scores of additional staff were hired and trained in the complex tasks needed to fill out the "packets" and to develop solutions in mediation.

The hardest year was 1989, my first year as Commissioner. We had an average of 48 farmers working with our program per county! And, every one of them was in crisis. But the Farm Credit Counseling/Agriculture Mediation Service made a huge difference. We saved many farmers and farm families from foreclosure of their farms and loss of their homes and livelihood. I am very proud of that work and intend to write about it in greater depth in the near future.

Starting Marketplace of Ideas and Marketplace for Kids

Leading up to the 1988 election, I knew that main street merchants were suffering as much as the farmers because of the farm crisis and the terrible 1988 drought. Also, it was apparent that farmers needed to diversify so they wouldn't be so dependent on one or two crops that were subject to swings in prices over which they had no control. During the 1988 campaign, I had promised a number of activities to stimulate economic recovery in the rural areas of the state and diversify farm income.

The genesis of these ideas was the *Alternatives for Agriculture* study that Dr. Curt Stofferahn wrote in 1987 for the North Dakota Economic Development Commission. One of the concepts identified by Curt was a "showcase" that would highlight agricultural diversification ideas and successes. By November 1989, Senator Kent Conrad and I launched such a showcase. We called it "Marketplace of Ideas" and it eventually became

Minot Daily News **photo of Agriculture Commissioner Sarah Vogel and singer Willie Nelson promoting Farm Aid at the state fair.** (Sarah Vogel photo collection)

the state's – and the nation's – largest rural economic development conference.

The defining principle of Marketplace of Ideas was that it would be a showcase for ***ideas*** that would be freely shared by the real people (farmers, rural entrepreneurs) that actually ran new, forward-looking businesses. The people selected for the "idea booths" would mingle with Marketplace attendees and would share their challenges, successes, failures, lessons learned and advice with the goal of helping others learn how to start similar businesses and avoid errors in doing so.

Our vision was that it would not be just another trade show where farmers would kick tires and agribusiness would induce farmers to buy expensive services or products. The "idea booths" were free, and they were coupled with a wide array of workshops about new crops, new businesses, new business methods and other subjects taught by experts – all with the goal to generate additional farm income.

The first Marketplace had 70 idea booths (there were buffalo ranchers, ranchers that hosted visitors in log cabins, people that turned wheat sheaves into art, people who made jams and jellies from the wild berries growing near their farms; organic farmers and many more), 30 sponsoring organizations, scores of workshop leaders and 700 attendees. It was a huge success. The second Marketplace was held in January 1991 and we doubled the participation to 1,500 people, and the participation doubled again for Marketplace '92. During the remainder of my time in office, Marketplace attendance averaged about 4,500 people per event.

The main product of Marketplace was a sense of hope! I remember visiting with a young farming couple after Marketplace '91. They said that when they had arrived, they felt that they were without hope and without choices, but after attending Marketplace, they realized that they had many options and it was going to be very hard to choose amongst them! What a contrast to the bleak outlook that was prevalent at the time.

Marketplace also created the opportunity for what I called "Marketplace Moments." An example of a Marketplace Moment was when the chocolate candy maker met the chokecherry jam maker and they decided to cooperate on chokecherry jam-filled chocolates, which became a bestselling product for each of them! Another Marketplace Moment was at a seminar on bison ranching where someone passed around a yellow legal pad so people in the room would write their names and addresses so they could stay in touch, and this list led to the formation of the North Dakota Bison Association, which in turn led to the bison processing plant in New Rockford.

A new term was created: "Co-op Fever," and it was born at Marketplace. Many cooperatives and associations were formed at Marketplace over the years; some were massively successful, others were not, but the spirit of entrepreneurship and possibilities were endless. As the years went by, the day of Marketplace was preceded by the annual meetings of many cooperatives and associations so that their membership could take advantage of the classes and idea booths at Marketplace. It was the place to be!

Marketplace could not have occurred but for the leadership of key staff at the Ag Department (Jeff Weispfenning) and Senator Conrad's office (Lynn Clancy and Milo Candee) and the total dedication of every person on Kent's staff and my staffs. And, we couldn't have done it without the superb organizational efforts of Marilyn Kipp and her staff, who did the bulk of the work for Marketplace year-round. While Kent and I got the headlines and our pictures in the news as the official co-sponsors, these dedicated state and federal employees and private contractors did the work that resulted in very successful and fresh programs year in and year out. Marketplace, sadly, had its last big gathering in 2009[35] – but its 20-year run as a people-powered economic development engine was extraordinary.

Reflecting back on why the annual Marketplace conference ceased, I think that after two decades of promoting diversification, new crops, new business startups and new ideas, an annual event was no longer necessary. I think the message of Marketplace irrevocably changed the economic psyche of North Dakota to unhesitatingly embrace diversification and entrepreneurship. And that is not its only legacy: It also left a vibrant non-profit association (Marketplace for Entrepreneurs/Marketplace for Kids Inc.) and a thriving program called Marketplace for Kids (started during my second term) that is still going strong and creating impetus for success for the next generation![36]

I Worked to Create Excellent Environmental Programs for North Dakota Farmers

Project Safe Send Was Created to Meet Pressing Needs of Farmers

Project Safe Send was created in the third year of my first term to deal with an injustice inflicted by pesticide companies and the Environmental Protection Agency. For many decades, farmers and ranchers were told that a certain product (for example, DDT or arsenic) was safe to use, and the farmers would buy these products. Later on, many of these products were found to be unsafe and the use of that product was prohibited for all crops, or for some crops. When a chemical was banned, however, no thought was given to helping the farmers who were stuck with banned, hazardous and unsafe products that could no longer be used. Legal disposal by the farmer who was stuck with a banned product was prohibitively expensive, if not impossible.

The more I learned about this problem, the more I grew to respect the farmers and ranchers of North Dakota. Rather than just dumping the products in a local land fill or pouring it into a coulee, the farmers and ranchers of North Dakota kept these products safely stored and away from the land and the water of North Dakota. As years passed, however, storage containers deteriorated and labels faded and became illegible. And, farmers retired or died, and the banned and hazardous chemicals were part of the "inheritance" of the next generation or the next buyer of the farm. What to do?

The Agriculture Department folks, especially the pesticide enforcement staff, were unhappy with this situation and resolved to develop alternatives for safe and affordable disposal. We did research on what other states and provinces were doing and found several worth adapting to our needs. We learned what legal disposal would cost. We found contractors who had the necessary permits and equipment for legal disposal (generally super high heat incineration).

The conundrum was how could the disposal costs (which were very expensive) be funded – obviously, it was past the capacity of the farmers to pay for disposal, and the state didn't have any spare cash, either. There was no federal program and no industry program for this type of disposal.

Jeff Weisphenning came up with the solution. Every pesticide sold in North Dakota must be registered with the state of North Dakota annually, and the cost of registration in the early 1990s was low, much lower than in our neighboring states. Jeff's idea was that if North Dakota's registration fees were increased to the same level that our neighboring states charged, the Department of Agriculture could hold free collections across the state for the banned and hazardous chemicals. The cost of the disposal would be paid by the state from the increased pesticide registration fees. It would be free for the farmers.

When we raised these ideas with members of the pesticide industry of North Dakota and the farm groups, we found they were very supportive. Even the national pesticide companies saw the merit in this program and didn't fight the fee increases. With the 1991 Legislature's blessing and the new source of funds, we selected contractors with the appropriate licenses and approvals and began widespread advertising of the program – now called Project Safe Send at the suggestion of one of the task force members – and carefully prepared for the first collections to occur the following year.

I went to watch the collections for the first time in 1992, and also in 1994 (there was no 1993 collection), 1995 and 1996 (my last year) and was thrilled as long lines of farm trucks and cars brought massive quantities of banned and hazardous chemicals to our collection sites. In many conversations with farmers and ranchers on those collection days, the universal emotion of the farmers was deep relief that they finally could legally and properly dispose of the products. The first year, we had 400 participants and collected about 75,000 pounds of chemicals. By 1996, we had collected 250,000 pounds of chemicals from over 1,000 individuals.

I am happy to say that Project Safe Send is still in operation and has even expanded. It remains a safe, non-regulatory and free program – just as it was designed by my team and our advisory team back in 1991. In the two decades since it started, Project Safe Send has collected over 3,000,000 pounds of banned, hazardous and unusable pesticides from thousands of North Dakotans.

As stated by Doug Goehring, the current Agriculture Commissioner, in his 2011 Project Safe Send Report to the Legislature: "What would be a difficult, expensive and possibly dangerous undertaking for individuals has become easy and affordable. The program is a model of sound public policy for dealing with complex environmental issues."[37]

Promoting Biological Control of Leafy Spurge

When I became Commissioner of Agriculture, I anticipated that some of the programs would be fascinating and fun to work on. The Noxious Weed program was decidedly not included among them. But as I learned more about noxious weeds and their impact on the state's farmers and the means to control noxious weeds, it became one of my favorites.

The worst weed on the North Dakota Noxious Weed list was leafy spurge (Euphorbia esula). Spurge had started as an ornamental flower brought from Europe to decorate gardens and cemeteries. But in the U.S., it had no natural enemies and spread widely. It exudes a sap which is irritating, even toxic, to cattle and renders infested land unusable except for sheep. Leafy spurge was (and still is) a plague.

Early in my first term, I had an unexpected vacancy in the Weed Director position and Cindie Heiser (she later married and her last name became Fugere) applied. Cindie had worked at the National Park Service, had ranched in the Badlands, and run a bar in Grassy Butte. She also had a degree in ecological science from Michigan. I hired her. When she started work, many of the weed officers and weed boards were surprised to meet her. She wasn't in the mold of other weed officials. But she stuck it out, worked hard and won their respect.

She studied the bio-control research of Dr. Neal Spencer, who worked for USDA in Sydney, Montana. He told Cindie about flea beetles whose only sustenance was the roots and leaves of leafy spurge and that rigorous federal research showed that the beetles could be safely used to combat leafy spurge. The barrier to widespread use of these flea beetles was that even though they were reproducing on governmental study plots, the bugs weren't yet being shared with private landowners.

In the early summer of 1991, Cindie found a source of these beetles in Canada, got an import permit, and drove up there and back in one very long day. I met her in the evening at a gas station in Bismarck, where she unloaded a small beer cooler filled with what looked like pint ice cream cartons. Each carton contained around 500 tiny flea beetles (they are almost microscopic) and a handful of leafy spurge leaves on which they could survive until they were released. A few (less than 10 had been selected) county weed boards officials were anxiously waiting for Cindie's arrival so that they could "inoculate" patches of leafy spurge in their counties. This gas station meet-up and the releases that followed the next day were the first releases of leafy spurge beetles on private land in North Dakota.

As time went on, Cindie found more sources for beetles, and as the bug colonies grew, she led bug collection/harvest days where farmers would sweep fields with nets (Cindie even persuaded a local firm to make the nets) which were then used to inoculate more fields. These "bug days" were free, privately run and very effective!

From the first private distribution of a coolerful of bugs in little ice cream cartons on that summer evening in the gas station in Bismarck, the flea beetle program grew at an amazing rate. In 1997, a report by NDSU[38] examined biological weed control activities on a county level in four states. North Dakota was the clear leader: 30 North Dakota county weed boards (only 30 had responded to the survey) had distributed 85 percent of all the insects released within the four states. They had released 30.8 million insects and had inoculated 48,959 acres with insects. At least two-thirds of the inoculations were already known to be successful. This is a stupendous rate of adoption of a new technology so few years after the first bugs were privately released. It is another example of a safe, free and non-regulatory program.

Adoption of the Nation's First State Endangered Species Program

The Department of Agriculture website still brags about one of my early achievements: adoption of the first state-sponsored endangered species plan. Rather than fighting the EPA, we worked with them and developed a plan that was workable for all.

The popularity of Project Safe Send, the quick acceptance of the "bug" program for leafy spurge and our early adoption of an endangered species program prove that North Dakota farmers and ranchers will readily abandon costly and toxic chemicals and will take a greener, more ecological approach if effective and affordable alternatives are made available by political leaders.

Supporting the Pride of Dakota Program With the Holiday Showcases

Pride of Dakota was a branding program for North Dakota-made products that was started by my predecessor, Kent Jones. I really liked working with the Pride of Dakota members and tried to help them increase sales and profitability however we could. One of the ways we did that was to start the Pride of Dakota Holiday Showcases. The idea of a Holiday Showcase came from the Marketing Division staff, John Sandbakken and Kaye Quanbeck Effertz. They proposed a special pre-Christmas show for Pride of Dakota products, thereby providing a ready market for the members' products.

The first Holiday Showcase was held in Bismarck, with beautiful decorations and entertainment. The aisles were so crowded with eager shoppers laden with sacks of gifts, it was hard to see the vendors through the crush. Many members sold out within hours. We knew we had a "winner." After a year or two of Showcases in Bismarck, we added another Holiday Showcase event in Fargo, which became even bigger than the show in Bismarck.

When it started, I made it a point to be among the first to arrive at the show, usually while companies were still setting up their displays and to be among the last to leave the show. These times were the best times to get insight and feedback on the needs and aspirations of the Pride of Dakota members so that our foreign and domestic marketing programs could be adjusted and improved.

The Holiday Showcase program still is a great success. I still try to attend each year, partly for "old times' sake" and to see old friends, and partly to buy fabulous North Dakota-made products.

Advocacy and Public Policy Work

My campaign slogan was that I would be an "advocate for agriculture." I took that commitment very seriously. One of my first actions was to add (within the existing Agriculture Department budget) a policy division.

During my two terms, I had some very smart policy analysts, including Sarah Nordby, Scott Carlson and Richard Quintas. We got a subscription to the Federal Register (the publication that carries all proposed rulemaking for the federal government) and read it daily. We were alert to proposed changes to regulations and fired off hundreds of comments on a host of issues: credit, crop insurance, swampbuster, sodbuster, foreign trade, economic development and many other topics. These comments made a difference to the outcome of many proposed regulations.

After I left office, I ran into a longtime USDA lawyer who told me that the department missed me. I was surprised and asked him why. He said that the North Dakota Department of Agriculture had submitted more comments to USDA than all of the other 49 states combined and that the folks at USDA had grown to rely on good feedback from us!

We weren't just reactive; sometimes we demanded new programs or new rules to provide better service to North Dakota farmers. For example, we were upset that North Dakota had only a handful of acres devoted to canola even though our climate and conditions were well suited for canola. In contrast, Canadian provinces just to the north were booming with canola.

Though North Dakota farmers we visited with wanted to grow more canola, they couldn't. What explained the difference? Lenders required that any crops grown by indebted farmers (and most farmers were indebted) had to be insured by the Federal Crop Insurance Corporation. Sarah Nordby, who was part of the policy and research team, was passionately committed to changing this. She and I became virtual "pen pals" with the folks at the FCIC by the time I left office. And, we had success – after a while we had a canola pilot program for federal crop insurance in several northern-tier counties in North Dakota.

The success of the pilot program led to broader availability, and as soon as crop insurance was available for canola, farmers seized the chance to grow canola. According to statistics collected by Northern Plains Canola Growers and USDA, canola acreage greatly increased in North Dakota while I was Commissioner. It went from a negligible number of acres in 1987 (reported at zero), to 16,000 acres in 1992 (the year I ran for re-election) to 376,000 acres in 1997 (the year after I left office).

Many pieces of the puzzle needed to come together for this to happen (farmer advocacy, political support, USDA efforts to get a workable crop insurance policy, better insecticides and more seed varieties, to list a few), but Sarah Nordby and my shared vision of vast fields of canola and a new major crop for North Dakota has certainly come about. By 2012, canola had risen to 1,455,000 acres and North Dakota now raises 90 percent of all U.S. canola supplies. I believe that having a crop insurance policy and our many letters and petitions to FCIC were part of that success.

As part of our policy work, I also sponsored two big seminars during my second term to encourage women to run for election or to seek appointment to the many agricultural boards or commissions that exist in North Dakota. We recruited a vibrant group of women leaders to serve as panelists and speakers, and presented information on the steps women could take to become elected or appointed for every agricultural board, commission, grower group and agriculture organization. We had excellent turnouts of women from all corners of the state. (While these meetings were well-received and important, my successors as Commissioner of Agriculture did not continue them.)

For me, it was a joy to be in a room of women for a change, as most of the meetings I attended for the eight years I was in office were composed primarily of men. I used to say that because more than half of the farm land in North Dakota is owned by women, and women are equal partners in all farms owned by married couples, and women have to sign all the mortgages and promissory notes, women should be better represented in the leadership of agriculture organizations. This is still true today; though there has been progress, much more to advance women in agriculture can be done.

Revitalizing the Agricultural Products Utilization Commission

When I started my first term, I learned about a small agency that funded rather obscure technical research on a limited scale, mainly at NDSU. It didn't get much done for the amount of overhead it consumed, but several of us (Deputy Jeff Weispfenning, Representative Bob Nowatski and others) developed a plan to make it more effective so that it could help start new businesses that would use agricultural products in new ways.

We developed a better funding method for it from a rather odd source: the unclaimed gas tax refunds for farmers' off-road use of gasoline products! Under its new mission and a better plan for operating and an active volunteer board, APUC became the "little agency that could." It gave grants that helped to start the Dakota Growers Pasta Company (now among the nation's largest pasta makers), the North American Bison Cooperative and many others. As a member of APUC, I felt I had a "picture into tomorrow" as entrepreneurs came in with their pitches for support for their ideas.

The Industrial Commission

Being on the Industrial Commission was a highlight of my years as Agriculture Commissioner. It is hard to pick the best examples of my work on the Industrial Commission, but here goes.

Consumer-sized Flour Packages From the State Mill

While I had been campaigning for Commissioner, I often met women (and a few men) who said that they loved the flour produced by the State Mill but didn't want to buy it in 25- or 50-pound bags. Perhaps as a relic of home baking for large families, the Mill's smallest size bag that was available in groceries in 1988 in North Dakota was 25 pounds. Home bakers who knew of the excellent quality of North Dakota State Mill flour didn't want to buy it 25 pounds at a time; they wanted a smaller package which would be easier to handle and one that they could use while it was still fresh.

This made eminent sense to me, so I made a campaign pledge to make modern-day consumer-sized 5- and 10-pound sacks available when I got elected. It took some doing, but the Mill management and other members of the Industrial Commission were supportive. I was at the Mill when we watched the new bags roll off the new bagging equipment, and it was exciting to see how an idea could become reality. Oddly enough, based on feedback over the past 20 years, I think bringing back the 5- and 10-pound sacks was one of the most popular things I did during my tenure on the Industrial Commission. I received a plaque from the Mill when I left office: "Thanks for bringing back the Five Pound Sack."

The Mill remains one of the many great legacies of the NPL: it buys between 8 and 10 percent of the state's output of spring wheat and durum wheat; it is known for the fabulous types of flour it makes for the baking trade (it makes over 250 different varieties of specialty flours); and it even engages in e-commerce. Anyone can now order 5- or 10-pound sacks of all-purpose flour or bread flour, automatic bread machine mixes, pancake mixes and whole-wheat flour – online![39]

I think people in North Dakota generally take the Mill too much for granted and do not fully appreciate the legendary national reputation that the Mill has earned due to superb-quality wheat that has been precision-milled and supplied to discriminating commercial bakers in every corner of the U.S. for almost 100 years.

Here is an illustration. When I became Commissioner and I learned that the Mill supplied a vast proportion of the bakeries in New York City and provided the specially high-protein wheat for bagels, I then realized that there was a North Dakota connection to a "contest" that I had judged many years earlier. In 1967, when I started law school in New York City's Greenwich Village, I didn't even know what a "bagel" was. My law school classmates were appalled at my ignorance and started a contest to a) educate me about bagels and b) have me (I was a neutral party) judge the source of the best bagel. I received bagels from Manhattan, Brooklyn, the Bronx, Queens, Long Island and even New Jersey. I sampled them all, and though all were great, I eventually decided that the bagels from Brooklyn were best.

Little did I know that every one of these bagels was most probably made from North Dakota hard red spring wheat that had been milled into flour at the NPL-founded North Dakota Mill and Elevator. The Mill still provides flour to the most discriminating bakeries in the U.S.

Helping Management and Workers at the Mill Work as a Team for Greater Productivity and Profits

During my time at the Industrial Commission, I also helped Lieutenant Governor Lloyd Omdahl resolve a labor dispute between a former manager of the Mill and the union workers at the Mill. In a very misguided effort to be more economical, a former manager of the Mill – who had been hired just prior to my joining the Commission – had taken steps to try to "bust" the union that had represented workers almost since the Mill was started in 1919.

I was asked to meet with union members, many of whom were third-generation workers at the Mill. Though members of the Industrial Commission generally don't interfere in the management of the day-to-day operations of Industrial Commission agencies, I decided I needed to hear what the workers had to say. After listening to them in the basement of the labor hall, I was shocked at their treatment by this manager, and I profoundly disagreed with his goal of getting rid of the union, a goal that he had not bothered to share with the Industrial Commission members. I brought the issues to the attention of Governor Sinner (who delegated this issue to the very able Lieutenant Governor Lloyd Omdahl) and Attorney General Spaeth.

Under Lloyd's leadership, we had a number of meetings with the manager, the union and others, and investigated the situation thoroughly. We quietly reached a solution where the union would stay, would have better dialogue with managers, and under which the workers would get bonuses in years with profits, based on a formula that recognized their contributions to the success of the State Mill.

This profit-sharing system is still going strong, as is the union which works in strong partnership with the management. An August 7, 2013, a Grand Forks Herald story about continuing Mill profits ("ND State Mill Grinds Out Profits") said that the North Dakota General Fund would receive profits of $5.63 million for 2013, and each of the 132 Mill employees would receive a bonus check, averaging $10,000.[40] Members of the Industrial Commission (all Republicans) approved the bonuses and complimented the workers, saying that they deserved it.

The NPL vision of fairness to farmers, to workers and to sound business methods has met fruition at the State Mill.[41]

In 1989, Sarah Vogel was the first woman to serve on the North Dakota Industrial Commission. In this photo of the Industrial Commission, which was taken in Governor Sinner's office, Agriculture Commissioner Sarah Vogel stands with Attorney General Nick Spaeth behind Governor George Sinner. (Sarah Vogel photo collection taken by Knutson Photography)

Creating New Loan Programs at the Bank of North Dakota

One of the most significant accomplishments during my time on the Industrial Commission was playing a role in creation of two new lending programs, PACE ("Partnership for Accelerating Community Expansion") and Ag-PACE (a PACE program for farmers).

Governor Sinner had developed an idea to create a fund (the "PACE" fund) that would be used by the Bank of North Dakota (BND) to reduce or "buy down" the interest paid by borrowers for loans from private banks. A PACE loan would typically have a very low interest rate to be paid by the borrower, but it would nonetheless be very attractive for the local bank.

First, the local bank reduced its risk in the loan because BND would participate in the bank's loan by "buying" a large share of a PACE loan (for example, if there were a $100,000 PACE loan, the BND would provide $75,000 and the local lender would only risk $25,000). Second, it was a solid source of fee income for the local lender. The local lender would earn fees for managing the BND share of the loan.

Third, the local lender would have a lower risk of default because the borrower would have lower interest payments, thereby increasing the likelihood of successful payment of bills and profitable growth of the company. Finally, a PACE loan would be profitable to the lender because the lender would collect its regular commercial rate (partly paid by the borrower, partly from the PACE buy-down, and partly from a community match.) The community where the borrower's business would be located had to match part of the buy-down from any source other than the borrower. Finding this community match served as a community screening process for reliable, trustworthy borrowers. Without a community match, there could be no PACE loan.

I thought the PACE concept as outlined by Governor Sinner was brilliant. What I didn't like about the proposal was that the communities most in need of this type of program were least able to find a match: I had travelled every corner of the state and the little farm towns had been absolutely blasted by the drought, the loss of farmers, lower values for homes and closing of agriculture implement dealers, farm supply stores and restaurants. In some cases, half of the buildings on main street were boarded up. As the little towns emptied, younger and middle-aged people moved to Fargo, Bismarck or other larger cities, if they stayed in North Dakota at all.

I feared – realistically – that if BND PACE buy-down funds were made available exactly as proposed by Governor Sinner, the little towns would not be able to gather the requisite match before the PACE buy-down funds would be gobbled up by the larger towns and cities.

I raised this objection with Governor Sinner and Attorney General Spaeth. I said I liked the program as far as it went, but I wouldn't vote for it unless there was a way to lower the barriers to the use of the PACE program by struggling small towns. I argued that these communities needed this type of program but lacked the human and financial resources to raise the requisite 25 percent match.

After some fairly stiff debates about possible changes to his outline, Governor Sinner said that he wasn't per se opposed to the type of change I wanted if it would be easy to administer and relied on concrete measurements, rather than exercise of judgment by lending officers. I agreed that the program would be better if discretion were removed. I took it as a challenge and spent time discussing and researching the problem with a small team consisting of Jeff Weispfenning, Don Morrison (who worked at the Tax Department and who was detailed to this project by Heidi Heitkamp, who was then Tax Commissioner) and Tim Moore, who worked at BND.

After a lot of work, our little team came up with a community percentage factor. It was based on readily available public data: taxable valuation, population, employment, and taxable sales and purchases.

The communities in North Dakota were assigned to one of five quintiles based on this economic data. The community percentage factor then determined the amount of the PACE fund's buy-down of the interest rate buy-down. The BND would buy down 85 percent of the interest rate for the most stressed communities (e.g., Willow City), and this would go down to 65 percent for the least stressed communities (e.g., Fargo). We agreed that the ranking of communities would be periodically adjusted and communities would be reassigned to higher or lower quintiles if economic data showed improvement or decline.

When the program finally became public, the Industrial Commission was united in support of the PACE program with the graduated requirements. It had a successful and popular start, with use by large and small communities. The program continues today.[42] Since March, 1990 when the program started and up to December 31, 2013, there have been 695 PACE loans in all corners of the state and in large and small communities, totaling $466,254,798, with a negligible default rate. It has been credited with the creation of 11,346 jobs.[43]

After PACE was operational, my attention next turned to how to stimulate alternative crops and livestock and new business development on farms and ranches. The state was still suffering from the farm credit crisis, and many of the old ways of doing business (monocrop wheat; beef cattle) were no longer reliably profitable. New crops and new types of livestock, new on-farm businesses and new enterprises on farms were needed by many of our farmers if they wanted to stay on the land.

Accordingly, I proposed AG-PACE and it was readily adopted. AG-PACE had a similar interest buy-down feature as PACE, but no community match was required (a match wasn't possible because most farmers weren't living in a community). AG-PACE was made available only for non-traditional ventures. AG-PACE wasn't available to grow more wheat or raise more beef cattle but would be available for raising buffalo or starting a greenhouse, growing a non-traditional crop, for buying shares in a cooperative, or for most types of on-farm business (such as hairdresser, truck repair or fence contracting.)

AG-PACE became very popular very quickly: Bob Humann, who is now Chief Lending Officer of the Bank but who was then an agriculture loan officer, became known as "Buffalo Bob" because of the large number of AG-PACE buffalo loans he made. Ag Pace is still a strong program. Since it was started on July 1, 1991, there have been 1,016 Ag-PACE loans totaling $10,898,407 – with a negligible default rate.

Oil and Gas

The oil and gas regulatory function of the Industrial Commission was much less active between 1989 and 1996 than it is today. Nevertheless, we created some good practices and regulations.

A law requiring payment of royalties and payment of taxes on gas that was flared more than one year after the time of first production, *unless it would be "economically infeasible" for the operator to connect to a gas gathering line,* had been in effect for more than a decade. See NDCC 28-08-06.4. However, it seemed to me and others that the industry was still engaging in wasteful flaring of natural gas.

Accordingly, in 1993, the Industrial Commission (me, Attorney General Heitkamp and Governor Schafer) adopted a rule that defined what "economically infeasible" meant. See Admin. Code Section 43-02-03-60.2. Our rule appropriately said that the connection to a gas-gathering line was "economically infeasible" only if the direct costs of connection and operation **over the life of the well** are greater than the amount of money the operator is likely to receive over the life of the well for the gas, less royalties and taxes.

In an odd turn, I even became a class representative on two lawsuits that sought to enforce the flaring law, as interpreted by the regulation that I helped to write in 1993.[44] I believe that oil and gas companies active in North Dakota must follow the laws and regulations of North Dakota. Just like the rest of us.

Conclusion: Don't Depend on Politics for a Living

I didn't run for a third term, though I think I could have been rather easily re-elected. Instead, in November 1995, I gave 12 months' notice that I wouldn't run for a third term.

In the early days of the League, two terms were the maximum any NPL office-holder was supposed to serve. These NPL'ers believed that office holders who stayed in too long would become "spoiled" and start thinking about their own re-election rather than doing a good job for the people that elected them to office.

By the end of my two terms, I worried about becoming dependent on the job of Agriculture Commissioner and losing my skills as a lawyer. I decided that I would either run for another office (I considered running for Governor but pretty quickly abandoned that idea) or I would simply go back to practicing law.

In the end, I rather awkwardly combined the two goals and ran for office as an attorney who wanted to be a Justice of the North Dakota Supreme Court. I lost that campaign for the Supreme Court and deservedly so. I didn't have the same compelling motivation to serve the public in the 1996 election that I had in the 1988 and 1992 elections. Losing was OK. The winner – Justice Mary Maring – was well-qualified (I even said she was well-qualified during the campaign) and she has served 18 years on the Supreme Court with distinction.

Thanks to my loss, I was able to go back to my career as a lawyer and continue representing farmers and ranchers, Native Americans and the people of North Dakota.[45] My father used to tell me, "Never depend on politics for a living. Always have your own career." I think that is sound advice, which has served me well.

I hope that many people, especially women, will feel that they can contribute to the betterment of society by being active in politics at some point during their lives and careers. Politics is what makes the cities, counties, states and nation run well, or run ill, and it all depends on the people involved. It isn't necessary to be a career politician to make a big contribution. Please become involved for whatever period and in whatever position best suits you! And, if you do, the people-first principles of the Nonpartisan League are a time-tested basis for political morality and serve as a model for public service.

SIX

On the Job Working for You

By

Susan Elizabeth Wefald

North Dakota Public Service Commissioner
1993-2008

"I realized from the beginning that it was not my job to look after the large companies who came before the PSC. They had their own lobbyists and plenty of money to spend on cases before the Commission. My job was to make sure that the people, who were busy working at jobs and raising kids, had a strong voice when Commission decisions were being made."

Susan Wefald

Susan E. Wefald nee Benschop*

1947-Present

Public Service Commissioner 1993–2008

First Woman to Serve on the North Dakota Public Service Commission

Public Service Commissioner Susan Wefald - 1996
(SHSND 32227)

Personal Information

Born 1947 in Detroit, Michigan, and raised in Royal Oak, Michigan. Married to Robert (Bob), three children. In "spare time," enjoys gardening, hiking and playing her violin.

Party Affiliation

Republican

Education

Kimball High School, Royal Oak, Michigan; Received B.A. from the University of Michigan in Ann Arbor, Michigan; Received Masters in Public Administration from the University of North Dakota (2002).

Professional Experience Before Taking Office

Burleigh County Social Services case worker, 1971-72; Bismarck Meals on Wheels, first director, 1972-74; Village Family Service Center budget and credit counselor, 1983-93; Bismarck School Board, 1989-93, president, 1992-93.

Memberships Include

As Public Service Commissioner: National Association of Regulatory Commissioners, 1993-2008, member Electricity and Consumer Affairs committees; Mid America Regulatory Commissioners, 1993-2008, president, 2001-02. Organization of Midwestern Independent System Operator (MISO) States, first president, 2003-04, and board member, 2004-08, North Dakota Lignite Research Council, 2001-05

Other: Sakakawea Girl Scout Council, president, 1977-83, and Lifetime GSUSA Member and council volunteer; Bismarck-Mandan Symphony, first violin, 1976-present; Trinity Lutheran Church; American Association of University Women, 1972-82; Bismarck Veterans Memorial Public Library Board of Trustees, 2001-07.

*Bio contains information through 2008

I arrived at the Public Service Commission at 8 a.m. on January 4, 1993, in a carefully chosen outfit of navy blue blazer and blue and gold paisley skirt. I was excited about my new "job." The day before, I had come to my spacious office on the 12th floor of the Capitol building and "moved in." I had also previously submitted my official oath of office to the Secretary of State. I was ready for work when I walked in the door.

During my first week, I was planning to meet personally with staff members, study pending cases, learn Public Service Commission meeting protocol, attend the ceremonial swearing-in ceremony and the inaugural ball, and work on legislative issues. All of these things were on my plate and more.

I was 45 years old, the mother of Tom, 15; Kate, 19; and Sarah, 20, and the wife of Bob. I was president of the Bismarck School Board, and I would continue that work for six months, but I already knew that I could handle two elected offices for only a short time. My oldest daughter, Sarah, 20, had announced before Christmas that she was getting married the next summer in Bismarck, and we had just held an engagement party for her over the holidays. Just like many other North Dakota women, I had a full plate of responsibilities.

Events Leading Up to My First Day

I really didn't think that Governor-elect Ed Schafer would appoint me to the Public Service Commission (PSC or Commission). Until Bob lost his race for Supreme Court judge in early November 1992, I had not given any thought to statewide public office. I had watched Bob run three statewide campaigns – two for attorney general (a win and then a loss) and one for Supreme Court Justice (a loss). You learn a great deal about politics by being married to a politician, and I had decided after the 1984 election that I was not interested in running a statewide campaign. They entail a great deal of work.

However, I was comfortable running for the Bismarck School Board in community elections in June 1989 and 1992. I loved serving on the School Board and dealing with challenging education issues. At that time, the Bismarck School District was the largest in the state, serving over 10,000 students. When I won a new term in June 1992, my fellow members of the School Board elected me president.

Then, in November 1992, PSC Commissioner Dale Sandstrom was elected to the Supreme Court, and there was a vacancy on the Commission. I had worked at the Village Family Service Center (Village) for 10 years as a budget and credit counselor and was ready for a new challenge. I also knew that if selected, I would have to run for statewide office twice in the next four years.[46] I decided to apply for the opening on the PSC. So with Bob's strong encouragement, I sent in my resume and letter to Governor Schafer's

Description of Official Duties as Public Service Commissioner

Six-year term. Serves as one of three Public Service Commissioners. The Public Service Commission is a constitutional agency with varying degrees of statutory authority over: Electric and Gas Utilities, Telecommunication Companies, Energy Plant and Transmission Line Sitings, Railroads and Motor Carriers, Grain Elevators, Auctioneers and Auction Clerks, Weighing and Measuring Devices, Pipeline Safety, Coal Mine Permitting and Reclamation. Duties of the commission include making decisions on utility rate cases; issuing permits and supervising reclamation of coal mines; inspecting and licensing grain elevators; inspecting and siting gas and oil pipelines, testing public scales and siting electric transmission lines. (Note: Commission responsibilities kept changing over the 16 years Commissioner Wefald served on the Public Service Commission.)[47]

search committee.

Governor-elect Schafer never interviewed me, so I was very surprised when I received a phone call from Schafer in mid-December, asking me if I would accept the appointment. I was at a soybean convention giving farmers home budget advice when the call came through. I told him I would work hard to be a good Commissioner, and that same day, December 15, his first day in office, he announced my appointment, along with two other appointments.

I had two weeks to round up my work at the Village, prepare for Christmas, sell my utility stock that I had inherited from my parents, preside over School Board meetings and realize that I was going to be the first woman to serve on the PSC.

The North Dakota Public Service Commission

The Public Service Commission is the only executive branch department that is led by three elected officials. All three have equal responsibilities, and all decisions have to be made in public meetings. The Commission is responsible for regulating large companies in our state, and the writers of the state constitution did not want those regulatory decisions in the hands of just one elected official.

When I started my work as Commissioner in 1993, Commissioner Bruce Hagen (1961-2000) and Commissioner Leo Reinbold (1980-2003) were my fellow Commissioners. Commissioner Tony Clark replaced Bruce Hagen on the PSC in 2001. Commissioner Kevin Cramer replaced Leo Reinbold in August 2003 and both served with me until I retired from the PSC in December 2008.

I soon developed my own approach to the challenging new responsibilities facing me at the PSC.

The PSC deals with complicated and technical issues, and things are constantly changing. Often I felt like,

"What am I doing here – and will people figure out I don't know all of the answers or all of their names?!" My fellow Commissioners, and the industry people I met, all seemed to feel comfortable and powerful, and so I just kept reading and studying the cases that came before me and I kept asking questions. I knew I didn't know all of the answers, and I quickly realized that no one else did, either. So I decided early on that I would not pretend I knew all of the answers.

My goal was to be an excellent leader and boss so that other women would have a chance to serve after I left the Commission.

I had never been inside a grain elevator, so before I attended and spoke to the Grain Dealers' convention that first January, I visited the grain elevator near Bismarck. I asked "what is anhydrous ammonia" at a farmer's meeting. I asked questions about DC lines and AC lines, and went on inspections with my staff to coal mines. I read the mining laws and rules and asked the staff why a coal company shouldn't receive a notice of violation if I noted a problem at the mine.

The Legislature met from January to April that first year, and I prepared my own testimony on controversial telephone bills. In the first month, I was labeled a consumer advocate by the legislative telephone lobbyist Mel Kambeitz, and the title stuck. I learned more in the first six months on the PSC than I had learned in years, and my learning never stopped in my 16 years on the Commission.

I realized from the beginning that it was not my job to look after the large companies who came before the PSC. They had their own lobbyists and plenty of money to spend on cases before the Commission. My job was to make sure that the people, who were busy working at jobs and raising kids, had a strong voice when Commission decisions were being made.

However, I understood that companies need to have adequate revenues in order to provide good service to consumers. I worked to be fair to all parties who came before the Commission, which meant that I studied to understand every case that came before the PSC, reading reams of paper files on the cases before me and consulting with staff.

I also wanted every person or organization to feel comfortable before the Commission. Regardless of political party, I wanted people to get questions answered and get help when needed from the PSC.

Working With Bruce and Leo

Bruce Hagen was and is a true gentleman. Welcoming and friendly, he knew people all over the state. By the time Bruce left the Commission in 2000, he had served 39 years on the PSC, the longest-serving Commissioner in state history, and among the longest

Public Service Commissioners Reinbold (left), Hagen (center) and Wefald (right) visit the Falkirk Mine near Washburn in the mid-1990s. (SHSND 32227-02-82-01)

serving nationally. He saved every paper he read at the Commission, and some he didn't read. Periodically, with the help of Charlene Magstad, his assistant, he sent all of these papers to the University of North Dakota to its archives. Bruce and I enjoyed each other's company, although we didn't always agree on issues, especially in cases involving disputes between a rural electric and an investor-owned utility.

Leo Reinbold, affable and funny, was a former geography teacher at Valley City State who remembered his students all over the state. Teachers who knew Leo would bring masses of students during legislative sessions up to the 12th floor to meet Leo, see the collection of hats on the ceiling of his office and hear a few words about the PSC. Leo wanted the Governor to appoint someone else to the Commission, so when I arrived, he was lukewarm to me. That was fine with me since I had been told to keep an eye on Leo, since he might forget some rules, like ex-parte communications or accepting favors from industry. I knew that if one Commissioner on the PSC did not follow the rules, it could hurt the whole Commission.

In the early '90s, Leo was constantly invited as a humorous speaker at natural gas conventions, both instate and around the country, because he held the natural gas portfolio on the Commission and was on the natural gas committee at the National Association of Utility Commissioners. He loved an audience, and at PSC holiday gatherings, he would play Karnac, wearing a turban on this head (copying Johnny Carson) and Bruce would assist. Bruce and Leo were great friends.

On the Job as Commissioner

When I announced that I was running for office in January 1994, I started my speech with the following words:

> "I've been your Public Service Commissioner now for one year, and what a year it has been! It's been a year of testifying before the Legislature, of participating in interactive video public hearings, of studying and making decisions in rate cases, of studying and learning about re-vegetation standards while visiting all our coal mines, and of travelling with our weights and measures people to observe scale testing at grain elevators and pump tests at gas stations. This is the "short list" of the things I've been doing. I have taken this extra effort to fully understand the effects my decisions on the Public Service Commission have on people's daily lives. People tell me I have a great deal of energy … and I think I do, but I recall some evenings I've fallen asleep over my cup of tea at the kitchen table after supper!"

I loved the diversity of my work at the Commission. If there was a controversial case before the Commission, I would be busy reading and responding to emails and letters from concerned citizens. I held the consumer affairs portfolio, and so I paid special attention to the letters and phone calls that were coming in from the public and often took phone calls from the people who wanted to "talk to a commissioner."

As the holder of the coal mine permitting and reclamation portfolio, I enjoyed getting out into the field and seeing coal mining reclamation myself. I wore regulation steel-toed boots and a hardhat. I felt my eyes were the eyes of the people who did not have a chance to see reclamation first hand. I would travel in the mud-spattered pickup with our staff inspectors, and sometimes the federal inspectors who came to North Dakota, and ride and walk all over the mines, listening to the questions our staff had for the company coal mine reclamation expert. Between these visits, I read the mining regulations myself, and soon I was asking my own questions of the company mine staff. These experiences helped me understand the coal mine permit applications that came before the Commission, and also their reclamation plans.

My style as a Commissioner was to consult with various staff on a daily basis, usually the division heads. I not only consulted with the division heads, but also with other staff members who could answer a particular question. These visits kept me in constant contact with staff so that I could try to understand their jobs and their concerns.

Formal hearings are an important part of Commission work, but they do not happen very often. Most of the work was taken care of through informal hearings, which were held at least every other Wednesday in the afternoon. Commissioners, staff and industry parties gathered at a square table in the hearing room and shared thoughts on the agenda item(s) of the day.

When a formal hearing was required, such as a major rate case or hearing on a pipeline or wind farm siting, the hearing room would be filled with people and the Commissioners would preside from the "bench." Hearings could extend for several days to get all of the important information on the record. After each witness testified, the Commissioners asked questions to clarify matters. This broke up just listening to all of the testimony and gave us a chance to get involved at each hearing. We all enjoyed these question and answer periods, unless the hearing was going longer than expected!

Working With the Legislature

I loved being a state official when the Legislature was not in session. The Commission was in charge of business at the PSC, and no utility company could use the threat of an "end run" around the Commission by going to the Legislature during that time. Of course, I was realistic and knew that if industry considered any Commission decision "unfair," there could be a bill in the next legislative session addressing that issue.

In the mid '90s, the telephone companies, both the telephone cooperatives and US West (now Century Link) were trying to be deregulated as quickly as possible, and none of them had any competition. Cell phones had not taken off yet, and there was still the possibility of competition through other land-line companies. We have almost no competition between land-line telephone companies today, and there certainly was none then. However, the lobbyists for the phone companies worked hard convincing legislators otherwise, and every year there was a bill deregulating some part of their business.

The Commission wanted to determine when real competition was in place and then deregulate on a systematic basis. Often the whole Commission took a position on a telecommunications bill and presented joint testimony. However, sometimes I wrote my own testimony, and went down and tried to get the worst bills changed, or in a few cases, not passed at all.

In 1997, I wanted to defeat HB1067, which would deregulate US West and shield the telephone co-ops from competition. I found other likeminded individuals and organizations and, working together, we were successful. I wrote testimony and placed it on the desks of House members. John Dorso, House majority leader, was so mad that I was against "his" bill that he called me down to his office, reprimanded me like a school girl and refused to let me speak to the Republican caucus. However, the Democrats invited me to their caucus, and I went. The bill passed the House, 58-38.

In the Senate, I saw David Cruthers, the lobbyist for the telephone cooperatives, kneeling on the floor next to a Senator's desk, pleading with him to vote for HB1067. ATT and US West and their politically funded interest groups ran full-page ads in the paper supporting or denouncing this bill. US West demanded my office telephone records and accused me of calling people on my Commission phone about the bill. I replied that, yes, I had called people on my Commission phone about the bill, but they had called me first with questions about the bill.

A US West lobbyist also argued that I should not vote on any future US West cases that came before the PSC because I was working against his legislation. This statement made the front page of the Bismarck Tribune in March and was the subject of several newspaper editorials. Gary Nelson, Senate majority leader, and I were at odds about the bill. I spent hours writing testimony, preparing charts, talking to legislators, etc., and, of course, when HB1067 did not pass the Senate, the lobbyists for US West and the telephone co-ops were not happy. This created problems for the PSC in future legislative sessions.

It was very interesting working as a regulator in the 1990s when many legislators did not think there was any need for regulation. In fact, in the mid-'90s, the Commission had to appear before an interim legislative committee that was considering "doing away" with the PSC.

After the year 2000, energy bills started taking center stage. Again, I would often take "lone" positions on bills I thought were important. Wind farm siting is an example. For years, the North Dakota Century Code had stated that all electrical generation units 50 megawatts (MW) and larger were to be sited by the Commission. Florida Power and Light, a large wind developer in North Dakota, wanted this changed so that the Commission only sited wind farms 99 MW and larger. This was a big change, and I didn't agree with it. This legislation allowed very large wind farms to be built with little oversight. I prepared my own testimony about this issue, but my arguments were not accepted. The change went through. But even legislators did not like the results of this change, and after I left the Commission, people started saying, "Susan was right." Now as a result of legislation, the Commission sites all wind farms one-half MW and above.

Ed Schafer was supportive of me during legislative sessions. I remember him saying to a group of legislators, when referring to me, "You can be a Republican consumer advocate." To some Republican legislators, this was an "oxymoron."

In the end, I would say I had about a 50 percent success rate with the Legislature on bills that I really cared about. Sometimes legislators wanted me to change my position. I generally stuck with the position I started with because I was going to the Legislature to give expert advice. They made the final decision.

Lobbyists I Have known

Since the Commission is a quasi-judicial agency, ex-parte communication is not allowed. So contrary to public perception, there is no informal discussion of case issues with industry representatives while a case is being considered. All information about the case has to be on the record, and the record is in the case file or on tapes from official hearings. That does not mean that you can't talk to industry reps while you are considering their case, but you can only talk about the weather, your family and other interests that you might share.

I loved attending legislative socials during the legislative session. One favorite was the Rural Electric Cooperative dinner hosted by Dennis Hill: no speeches, just a few introductions, a good dinner, legislators and lots of interesting people with whom to visit. Commissioners were also invited to speak or moderate panels at industry conferences. Every January, the Grain Dealers, led by Steve Strege, held its 800-plus person conference. All three PSC Commissioners would always be speakers at the conference. The Lignite Council, headed by John Dwyer, held its large meeting every fall. Usually Commissioners were part of the program.

All of these events were male-dominated. As a woman, I was in the minority at the formal sessions without spouses. In fact, at many smaller North Dakota industry meetings, especially lignite or pipeline meetings, I was often the only woman present.

Early on, I realized that all industry lobbyists liked me, not because of my charm or wit, but because I was a Commissioner and I might soon be making an important decision on something that mattered to their company! That helped me keep things in perspective when I would be talking and a group of lobbyists around me would be hanging onto my every word!

There were also Commission policies limiting gifts from industry. It was a standing joke between Commissioners and staff that John Dwyer, Lignite Council, always sent each Commissioner a small pail of licorice "coal" candy at Christmas. We would try to "share" it with staff, but had no luck. It made a great "cough drop" in an emergency.

Working With Tony and Kevin

Tony Clark was a smart, political and articulate Commissioner. A young father, he would bring his boys up to the Commission offices for short visits while he was working. He studied our casework and helped the Commission receive more money from the Legislature. He had the telecommunications portfolio and soon was an expert in this area. He was great friends with Kevin Cramer from the day Kevin arrived, and they voted together on almost every issue that came before the Commission. Tony and I had a good working relationship at the Commission, but we were not friends.

In general, I enjoy working with men, and I got along well with the men who were on staff and my fellow Commissioners that I met at national meetings. I also had an easy-going, friendly relationship with the men I served with on the Bismarck School Board. But Kevin and Tony kept their distance from me. Trust is an essential element for friendship, and there was no trust between me and Kevin or Tony.

Kevin Cramer was a cheerful, helpful Commissioner. He didn't like attending meetings and was always saying that he liked to know just the "big picture," not a lot of details. He felt the same way about Commission administration. I am just the opposite. I loved

Public Service Commissioners Tony Clark (left), Susan E. Wefald (center) and Kevin Cramer (left). Susan Wefald was serving as President of the Commission in 2006.
(SHSND 32227-02-70-02)

to delve into the details in the cases that came before the Commission. He loved hosting radio shows and helping raise funds for various organizations.

Open Meetings

Having served on the Bismarck School Board for four years, I was familiar with the rules for open meetings. The PSC is a state office run by three elected officials, and open meetings are required for every group decision. That means that whenever the Commission either makes a final decision or is in the process of deciding what a decision might be, an open meeting must be held.

Open meeting laws are great for the public, and they also ensure that each Commissioner knows what is going on, both within the agency on administrative matters and on policy matters. However, there are also drawbacks. I could never go into one of my fellow Commissioner's offices and visit about a case that was before the Commission. All communication about cases had to be at a public meeting, which was noticed, and usually someone from industry was in attendance at the meeting. Often, a whole group of interested industry people were in attendance. An open meeting does not mean that people who attend are able to participate in the discussion. They are there to observe.

For example, for an important rate case decision, the Commission would usually meet three or four times after the hearing to work on the wording of the final order. Present at the discussion table would be the three Commissioners and staff assigned to assist the Commission on the case. Sitting in on the open meeting would be PSC staff assigned to represent consumer interests, representatives from the company affected by the rate case, individuals interested in the case and a media person.

Very soon I learned not to be intimidated by the number of industry people in the room for important policy discussions. I learned to say what needed to be said, regardless of who was in the room listening to the meeting.

I also learned quickly that I needed to be well-prepared for these meetings, and plan what points I wanted to make, and decide when to stand firm and when I was willing to compromise. These meetings were also taped and sometimes broadcast, so there was not a lot of chitchat.

As a new Commissioner, I was fortunate that Bruce and Leo were willing to hold many meetings about administrative matters. We held meetings reviewing all open cases before the Commission, creating a Commission policy manual, reviewing the Commission budget, determining raises for employees, organization of Commission staff and many other matters that affect a well-run agency. These meetings gave me a chance to really get to know the administrative side of the agency, and Bruce and Leo were open to my suggestions for change. When Tony and Kevin came to the Commission, they did not like to hold many administrative meetings. However, by that time, I had served on the PSC for eight years and understood agency administration. While I continued to study many of these things on my own, I adapted to fewer administrative meetings.

Formal PSC meetings, where we voted on all cases before us, were held at least once every two weeks. These meetings were fun and interesting. We usually voted on 20 to 30 cases every two weeks. Many of these "cases" were routine matters, but at every meeting, there were usually five to 10 important decisions. Each Commissioner had a turn to discuss each case and why they would vote for or against it. If there was a 5,000-acre coal mining permit on the agenda, I would be the first to explain the case, since I held the coal mine reclamation and permitting portfolio for over 11 years. I had the electricity portfolio for 16 years and the consumer affairs portfolio for 16 years, so I always had many important cases to explain at meetings.

I served on the Commission before PSC meetings were video broadcast, and so usually there would be at least 10 people from the public in attendance at the meetings. The people who usually attended were industry people affected by the Commission decisions and members of the media. PSC department heads also were present and occasionally someone from the general public.

Leo Reinbold, Bruce Hagen and I, in our official seats on the podium, all played to the audience. Leo and Bruce loved to exchange banter with the audience before and at the start of the meetings. Bruce would always give an update on the level of the water in Devils Lake. He had a personal interest in this because he had a farm near Devils Lake. Leo would tell jokes or tell how an obscure town in North Dakota got its name. He loved knowing where every grain elevator was in the state and describing their locations by naming another obscure town nearby.

I could not compete with their banter, and so I decided that I would give short, but complete information on each case that was in my portfolio. If there was controversy, I told about the issues that created the controversy. If there were a few facts that created human interest, I shared these. I did this to attract media attention to our cases, and generally after every meeting, there was at least one story in the news about the PSC.

Dale Wetzel, AP writer, showed up for most PSC meetings and grilled the Commissioners about any item on the agenda in which he was interested. Our formal meeting might last 20 minutes, and then Dale would spend 20 minutes asking questions. Although any Commissioner could answer his questions, the portfolio holder needed to be able to field most of the questions about a particular case. I didn't want to have to refer Dale to staff to answer questions, even though my fellow Commissioners Reinbold and Hagen had no qualms with doing this. I had to really do my homework those first months to accurately answer his many questions.

After 2003, Commissioners Kevin Cramer and Tony Clark were great friends and their offices were next to each other in our office space on the 12th floor. As odd man out in this trio, I was not part of many of their personal exchanges. In regard to open meeting laws, I watched carefully, and on one occasion publicly announced that they had discussed a case at their own press conference, where I was not asked to be present.

PSC Staff

Staff members were the only people with whom I could talk about cases before the Commission. Since I loved discussing these issues, I talked to staff a great deal. Over the years, the PSC has been blessed with a very knowledgeable and hard-working staff. Many staff members have worked most of their career at the PSC, which means that there is good continuity when Commissioners come and go.

When I was at the Commission, we had about 37 staff. Ironically, the smallest division was the Public Utilities Division, which had the most complex cases and a heavy workload. The Legislature just did not want to beef up this division. With three professionals and one administrative assistant, the Public Utilities Division was the smallest in the U.S. Two attorneys worked for the PSC, and they provided legal advice on cases from all of the divisions. One advantage of having such a small staff was that I was able to really get to know each staff member and his or her strengths.

Commissioner Reinbold Resigns

In spring 2003, Commissioner Leo Reinbold was accused of sexually harassing an employee he was with in the Capitol elevator. She worked for another agency in state government. Shortly after this accusation, several women employees of the Commission met with and told our attorney Bill Binek that they had also been harassed by Leo. On that same day, when Bill told me what our women employees had said, I spoke to Central Personnel and asked them to open an investigation of sexual harassment at the PSC. Commissioner Reinbold resigned in July.

All of these events were very difficult for me, especially since I worked closely with all of the employees at the Commission and felt deep regret that this had happened during my watch. Shortly afterwards, Governor Hoeven appointed Kevin Cramer to the Commission.

Running for Office

In our life together, my husband, Bob, or I ran in 10 elections over 24 years. Bob ran for Attorney General in 1980 (win) and 1984 (loss). I ran for Bismarck School Board in June 1989 (win) and 1992 (win). Bob ran for Supreme Court Justice in 1992 (loss). I ran for PSC in 1994 (win), and 1996 (win). Bob ran for District Court Judge in 1998 (win). I ran for the PSC in 2002 (win), and Bob ran for District Court Judge in 2004 (win). Between us, we have a great deal of political experience. Someone was always running for office in our house, and it kept us very busy over the years.

A statewide campaign takes hard work. I knew when I accepted Ed Schafer's appointment to the Commission that I would need to run in two elections in the next four years. Dale Sandstrom, who left the PSC to serve on the Supreme Court, had four years left in his term. At that time, any appointed official had to run in the next general election after they were appointed. Since I was appointed in December 1992, in November 1994, I ran for the remaining two years in the six-year term. Then in November 1996, I ran for my first full six-year term. In 2002, I ran for my last six-year term on the Commission. I served a total of 16 years on the PSC.

Julie Hill (1994 election) was my toughest opponent. A teacher who had run for Lieutenant Governor with Nick Spaeth in 1992, she worked hard. I would see her campaigning everywhere, and I liked her and respected her. I realized early in the campaign that I was very competitive, and I wanted to win the election. So I worked very hard as well, and I found that the "harder I worked, the luckier I was." The election results for that first election were Susan Wefald 126,526 votes to Julie Hill 100,512 votes.

I chose the campaign slogan, "On the Job, Working for You," when I ran for my first statewide election and used it for my election campaigns in 1996 and 2002 as well. I ran against Steve Tomac in 1996 and Bob Stefonowicz in 2002.

There is a fun part to statewide campaigns. You meet new people at county fairs, parades, festivals, dinners and events all across the state. I ate french fries at the potato festival in Grafton, climbed aboard antique farm equipment at a threshing show, rode in a horse-drawn carriage in Taylor at the horse festival and ate sauerkraut in Wishek. I attended electric and telephone cooperative annual meetings across the state, and I talked with the people who attended as they were waiting in line for dinner.

One day I was in my office late in the afternoon, and in walked an elderly couple. They were from Dickinson. They had found their way to the PSC on the 12th floor, bypassed the PSC front desk and came in to see me with their telephone bill in hand. I welcomed them, and we sat down and talked about their problem. After we had determined what to do, I asked them, "Why did you come to see me about this?" The man said, "We saw you in a parade, and we knew that you could help." That comment alone made all of the parade appearances around the state worthwhile!

I always felt it was better for me, as a woman, to campaign alone. I read and believed the adage that the public views a man candidate's wife as a "helpmate" and a woman candidate's husband as "in charge." So I usually left Bob home in the early years for this reason. Starting in 1998, when Bob was running for and elected District Court Judge, judicial rules did not allow him to be involved with political parties. He could not accompany me to any political event, including Republican dinners or even state conventions.

Judicial rules also mandated that I could not announce in a speech why Bob was not present, and some peculiar rumors sometimes circulated. One year, Republicans held a large dinner, and there was a fancy program that listed each Republican state official and the name of their spouse. Bob's name could not be listed on the program due to judicial rules. Some people started speculating that "Bob and I were separated."

I missed him at some of these large Republican events because Bob knew lots of people. But he could attend non-political events with me when I was not running for office. One of these was the reception that is held every other year in the Great Hall of the Capitol, when legislators and the public are invited to meet all of the state officials in a receiving line.

In 2002, after winning the election, I was looking forward to the swearing-in ceremony for state officials that is held before the reception. Just as we were leaving for the ceremony, Bob announced that he was having terrible stomach pains. I rushed him down to the hospital, dropped him off, went to my swearing-in ceremony and then participated in the reception. The good news was that Bob only had a kidney stone and felt better soon. The bad news was that I did not have him by my side to whisper names and hometowns as people I didn't know came through the receiving line. Our standing joke at home was that he never forgot a name and we both knew that I did not have that gift.

Each person who campaigns has their own style – there is no one right way to go about it. Although I could get out and visit with people for hours, I always needed some alone time (usually driving home in the car) to "regroup." I would never try to meet everyone in a large roomful of people. I would stand near the door or in another place I would be "seen" and then spend time talking one on one with a handful of people in the area. People in the room would see me and know that I was there, and I didn't have to rush when talking to the few I met. That was my "style," and it worked well for me.

Regional Activities

As part of my Commission work, I served as president of the Organization of MISO (Midwest Independent System Operators) States (OMS). In December 2002, Pat Wood, president of the Federal Energy Regulatory Commission (FERC), asked me to chair a task group to establish a multi-state organization to monitor and make official comments on the wholesale electricity markets that were being established to serve the Midwest. This was a daunting task, and people in the know thought that the 15 state utility commissions would not agree on anything.

I agreed to chair this project, and between January and May 2003, commissioners from the 15 states worked together, established bylaws and incorporated into the first organization of its kind. As the first president of OMS, I worked very hard the first year keeping everything organized and everyone informed, until we hired an executive director.

The result was that staff and the commissioners from the member states talked together on conference calls and filed substantive comments with the FERC on many important wholesale electric market issues that had a direct effect on the people who lived in their states. While on the OMS board, I learned more about wholesale electricity markets and the wholesale costs of electric transmission than I ever wanted to know and was constantly amazed as the whole industry made tremendous changes in just a few years. I continued to serve on the OMS board until I left the Commission in 2008.

Deciding When to Leave the Commission

I knew it was time to leave the Commission when I no longer wanted to organize another campaign to run for office.

Also, federal energy policies kept changing. It was very frustrating to try to create a good, stable regulatory environment in North Dakota when national laws and rulemakings had no set direction. I had always been a very positive person and found that I was becoming "cynical" as I dealt with constantly changing federal energy policy. In January 2008, I announced that I would not run again for the PSC.

At the 2008 state Republican convention, I was nominated to be an "elector." When North Dakotans voted for John McCain, they actually voted for me and two other electors. In December 2008, in the North Dakota Secretary of State's office, I cast one of our state's three electoral votes for Senator John McCain.

The PSC staff organized a wonderful late-afternoon reception for me in December 2008 which was held on the top floor of the state Capitol building. I could have chosen to have the reception in the Great Hall of the Capitol but preferred the more intimate setting on the 18th floor. My husband, Bob, Governor John Hoeven, my fellow Commissioners and others were part of the program, and it was great to greet my whole family and the many others who attended.

I loved serving the people of North Dakota for 16 years, and it was difficult to say "goodbye."

SEVEN

Education is Priority One

By

Kirsten Baesler

State Superintendent,
North Dakota Department of Public Instruction
2013-Present

"My love of learning and young people influenced my choices of public service toward activities that contributed to helping children grow emotionally, physically and intellectually. I was following my parents' example to serve 'where I could best serve.'"

Superintendent Kirsten Baesler

Kirsten Baesler nee Schafer*

1969-Present

Superintendent of the North Dakota Department of Public Instruction 2013–Present

Superintendent of Public Instruction Kirsten Baesler – 2013
(Kirsten Baesler photo collection)

Personal Information

Born 1969 and raised in Flasher, North Dakota. Three children. In "spare time," enjoys running and lifting weights.

Education

Flasher High School. Earned two associate degrees from Bismarck State College; Bachelor's degree in Education from Minot State University; received master's degree in Education and Library Information Technology from Valley City State University.

Party Affiliation

Elected on No-Party Ballot but endorsed by the Republican Party

Professional Experience Before Taking Office

Bismarck Public Schools, 22 years as an instructional assistant to students with intellectual disabilities, a classroom teacher, library media specialist, technology integration specialist and vice principal; Mandan Public Schools, board member, 2004-13, president, 2006-13; North Dakota School Boards Association, southwest regional director; North Dakota Educational Technology Council, governor-appointed member.

Memberships and Committees

Other: board member for several local nonprofit organizations[48]

*Bio contains information through 2013

As I began my own path in education, I did not realize I would eventually become the State Superintendent of the North Dakota Department of Public Instruction. I am humbled to have been elected to this position, and I am extremely grateful to have the opportunity to advocate for the best possible public education for North Dakota's children. My entire adult life has been dedicated to helping children grow – intellectually, physically and emotionally. I believe that public education is the greatest American institution this country ever created. Our children are the future of our state and our nation, and they deserve the opportunity to succeed and prosper regardless of their cultural or economic backgrounds.

My experiences as a teacher, vice principal, school board member and president, and my work with state and federal legislators advocating for public education, were each instrumental in leading me to this office. I am passionate about public education and understand how very important it is to prepare our children for their futures.

To better understand how amazing I find my journey to this elected position, it is helpful to know the foundation that shaped the person I've become and the road that brought me to the office of state Superintendent. There were many people, experiences and activities that guided me on this path. I was blessed with parents who nurtured my love of learning, six older siblings who supported me in everything I did, and a community of people who encouraged me and expected me to always do my best.

A Firm Foundation

I grew up in the small town of Flasher, in southwestern North Dakota. Flasher is typical of rural North Dakota towns that are home to Class B schools. I attended school with basically the same group of classmates from kindergarten through high school. Our parents and relatives attended all of our school activities and sporting events and watched over all of us, not just their own families' children.

I am the youngest of seven children, raised by loving parents who provided guidance and, when it was needed, discipline and redirection. We were held accountable for our actions and learned that we were expected to do our best in all that we did, whether it was chores, schoolwork or other activities. My parents taught by nurturing, loving, helping and mentoring. They provided examples of servant leadership long before I ever heard the term.

My parents were also my first teachers. My late mother, Ardys (Zempel) Schafer, instilled the love of learning in all of her seven children. She shared facts from the family's encyclopedia set and used "big words" to help us build our vocabularies. When one of us would ask, "Mom, how do you spell … ?" she would send us to get the dictionary so we could look up the word, or we would look it up together.

While my mother infused in us the love of learning, my father, John, was a living example of the art of communication and service to others. My dad was a rural mail carrier and a member of the North Dakota Rural Letter Carriers Association (NDRLCA). He served as the state steward of that organization, representing members in grievance and arbitration cases. The conventions were family events that included the carriers' spouses and children. I ran for office for the first time and was elected as an officer of the Junior Association. As officer of the Junior Association, I had the opportunity to learn about policy issues and see Dad's communication and problem-solving skills in action. It wasn't a matter of who won or who lost; the intent was to reach a compromise so both sides would end up benefitting in some way.

Both of my parents taught me love of our country – to take pride in our freedoms, to remember how they were earned and are defended, and the great price that was paid for our nation's citizens to enjoy them. Both of my parents were active in the American Legion; my father as a member of Post 69 and my mother as a member of the Auxiliary. My siblings and I were signed up practically at birth, and I am a proud member of the American Legion Auxiliary to this day.

My early exposure to both of these organizations – the Rural Letter Carriers Association and the American Legion – helped me learn how to set goals and to work with others to problem-solve and design solutions to reach those goals. Even more importantly, I learned to listen, not just superficially, but to truly hear – and understand – what others have to say. This is such an important skill and one we should all take time to practice.

Perhaps the most important lesson my parents instilled in me was the responsibility that each of us has to help others. Both of my parents demonstrated public service through actions as well as words. I was raised knowing that each of us has a duty to be involved and to give back to our communities, our state and our country. There was never a question of *if* I would serve; the question has always been "How can I best serve?"

Preparation is the Key

Public service is not always easy. As a young mother, it seemed like I was in constant conflict trying to balance life, work and family. I had three young boys – the youngest two are twins – while I was working and going to college. I soon learned to become involved in things that complemented each other. I volunteered as a Sunday school teacher, Cub Scout leader and a youth park and recreation coach because these opportunities to serve were also opportunities that allowed me to be involved in my children's activities.

I always worried if I could really be a good mother while working and going to school.

Superintendent Baesler doing what she loves best – helping children learn.
(Kirsten Baesler photo collection)

But my children were my inspiration, and I knew that I had to prepare myself for any opportunity that may come my way. I knew by attending school and working that I would be setting a good example for my sons.

With positive reinforcement from my family and other early mentors, I earned my degree and continued my professional career in education.

While both people and past experiences helped me along my path, public service, volunteer and work-related activities were also an essential part of the equation. I've heard it said that "luck is preparing yourself for the next opportunity." This has proven to be very true for me. The experience I gained through volunteer positions – together with building a reputation for having a strong work ethic, following through on my commitments, and having a positive, nurturing attitude – I increased my opportunities. After being initially hired as a teaching and library assistant, I rose through the system at Bismarck Public Schools and was hired as a classroom teacher, library media specialist, technology integration instructor and then vice principal.

My love of learning and young people influenced my choices of public service toward activities that contributed to helping children grow emotionally, physically and intellectually. I was following my parents' example to serve "where I could best serve." I didn't realize I was also preparing myself for my next opportunity by developing skills and knowledge that would improve my ability in future positions. Looking back, I can honestly see the truth in the saying, "we get much more out of volunteer service than we put in."

My years with the Bismarck Public School system continued to fuel my passion for public education. I went on to earn my master's degree in Education and Information and Library Technology from Valley City State University. When an opportunity that allowed me to combine my love of classroom instruction with a vice principal position arose, I gladly accepted and continued my growth as an educator and as a leader.

I have spent my entire adult career in education. However, my career has consisted of a series of individual positions: classroom aide, teacher, librarian, technology coordinator, media specialist, vice principal and school board president, each providing an opportunity to learn and to grow.

My passion for education drew me to new and different experiences within my chosen field, but that may not always be the case. You may find that your passion draws you in a totally new direction. A willingness to explore new territory, learn new skills, and apply the skills and knowledge you have may lead you to prospects that may not appear to relate to your current career or expertise. When opportunity knocks, be brave – step out of your comfort zone and accept the challenge.

Servant Leader in Training

Among the most valuable leadership lessons I've learned is to strive to be a servant leader. Becoming a servant leader is a lifelong process, so I consider myself to be a "servant leader in training." A servant leader's primary focus is on the growth and well-being of people and the communities to which they belong. Rather than striving for the position, power and authority of traditional leadership, servant leaders share power, put the needs of others first, and help people develop and perform to the best of their abilities.

A servant leader takes responsibility for outcomes, congratulating all and sharing the joy of accomplishments, and being accountable when things don't go as well. There's a quote from author Jim Collins that sums this up well: "When things go well, we should look out the window and look for people to thank and recognize, ensuring that the praise is spread around and that people get credit when it's due. When things go wrong, we need to look into the mirror and analyze our actions to see if we could have done something differently, taking responsibility and learning from the experience."

The servant leadership concept was modeled by my parents in everything they did. My mother and father led by example as they nurtured, encouraged, taught and guided my sisters, brothers and me, and as they served their community. As I mentioned earlier, I didn't yet have a name for the concept; I simply knew from my parents' example that I had a responsibility to serve others and to contribute to the greater good.

Over the years, the benefits of servant leadership have been reinforced for me time and time again. The best leaders I've known and admired – those who I consider to be the most successful – practice servant leadership not just part of the time, but all of the time. The path of servant leadership is a lifelong journey of growth, accompanied by an open heart and an open mind. Everyone we come into contact with has at least one lesson for us. And, when we are honest with ourselves, we will learn by objectively examining our own actions and experiences, identifying the positive areas we should continue to develop as well as the negative areas we need to actively work to change.

The Road to the Capitol

As a result of my work as a school administrator, as president of the Mandan Public School Board and as a regional director for the North Dakota School Board Association, I understood the value and importance of sound educational policy. I recognized the critical role of the state Superintendent in developing, advocating for and implementing policy to ensure that our state provides the best possible public educational system for our children. While I thought it would be rewarding to be that advocate on behalf of our state's children someday, I had not seriously considered entering the race for office.

My thought process changed drastically in early 2012. I was on my way to Dickinson for one of my son's basketball games when I got a call asking if I would consider running for the office of Superintendent of Public Instruction. I admit I had to give the question a lot of thought before I could respond. My parents taught me to fully consider my public service choices to ensure that I not only had the experience necessary to effectively do the work but also had the time to fully commit to the responsibilities. I had many serious and insightful conversations with family, mentors, colleagues and generous people who had experience with the campaign process before I agreed to run.

The First Steps

I knew that there would be more to campaigning than meets the eye, and the work began soon after I made the decision to run. The day I announced my candidacy was a whirlwind of news conferences held in both Bismarck and Fargo. That was the first of many road trips I would make in the months before the November election.

The next step was to attend the Republican Party convention to seek a letter of support. I was familiar with the convention procedures and protocol, but the extra dimension of hosting a hospitality room, visiting with delegates and meeting party leaders took the experience to a whole new level. Even though I appreciated the delegates' level of interest in public education and their specific questions, asking for their support was not something I was used to doing. I was taught to be humble and to share credit for work well done. Campaigning required me to assertively promote my qualifications and skills, an approach to which I am still adjusting.

The vote for Superintendent was scheduled for Saturday afternoon. Voting for other offices took longer than expected and many delegates were leaving the floor. We were given the option of going forward with the vote on Saturday or waiting until Sunday, when the full contingent of delegates would be voting. We opted to wait until Sunday. I had been mentally prepared for the vote to occur on Saturday and then had to mentally regroup, rearrange thoughts and prepare myself for a Sunday vote.

Giving my speech was exhilarating! I always appreciate having the opportunity to talk about education. Receiving the letter of support, and having my family and dear friends there to share it with me, was a true highlight of the journey. One of my favorite photos from the campaign is of my dad sharing that landmark convention moment with me.

The Campaign Trail

Looking back, the months of campaigning are a blur of parades, speeches, fundraisers, more parades, more speeches and, finally, a weekend spent aboard a bus with my fellow statewide office candidates, office holders and staff, traveling to all corners of the state. People sometimes ask, "What did you do during your campaign?" The question prompts memories of all of the activities. I smile and say, "What didn't we do?" In addition to the miles traveled, parades, fundraisers and other events we attended or participated in, my campaign team made phone calls, created and managed a website and a Facebook page, tweeted, passed out palm cards and buttons, hung banners and spent many memorable nights stuffing envelopes in a friend's kitchen.

This wonderful group of people – self-named "Team Baesler" – did anything and everything to get the word out to North Dakota voters. I am so very grateful to this group of friends, most of whom I knew from other educational endeavors. I met my treasurer through educational technical grant programming, my campaign manager through Building Up Schools for Youth (BUSY) in Mandan, and my webmaster was a school information technology consultant. Add to this mix my incredible family – my sisters, my brother, my sons, my dear friend and, of course, our parade star, my dad.

Dad was in almost every parade we entered. Our parade entry was our treasurer's pickup truck, decorated with bunting and campaign posters, and a frame in the truck bed that was used to hang the campaign banners so they could be easily seen by the crowds along the parade route. Dad was 82 years old, so he would ride on the tailgate of the truck wearing his American Legion cap and holding a sign he made that read, "Please Vote For My Daughter." What a trooper!

I was also blessed to have a cadre of advisers, both formal and informal, who guided me through the ins and outs of my first political campaign. Republican Party staff and experienced members generously guided Team Baesler throughout the process. Current office holders and longtime volunteers shared a wealth of experience, gave excellent advice and included me in activities with other candidates. Our informal advisers were wonderful people who gave freely of their knowledge, experience, skills, time and talents. I am grateful for their help and support throughout the process.

"Process" is a mild word for what happened between March and November 2012. A better way to describe a statewide campaign is to say it is like riding a roller coaster. There were some incredibly wonderful highs and some equally challenging dips in the track. I loved the parades. It was wonderful to meet people and hear what they had to say. I also appreciated all of the great opportunities I had to learn about educational needs, concerns and ideas from people all over the state, whether in person, via email or through social media. It was amazing to me how Team Baesler grew from three friends and my sisters walking in the Band Day Parade to an organized group with banners, decorations, music and candy buckets personalized with campaign stickers.

These wonderful high points were balanced by the challenges of campaigning. Oddly enough, parades are also at the top of this list. We had a lot of early mornings and long miles, learned to avoid the "land mines" left by the mounted entries, and had a banner nearly take off like a kite in the wind during the Grand Forks Potato Bowl Parade. Another difficult area for me, personally, was fundraising. From my earliest years, I was taught to be self-sufficient, so it was hard for me to ask for help and especially difficult to ask for money. On a positive note, I received some lovely notes from supporters, some of whom would send a few dollars each month as they could. And the in-person fundraising gatherings offered opportunities to meet new people, make new friends and reconnect with friends I hadn't seen in awhile, all of whom shared my passion and enthusiasm for making our public education system even better for our children.

None of the events leading up to election night, including the state convention and primary election, prepared me for election night in November. My desire to be in a position of making sure our children get the best education possible to prepare them for college and careers made waiting for the outcome truly excruciating. The thrill and joy of being told it was time for my acceptance speech was beyond description. Sharing the stage with my father, my sons, my siblings and Team Baesler is a memory I will treasure forever.

Taking Office

My first days in office were not nearly as glamorous as you might expect. I went through the same process as any employee new to state government. I read the employee handbook, workforce safety information, and agency policies and procedures, and was issued keys and my identification card.

The swearing-in ceremony was surreal. I don't think it really even sunk in at the time. The reception following in the Great Hall of the Capitol was equally a blur. What stands out is how phenomenal it was that my father, my children, my siblings and my dear friends were able to share it with me.

I was fortunate to have the benefit of my predecessor's cooperation and support, and support from Governor Jack Dalrymple. I received an invitation from the Governor around midnight on election night – just after my acceptance speech – to attend a meeting the following morning at 7 a.m. to discuss education funding and the Governor's budget. The retiring Superintendent, Dr. Wayne Sanstead, had also invited me up to his office before the election to meet the North Dakota Department of Public Instruction (DPI) staff. In the weeks that followed, existing leadership personnel included me in important conversations with the U.S. Department of Education and in unit planning, so I was able to hit the ground running on January 2, 2013.

It was – and continues to be – important for me to rely on North Dakota DPI staff members and others who know the system of public government. There were many wonderful people, including retirees, who offered words of

Description of Official Duties as State Superintendent of Public Instruction

Four-year term. The State Superintendent is responsible for the enforcement of all state statutes and federal regulations pertaining to the establishment and maintenance of public schools and related education programs, including adult education, special education, state English language learner program, child nutrition and food distribution programs.

Member: State Board of Public School Education, State Board for Career and Technical Education, Board of University and School Lands, Teacher's Fund for Retirement, Children's Services Coordinating Committee, Education Technology Council and High School Activities Association, and supervises the North Dakota School for the Deaf, North Dakota Vision Services/School for the Blind and State Library.[49]

wisdom, support, insight and historical perspective about moving educational initiatives forward and the joys of doing so successfully.

Even so, the learning curve was steep, especially with the legislative session starting only six days after I took office. While my past experience of working with North Dakota's congressional delegation in Washington, D.C., and North Dakota state legislators on various issues was helpful, participating in a session of the North Dakota state Legislature as state Superintendent was a very different experience. As an advocate in our nation's and state's capitals, I prepared and delivered testimony to encourage our legislators to support viable education policy that would benefit students, teachers and school systems. As Superintendent, I had to present and defend not only proposed public education legislation, but also the North Dakota DPI's entire budget. It is a very interesting process, with many, many hours invested by legislators, state agency leaders and agency employees.

The work is challenging, intense and sometimes uncertain, but always wonderfully rewarding. My vision was to put forth proposals in policy areas that have risen to the top of my priorities during more than 20 years of experience working with students. I proposed policy changes that I thought would make the biggest differences in students' lives and in their academic achievement. As expected, a proposed early childhood funding bill met with some resistance. My challenge was to communicate that early childhood education would pay for itself in the long run. The increased initial investment in the pre-kindergarten years will lead to cost savings due to a reduced need for remediation and additional services in elementary, middle and high school.

A version of the legislation passed and – for the first time – state law allowed local dollars to be spent on early childhood education programs. The testimony and discussion regarding this bill helped our legislators to realize that there is need to further examine early childhood education and child-care services in North Dakota and resulted in a mandate for a study of this topic, led by the North Dakota Department of Public Instruction. Ideally, the results of the study will lead to increased support for our youngest learners at a time in their lives when they can benefit most from these services and programs.

Another important piece of legislation introduced during the session was a major education bill in the Governor's budget that drastically changed education funding in the state. The North Dakota DPI budget, which included the new funding formula, was one of the last bills to be approved at 2:00 a.m. on the last day of the session.

In addition to preparing testimony and testifying, I was meeting with more than 100 North Dakota DPI employees, attending unit meetings, sharing thoughts and direction, and explaining the rationale behind restructuring the management team. At the time I took office in January 2013, the Superintendent was the only elected state leader who did not have an appointed deputy. Recognizing the need to increase the department's strength in business management, a deputy superintendent with extensive state agency and government experience was appointed. The existing assistant superintendent, who has more than 30 years' experience as a principal and superintendent, continued in his role.

First Year Highlights

After the session, we began working on implementing the new laws and my expectations for the North Dakota DPI and its role in serving our schools. The focus shifted from the legislative session to department restructuring, management and creating better efficiencies. We also increased emphasis on customer service to our local school districts and to how we can help increase student achievement. Student achievement is the most important priority for me as state Superintendent. It is essential that we analyze what can be done at the state and local levels to better prepare all students for their success beyond high school.

As with any position, there are areas that provide satisfaction and areas that provide challenges. The challenges include trying to provide adequate support and resources to a very diverse group of school districts with student populations that range from a school district in eastern North Dakota that has over 11,000 students to a school district in western North Dakota that only has three students. The challenges in every district are very different, but very real. Regardless of the size of the district or where it is located, all students' needs are vitally important.

The satisfactions of serving as state Superintendent far outweigh the challenges. My greatest satisfaction comes from being able to have a positive effect on the futures of North Dakota's 110,000 public school students, being able to provide better opportunities for them this year than they had last year, and helping to create a bright future for our North Dakota young people.

Serving as state Superintendent has lifted my passion for public education to a whole new level. It has affirmed for me the critical importance of bringing good educational opportunities to this generation of students. Young people of today are unique, intelligent and special. They depend on us as leaders to make decisions that will positively impact their future.

There are many conversations throughout the state about many different issues, but I am even more convinced that the most important issue we have facing us today is the care and support of our young people's futures. There is a lot of work that needs to be done in individual classrooms and individual buildings to make that focus a systemic and constant reality and provide high-quality educational opportunities for every student in our state. But I am confident we can meet the challenge.

After nearly 14 months in office, I am only beginning to understand the level of respect and admiration that North Dakotans have for their elected office holders. I have always been committed to education and I approached my new position as a job to do with work to be accomplished. The pomp and circumstance of being an elected official was not something I aspired to or even expected. I have come to understand that ceremony is an important part of the position, and I am learning to embrace that aspect as well.

Having said that, I know that the real heroes are the people in our schools who are doing their jobs well, embracing new ideas and methods, teaching and challenging our students to be their best. My respect and admiration for them continues to grow each day.

Guiding Principles

I am inspired by a story from Rev. Dr. Patrick T. O'Neill about the Masai tribe.

"Among the most accomplished and fabled tribes of Africa, no tribe was considered to have warriors more fearsome or more intelligent than the mighty Masai. It is perhaps surprising, then, to learn the traditional greeting passed between Masai warriors is 'And how are the children?'

"This is still the traditional greeting among the Masai today, acknowledging the high value that the Masai always place on their children's well-being. Even warriors with no

This Masai shield was a gift to Baesler in honor of the Masai greeting – "And how are the children?" – that helps to guide Baesler's vision for North Dakota children.

(Kirsten Baesler photo collection)

children of their own always give the traditional answer, 'All the children are well,' – meaning that peace and safety prevail, that the priorities of protecting the young, the powerless, are in place. That Masai society has not forgotten its proper functions and responsibilities. 'All the children are well' means that life is good. It means that the daily struggles for existence do not preclude proper caring for their young."

O'Neill asked, "How might it affect our own children's welfare if, in our culture, we took to greeting each other with this same daily question: 'And how are the children?' Would it begin to make a difference in the reality of how children are thought of or cared for in this country – in our community? What if every adult among us, parent and non-parent alike, felt an equal weight for the daily protection of the children? Would we then be able to say without any hesitation, 'The children are well'?"

This profound question "Are the children well?" drives my decisions on a daily basis. As does the quote, "Be kinder than necessary to everyone you meet because you never know what kind of battle they may be facing."

Will You Be Next?

When something affects the community, the state or the nation, it is a woman's issue – women should be a part of the process when decisions are made about the issues.

My path to a statewide office was not remarkable or extraordinary. It was built on a solid foundation guided by good mentors, supported by a commitment to lifelong learning, service to others and preparing myself for the next opportunity.

Women Supreme Court Justices Address Important Issues

1985-2013

EIGHT

An Inspiring Justice

Beryl Levine

North Dakota Supreme Court Justice
1985-96

By
Cody Stanley

"I thank you, Governor, and I plan to spend the rest of my career proving that you made the right decision."

Beryl Levine to Governor George Sinner, 1985

Beryl Levine nee Choslovsky*
1935-Present

Supreme Court Justice 1985-96

First Woman to Serve on the North Dakota Supreme Court

Supreme Court Justice Beryl Levine - 1988
(Renner Photography - Supreme Court photo collection)

Personal Information
Born 1935 and raised in Winnipeg, Canada. Married to Leonard, five children. In "spare time," enjoys playing the card game contract bridge.

Party Affiliation
Elected on No-Party Ballot

Education
Saint John's High School, Winnipeg, Canada; received B.A. from the University of Manitoba, Winnipeg, Canada; attended North Dakota State University and Moorhead State College; awarded J.D. from University of North Dakota, Grand Forks, and awarded Order of the Coif.

Professional Experience Before Taking Office
Private practice with Vogel, Brantner, Kelly, Knutson, Weir & Bye, Fargo, 1974-85; member of the following committees of the Supreme Court: Joint Procedure, Continuing Legal Education Commission, Court Services Administration.

Memberships include
As Justice: Governor's Commission on Children and Adolescents at Risk, member, 1985-86; Commission on Victims and Witnesses, representative of judicial branch; National Association of Women Judges, director; Supreme Court Judicial Planning Committee, chair.

Other: Hospice of the Red River Valley, board member; North Dakota Women's Caucus; National Women's Political Caucus; Women's Network of the Red River Valley; Hadassah; Tempe Beth El; North Dakota Century Club; American Civil Liberties Union; Cass County Bar Association, president; North Dakota State Bar Association; American Contract Bridge League; Plains Art Museum; UND Foundation.[50]

*Bio contains information through 1996

Beryl Levine can still recall the time and place she first read *The Feminine Mystique*. It was 1963 and she was 28 years old. She was sitting on a beach in Gimli, Manitoba, while her children played nearby. As she read the book, she realized that Friedan was talking directly to her, explaining exactly what was happening to Levine and countless other middle-class women. According to Levine, the problem middle-class women faced was that they felt guilty about wanting more out of life. By Levine's own admission, she had a good life and a husband who cared for her and gave her whatever she needed. However, mentally her "brain was atrophying." Written by Betty Friedan and published in early 1963, *The Feminine Mystique* awoke thousands of women's minds to realities and possibilities that they had never contemplated before. Beryl Levine was one of these women.[51]

Preparing for the Bench

Beryl Levine was born on November 9, 1935, in Winnipeg, Canada. She was the second oldest child, with two younger sisters and one older brother. Her father, Maurice Jacob Choslovsky, was a Russian Jewish immigrant, and her mother, Bella Gutnik, was Canadian. Neither of her parents attended college, but this did not stop them from creating and maintaining a comfortable middle-class home for their family.[52]

The desire for and support of education and knowledge in general was stressed a great deal by Levine's parents. Beginning when she was a teenager, Levine knew that she would attend college when she was finished with high school. In 1952, she began to attend the University of Manitoba while still living at home with her parents, as was the custom of the times.[53]

In early 1955, at age 20, Beryl met her future husband, Leonard, and they married three months later. Soon after this, the realities of being a young married woman in the 1950s forced Beryl to put her education on hold for her husband's career. In his desire to become a doctor, Leonard needed to move in order to go to medical school. Compounding this were her responsibilities as a young wife, who, in 1956, gave birth to her first child. For approximately the next 10 years, Beryl's primary job was that of caretaker of the Levine household. She was responsible for her children's primary care and she also maintained the house while her husband furthered his career. Beryl did not totally forgo her collegiate aspirations because she took a few independent study classes now and again. However, unless she moved back to Winnipeg, first from Grand Forks and later Fargo, for a few key classes, she could not earn her bachelor's degree.[54]

In 1963, two events occurred that were fundamentally important in her ultimately becoming a lawyer. First, during that summer, Levine and her young children moved in with a friend in Winnipeg so that she could finally finish her undergraduate degree.

All she had left was two philosophy classes that had to be taken at the University of Manitoba. She passed these two classes and, by the beginning of 1964, she had earned a bachelor's degree with a major in Philosophy and a minor in Political Science. The second major event of 1963 for Levine occurred when she read *The Feminine Mystique*.[55]

It should be noted that Levine did not have the practice of law singled out from the start as the field she wanted to pursue. There were no other members of her family who were in the law or politics. Levine always had a general interest in current events and the desire to somehow make the world a better place. What she came to realize over the next few years was that the field of law had a great impact on the everyday lives of many people, and she saw that lawyers had a great opportunity to help people resolve life's problems.[56]

It was at this time that the Levine family decided to not move back to Canada and to stay in the U.S. permanently. A primary motivator for the move was that Canada had just introduced what is in today's popular culture called "socialized medicine" and there was a great deal of apprehension in the Canadian medical community as to what this meant for the practice of medicine. Leonard wanted to move to California, but this would have been too far away from home for Beryl. North Dakota was settled on as a compromise because of their relative familiarity with the region and its close proximity to Winnipeg.[57]

By 1970, Levine was ready to take on new challenges. With her husband's full support and planning for the needs of their five children, who ranged from a toddler to teenagers, she began looking for the next step in her life. Levine realized that if she became a lawyer, she would have an opportunity to satisfy the feeling of not having a fully complete life as described by Friedan in *The Feminine Mystique* and she would be able to put her pragmatic philosophy of resolving conflicts to use.[58]

Levine soon realized the magnitude of her decision and the effect it had on her family. First, in order for the Levine household to continue functioning in her absence, they had to hire a housekeeper. Next, Levine had to accustom herself to the 75-mile drive from Fargo to Grand Forks, which she had to make every day. Probably her toughest challenge, however, was understanding the language that was used in the legal profession. By her own admission, it took her the better part of her first year to fully understand and be comfortable with that language.[59]

When asked if she experienced any gender-based discrimination in law school, Levine had an interesting answer. When she entered law school, Levine was about 10 years older than the other women in her class and, in addition, her hair was prematurely turning white. These two things combined made her appear more like a safe maternal figure to the men in law school and not as a female who was trying to encroach on a male-dominated field. However, the male students viewed the other female students as competitors and not as equals.[60]

By graduating first in her class in 1974, Levine proved that she was very serious about her studies. After graduation, she began working at the Vogel Law Firm in Fargo. Her specialization was family law, an area in which many of the first female lawyers practiced. Levine did not practice solely in the field of family law; she practiced in business and malpractice law as well as several other fields. She even argued a couple of cases before the North Dakota Supreme Court.[61]

Levine realized that as one of the few women in the law, her actions would be closely scrutinized and that if she failed, her failure could be used against other women trying to enter the law. However, there was a positive side to this double standard; because her work was exceptional, it meant that she became known not just for being a woman who was a lawyer, but for being a good lawyer.[62]

Governor Sinner Appoints Beryl Levine to the North Dakota Supreme Court

The ultimate opportunity for Levine to illustrate that women were capable of working at every level of the law came at the end of 1984, when two openings appeared on the North Dakota Supreme Court. The first appeared in November with the retirement of Justice Vernon R. Pederson, and the second came in December with the sudden death of Justice Paul M. Sand. These two openings on the Court presented a unique opportunity for the newly elected Governor George Sinner, who had just defeated the incumbent, Governor Allen Olson, to mold the bench in a way that he deemed appropriate to his judicial vision.[63]

The Judicial Nominating Committee produced a list of eight candidates for Governor Sinner to choose from. Levine, age 49, had been practicing law for 10 years by this time and she knew that she had the experience necessary to be a Supreme Court Justice, so she applied for one of the openings. She desired to be a justice because of the unique opportunities that it presented for her as a woman and as a lawyer.[64]

Governor Sinner wanted to advance women's rights in North Dakota. The 1970s and early 1980s were a time of great advancements for women's rights, and Sinner believed that North Dakota needed to stay in step with the rest of the nation in this area. There was some pressure from the Democratic Party to nominate a woman to the Court, but the primary impetus came from Sinner himself. The governor was influenced by his Catholic faith and the inequality that he saw within it; the word Sinner used to describe women's position in the church was "shameful." Also, he saw that women in society in general had never experienced equal protection under the law. Sinner was going to nominate a woman even before Levine's name came up.[65]

Why Governor Sinner choose Beryl Levine is important in illustrating that hers was not a token appointment and that she represented the best candidate produced by the North Dakota legal community. The right judicial temperament for a court was the primary characteristic Sinner looked for in all of his judicial appointments. What this meant was that the candidate did not identify himself or herself with an issue that could cause public controversy, and Levine filled that bill. Sinner believed that when a judge made

New justice maintaining two homes

Levine, family spending lots of time on I-94 between Fargo and Bismarck

By JEFF MEYER
Associated Press Writer

MAY 4 1985

FARGO — After three months on the bench, North Dakota Supreme Court Justice Beryl Levine is still adjusting to the rigors of her new job and the difficulty of maintaining two households.

"It's challenging, but I like that," Levine, the first woman named to the high court, said during a recent trip to Fargo, where her husband, Leonard, and youngest son, David, live in a modern two-story home.

Levine's appointment to the Supreme Court in January surprised some in the legal profession. She took the bench with only 10 years' experience, a relatively short career for judges.

Many privately questioned whether it was her qualifications as an attorney or the fact that she is a woman that won her the appointment from Gov. George Sinner.

Levine, 49, dismisses the charges of tokenism and says she is out to prove she belongs on the court.

"I want to show people that I can be a fair and impartial judge," she said. "But I do think it was high time a woman was appointed, even if it was a leap of faith. My hope, my aim is to prove he (Sinner) was right."

Levine and Herbert Meschke were named to replace Justice Vernon R. Pederson, who resigned last November, and Justice Paul M. Sand, who died in December.

The vacancies became a heated issue in January when former Gov. Allen I. Olson and Sinner clashed over who was the legal governor and who would be able to make the appointments.

Because he husband has a successful 21-year urology practice in Fargo, the Levine and her family have decided to keep two homes — one in Fargo and the other in Bismarck. They plan to continue doing so for as long as Beryl serves on the court.

Levine is filling a term that has four years to go before expiring. She stands for election next year for the right to fill out the remainder of the term and then will have to face re-election to full 10-year terms.

"It's working out well," says her husband, 56, who works out of the Fargo Clinic. "We take turns traveling, so we see each other just about every weekend."

David, who is an 18-year-old senior at Fargo South High School, jokes that "the interstate is our connecting driveway." And he says "you get to know where every shrub and sign are."

"We make much more of our time together than we ever did," said Beryl, who lives in a rented two-bedroom apartment near the state Capitol during the week. "And doing a lot of driving gives you time to sort out the issues."

The Levines have four grown children.

Levine admits she has a lot to learn about the interrelationship of the government and the judiciary and is still wide-eyed with awe over "how smoothly it all works," but believes that will soon pass.

"It's a tremendous responsibility, when you think about it," she said. "But the privilege is greater."

AP Laserphoto

North Dakota Supreme Court Justice Beryl Levine at her family's Fargo home with her husband, Leonard, and son David.

The *Bismarck Tribune* interviewed Justice Levine about the challenges of commuting between Fargo and Bismarck. Photo shows Justice Levine with her husband, Leonard, and son David. (May 4, 1985 - *Associated Press* photo file)

himself or herself the center of an issue, it took away from his or her ability to serve the people.

The second sentence of the Declaration of Independence states, "That to secure these rights, Governments are instituted among Men, deriving their just powers from the consent of the governed." Sinner saw Levine as a justice who would fully represent the idea of securing the rights of the people due to the fact that she represented a section of the people which historically were silent in the law. Through this increased representation, the Court would add to its legitimacy.[66]

Also, Levine had the ideal personal and political connections to make her known in the circles in which Sinner traveled. Sinner's personal legal councilor was John Kelly, who also worked at the Vogel Law Firm, and the Vogel Law Firm also represented Meritcare Hospital, where Levine's husband, Leonard, worked. Because of these personal connections, Sinner had a deeper and more complete understanding of Levine's work ethic and intelligence.[67]

Governor Sinner informed all of his judicial appointments through a phone call as soon as he made his decision. The governor called Levine on the morning of January 16, 1985, to ask her to be the next member of the North Dakota Supreme Court. Her son David answered the phone, realized that it was the Governor and handed the phone to his mother. The phone call was short and to the point, and culminated in her telling the Governor, "I thank you, Governor, and I plan to spend the rest of my career proving that you made the right decision."[68]

Description of Official Duties as Supreme Court Justice

Ten-year term. Serves as one of five justices. The North Dakota Supreme Court is the highest court for the state. It has two major types of responsibilities: (1) adjudicative and (2) administrative. In its adjudicative capacity, the Supreme Court is primarily an appellate court with jurisdiction to hear appeals from decisions from district courts. It also has original jurisdiction in certain matters and can issue original and remedial writs as are necessary to exercise this authority. In its administrative capacity, the Supreme Court has major responsibilities for ensuring the efficient and effective operation of all courts in the state, except federal and tribal courts; maintaining high standards of judicial conduct; supervising the legal profession; and promulgating procedural rules that allow for the orderly and efficient transaction of judicial business.[69]

Justice Levine's Role in Marriage and Divorce Law

The appropriate place to begin examining Justice Levine's views on marriage and divorce is with her dissenting opinion in the case of *Gravning v. Gravning,* decided in 1986. This dissenting opinion was unmistakably Justice

Levine's clearest articulation of the Primary Caretaker Doctrine. Furthermore, it was from this case that Levine built her future attempts to get the Court to adopt the Primary Caretaker Doctrine.

The Primary Caretaker Doctrine, if a court adopted it, would automatically grant physical custody of a child to the parent who was the primary caretaker of the child. In *Gravning v. Gravning*, Levine articulated a general statement to which the court would conform, if it used the Primary Caretaker Doctrine: "the primary caretaker is the parent that provides the child with daily nurturance, care and support." [70]

The primary caretaker is the parent who is in charge of preparing meals, grooming the child, taking care of the child's clothing, creating situations for the child to have social interactions with his or her peers, dispensing discipline to the child when need be, educating the child in normal manners and helping the child in other ways that produce the social and emotional education for the child. Levine did not create the Primary Caretaker Doctrine; it was first put into law in other states before this case. In Minnesota, the doctrine was adopted in 1985 in the case of *Pikula v. Pikula*. Minnesota law was an important reference point for Levine because of Minnesota's proximity to North Dakota.[71]

The facts of this case are as follows: Nancy and Greg Gravning were married in 1982 and they divorced in 1985. During their marriage, they had two children, Gabriel, born in 1982, and Amanda, born in 1983. The trial court awarded custody of Amanda to Nancy, contingent on Amanda's continuing work toward an education and/or her acquiring gainful employment. Greg was awarded Gabriel, with his custody contingent on his maintaining employment, not using alcohol and continued living with his parents. Also, each month there were to be two consecutive days of joint visitation alternating each month between Greg's and Nancy's residence so that the children would have contact with each other.[72]

Both Greg and Nancy believed the trial court to have been in error in that they both thought that they should have sole physical custody of the children. Also, Nancy believed that the financial settlement was inequitable and that it should be redressed. Greg as well believed that the financial settlement was excessive but that it should be redressed in his favor.[73]

The first issue that the majority addressed was the custody question. The court stated immediately that the Tender Years Doctrine was no longer the standard that guided them. The case of *Odegard v. Odegard*, in 1977, eliminated the Tender Years Doctrine in North Dakota. Now the standard that was to be used was "determined by the court's consideration and evaluation of all factors affecting the best interests and welfare of the child." This was the test that the majority used to come to their conclusion that the split custody arrangement was the correct route to take. The final justification for their decision was a section of North Dakota Century Code 14-09-06 that states that parents "have equal rights" in the "care, custody, education and control" of minor children. In the eyes of the majority, the only way that the law could have been satisfied was by the current arrangement as articulated by the trial court.[74]

Justice Levine viewed the facts in a much different manner than the three male justices who made up the majority. Justice Levine began her dissent by stating that the trial court did not make its justification for split custody obvious and that it left her with more questions than answers about their decision. However, she made it well known that she was aware of the difficult task a trial court has in deciding who should receive custody.[75]

It was at this point that she began her argument for the Primary Caretaker Doctrine. Since both Nancy and Greg were equally fit to be the parents, then the court needed to establish which one was the primary caretaker. In this case, Levine saw Nancy as the primary caretaker. Next, Levine gave four reasons why the benefits of Primary Caretaker Doctrine outweighed the negative side effects in this case. First, she believed that "the intimate interaction of the primary caretaker with the child creates a vital bonding between parent and child." The second factor was that it adds a level of certainty to custody actions. Levine saw this as the only real way a judge can knowingly and directly affect the child's life in a positive way. Third, the negotiating process of the primary caretaker is aided in the financial settlements that are created when a marriage ends. The primary caretaker will not be able to be threatened with financial ruin by the non-primary caretaker and therefore will get a more equitable arrangement. Fourth, the Primary Caretaker Doctrine at its implementation is gender neutral because it is possible for a man to be the primary caretaker.[76]

In interpreting the law, Justice Levine always sided with what she thought was the best interest of the child, with the effects it had on the parents always coming in second. When interviewed, Levine stated that one of her main goals with the Primary Caretaker Doctrine was to add a level of stability and civility to the divorce proceedings. When talking about divorce and what it did to the former couple, Levine made sure to point out that divorce is an ugly process and that the Primary Caretaker Doctrine would shield the child from some of the battles that were bound to ensue between his or her parents. Levine did not stop trying to implement the Primary Caretaker Doctrine she enunciated in *Gravning*.[77]

The next area of divorce law on which Levine had a great deal of impact was spousal support. With the elimination of fault-based divorce and the adoption of no-fault divorce, the dependent partner lost the legal grounds to achieve a level of financial security after a marriage ended. A vast majority of the time, the woman was the one who was at risk of entering poverty or approaching it after a marriage ended.

Now that the nature of marriage had changed to a more egalitarian model, so did the way that judges viewed alimony. Levine saw marriage as a partnership in which economics played a very important role in regard to who worked and who did not, and also what type of work each partner did. Often, her differing perspective came out in the battle between when to use rehabilitative support or permanent support. Rehabilitative support lasts only until the spouse who was disadvantaged by the divorce is able to achieve a level of financial self-sufficiency. Permanent support is awarded to an individual that was so financially damaged by the divorce that she or he will never be able to achieve an equitable financial situation on her or his own.[78]

In 1987, in the case of *Dick v. Dick*, Levine wrote a lone dissenting opinion that clearly articulated her legal views on the issue of alimony. It also showed how her perspective on the matter was clearly different from what the court used and was in the custom of using.

The facts of the case were that Maxine Dick married Keith Dick in 1969. They did not have any children in the course of the marriage, and during the marriage, Maxine had intermittent employment, usually a part-time job with no advancement opportunity. Usually her employment was a secondary source of income used to augment Keith's. Maxine appealed the trial court's distribution of marital property and also the lack of alimony awarded to her. Maxine was awarded approximately one-half of the marital assets value after all debts were paid, which equaled around $85,000, and $1,000 per month for the last four months of 1986. Keith received the other half of the marital assets and also his Pioneer seed business, which was deemed to have no tangible assets beyond the client list. Also, Keith was awarded the assets he brought into the marriage.[79]

The four-member majority viewed this ruling by the trial court as adequate for both parties and that there were no glaring errors. Justice Levine wrote a dissenting opinion that disagreed with the majority on almost every point. Levine did not see Maxine's periodic employment as having the necessary weight to support her. Also, Levine argued that Maxine did not have the opportunity to pursue a career that fulfilled her needs and inner desires. Furthermore, Levine blasted both the majority and the trial court for not giving Maxine's desire to pursue an education the importance that it deserved. By not doing this, Levine believed that Maxine was being denied the opportunities that the marriage had given Keith and that the court had a duty to give her the same chance at life.[80]

Dick v. Dick was by no means the last time Levine voiced her position on spousal support. In *Weige v. Weige,* Levine wrote a concurring opinion that was meant to get the court to re-evaluate its stance on its awarding of permanent versus temporary rehabilitative spousal support. Larry Weige was appealing the trial court's ruling that gave his ex-wife, Dianne, both temporary support until she received a college degree and then permanent support at a reduced amount until her death. The majority affirmed the ruling because of Dianne's disadvantaged position due to the duration of the marriage and her total lack of skills necessary to achieve financial independence.[81]

Levine agreed with the court's decision, but she felt it necessary to write a concurrence because she did not believe the court truly understood the effects that inadequate spousal support had on the person receiving it. Also, she wanted to address the fact that the court had a strong bias in favor of temporary support and that it did not give permanent support the weight it should have. In addition to this, Levine thought that the court needed to re-examine its precedent that held that as soon as a person remarried that support should end. Her justification for this was that marriage was a contract two people decided to enter into, the results of which will impact a person for the rest of her or his life. Just because a person makes the choice to enter into a new marriage, there is no reason that this new contract should affect the previous contract. They were two separate entities in Levine's eyes.[82]

Justice Levine's Work Against Gender Discrimination

Justice Beryl Levine worked diligently to correct gender inequality in North Dakota. Because of Justice Levine's powerful position as a state Supreme Court Justice, she had the ability to develop policy and the means to articulate legal thinking to directly combat gender inequality.

In 1985, the year she became a Supreme Court Justice, Levine joined the National Association of Women Judges (NAWJ). In that same year, Levine attended her first NAWJ meeting in Minneapolis, Minnesota. The NAWJ was still very small at that time due to the few female judges in the country. However, it did not stop them from asking the question, "What does it mean to be a woman within the legal system, either as a lawyer or as a citizen using the system?" To answer this question, the NAWJ members were forming state commissions in their respective states.[83]

After learning about these state commissions on gender bias, Levine wanted to form a similar commission in North Dakota. From the very beginning, Levine, according to Chief Justice VandeWalle, had the support of all the members of the North Dakota Supreme Court and was poised to go ahead with the creation of the commission. The State Bar Association of North Dakota also supported the creation of the commission. However, due to a tax referral in 1989, there was no funding to start a commission until 1994. During the interim, Justice Levine was the driving force keeping the commission idea alive in North Dakota. She was able to do this because of her powerful position as a state Supreme Court Justice and her personal connections within the legal community.[84]

Levine was able to recruit Fargo attorney Sara Andrews Herman to co-chair the commission, and in Levine's words, Herman became "the real driving force"[85] behind the work of the commission once it started. This commission was the first of two commissions. The goal of the first was to be a fact-finding enterprise. The members were not charged to prove any point specifically, but to ask questions and do research that would allow for the current situation of North Dakota's legal system and how it treated women to be documented. The first commission was called the North Dakota Commission on Gender Fairness in the Courts.[86]

One key element that the first commission articulated and that Levine herself worked very hard to eliminate was the use of terms of endearment by either male judges or lawyers for women in courtrooms. An example of a term of endearment would be if a judge called a female council in a case "honey" or "dear." Now, from the judge's partial perspective, this might be perfectly OK or even a good thing. However, from the woman's perspective, it degraded her in the eyes of those in the court and possibly how she saw herself. In an interview, Sara Andrews Herman commented on how Levine, in meetings of the commission, would get agitated with male commission members who saw nothing wrong with those terms of endearment and did not understand a woman's perspective on the issue.[87]

Another finding of the first commission was that rural women in North Dakota often lacked the means to acquire representation in the court. Compounding this was the practice, once again often in rural communities, of judges not allowing women to represent themselves when they could not get a lawyer. This lack of representation in the legal system for women in rural areas of North Dakota illustrates the fact that women were not treated equitably under the law. In the eyes of the commission, in order for women, or anyone else, to receive justice, there must be equity in the law.

The concept of partial perspective was an important theme running throughout the commission's findings. Women and men perceived the activities in the courtroom differently due to their unique experiences. The commission's final report frequently made special note of how men and women both need to view things from each other's point of view in order for justice to be carried out. This conclusion reflected a sentiment that Levine expressed in many of her legal writings and also in her interview.[88]

Justice Levine also wrote several case opinions that had an effect on women's position in North Dakota. *Swenson v. Northern Crop Insurance and John Krabseth* was a case in which Levine was able to articulate a woman's perspective on gender discrimination. It was also important for the state as a whole in addressing the continued existence of sexual discrimination.[89]

The facts of this case are as follows: Catherine Swenson started working for Northern

The 1985 Supreme Court. Front from left: Justices Levine, Erickstad, Meschke; Back from left: Justices Gierke and VandeWalle (D'Joyce Photography – Supreme Court photo collection)

Crop Insurance Inc. (NCI) in February of 1986 as a secretary. Her only co-worker at that time was office manager Rick Wallace, who resigned in December of 1986. Wallace recommended that Swenson take his position as office manager. Swenson went to John Krabseth, who was NCI's general manager, and asked to be considered for the job. Krabseth response was that he wanted a man "fresh out of college" for that job and that he did not want a woman. However, NCI's board of directors thought differently and they gave the job to Swenson.[90]

Swenson's salary was increased from $7.50 to $10.00 per hour. Shortly after her promotion, Krabseth reorganized the office structure and, in the process, eliminated Swenson's new position. Swenson was demoted to a secretary and her pay was decreased to $6.00 per hour. Two new office positions of program specialist and computer operator were created. For each one, a man was hired, each being paid a higher wage than Swenson was when she was the office manager, even though each one did work that was comparable to the former office manager position. Also, Swenson was never offered either job before her demotion. Once these events transpired, Krabseth began avoiding Swenson, refusing to discuss the issue with her.[91]

Swenson terminated her employment with NCI and brought suit against NCI and Krabseth in the District Court for Williams County, North Dakota. She sued them on three grounds. First, she claimed that NCI and Krabseth were guilty of gender discrimination in violation of chapter 14-02.4 of the North Dakota Century Code, (N.D.C.C). Second, Swenson believed that they had violated North Dakota's Equal Pay Act. Third, that the actions of NCI and Krabseth constituted intentional infliction of emotional distress. The trial court ruled against Swenson on all three grounds and simply dismissed the suit. Swenson appealed to the North Dakota Supreme Court.[92]

The North Dakota Supreme Court's opinion of the case was written by then-Chief Justice Ralph J. Erickstad. The Court ruled that on the first issue, Swenson lacked the grounds for a suit. Under North Dakota law, in order for a company to be classified as an employer and subject to anti-discrimination laws, they must have 10 or more employees, but NCI did not. Swenson then tried to argue that the law was unconstitutional, but because she did not bring that issue up enough when the case was heard at the district court level, the court had no legal right to rule on its constitutionality. Had Swenson made the unconstitutionality of the law a major issue in the district court brief, it would have been able to be ruled on.[93]

On the second issue, the Court ruled that NCI and Krabseth violated North Dakota's Equal Pay Act. The main fact that proved this for the Court was the disparity in Swenson's pay versus that of male employees. Also taken into account were the discriminatory statements made by Krabseth in regard to what women should be paid. Krabseth repeatedly stated that a woman should not be paid as much as a man and that he wanted men to be employed by NCI instead of women.[94]

The third issue, of emotional distress, was the only one of the three areas on which the justices varied in their rulings. The majority ruled that NCI and Krabseth had caused intentional emotional distress. The two pieces of evidence that caused them to come to this conclusion were Krabseth's sexist comments and the power relations between Swenson and Krabseth. Krabseth was in a position at NCI that gave him a great deal of power over Swenson's job and, through that, her very livelihood. This power gave any actions that he took which were derogatory toward Swenson a greater weight.

Justice Levine agreed with the majority on every point except one. Levine was not willing to agree that the case should have been put to a jury. Instead Levine believed that the case should have been granted summary judgment. Summary judgment is rendered when the facts of an issue are so clear and undisputed that there is no need for a trial. All that is needed for justice is for a judge to rule on how the law should be applied to the facts at hand. Levine's position here illustrated that, from her perspective, the facts at hand were of such clarity in their illegality that a trial was not needed. Levine contended that for Swenson to get a fair trial, she would have needed to eliminate all the jurors who still held antiquated beliefs about women. Levine saw this as an injustice because it placed an undue burden on Swenson. Therefore, the only way that Swenson could have received justice would have been through a summary judgment.[95]

Afterthoughts

Beryl Levine retired from the North Dakota Supreme Court on March 1, 1996, at age 61. She served on the Court for 11 years and one month. During her time on the Court, she allowed women to have a voice in a way they never had before. Levine could not speak for all women, but she was able to allow for women in general to have an avenue to an agency open to them that was not there before. In addition to this, Levine was able to allow minorities in North Dakota to believe that anyone can become a part of the institutions that shape people's legal rights. Ultimately, Levine made it seem normal and natural for women to be on the North Dakota Supreme Court. This could be her most important contribution.

Justice Levine currently resides in Palo Alto, California.

Excerpt From Beryl J. Levine's Application to the Supreme Court 1984[96]

1.

Background

I am 49 years old, a woman, wife, mother and attorney, who has experienced to date the best of all worlds – family and career.

I am married to Leonard (Leo) Levine, a physician, and we have five children of whom we are extremely proud: Susan is 28 and an investment banker, fluent in Chinese, who lives and works in New York City and travels extensively in Asia; Marc is 27 and a resident physician in internal medicine at the University of California San Francisco; Sari is 25 and a fourth-year medical student, at Washington University in St. Louis where she will graduate in May and then enroll in a urology residency at Yale or the University of Pennsylvania; 20 year old Bill is a pre-med student at Stanford University in California; our youngest son, David, is a senior at South High presently working on his applications for college. He is interested in computer technology as it applies to law and medicine.

I grew up in Winnipeg, Manitoba, the second child of four and eldest daughter of Russian immigrant parents, now deceased, whose warm and loving care was exceeded only by their emphasis and encouragement that we strive for the unattainable and reach for the stars.

I graduated from St. John's High School with highest honors and a variety of scholarships. Then, while a junior at the University of Manitoba in Winnipeg, I met, and in short order, married, my husband. In June, 1955, we moved to Cleveland, Ohio, for his residency training program in urology. I worked as a nursery school teacher and went to night school in what was to be but the beginning of my long odyssey toward obtaining a college degree.

Leo completed his residency in 1959 and the Levines, by then, all four, moved to Grand Forks, North Dakota, where Leo became a member of the Grand Forks Clinic and I became a member of a number of community organizations in which I participated rather actively while also mothering and caring for our small children. Our third child, Sari, was born in Grand Forks, followed by a little son who died at the age of three months. Grieving, we welcomed the invitation from the Fargo Clinic for my husband to join its ranks, and in September, 1964, we moved to Fargo, which has been ever since our home. Also by 1964 I had accumulated, finally, enough credits to earn a Bachelor of Arts degree from my alma mater, the University of Manitoba.

The '60s for me were highlighted by my family and community involvement. During that period I became a fairly good duplicate bridge player. I also attended both North Dakota State University and Moorhead State College on a part-time basis, working for a Master's Degree in political science. Then, in 1971, my husband and I discussed at length my future. I was 35 years old – mother of five – whose children while growing up were naturally growing more independent, thereby freeing more of my hours than I knew what to do with. So, because of a long abiding interest in politics and because of the desire to be able to work at a profession for thirty years or so, we decided that law school would equip me with a profession I could both master and enjoy. The law appealed to my strong sense of pragmatism - in an imperfect world, best to resolve disputes and move on.

So, I enrolled as a law student at UND in September, 1971. I remember being summoned to the office of the Dean shortly before freshman classes were to begin. I remember his skepticism when he first met me - in his perception a 35 year old doctor's wife, spoiled, frivolous – I made up my mind that day that no one would ever have cause to doubt either the depth of my commitment to my profession or my ability to attain the knowledge, skills and judgment necessary for good and decent lawyering. Toward those ends I have always studied hard and worked hard. I see myself as a student of the law and the Supreme Court as a vehicle for reflection on the law and its applicability to the case on review. I see also my appointment to the Supreme Court for me, as a woman, to be yet another remarkable statement about this country, this state, and our community and the opportunities they provide for qualified, interested people. Doubtless, my appointment to the Court would be among my greatest personal achievements. Of far greater significance, it would send a clear and resounding signal to competent, qualified women in this state who seek and strive and stretch, that doors are indeed open and nothing is foreclosed merely because of gender.

2.

Education

I received my Bachelor of Arts degree from the University of Manitoba in 1964. I did graduate work in political science at North Dakota State University and Moorhead State College. Thereafter, I enrolled at UND Law School and commuted daily to law school throughout the three year degree program. Obtained my J.D. degree in 1974, with distinction, graduating first in my class and winning a variety of prizes and awards. I was also elected to membership in Order of the Coif.

3.

Legal Experience

In September, 1974, I joined the law firm headed by Philip and Mart Vogel in Fargo, in which I am now a 100% shareholder. Indeed, the one misgiving I have about seeking appointment to the Supreme Court is leaving my law firm and the men and women I have worked with, confided in, learned from, and celebrated and commiserated with over these many years. They have been very good years spent with very good people.

I have been engaged in civil trial practice for these past ten years and have worked extensively in the areas of family law, tort litigation with a recent emphasis on professional malpractice defense work, some juvenile work, bankruptcy cases and commercial law.

I have had the singular good fortune to apprentice with and learn from Mart Vogel. His talent as a trial lawyer is surely well known throughout the state. His integrity and decency are reflected in every aspect of his practice and life and I consider him to be my mentor and model.

As a law student, I served as a clerk for Judge Ralph Maxwell, who was then a Cass

County District Court judge. I also served an internship in my senior year at law school in the Cass County Juvenile Court and the Office of Legal Assistance of North Dakota, here in Fargo, alternating between the two facilities.

I have lectured to UND medical students once a year on the legal issues confronting young physicians and have also spoken to many women's groups, clubs and students on a variety of topics, most commonly concerning the legal rights of women.

I presently serve as a member on the Joint Procedure Committee and in the past have served on the C.L.E. Commission and on the Court Services Administration Committee. I am also a member of the Law School Visitor's Committee.

Over these past ten years I have met with many young women interested in the profession of law and have advised them on how to achieve their goals.

NINE

Working to Improve Our System of Justice

By

Mary Muehlen Maring

North Dakota Supreme Court Justice
1996-2013

"Over the past 17-plus years, I have written approximately 820 majority opinions, dissents and concurring opinions. I have enjoyed the research and crafting of opinions very much."

Justice Mary Maring

Mary Maring nee Muehlen*

1951-Present

Justice North Dakota Supreme Court 1996–2013

Supreme Court Justice Mary Maring
(Supreme Court Photo Collection)

Personal Information

Born 1951 in Devils Lake and raised in farming communities of Penn and Devils Lake, North Dakota. Married to David, two children. In "spare time," enjoys running, skiing, scrapbooking.

Party Affiliation

Elected on No-Party Ballot

Education

Devils Lake High School; received B.A. Moorhead State University, graduated summa cum laude; awarded J.D. University of North Dakota School of Law.

Professional Experience before taking office

Law Clerk for Minnesota District Court Judge, 1975-76; practiced law Stephanson, Landberg and Alm, 1976–82; partner in Ohnstad, Twichell, Brietling, Rosenvold, Wanner, Nelson, Neugebauer & Maring PC, 1982-88; partner Lee Hagen Law Office, 1988-91; Maring Law Office PC, 1991-96.

Memberships and Committees Include

As North Dakota Supreme Court Justice: North Dakota Judicial Conference, chair; Gender Fairness Implementation Committee, chair; Study Implementation Committee of the Juvenile Drug Courts in North Dakota, chair; Joint Procedure Committee, chair; Judicial Education Commission, chair; Juvenile Drug Court Advisory Committee. Member of Juvenile Policy Board, the Commission to Study Racial and Ethnic Bias in the Courts, the Administrative Council and the Alternatives to Incarceration Interim Legislative Committee.

Other: International Society of Barristers; Clay County Minnesota Bar, president; East Central Judicial District Bar Association, president; North Dakota Trial Lawyers Association, president; Board of Governors of the State Bar Association of North Dakota.[97]

*Bio contains information through 2013

A New Opportunity

In January 1996, my life and my family's life changed. Justice Beryl Levine, who was the first woman to sit on the North Dakota Supreme Court, announced her retirement from the Supreme Court, and I decided to apply for her position. This decision was not an easy one for me. I started the Maring Law Office on May 1, 1991, and had invested a lot of physical and emotional energy into setting up the office. My family was entrenched in Fargo and my sons were both still young. Yet, my husband, Dave, and I decided that the opportunity may not come my way again.

I applied for the position and, on March 1, 1996, Governor Ed Schafer appointed me to the Court. By April 15, 1996, another lawyer filed to run against me in the November general election, and I found myself in a statewide race for my seat on the Court. It was a tough next few months. I was either working or campaigning. I found out how difficult it was to conduct a statewide campaign because of the travel required across the state. I put a lot of miles on my vehicle. I visited many places in North Dakota and met many wonderful people. My mom, my husband and two sons came with me to many events. Fortunately, in November, I was successful and was elected by the citizens of the state to sit on the North Dakota Supreme Court. I would only be able to fill out Justice Levine's term, which had two years remaining, before I would be on the ballot again in 1998.

Because my re-election in two years was uncertain, my husband and I decided that I would commute from Fargo to Bismarck while he and our two sons remained in Fargo. It was also important for our oldest son, Christopher, to finish high school at Fargo South High School. This decision turned out to be very hard on us as a family. I would leave for Bismarck Monday morning very early and stay the week, then come home on Friday or, sometimes, Thursday night, depending on the Court's schedule. We missed one another very much during that time.

Election to a 10-Year Term

In 1998, I did not have any competition for my seat on the Court, and I was elected to a 10-year term. My oldest son, Christopher, went off to college at Georgetown University, Washington, D.C., in the fall of 1998. My husband, David, our son, Drew, and I moved to Bismarck. David opened a branch office of the Maring Williams Law Office in Bismarck. Our son Drew started middle school at Simle in Bismarck. Moving a family to a new city is not easy, and we had some difficult adjustments to make. It was especially hard on our youngest son who had to make all new friends and try to fit in at age 13.

Election to my first 10-year term in 1998 was a very important event. I believe that the length of the term for the North Dakota Supreme Court justices is critical to protect

Justice Maring with her husband, David (left), and former Governor Schafer (right), who appointed Justice Maring to the Supreme Court in 1996. (Supreme Court photo collection)

the justices from the pressures and whims of society. It allowed me to focus and concentrate on the work at hand.

The fact that I was appointed to fill out Justice Levine's term on the Court on March 1, 1996, but then had to run in a statewide election the following November, caught the attention of some North Dakota legislators. A constitutional amendment to Article VI of the North Dakota Constitution resulted in a newly appointed judge having the ability to serve two years in office before having to stand for election.

This amendment, I believe, has provided added encouragement for lawyers to seek appointment to judicial positions in our state. Before the amendment, the concern of those interested was that a candidate would need to leave her private practice with the possibility of losing the judicial seat to a challenger before having an opportunity to establish a sound reputation as a judge.

The issue of whether North Dakota judges should be elected by the citizens of North

Dakota or vetted by a merit selection commission and then appointed by the Governor remains somewhat controversial. Unfortunately, there is not a good answer.

Description of Official Duties as Supreme Court Justice

Ten-year term. Serves as one of five justices. The North Dakota Supreme Court is the highest court for the state. It has two major types of responsibilities: (1) adjudicative and (2) administrative. In its adjudicative capacity, the Supreme Court is primarily an appellate court with jurisdiction to hear appeals from decisions from district courts. It also has original jurisdiction in certain matters and can issue original and remedial writs as are necessary to exercise this authority. In its administrative capacity, the Supreme Court has major responsibilities for ensuring the efficient and effective operation of all courts in the state, except federal and tribal courts; maintaining high standards of judicial conduct; supervising the legal profession; and promulgating procedural rules that allow for the orderly and efficient transaction of judicial business.[98]

Serving as a Justice on the North Dakota Supreme Court

When I first arrived at the North Dakota Supreme Court, I served with Chief Justice Gerald W. VandeWalle, Justice Herbert Meschke, Justice William Neumann and Justice Dale Sandstrom. Justice Sandstrom and I were in the same law school class of 1975 and knew one another. I also knew Justice Neumann because of the contested election he ran for his seat on the Court. I soon learned to know and respect them all very much, including the more recent additions to the Court: Justice Carol Ronning Kapsner and Justice Daniel Crothers.

When I started my position on the Court, Keithe Nelson was the State Court Administrator and Penny Miller was the Clerk of the North Dakota Supreme Court. The Chief Deputy Clerk of the Court was Colette Bruggman. The staffs in the North Dakota Supreme Court's administrative office and the clerk of court's office were extremely helpful to me. There are no schools a lawyer can attend to learn how to become a competent appellate judge. Other than opinion writing courses for appellate judges, the training is on the job.

The primary work of the five North Dakota Supreme Court Justices is deciding cases properly appealed to the Court. This work entails an enormous amount of reading, including briefs, records and appendices. It also includes a great amount of research and writing. Over the past 17-plus years, I have written approximately 820 majority opinions, dissents and concurring opinions. I have enjoyed the research and crafting of opinions very much.

My Court hears oral arguments of the parties or their lawyers in the majority of the cases brought to it. Over the course of my time on the Court, I have heard approximately 3,800 oral arguments. I am asked all the time about the worth of oral argument. In most cases, it does not make a difference in the outcome of the case. There is always that rare case, however, when oral advocacy turns the Court around. Personally, if I were the attorney for a party, I would not be inclined to waive oral argument.

Another duty of my position is the administration of the North Dakota Judicial System. The justices meet every week to take care of matters that arise concerning the administration of the courts. These matters can range from the enactment of policies to security issues. In addition, each of the justices chairs one or more committees dealing with the improvement of the administration of justice and the courts in North Dakota.

Working to Improve Our System of Justice

The committees we chair and serve on are very important to the work of our court system and its future. Personally, I have enjoyed all the committees I have served on or chaired. These committees do a lot of very substantive work that ends up in recommendations to the North Dakota Supreme Court for proposed changes to improve our system of justice.

Gender Fairness

In 1997, the North Dakota Supreme Court created the Gender Fairness Implementation Committee by Administrative Order 7. Chief Justice VandeWalle asked me to chair this Committee. The Committee addressed 33 recommendations in six categories, and identified which ones should be referred to other committees and which ones the Committee should implement itself. After addressing all of the recommendations, the Committee completed a report to the North Dakota Supreme Court.

In 2006, the Committee conducted a 10-year study of the progress made by the implementation of the recommendations. This report was published in the North Dakota Law Review.[99] In addition, through a grant, the Committee oversaw the creation of a domestic violence bench book for use by our trial judges. This bench book was originally drafted by Jeanne McLean, a professor of family law at the University of North Dakota School of Law.

Court Unification

When I arrived at the Court in 1996, court unification had just taken place a year earlier on January 1, 1995. This legislation elevated all of the county court judges to district court judges. The North Dakota Legislature, in addition, decided that this resulted in too many district court judges and it mandated a reduction in the number of judges from 56 down to 42.

Justice Maring on the bench with Justice VandeWalle. (Supreme Court photo collection)

My Court was able to accomplish this reduction by retirements and by deaths with the exception of one judgeship, which had to be abolished in the Southwest Judicial District. This was done to meet the deadline set by the Legislature. It was a difficult decision for our Court. We also were faced with trying to efficiently use the 42 judgeships we had by relocating judges to districts with greater need. The five of us on the Supreme Court did not always agree on these difficult decisions.

Now, in 2013, we are adding judgeships due to the oil boom in the state and the increase in case filings in our courts. As of December 2013, we have 47 district court judges and five Supreme Court justices. In 2012, the Supreme Court's civil filings increased approximately 21 percent and the criminal filings increased approximately 22 percent. This has placed pressure on the Supreme Court staff and the justices to keep up with the caseload.

Administrative Reorganization

Another major change that occurred during my time on the Court is the administrative reorganization of our district courts. Through the enactment of Administrative Rule

22, our seven judicial districts were organized into four separate administrative units. The Court hired a professional trial court administrator for each unit. This removed a great amount of administrative duties from the presiding judges and freed up time for them to perform their essential duty of judging.

Mediation

Mediation also has taken hold in our trial courts to address the needs of families. This program was piloted in 2006. Today, it is available in all our district courts and has a high user satisfaction rate. In January 2014, our Court will begin an appellate mediation program to try to amicably resolve family law and probate cases on appeal to the Supreme Court before the case is argued to the Court.

I am, personally, a strong advocate of mediation to help settle disputes in the family law and tort areas. I have advocated for some form of court-annexed mediation since I joined the Court. Fortunately, Chief Justice VandeWalle and the other justices have been like-minded and mediation is now a reality in our court system.

Chairing the Joint Procedure Committee

The North Dakota Supreme Court is responsible for promulgating all of the rules of court that govern proceedings in the North Dakota courts. It is also responsible for all the discipline of lawyers and judges.

I had the opportunity to chair the Court's Joint Procedure Committee, which reviews, revises and recommends changes to the N.D. Rules of Civil Procedure, Criminal Procedure, Evidence, Rules of Court and any other rules referred to it by the Supreme Court. The Committee meets three times a year and is one of the Court's standing committees. The members were prepared and hard-working lawyers and judges, and it was a privilege for me to work with them.

Creating a New Case Management System

The North Dakota Supreme Court replaced its case management system during my time on the Court. This was a major undertaking because we moved our system completely away from a paper system to an electronic system, known as Odyssey. The adoption of electronic filing, serving and file maintenance brought with it a need to make major changes to our rules of procedure. We dealt with these changes in the Joint Procedure Committee and will continue to deal with necessary rule changes in the future.

Legal Counsel for Indigents

In 2005, the Legislature enacted NDCC ch. 54-61, creating a new executive branch Commission on Legal Counsel for Indigents. This legislation transferred the responsibility for indigent defense services from the judicial branch to the executive branch and the new Commission. Our Chief Justice VandeWalle should be given much credit for this important change. Our trial courts and our Court have experienced a tremendous increase in criminal cases where the defendant is unable to pay for an attorney. The conflict that could be present by involving the judiciary in indigent defense contracts was eliminated by the creation of the Commission.

Working With Parties Who Represent Themselves

The Supreme Court and the trial courts have also experienced an increase of cases in which one or more of the parties represent themselves. In 2012, 23 percent of the cases filed in the North Dakota Supreme Court had at least one party self-represented. Lack of knowledge and understanding of our court rules makes self-represented cases more difficult and time-consuming for our clerk of court offices and our trial judges.

Therefore, my Court requested funding from the 2013 Legislature to establish a citizen access coordinator. This individual will develop aides, forms and instructions to assist those parties who want to represent themselves in our court system. Access to justice by those who cannot afford a lawyer is a constant concern for our Court.

Juvenile Policy Board

I also had the opportunity to sit on our Juvenile Policy Board for nine years. During the time Judge Debbie Kleven chaired the Board, we reviewed the Uniform Juvenile Court Act, NDCC ch. 27-20, and drafted the first juvenile court rules. We proposed revisions to the act, which were passed by the 2007 Legislature. My Court approved and enacted the juvenile court rules. The Board also developed a best practices manual, which was adopted in 2005.

Creating a Strategic Plan for the Education of Our Judges

As chair of the Judicial Branch Education Commission, I sought to develop a strategic plan for the education of our judges and all of the judicial branch employees. Our Court was fortunate to have Lee Ann Barnhardt join our administrative staff as the Director of Judicial Branch Education. Lee Ann Barnhardt, Judge Steven McCullough, Sean Peterson, a juvenile court officer, and I attended a leadership conference at the University of Memphis. At that conference, we drafted the skeleton of a strategic plan. Under the guidance of Lee Ann Barnhardt, our Committee completed the plan in 2007.

This plan is still guiding our judicial branch education. We have trained our own employees to teach within our state. This has proven to be a plus not only for those who are taught, but those who teach. The dedication and competence of our Director Lee Ann Barnhardt cannot be overstated.

Initiating a Judicial Education Program for High School Teachers

In 2006, our Court started a civic education outreach program for high school teachers. We hold the program at the North Dakota Supreme Court for 1½ days. I was able to develop the program as my project for the Institute for Excellence in Judicial Education.

The teachers who are invited to attend are history, social studies and government teachers. Our Court chooses a U.S. Supreme Court case dealing with a First, Fourth or Fifth Amendment issue. The first day of the program is dedicated to general constitutional law and principles of our judicial system. The end of the day is devoted to very specific constitutional issues. The second day, the teachers step into the shoes of an appellate court judge. They are provided with the facts of the case; they hear an abbreviated oral argument by lawyers; the teachers then divide up into courts of five justices and decide the case by applying the law.

After their decisions are reported, they are told how the U.S. Supreme Court decided the case and why. This program has been well-received by the teachers who attend, and my colleagues and I enjoy the time with the teachers as well. All five of the justices teach at some point during the program. We have now held five of these programs, which are known as the Justices Teaching Institute.

Starting a Juvenile Drug Court Program in North Dakota

One of the initiatives implemented during my time on the Court was the juvenile drug court program. In 1997, I attended the National Association of Women Judges conference in Salt Lake City, Utah. One of the sessions was on drug courts and how successful they were in helping young people successfully treat substance abuse and avoid recidivism.

After returning and visiting with Chief Justice VandeWalle, he agreed to have me form a study committee of stakeholders, who would be necessary to the implementation of a juvenile drug court program. We concluded we should pilot two juvenile drug courts, one in Fargo and one in Grand Forks. The program has proven successful on many levels, including reduced recidivism, increased treatment success, improved school achievement and improved family relationships.

We now have juvenile drug courts in Fargo, Grand Forks, Devils Lake, Jamestown/Valley City, Bismarck and Minot. Our state coordinator, Marilyn Moe, has done a phenomenal job for this program and it continues to depend for its success on her expertise and enthusiasm. Marilyn Moe conceived of and coordinated our Upper Midwest Drug Court Conference, which has enjoyed great success. The teams that participate in running these treatment courts are dedicated to youth who come into the juvenile court system primarily because of a substance abuse problem. My admiration and gratitude to them is unending.

Thoughts on Serving as a Supreme Court Justice

I did not understand, as a lawyer, what it would entail to be a judge, both professionally and personally. I thought as an appellate judge, I would be researching the law and writing opinions rather leisurely. That is not reality. The number of cases, the amount of reading and the significant cases of first impression are at times overwhelming because of the amount of time needed for consideration. This means that, as a justice, I never go anywhere without briefs and law to read. I read nights and weekends. I read on the airplane and in the car when I am a passenger. I read on vacation. Because the work is rewarding, it makes it all worthwhile.

I have been able to contribute to the improvement of our judicial system in ways I never would have were I not a judge. There is a certain amount of power and prestige that comes with being a judge. I am humbled by it and hope that I have done the work as well as I am able.

Personally, I did not fully contemplate what my position as a judge would mean for my family. I did not think about the restrictions on both their activities and my activities, which are in our Code of Judicial Conduct. Most citizens have no idea how many limitations are placed on judges by our Code. Our families are affected in many ways also. Our work interferes at times with the amount of time we can spend with our families. In addition, we deal with various levels of threats from unhappy parties, primarily defendants in the criminal system.

As of December 31, 2013, I have officially retired from the North Dakota Supreme Court. I have served with some of the finest jurists and people. I could not have spent the last 17 and three quarters years in a more rewarding career.

TEN

A Life in the Law

By

Carol Ronning Kapsner

North Dakota Supreme Court Justice
1998 – Present

"We research the law on the issues that come before us, hear the arguments from the lawyers or litigants and issue our written decision in the case. If one enjoys being a student, and I do, it is virtually the perfect job."

Justice Carol Kapsner

Carol Kapsner nee Ronning*

1947-Present

Supreme Court Justice 1998-present

Supreme Court Justice Carol Kapsner - 2007
(Supreme Court photo collection)

Personal Information

Born 1947 in Bismarck and raised in Underwood and Bismarck, North Dakota. Married to John, two children. In "spare time," enjoys needlework and quilting.

Party Affiliation

Elected on No-Party Ballot

Education

Saint Mary's High School, Bismarck; received B.A. from the College of St. Catherine in St. Paul, Minnesota, Phi Beta Kappa; began graduate studies in English literature at Oxford University and completed M.A. at Indiana University as a Woodrow Wilson fellow and Indiana University fellow; awarded J.D. from University of Colorado.

Professional Experience Before Taking Office

Started law firm of Kapsner & Kapsner in Bismarck in 1977 and remained in private practice until 1998; president of the Burleigh County Bar Association, 1980; Board of Governors of the State Bar Association of North Dakota, 1993-95; Bar Association appointee to the Judicial Conference, 1988-98.

Memberships and Committees Include

As Justice: Judicial Planning Committee, chair, 2008-present; Commission to Study Racial and Ethnic Bias in the Courts, co-chair, 2009-2013; Court Services Administrative Committee, member, 1998-08, chair, 2004-08; Judicial Education Commission, 1998-04; Committee on Tribal and State Court Affairs, 2002-10; Personnel Policy Board, 2004-2013; ABA Standards Review Committee, 2004-08; ABA Accreditation Committee, 2012-present.[100]

*Bio contains information through 2013

I never intended to go to law school. Teaching the nuances of the poetry of Richard Wilbur and John Donne seemed the right career for me. Yet in the middle of graduate school, doing a master's degree in English literature, I found my husband's studies in the law equally fascinating and that began the process of change that led me to become a Supreme Court justice.

My North Dakota Heritage

I am a product of North Dakota. My grandmothers are reflective of the heritage of this state. My father's mother, Ingeborg Hjelmstad Ronning, a rather austere but music-loving woman of Norwegian Lutheran roots, homesteaded in her own name near Ryder, North Dakota. Her husband died as a young man and left her with four children, the youngest being my father, who was then only 3 years old. She ultimately lost her farm. She was frightened by the loss of her resources. But she kept her family together, raising them through the difficult times of the 1920s and '30s, without government assistance, undoubtedly with the kindness and generosity of friends and family, but mostly through her own endurance.

My mother's mother was Nellie Dolan Scott. She was an Irish Catholic who bore 14 children and raised 12 to adulthood in the Douglas, Drake and Underwood areas of North Dakota through those same tough years. She had a dozen children of her own - yet she was always known to be the one person available when neighbors needed help or nursing through illness. Her children say that there was never enough money but there was always enough food and always a welcome in Nellie's home for anyone who came there. I think of these two women as reflective of these prairies, with their strength and their endurance.

Growing up in Bismarck and Underwood, North Dakota, my early childhood was as close to the idyllic small-town life as the movies could depict. I have a sister, Connie, six years younger, and a large, close extended family on both my mother's and my father's sides. There was a sense of security, relationship and belonging in my very early years that should be a part of every child's life. My parents gave us a great deal of freedom. They, especially my father, seemed free of gender expectations. Whatever job needed doing, whether it was washing dishes or mixing cement, was the job of the person available to do it.

Learning to "Think" and "Challenge"

My sister and I were educated in the Catholic schools in Bismarck through high school. I was a good student and school came easy to me because I liked to learn. I do credit much of my later success to the experience I had at St. Mary's Central High School. The school at that time was "tracked" based upon intellectual ability and academic performance. Students who were expected to perform at a certain level were grouped together and were not allowed to participate in extracurricular activities unless that level was reached. This is the sense in which I credit my experience for later success. The social segregation resulting from tracking was not commendable, but I am not sure that we who were benefitted by tracking were as aware as we should have been of that fact.

Despite the school being parochial, I remember high school as a time when it was expected that one "think" and "challenge." Perhaps this memory is the legacy of the greatest teacher I have ever had: Sister Barbara Ann Gehrki. She taught literature at the high school to those students in the accelerated track. Sr. Barbara Ann expected students to have opinions about what they read. But opinions were not sufficient – one had to justify the opinions she held and be ready to defend them based on critical thinking. Good preparation for the work of a Supreme Court justice.

In senior religion class – a class where a variety of opinions were rather freely communicated - I was assigned to read *The Feminine Mystique* by Betty Friedan and report on the book to the class. It was indicative of the atmosphere of the school in 1964-65 that I was assigned to read a book newly published relating to the release of women from their stereotypical roles. Sitting in the class when I reported on the book was John Kapsner, who would become my husband four years later. John has "evolved" greatly from the comments that he made in class that day.

I attended the College of St. Catherine in St. Paul, majoring in English literature. The college was a women's college run by an order of nuns whose focus on education for women had created an outstanding institution. I attended college on a National Merit scholarship based upon my high school grades and testing performance. This was fortunate because, by this time, my parents had separated and, during my sophomore year, my father died. The scholarship, coupled with the veterans benefits from my father, meant my education did not have to be interrupted. I majored in English and intended to become a college professor of English literature.

During college, John and I began dating. John attended St. John's University in Collegeville, Minnesota, and would travel to see me each weekend. John had always planned to become a lawyer and we had to look for graduate schools that would provide us both with the programs we needed. At graduation, I got a fellowship to attend Oxford University to study 17th century English literature to start my graduate studies. It was a summer program, so I left for England after graduation in May, leaving my mother and John to plan a wedding that would take place in late August. Our "honeymoon" was our trip with a U-haul trailer to Indiana University, where we both would study starting in September.

I had a Woodrow Wilson fellowship and an Indiana University fellowship and John had a Law School scholarship. We were married graduate students, living on $275 per month, and we got pregnant within two months.

Our older daughter, Miki, was born the following July, by which time I had finished the course work for my master's degree, which I was awarded in January 1971. I dropped out of graduate school while John completed law school. This was the period when I "caught the bug." I decided that rather than complete my studies in literature, I would go to law school at some point. We had our younger daughter, Caithlin, in 1972 and moved back to North Dakota, where John worked in the Attorney General's office and I stayed home to care for our children.

In early 1974, we moved to Colorado so that I could attend law school while John worked at the Environmental Protection Agency. Attending law school with two preschool children meant that every day was completely scheduled. There was time for school and time for children and time for studying and not much time for sleeping. We would probably have stayed in Colorado, but during my last year of law school, my mother got cancer and we knew that we would be returning to North Dakota to care for her.

Kapsner and Kapsner

I was admitted to the bar of North Dakota on October 7, 1977, and on that day, John and I signed our partnership agreement and opened the firm of Kapsner & Kapsner in Bismarck. We had gross income of $354 the first month we practiced together. Fortunately, John's expertise in environmental law resulted in him being hired almost immediately by a large mining company, which kept him busy and our firm financially stable for several years.

Like many lawyers in North Dakota my practice was very general. I have often said that I have done everything from adoption to zoning. This was fortunate from the perspective of a justice who is, of necessity, a generalist and must deal with cases over the full spectrum of the law. For 22 years, with the exception of one year, I practiced law with John, who likes to say that we get to count our marriage in dog years since we spent 24 hours a day together during that time.

The first years of practice, I also taught business law at what was then Bismarck Junior College. I tried to be active in the local bar association and served in the offices of that group and as president in 1980. I also served on committees of the State Bar Association and on the Board of Governors of the State Bar Association from 1993 to 1995. Probably the most interesting service was an appointment to the subcommittee of the Attorney Standards Committee, where I served from 1986 to 1994. This subcommittee drafted the Rules of Professional Conduct. The President of the State Bar Association also appointed me as a bar-representative member of the Judicial Conference, a conference of all the judges in the state. Attending the biannual meetings of the conference gave me an understanding of the close relationship of the bench and bar of the state, but also an understanding of the differing perspectives of attorneys and judges.

Private practice is a rewarding and exhausting experience. It profoundly changes you as a person. People bring you their problems, hope that you will take them on and expect you to care about those problems. The people who bring you these problems often have little perspective on either the problem or the potential for solution. I tried to make it a rule never to distance myself from a client and never to be less than honest with a client, even when it meant telling a client what that person did not want to hear. There were extraordinary people and extraordinary cases that will always be with me.

The successful private practice of law also makes serious and continuing demands on one's private life. Frequently, the private life gets rearranged for the needs of the practice. When our children were young, I routinely went to the office at 4:30 or 5:00 a.m. because at that hour the phone didn't ring. That schedule allowed me to spend time with our children in the evening. Either John or I was always at the office on Saturday.

The 1980 Association of Retarded Citizens Lawsuit

The case for which our firm was most known was a case early in the career of Kapsner & Kapsner. *ARC v. Olson, et al.*, a case seeking to deinstitutionalize the developmentally disabled citizens of North Dakota, was filed in September 1980. It wasn't intended to be the kind of case it turned out to be. Parents of institutionalized children wanted to stop the construction of a food service building to get more money devoted to services for their children and asked if our law firm would represent them. The firm would, but after research, we thought it a waste of resources; the problems were so profound that greater relief should be sought.

Before the lawsuit, people who were at the time described as "retarded" were warehoused at two facilities in Grafton and San Haven, North Dakota. The lawsuit sought multiple forms of relief for these citizens, describing the conditions of their lives as unconstitutional. It was the kind of lawsuit that John was completely suited to oversee. It required experts in various fields to review the state's actions and testify, and it needed substantial briefing of the constitutional issues to explain how the conditions of the individuals confined demonstrated the constitutional violation. It was expensive to bring and there were times when the work of every person in the firm was focused on that lawsuit. One of the experts hired to review the situation gave us what proved to astonishing advice: Go to the institutions. Take your staff and see how they react to the situation there. Only then will you have a sense of the real-world response to your lawsuit.

I went with the attorney at the firm who was doing only that litigation, and we took our secretaries to see the conditions at the institutions. It was a lesson in how, without any malevolent intent, humans are capable of creating for others the most degrading of conditions. It was terrifying. We toured the wards of adults who were described as profoundly retarded. They were unclothed. They spent their days in groups in large, empty rooms made of concrete blocks with virtually nothing to do. When we entered, they swarmed around us. We were a distraction. From the muddled sounds in that room and from the center of the group of men, I heard, "Hello, my name is Jerry." To this day, I do not know if that is the only communication Jerry was capable of. To this day, I do know that even if it was the only communication Jerry was capable of, it was wrong to be required to live as he was living.

We visited the wards of less disabled individuals, some of whom had been there for decades but who could have functioned well in a community setting. I cannot forget the woman who must have been in her 40s or 50s and had been institutionalized since childhood, who proudly had me read the cherished card from her mother, signed by her mother, "Sincerely, Mrs. John Doe." I cannot forgive the mother nor forget the woman who cherished the card.

There were also some individuals who were medically fragile and did need assistance. There were an unquantifiable number of stories during the visits, including the stories of the staff who wanted to do more. As a lawyer, you come to realize that there are situations and institutions that will not change unless someone uses the judicial system to bring that change about. It is people who get caught in the inertia of the status quo. It was two terrifying visits that highlighted this lesson for me. Ultimately, the institutions were visited by 13 experts who testified for us and we accumulated over 100 hours of video tape.

The ARC lawsuit was not a popular lawsuit. It cost the state of North Dakota tens of millions of dollars to provide community services, deinstitutionalize 90 percent of people at the institutions and provide adequate staffing, training and education. After the fact, it seems unlikely anyone would want to go back to things as they were. However, having been one of the lawyers who caused the state to incur such enormous costs was not necessarily going to be favorable to becoming a judge. When my name was proposed as a Supreme Court justice, there were people who opposed my appointment for this reason.

On the Bench – From left to right, Justices Kapsner, Sandstrom, VandeWalle and Crothers listen while Attorney General Wayne Stenehjem addresses new lawyers during an admission ceremony. (2006 - Supreme Court photo collection)

Seeking Nomination as a North Dakota Supreme Court Justice

I practiced law for 22 years and always enjoyed the courtroom as a trial attorney. I never thought about becoming a trial judge. An appellate judge always seemed the right fit for me. I describe an appellate judge as being a student of the law. North Dakota Supreme Court justices are given roughly 30 legal cases each month for 10 months of the year. We research the law on the issues that come before us, hear the arguments from the lawyers or litigants and issue our written decision in the case. If one enjoys being a student, and I do, it is virtually the perfect job.

When Justice Herb Meschke announced that he was retiring in 1998, I felt the time was right for me to apply for the job. I knew I had the academic background for the work. I had suitable experience both as an attorney and within various professional organizations. During the last years of my practice, I had represented organizations that had statewide membership, which I felt would be of assistance during an election.

The first step to getting an appointment is applying to the Judicial Nominating Committee, a committee of lawyers, judges and lay persons who interview people who are interested in judgeships that open up when a sitting judge retires before a term is completed. That committee does background checks, conducts interviews and sends a list of nominees to the governor, who then makes an appointment from the list of nominees. I was one of three names forwarded to Governor Ed Schafer for the open position.

The other two names forwarded to Governor Schafer were formidable:- one of the state's most respected trial judges and one of its most respected legislators. There was an additional issue. Governor Schafer had been my client for his individual interests. Although he would certainly be familiar with my legal ability, would he be less likely to appoint me because of the past relationship? I knew him well enough to know that he would not be more likely to appoint me as a result of it.

There was also the issue of whether a governor would be less likely to appoint a second woman to the Supreme Court. Justice Mary Maring had been appointed by Governor Schafer two years earlier to fill the term of Justice Beryl Levine when she retired and Justice Maring had then run a successful campaign in a contested election. With Ed Schafer, one always needed to be direct, and during his interview with me as a candidate, I decided to approach the subject directly. I told the governor that I didn't want the job because I was a woman, but I didn't want to not get the job because I was a woman.

I shouldn't have been surprised that he found that issue irrelevant and his concerns were whether I had thought about what I would be doing to get myself elected after serving for two years - if I got the job. I mapped out the election strategies I had indeed been thinking about. The next several days were tense. I remember one of the other candidates calling me and asking how I felt. We commiserated on how nervous we both were. The call came from the governor about 8:00 o'clock at night. "Come to the Capitol tomorrow morning at 10:00. I'm appointing you."

The 2000 Election for Supreme Court Justice

After serving two years, an appointed judge must run for election. My first election was in 2000 and it was a contested election. Judicial elections in North Dakota are unlike other elections. Judges run on no-party ballots. But unlike other no-party offices, judges may not get the endorsement of political parties and do not get funding from political parties. Judges are restricted by our judicial canons from knowing who has contributed to our political campaigns. Judges must seek contributions through a committee and that committee must keep those campaign contributions separate from the judge. As a practical reality, the judge also ends up spending a substantial amount of his or her own money on a contested political campaign and must decide how much money he or she is willing to spend.

In the year 2000, in addition to doing my judicial work, I traveled the state putting

Justice Kapsner and Justice Crothers visit a classroom in West Fargo.
(2012 - Supreme Court photo collection)

over 27,000 miles on my car, participated in over 20 parades, talked to as many organizations as possible and wouldn't trade the experience for anything. You learn a lot about the people of North Dakota and about the state of North Dakota when you run for a statewide office. Asking people to vote for you was one of the hardest things I had to learn to do. Being naturally introverted, it seemed rude to talk about yourself and tell someone that you were worthy of his or her vote. I got over it. I had to get over it. I knew that had happened when I was in a line to get tickets for a movie on a night when I was giving myself a "vacation" from campaigning. I introduced myself to the other people in line and asked for their votes. I remember John looking at me and saying, "Who are you? This isn't the woman I married." I had learned the dance of politics. It was necessary if I wanted the job. And I wanted the job.

One 2000 campaign experience that still makes me laugh, and puts things into perspective, occurred in Beulah, North Dakota, during a parade. As usual, candidates walked during the parade. The day was very hot and the parade route went up a hill. I had gotten separated from my car and from my source of candy. A boy of approximately 6 years approached me. I apologized that I had run out of candy and only had a card to give him. I explained that he was too young to vote but that he should be sure to vote when he was old enough. He looked at me critically and said, "That's OK. You'll be dead by then." It's now 2014, I'm still in office and he's undoubtedly old enough to vote.

This is a BIG, beautiful state. My good friend Becky Quanrud agreed to be my campaign manager and we spent the spring, summer and early fall exploring North Dakota on the campaign trail. We rode the carousel in Wahpeton. We learned that the fastest way from Gwinner to Bowman is through South Dakota. We decided to find out which café made the best BLT in North Dakota. We tasted as many tomato recipes as possible in Minot. We ate sauerkraut in Wishek and lutefisk in Washburn. We visited the house on the island in Grafton. We saw the quilts at the county fair in Watford City. We truly tried to enjoy meeting the people and seeing the state. But perhaps my election in 2010 was better – it was uncontested.

Description of Official Duties as Supreme Court Justice

Ten-year term. Serves as one of five justices. The North Dakota Supreme Court is the highest court for the state. It has two major types of responsibilities: (1) adjudicative and (2) administrative. In its adjudicative capacity, the Supreme Court is primarily an appellate court with jurisdiction to hear appeals from decisions from district courts. It also has original jurisdiction in certain matters and can issue original and remedial writs as are necessary to exercise this authority. In its administrative capacity, the Supreme Court has major responsibilities for ensuring the efficient and effective operation of all courts in the state, except federal and tribal courts; maintaining high standards of judicial conduct; supervising the legal profession; and promulgating procedural rules that allow for the orderly and efficient transaction of business.[101]

Reading, Thinking and Writing

The judicial aspect of the job from the very beginning was exactly as I expected it to be. It involves the research, critical thinking and writing that I expected. Many observers equate the judge's work with what happens in the courtroom, but it is actually the time spent reading, thinking and writing in places other than the courtroom that is the bulk of our work. It's not a job that can be done in a 40-hour work week, but it is challenging and satisfying.

What is less known is the administrative side of a justice's work. The Chief Justice is responsible for the entire judicial system of the state, and the Court sits in an administrative conference once a week to handle the supervisory issues of running the judicial system. During the first two years I was on the bench, the Court had the additional and unusual problem that it was charged with reducing the number of trial judges. By statute, trial judge numbers had to be reduced to 42 by the year 2000. Each time a judge retired or decided not to run, the judicial needs of the entire state had to be reviewed to determine how to assign judicial resources to meet the mandate. We spent a great deal of time looking at the demographics of North Dakota. Those demographics looked very different at that time than they do during the Bakken explosion. Recently, the Legislature has had to increase the number of judgeships.

Education about the government and particularly about the judicial system is an important focus of the outreach efforts of the Court. The Court travels to the University of North Dakota law school each year to hear cases, which the law students can observe, and also to judge the school's moot court competition. The Court also travels, usually four times a year, to high schools around the state to hear cases in the high school gym or auditorium so the high school students and the people from the community can see an actual case being heard. The justices regularly participate in the "We, the People" contest, a program which tests high school students' knowledge about their government, as judges for the state competition.

In addition to the judicial work, each justice serves on or chairs several committees. Most recently, I have co-chaired the Commission to Study Racial and Ethnic Bias in the Courts and chaired the Judicial Planning Committee. The Commission to Study Racial and Ethnic Bias in the Courts was created by resolution in October 2009. It involved a statewide study to determine whether bias was perceived in the treatment of racial and ethnic minorities in the state court system.

The commission conducted a number of hearings and studies over the period March 2010, through April 2012 and filed a report with recommendations to the Court on its findings. The result is the creation of an Implementation Committee to follow through on the recommendations of the Commission. The Judicial Planning Committee exists to identify challenges to the judicial system and to make recommendations to the system for changes to adapt to future needs. The planning committee filed a report recommending changes to the judicial districts of the state, some of which have recently been implemented.

As a member of the American Bar Association, I have served on the Standards Review Committee, a committee which drafts the standards for the accreditation of law schools. I have participated on site team inspections, which go to law schools to do evaluations of whether the law school is in compliance with the standards and report findings to the Accreditation Committee. I now serve on the Accreditation Committee of the American Bar Association. Service on national committees like these helps a judge understand how legal education and the practice of law are evolving around the country. It is also important to offer your services to your profession.

Final Thoughts

Constantly working with words and intangible concepts, I find it is absolutely necessary to have an outlet that is completely tangible. For me, that is needlework and quilting, and I try to do some every day. I need to experience the process of planning, executing and touching a tangible piece that I have produced as a counterbalance to the work of a judge. I belong to guilds that support the needle arts and take classes in the techniques that I enjoy. Once a year, I go on a weeklong retreat where the entire time is devoted to needlework.

When I look back at how my life might have been so different had I pursued the first career of English professor, I think about how both poets and lawyers love words and how they use them in such different ways. As lawyers and judges, we try to use words for their precision, their conciseness and their lack of ambiguity. Poets, on the other hand, look for the word with the richest, most complex, nuanced and suggestive meaning. I continue to think that perhaps there will come a time when I can share my love of poetry, particularly the poetry of Richard Wilbur, by teaching a class or two.

Charting a Path in the Early Years

1893-96

ELEVEN

"A Bright, Active, Public-spirited Woman"

Laura J. Eisenhuth

The First Woman Elected to Statewide Office in the United States
Superintendent of Public Instruction
1893-94

By
Susan Wefald

"… there ought to be at least one bright, active, public-spirited woman on every school board."

Laura Eisenhuth, 1894[102]

Laura J. Eisenhuth nee Kelly*

1859-1937

State Superintendent of Public Instruction 1893-94

First Woman Elected to Statewide Office in the U.S.

State Superintendent of Public Instruction Laura Eisenhuth
(North Dakota Department of Public Instruction photo collection)

Personal Information

Born 1859 at Blenheim, Ontario, and raised in Dewitt, Iowa. Married to Willis. In "spare time," enjoyed painting and sketching.

Party Affiliation

Democrat

Education

Dewitt, Iowa, public schools

Professional Experience before taking office

Twelve years of teaching experience, including teaching at DeWitt High School, Iowa, and Carrington, North Dakota, Public Schools; Foster County Superintendent of Schools, 1888-92; State Institute Conductor, 1891-92.

Memberships include

North Dakota Educational Association, Vice President, 1891.

*Bio includes information through 1894

Laura Eisenhuth, the first woman elected to statewide office in the U.S., was 33 years old when she entered the State Capitol Building in Bismarck and took her oath of office. [103] The date was January 3, 1893. Superintendent Eisenhuth was the fourth person to serve as state Superintendent of Public Instruction in the new state of North Dakota.[104] At the end of that busy first day, she sat down and wrote her first entry in the Superintendents Record, in which she recorded each day's activities while she was in office:

> *"I, Laura J. Eisenhuth, took the oath of office and filed my official bond as State Supt of. Public Inst. Appointed Willis R. Bierly as Chief Cherk in the Dept. Received from my predecessor through Mr. Cathro the keys of the office and $25.00 Amt. due for Reading Circle Fund."* [105]

During her time in office, she reorganized important office responsibilities and proposed many improvements to the state school system, some not enacted until after she had left. Although Laura Eisenhuth served only one term as Superintendent of Public Instruction, she left a model of an efficient, energetic office holder for other women seeking political office.

An Experienced Teacher and County Superintendent

Laura Kelly Eisenhuth was born in Blenheim, Ontario, Canada, on May 29, 1859, the daughter of Thomas and Nancy Kelly.[106] In 1863, her family moved to eastern Iowa and settled in DeWitt, where she grew up with her four siblings, Mary, Thomas, Fredrick and Edward. [107] An 1895 article in the Fargo paper, *The Record,* stated she was educated in the best schools of that state, but there is no mention in *The Record* or other sources that Laura attended any normal school (a two-year school, beyond high school, which provided teacher training) or college.[108] For 11 years, she was a successful teacher in the Iowa schools, starting teaching at the age of 18.

Laura Kelly, like many others, was drawn to northern Dakota Territory during the great Dakota boom. She described her move to what would soon be North Dakota in a one-page autobiography written in 1937:

> "My first trip to North Dakota was made in June 1885, and at that time [I] located on a pre-emption claim of 160 acres near New Rockford. Returned to duties as teacher at DeWitt High School that fall. Returned to North Dakota in the summer of 1886 and again in the summer of 1887, and in the fall of 1887 was married to Willis Eisenhuth.[109]

Laura Eisenhuth was 28 years old in 1887. Her husband, Mr. Willis H.B. Eisenhuth, known also as Joseph, was originally from Pennsylvania and was a farmer and druggist in Carrington.[110] He was also a staunch Democrat.[111] Laura later also described herself as a "member of the minority Democratic Party."[112]

Two weeks after the couple settled in Carrington, the School Board came to Laura and asked her to become the teacher at the Carrington School because the teacher hired that fall had quit. Mrs. Eisenhuth took over a one-room school with a class of 80 students, and two weeks later, the School Board asked her to continue for the full school year. Years later, Laura recalled, "They said I was doing splendidly and as they employed a hired girl to do my housework I accepted."[113]

By June 1888, the *Carrington News* endorsed Mrs. Eisenhuth for Foster County superintendent of Schools, and in the June election, she won by a majority of four votes. [114] She gave "so satisfactory an administration of the office that she was re-elected in 1890, carrying eleven of the thirteen election districts of the county."[115]

A few personal descriptions of Laura Eisenhuth survive. Bertha Grant, a writer who knew Mrs. Eisenhuth, described her in 1894 in an article for *Western Womanhood*, the publication of the North Dakota Women's Christian Temperance Union. The article, titled "Wives and Daughters of the Administration," described Laura as:

> "... tall and slight, with mild dark eyes, full of expression and soft, wavy brown hair. Her firm, cordial handclasp is earnest of her good will toward men and assure the visitor of her sincerity. Although a delicate and spiritual woman, Mrs. Eisenhuth has, to an unusual degree, the quality of patience and determination, and of fortitude ... Mrs. Eisenhuth is, above all, a womanly woman, devoted to her husband, her business, and her home, and her personal magnetism is recognized by all so fortunate as to make her acquaintance ... She has a fondness and taste for painting and sketching, and when she has an occasional spare moment to devote to her own amusement it is given to her oils and pastels."[116]

The difficulty in finding a category for an office-holding woman is evident, as well as the need to reassure readers that Eisenhuth remained a "womanly woman."

When Mrs. Eisenhuth was elected Foster County Superintendent of Schools in 1888 and 1890, she was following in the footsteps of Dakota Territory pioneer Linda Slaughter. Mrs. Slaughter had first been appointed to be Burleigh County Superintendent of Schools in 1873, and then had been elected to that position in 1878-82.[117] In the years after Mrs. Slaughter, other women were elected county Superintendent. By 1888, there were about half a dozen women superintendents in northern Dakota Territory. Six years later, in 1894, when Laura Eisenhuth was state Superintendent of Public Instruction, she called attention to the fact that "we have now eleven lady county superintendents out of thirty-nine, and all doing excellent work; their natural aptitude to teach and their love for little children giving them a peculiar advantage."[118]

As noted above, women could be elected county Superintendent of Schools while Dakota was a territory. They had been voting in local school elections and on school issues since 1883. In 1889, a new constitution was drafted for the new state; article V, section 128, provided that women could now be elected to state school positions:

> Any woman having the qualifications enumerated in section 121 of this article, as to age, residence and citizenship, and including those now qualified by the laws of the territory, may vote for all school officers, and upon all questions pertaining solely to school matters, and be eligible to any school office.[119]

The 1889 constitution also established the office of state Superintendent of Public Instruction and determined the state Superintendent would be an elected official with a two-year term. Now North Dakota women could vote and run for election in a statewide race. While county elections for school Superintendent were usually held in June, state and congressional elections, including the state Superintendent of Public Instruction, were held in November.

The North Dakota Political Scene

Laura Eisenhuth entered North Dakota state politics at a very volatile time. North Dakotans elected a different governor every two years during the first 10 years of statehood. Although Republicans won every election except one during that period, Republican conventions, dominated by the political boss Alexander McKenzie, regularly nominated new candidates to state office.

In 1890, the populists, prohibitionists and members of the Farmers Alliance formed a third party – the Independent Party. The message this party offered voters included free silver, government loans on real estate and stored crops, woman's suffrage and direct election of U.S. Senators.[120] The Independents endorsed Mrs. Eisenhuth for state Superintendent of Public Instruction. Because of her "success and popularity as an educator," she had already been nominated by the Democratic state convention.[121] She may have been endorsed to attract new women voters to the Democrat and Independent Parties, although women could not vote for any other offices on the state ticket.

In early October 1890, the Women's Christian Temperance Union held their first North Dakota convention. Susan B. Anthony was the featured speaker and a large crowd gathered to hear her remarks. The Jamestown Weekly reported, "Mrs. Laura Eisenhuth, the first lady candidate on a North Dakota state ticket was then introduced … and was greeted with loud applause. She urged upon the ladies the necessity of voting in the upcoming election."[122] This must have been a thrilling moment for Laura. Her Republican opponent was John Ogden, a well-known educator in the state.[123] Unfortunately for Eisenhuth, it was a Republican year in North Dakota politics and Ogden won, as did every Republican candidate for statewide office in 1890.[124]

Mrs. Eisenhuth continued to build her statewide reputation as an educator during the next two years. John Ogden, the new state Superintendent of Public Instruction, chose five state educational leaders to conduct one-week institutes (mandatory training sessions) for teachers throughout the state in 1891-92.[125] He selected Mrs. Eisenhuth to conduct 13 institutes. She received good reviews for her workshops, including one from Kidder County in July 1892, which stated, "Mrs. Laura J. Eisenhuth conducted the institute in her highly interesting manner, following the plan laid down in the institute manual."[126] Conducting institutes kept her very busy travelling around the state and also provided her with the opportunity to demonstrate that she was a leader in North Dakota educational circles. She was also elected vice president of the North Dakota Education Association in January 1891.[127]

By June 1892, Laura Eisenhuth was in the thick of politics. She ran for a third term as Foster County Superintendent, but this time things did not go so smoothly. She lost the election by a few votes and demanded a recount. The *Bismarck Weekly Tribune* reported, "Mrs. Eisenhuth appeared and demanded another canvas of the votes, including those of the disputed township. The auditor refused to make it, and the case was carried to the courts." In late summer, the judge ruled in favor of Mrs. Eisenhuth, a recount was held, and she won by a majority of eight votes.[128]

Also in mid-June of 1892, 300 people attended the Independent Party convention in Valley City, where the party nominated a full slate of candidates, including Laura for state Superintendent of Public Instruction. [129] She was also endorsed by the Democrat Party.[130] Her Republican opponent was J.M. Devine, superintendent of schools in LaMoure County.[131] He had also been chosen by John Ogden to participate in 15 state institutes in 1892 as a "state lecturer," a featured speaker on the institute program.[132]

In August 1892, Mr. Eisenhuth began publishing a Democrat newspaper, *The Citizen*, in Carrington. In the nine issues that were published between August 12 and December 2, 1892, Mrs. Eisenhuth edited and wrote material for the "Educational Column." "Education should be above politics," she wrote in the first issue, "and it is my intention to keep this column so."[133] She was true to her word, and in the issue just previous to the election wrote only about how "Each office, its qualifications and duties should be taught in a non-partisan" manner.[134]

Eli Shortridge, the Independent candidate for governor, campaigned vigorously, and during the final days of the campaign, a worried Republican National Committee sent money to North Dakota to defeat the Populists. [135] This effort was largely unsuccessful, as the Independent Party won every office except Secretary of State.

Although the election was held on November 8, election results came in very slowly in 1892. It took over a month to tally all of the votes and finally, on December 16, the final abstract was printed in the Bismarck *Daily Tribune*. Laura Eisenhuth: 19,078; J.M. Devine: 17,343.[136]

Description of Official Duties of Superintendent of Public Instruction

Two-year term. Preserve in the office miscellaneous documents (books, maps, school reports, etc.); general supervision of the public schools of the state; prepare and furnish school supplies; responsible for teacher examinations and issuing or revoking state certificates; prescribe a course of study for public and State Normal Schools in the state; prescribe rules for and assist at teacher institutes in the state; advise county superintendents; keep a record of all official acts; print the school laws; hold a conference with the county superintendents; prepare a biennial report and print and distribute 2,500 copies.[137]

Member: Board of University and School Lands, secretary; Normal School Board.

Superintendent Eisenhuth's First Month in Office

A week after the election results were announced, Laura Eisenhuth was in Bismarck, preparing to settle in for her new duties. Finding a place to live was an early priority. On December 23, 1892, the *Bismarck Weekly Tribune* noted these comments of Mrs. Eisenhuth:

> "I find houses scarce and hardly know where to go. I presume we will be obliged to take temporary quarters this winter and wait until spring for a permanent location. When I located at Carrington, I hesitated between Carrington and Bismarck, but was finally urged by Senator Casey to locate at Carrington." [138]

After only about a week in which to settle in a new home and city, she took office. With a staff of only two people, it was a daunting task for Superintendent Eisenhuth to take on the responsibilities of her department. During her first month in office, she hit the ground running, taking care of the myriad duties that confronted her as a state administrator. During that first month, her work included drafting education bills, answering the questions of a legislative investigating committee, preparing for and participating in important meetings of the Board of University and School Lands and the Normal School Board. She also attended to administrative functions such as sending out large mailings to school districts and county superintendents and organizing the state educational library. Juggling all of these duties at the same time required good administrative skills, which Eisenhuth had honed during her time as a county superintendent.

Fortunately for us, every day Superintendent Eisenhuth was in office, she, or a person in her office, recorded a short notation of what duties were accomplished that day in a very large record book, preserved in the State Archives in Bismarck. The record of the month of January 1894 is written in Mrs. Eisenhuth's own hand. Her notations in her first month (January 4 through February 4, 1893) indicate she made a good start on important work she would continue to deal with throughout her term in office. [139] Excerpts from the Superintendents Record are included to illustrate how she juggled these various responsibilities, concentrating especially on her first month in office. Some later excerpts incorporate activities that occurred later in the year, such as teacher training.

Board of University and School Lands

January 5 – Conducted correspondence. Indexed Secretary's Record of University and School Lands. Called a meeting of normal School Board for Jan 10.

Jan 30 – Conducted correspondence. Meeting of U and S Land Board. Meeting adjourned until Jan 31 10 A.M. owing to the illness of the Gov. Assorted letters in regards to bonds and lands and made list of lands for sale, lease & hay permits.

It was not business as usual for the Board of University and School Lands in January 1893. Questions had been raised about how the board issued bonds, and so a legislative committee had decided to investigate the actions of the board under the previous administration.[140] Superintendent Eisenhuth, as secretary of the board, had responsibility for the records of the board in 1893-94. She found them in disarray.[141] The Governor, the Secretary of State, the Attorney General and the State Auditor were also members of the board.

At the time of statehood, Congress endowed education in North Dakota with land grants, including two sections of every township that were under the jurisdiction of the Board of University and School Lands – 3,049,465 acres in all. [142] The Legislature established a minimum sale price of $10 an acre, so the state had a potential education endowment of more than $30,000,000.[143] In 1893-94, the Board of University and School Lands invested the income that was produced from renting or selling school lands in school district bonds, state bonds and farm contracts.[144]

In January, Superintendent Eisenhuth did much of the recordkeeping herself, probably so that she could become very familiar with this important part of her work since she had to prepare information for the legislative investigating committee and prepare for and participate in board meetings. In her first month of office, she spent time on 21 days on board activities. In February, she arranged for a part-time clerk to do the recordkeeping.

The Legislature had changes in mind. Even though the legislative investigating committee found "nothing crooked" when it ended its investigation and made its report in February 1893, by March 1893, the Legislature had established a staffed Land Department with an appointed Land Commissioner. [145] Superintendent Eisenhuth had lobbied the Legislature to place the school land responsibilities under the supervision of her office, but to no avail.[146] Superintendent Eisenhuth continued her work as secretary of the board, which she found interesting but time consuming. In the first 18 months of her term, there were 118 meetings of the Board of University and School Lands, and she attended all but three.[147]

State Educational Library

Jan 9 – Conducted correspondence. Met with State officers in the Governors private room to discuss the policy of Attorney General. Continued the arrangement and listing of Library. Drafted two bills. Reviewed two School bills. Copied Land Lists.

The library Mrs. Eisenhuth refers to in the Superintendents Record is the State Educational Library, the lending library established by her predecessor for the use of teachers and county superintendents across the state. Although there were some private lending libraries, there were no public libraries in North Dakota at that time; the first public library was established in 1897 in Grafton.[148]

During her first month, Eisenhuth took on the project of arranging, listing and checking all books in the library. Her Superintendents Record entries show that she worked on tasks related to the library 14 days in her first month in office, and on January 24 she wrote, "Finished checking library." The next day she noted, "Found sixty six, 66, volumes missing." It probably gave her great satisfaction to actually be able to start and finish one part of her work in that hectic first month.

However, difficulties with the educational library continued throughout her term. In late 1894, Superintendent Eisenhuth noted that the library:

> "is used wholly by the people of Bismarck, is a caricature on a state educational library, and is a great trouble to take care of with the limited clerk hire in this office. The State has no right to furnish a library and librarian for the benefit of any one city, and there have not been more than twenty-five people in the last two years who have taken biographies, histories, books of reference, or pedagogical works. The light literature and children's stories have been so thoroughly read that they are worn from use."[149]

In 1907, the Legislature established the Public Library Commission to provide statewide library services. The state educational library and libraries maintained by other state agencies were incorporated into a single public library under the direction of the State Superintendent of Public Instruction. Reorganized several times, it now exists as the North Dakota State Library and remains a division of the North Dakota Department of Public Instruction, under the direction of the state Superintendent.

Working With the Legislature

Jan12 – Helped draft a bill for the certification of the State Normal School graduates, and one for free text books.[150] *Conducted correspondence and continued work on School Lands and in Library.*

Superintendent Eisenhuth started her term just as the 1893 Legislature started its session. Like any new state official, she had to dive into the work of her office and take care of legislative matters. Her entries in the Superintendents Record reveal that she drafted bills (January 9, 11, 12, 14), reviewed bills (January 7, 9, 13 and Feb 2), turned over books and records to an investigating committee (January 25), notified county superintendents of school bills introduced (January 26), and was called into investigating committee rooms to turn over letters pertaining to school bonds (February 4). The legislative session kept her busy.

Later in her two-year term, she included legislative recommendations in her 1894 Biennial Report. One of her recommendations related to better sanitary conditions for pupils in the public schools.

> "I cannot place too much emphasis upon the necessity for a law providing that every school house be furnished with separate outhouses, ... and that a system of inspection be made obligatory on the part of teachers and school officers. I ... wish to call your attention to the fact that our present law barely mentions them and provides no safeguard whatever. . . .
>
> | Number of schools having | No privy, 1893 | 25 |
> |---|---|---|
> | | Only one privy, 1893 | 397 |
>
> I need scarcely add anything to the figures given, they speak volumes as to the thoughtlessness of parents and officers upon the greatest moral question now affecting schools, and if the condition of those buildings could be reported you would be shocked to find the great wrong that is being done our innocent little ones in the most important time of their lives. ... The abominations that are left standing from year to year at a school house, would not be tolerated for a single day at any decent home. This is not a

subject alone for teachers to look after, but parents, and first of all legislators."[151]

Superintendent Eisenhuth's strong words made a difference. In 1895, the new state Superintendent drafted a bill which mandated two "convenient water closets or privies" for each school, which had to be "entirely separate from each other, and having separate means of access." School officers had to keep the same in a "clean, chaste and wholesome condition" or face removal from office or loss of state funds. The bill passed and went into effect immediately.[152]

Correspondence in 1893

Jan 17 – Conducted correspondence. Filled orders Supt's Supplies. Continued library work. Prepared a mimeograph letter to clerks in regard to School Lands, sale of bonds and apportionment.[153]

Jan 18 – Printed directed and folded six hundred of the letters to clerks. Conducted the usual correspondence. Filled orders for Co Supt's Supplies.

Preparing 600 letters with such a small staff in the 1890s was a significant task. And that was only one-half of the letters that had to be mailed to the 1,199 school district clerks in 1893. Today, with modern computers and copying machines, it is difficult to imagine the offices in the North Dakota State Capitol Building in the 1890s. They were equipped with steam heat, a telephone, typewriters and mimeograph machines. [154] Offices were lit by kerosene or gas lamps and had wooden floors and oak furniture.

However, telephone service was only available locally, since communities in the state were not connected by telephone lines. Therefore, almost all communication was by mail. Laura noted every day in the Record "letters answered" or "conducted correspondence." The mail was her only communication link with the county superintendents and other constituents across the state, and good communication was a vital component of her job.

Superintendent Eisenhuth's Staff

Jan 14 – Had interview with Gov. Shortridge in regard to deputy and clerk. Answered letters. Continued work on library and School Lands. Mailed biennial reports at Mr. Cathro's request. Drafted bill for teachers' institutes.

Feb 4 – Mr. Bierly severed connection with this office and returned to Grand Forks. Called into investigating committee rooms to turn over letters pertaining to school bonds. Conducted correspondence. Appointed Mr. Eisenhuth my deputy by sanction of Governor to date from Feb. 1st. Was empowered to employ clerk to be paid from Interest and Income Fund to do the work of the U. and S. Land Board. Referred the despoiling of timber claims to Atty. Gen. Standish."

One of the most important duties of an office holder, though not often recognized in historical accounts, is dealing with staff needs. On January 14, 1893, Laura met with the Governor to discuss the needs of her department in regard to staff, and changes followed quickly.[155] The Superintendents Record entry of January 24 included, "discharged and paid Miss Bearer."[156] Miss Bearer was a holdover from the previous administration. It was not unusual for a new state official with a different party affiliation to replace employees in the office. In this case, Superintendent Eisenhuth was a Democrat, and she needed people around her she knew she could trust. [157] Miss Bearer's replacement is first mentioned on May 5: "Dictated correspondence to Miss Gray."[158] The descriptions of Miss Gray's work in the Record reveal that Miss Gray was a great help with the work of the Department of Public Instruction, including being "in charge" of the office when the Superintendent and her husband travelled to the Chicago World's Fair for 19 days in 1893.[159]

On February 4, 1893, Eisenhuth wrote that Mr. Willis Bierly, whom she had appointed Chief Clerk/Assistant Superintendent of the department on her first day in office, January 3, 1893, "severed his connection with this office and returned to Grand Forks." [160] He had only served her administration for one month, and may have been hired on an interim basis.[161] The same day Laura noted, "Appointed Mr. Eisenhuth my deputy by sanction of Governor to date from Feb. 1st."

The Record indicates Deputy Eisenhuth helped Laura visit school districts all over the state. By the fall of 1894, the *Bismarck Weekly Tribune* wryly noted when Mr. Eisenhuth attended an institute in Ellendale, "Mrs. Eisenhuth is to be congratulated upon the possession of a husband to whom she can entrust her political interests upon an occasion of this kind."[162] Superintendent Eisenhuth was not the only state official at the Capitol in 1893 to hire a family member as staff. Attorney General Standish and State Treasurer Normland both hired their wives as staff members as well. As a result of this practice, Republicans raised nepotism as a campaign issue in the 1894 election.[163]

Superintendent Eisenhuth was convinced that the Department of Public Instruction needed more employees. One early addition was noted on February 4, 1893, "Was empowered to employ clerk to be paid from Interest and Income Fund to do the work of the U. and S. Land Board."[164] On February 6, she wrote, "James Murphy worked ½ day as clerk in writing letters to applicants for purchase of bonds. "This was followed by similar entries on February 7 and 8.[165] James Murphy is not mentioned again in the Record, but he was probably the clerk hired to assist the Superintendent with her University and School Lands work. Eisenhuth continued to press for a larger staff. In the 1894 Biennial Report she wrote:

A group photo of the participants of the 1894 Cass County teacher institute. Superintendent Eisenhuth is the second person from the left.

(Porterville Collection NDIRS MSS296.197.8)

"The duties of this office are onerous in the extreme. Few realize the amount of work, real plodding, continuous work attached to, and inseparable from, the office of State Superintendent in this State. The duties of the secretary of the Board of University and School Lands require, and should have, the entire time of one efficient experienced person.

And there can be no greater mistake than so limiting the clerical force so that the State Superintendent is compelled to do clerical duty as has been the necessity since statehood. The educational work of the State would be much more satisfactory if the State Superintendent could be free to supervise every branch of the work in the State, visiting, encouraging, enciting the workers in each county, strengthening weak places, kindly pointing out errors, gathering comparisons, and ideas for still greater advancement, and studying the systems of other states in order to keep our own in the front ranks."[166]

Travelling the State to Visit School Districts

June 8 – Conducted Correspondence. Mr. Eisenhuth went to Dickinson Institute. Mrs. Eisenhuth visited Minnewauken Institute and addressed school officers in the afternoon and citizens in the evening.

Connecting with people face to face is an important part of the life of any state official, and Superintendent Eisenhuth made sure that she or her deputy attended educational events all over the state. Entries in the Superintendents Record in early June 1893 indicate that Superintendent Eisenhuth and her deputy had a very busy travel schedule, especially when you consider that they were using train or horse and buggy as transportation!

For example, on June 6, Mrs. Eisenhuth spent the morning in Pembina, about 350 miles northeast of Bismarck, and travelled 65 miles south to Grand Forks for the evening. On June 7, she travelled 76 miles west to Devils Lake, where she attended the Devils Lake Institute and that evening presented diplomas to the graduating class. On June 8, the state Superintendent travelled 20 miles west to the Minnewaukan institute and addressed school officers there in the afternoon and citizens in the evening. Then, on June 9, she travelled 180 miles back to Bismarck. During the same time period, Deputy Eisenhuth spent June 6 in Cooperstown, 160 miles northeast of Bismarck. On June 7, he travelled 60 miles southwest to attend an institute at Jamestown. On June 8, he travelled 200 miles west to attend the Dickinson institute.

Balancing Work with Other Interests

Mrs. Eisenhuth did have a life outside of the Capitol building. In Bertha Grant's 1894 article, "Wives and Daughters of the Administration," she reassures readers that Laura Eisenhuth still had a proper social life.

> "Mrs. Laura J. Eisenhuth, our State superintendent of education, has official duties that occupy nearly all the hours of daylight, but when she leaves the Capitol Mrs. Eisenhuth has a social life that is as dear to her friends as it can be to herself. Her public life, so rich in its results and so far reaching in its influence, we mention only as an example of the broad educational and moral strength so highly developed in her character."
>
> "Notwithstanding her official duties, Mrs. Eisenhuth directs the affairs of her household, and manages to have congenial spirits meet with her at dinner or during evenings, and is a delightful hostess."[167]

The Eisenhuths also managed a few vacations during her term in office. In August 1893, the *Bismarck Weekly Tribune* reported that Mr. and Mrs. Eisenhuth joined a party of 12, including Governor and Mrs. Shortridge and their daughters, for a camping trip to Spirit Lake. They took a train from Bismarck for the several-days trip, which included fishing.[168] In October 1893, the Eisenhuths also traveled to the Chicago World's Fair, where Laura participated in "North Dakota Day" on October 10, along with many other state officials.[169]

Superintendent Eisenhuth's Recommendations

Along with continuing the responsibilities examined above, an additional duty in 1894 was the development of a 500-page biennial report, filed at the end of 1894, which gave an update on the state of the public school system in North Dakota. The report included 33 pages of Superintendent Eisenhuth's recommendations to improve education in the state and enables us to understand her concerns at the end of her two-year term. Her recommendations were extensive and covered more than 30 different topics, including discrepancies she found when examining financial reports of the Dakota Territory Superintendents of Public Instruction. The recommendations of her predecessor and the Superintendent that followed her each covered only half the topics of Superintendent Eisenhuth.

Laura Eisenhuth did not mince words when she made recommendations. Whether her practice of using strong words, as demonstrated in this report, contributed to her defeat in the election is subject to debate, as many people like a political leader who "says it like it is." The report's main audience was the Governor, the Legislature and county school superintendents. As a public document, it was also available to any member of the public who was aware of and requested to read it. Excerpts are included below:

> "I wish to call attention not only to the strongest points in our system but to truthfully cite our weakest points with such suggestions as can only come from one whose thoughts and interests have for two years been completely centered upon this work. ... If I cut deep in places I do so with the same intent and purpose that a wise physician probes a wound."[170]

Compulsory Education

> "Our compulsory education law is almost a dead letter. ... You will notice by the statistical report that there are 2,375 children who did not attend any school during the year ending June 30, 1892 and 2,139 who did not attend any school in 1893. ... If the law could be so changed as to have the teacher ... report at the end of the term, all pupils that have not attended the required twelve weeks and the district be deprived of the pro rata apportionment for every pupil of required age not attending and not excused."[171]

Health of Pupils

"Our school houses in a majority of district schools have been built without regard to ventilation. The one thought has been to keep them warm and as a result the children sit through the winter term with hot heads and cold feet, breathing in vitiated air ... . It is imperative that a plan of a one-room building lighted, heated, and ventilated properly, be furnished by the State, and that school boards be compelled to build all new school houses according to this plan as soon as possible and to re-arrange old buildings so that they can be properly heated, ventilated and lighted."[172]

Kindergarten

"I would respectfully recommend that a kindergarten be established, in connection with every public school, in villages of 300 inhabitants and over.[173] ... Our kindergarten schools, to be effective in elevating the masses, must be free. [174] ... And what a boon to the laboring mother, who leaves her helpless little ones while she earns their scant clothing and living, fear for their safety, adding to her over-burdened hands the haste of anxiety."[175]

Most North Dakota children in the 1890's attended rural one room schools. At McKenzie School, Burleigh County, students posed for a group photo in 1895 outside their school house. (SHSND 11048-08)

School District Officers

"There are in the state 1199 school districts .... That the school district board shall consist of three members ... . And here I would add that there ought to be at least one bright, active, public-spirited woman on every school board."[176]

1894 Campaign

This must have been quite the campaign. Laura Eisenhuth, the incumbent State Superintendent of Public Instruction, was a known leader in educational circles. She was again nominated by the Independent and Democrat parties in the summer of 1894. Emma Bates was nominated in July by the Republican Party and endorsed by the Prohibition Party. Miss Bates was on the faculty of the Valley City Normal School in the Department of English, Literature and Latin. She had many other professional credentials in education as well. Both of the women came to North Dakota in 1887. Seven years later, they were vying to be the state's highest education officer.

Both were known to be excellent public speakers. An 1894 article in *Western Womanhood* said of Miss Bates that "With measured speech, and countenance aglow with the interest of her subject, she holds the attention of every hearer and seldom fails to send home the shafts of conviction to the heart."[177] Both women were well-known around the state in educational circles, and both received their State Professional Certificates (valid for life) in November 1892. Only 24 people in the state had this certificate at this time.[178] In 1891-92, both had been chosen by State Superintendent of Public Instruction John Ogden to conduct county institutes around the state. By the time the 1894 election rolled around, Laura and Emma were well-acquainted with each other.

Both women were busy that fall addressing audiences. *Western Womanhood* reported Mrs. Eisenhuth "has been delivering some interesting addresses in different parts of the state."[179] The Women's Christian Temperance Union invited the two candidates to speak at their North Dakota convention. Mrs. Eisenhuth spoke on "The Child in the Home and School." Miss Bates spoke on "Motherhood."[180] Just like today, organizations liked to give their members a chance to hear both candidates.

Laura Eisenhuth lost the election to Emma Bates in November: Emma Bates – 26,089, Laura Eisenhuth – 20,268.[181] The Republicans swept back into office, winning every statewide election.[182]

Although she lost the election, Superintendent Eisenhuth was recognized for the work she had done while in office. In December, members of the North Dakota Education Association presented her with an "elegant solid silver tea tray, sugar bowl, creamer, and spoon holder with a set of spoons."[183] In 1895, *The Record*, a North Dakota magazine, noted that Laura Eisenhuth gave "an able and conscientious administration of her office, earning the warmest commendation from the other members of the state administration as an untiring officer and a most efficient executive officer. North Dakota was the first state to choose a woman for an office so high, to a position so responsible, and the people of the state were not dissatisfied with the experiment, as evidenced by their votes at the last election."[184]

After Leaving Office

After her term of office ended, Mr. and Mrs. Eisenhuth moved back to Foster County. Laura Eisenhuth must have been disappointed when she lost because she ran for state Superintendent of Public Instruction in 1896. She was endorsed by the Fusionists, the coalition of Independents and Democrats who hoped to wrest control from the Republicans. This time she had two opponents, Emma Bates, who did not get the Republican endorsement and ran as the Prohibition Party candidate, and John Halland, Republican. Laura made a good showing, but she lost the election by over 5,000 votes: John Halland – 26,912 Laura Eisenhuth – 21,427, Emma Bates – 3,011.[185]

Mrs. Eisenhuth did not run for state office in 1898, but she ran one last time in 1900 as an Independent-Democrat. Her opponent was J.M. Devine, whom she had beaten in the 1892 race, and who recently had served briefly as governor. She lost the election: Devine 40,828 votes, Eisenhuth 25,493 votes.[186] In all, Laura Eisenhuth had run in five statewide races for Superintendent of Public Instruction and been active in North Dakota politics for over 10 years.

Laura and Willis Eisenhuth had no children. In 1902, when she was 44 years old, her husband died after an extended illness.[187] In September 1903, the *Bismarck Weekly Tribune* reported, "Mrs. Laura Eisenhuth is assistant principal of the high school at Carrington."[188] A few years later, she married Ludwig Alming, a farmer near Carrington, and in 1909, the couple moved to Medford, Oregon, where Laura lived until her death on September 30, 1937. She was 78 years old.[189]

Thoughts on Laura Eisenhuth Being the First Woman Elected to Statewide Public Office in the United States

Mrs. Eisenhuth brought to the job of Superintendent of Public Instruction a keen mind, strong administrative skills, and the practical experience of being a classroom teacher and county superintendent. In 1893 and 1894, she wrote new curriculums for the teacher institutes, which were well-received. Her goal was to share methods, facts and broad, new ideas with the institute participants.[190] She wrote a new course of study for schools across the state.[191] She encouraged "young people's reading circles." With two professors of education, she drew up a recommended list of books for students of all reading levels for this project.[192] She prepared an indexed comprehensive biennial report, which contains a treasure trove of information about education in the early days of North Dakota. She was a very dedicated and informed secretary of the Board of University and School Lands and she submitted the first biennial report of the board, which included her thoughtful recommendations. [193]

Mrs. Eisenhuth wrote the following words just before she retired from state office. She understood while she was serving the people of North Dakota that she was "making history."

> *"Being the first woman to hold a position of this kind I have realized that even my warmest friends have looked upon my work as an experiment, and that the novelty of my position might have made my relationship with the other officers strange and constrained; that such has not been the case in any instance is a matter of deep gratitude to me. I have endeavored to discharge the duties of this office with an eye single to the benefit of education and in such a manner that it would reflect credit upon womankind; that I have been successful in even a greater degree than I had hoped for, I have been warmly assured.*
>
> *For two years, I have given all the thought, energy, and enthusiasm I could command to the discharge of my duties. The work has been to me a source of great pleasure and satisfaction.*
>
> *I retire from office with a very great interest in the progress of our schools, with a warm friendship for my fellow educators, and a sincere desire for the welfare of the State and the prosperity of her people.*
>
> *The appropriation for clerk hire is insufficient, but by strict economy and extra labor on my own part, and the kindness of the Board of U.&S. Lands, it has not been overdrawn.*
>
> *There is no deficiency and a balance in the travelling expense fund reverts to the treasury,*
>
> *Respectfully submitted,*
> *Laura J. Eisenhuth,*
> *State Superintendent of Public Instruction"*[194]

TWELVE

Inspiring People to Support Education

Emma F. Bates

State Superintendent of Public Instruction
1895-96

By
Susan Wefald

"It is not the higher education of the few, but the right education of the masses that determines the safety, strength and prosperity of a nation."

Emma Bates, 1895[195]

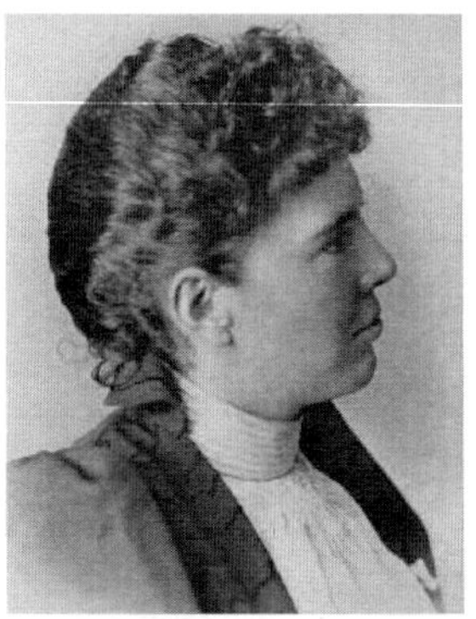

Emma F. Bates*

1854-1921

State Superintendent of Public Instruction 1895-96

First Republican Woman, along with Estelle Reel of Wyoming, to be Elected to Statewide Office[196]

State Superintendent of Public Instruction Emma Bates
(SHSND 361-12)

Personal Information
Born 1854 and raised in southwestern New York. In "spare time," was a writer.

Party Affiliation
Republican

Education
Free Academy and Union School, Forestville, New York; attended Allegheny College in Pennsylvania and National School of Oratory in Philadelphia, Pennsylvania.

Professional Experience Through Time in State Office
Seminary of Western Pennsylvania at Clarion, Pennsylvania, head of the Department of Elocution and Literature; Collins, New York, Graded School, principal; Clarion, Pennsylvania, High School, teacher; Territorial Normal School at Milnor, North Dakota, assistant principal, 1887-89; Sargent County, teacher; Normal School at Valley City, North Dakota, faculty (including four months as interim president), 1891-94; State Institute Conductor, 1891-93; Western Womanhood, editor in chief, December 1895-August 1896.

Memberships Include
As State Superintendent of Public Instruction: National Educational Association, vice president, 1896.

Other: Women's Christian Temperance Union; Order of the King's Daughters; North Dakota Women's Suffrage Association; North Dakota Educational Association.

*Bio includes information through 1896

For Miss Emma Bates, an accomplished public speaker at 40 years old, this was a new experience. She had just been nominated by J.M. Devine to be the Republican candidate for State Superintendent of Public Instruction on the 1894 November ballot.[197] Mr. Devine described Miss Bates in his nomination speech as a "conscientious, truthful, free and bold woman."[198] When the Republicans cast a unanimous ballot to support her as their candidate, she stepped up to the convention platform to give her acceptance speech to the delegates.

The *Jamestown Weekly Alert* reported, "Her acceptance speech was carefully prepared and delivered." After she thanked everyone, she said "... the glory of the Republican party was its fairness to women," and that as far as she knew, she was the first woman to receive such an endorsement in the U.S. by the party. She longed to see woman's suffrage an accomplished fact. She closed her address by reference to the chivalry of the knights of old in pinning their colors on their lady love and referred to a "similar ideal ceremony expected by the Republican Party in 1894 in North Dakota."[199]

Her opponent was incumbent State Superintendent of Public Instruction Laura Eisenhuth. Emma Bates was ready and willing to campaign across the state of North Dakota to win the election. She couldn't know that after two successful years in office, she would feel very frustrated with her fellow Republicans.

From New York to North Dakota

When Emma F. Bates, age 33, arrived in North Dakota in 1887, she was an experienced educator. Emma, the only child of Charles and Juliette Bates, was born in 1854 and raised in the southwestern corner of New York, where her father was a farmer.[200] She attended Forestville Free Academy and Union School in Forestville, New York.[201] She then moved to northwestern Pennsylvania, where she attended three semesters in 1878-79 at Allegheny College, connected with the Methodist Church.[202] Overwork brought on a long and severe illness, which prevented her from completing college.[203]

When she recovered, she took special training in elocution at the National School of Oratory in Philadelphia and then became head of the Department of Elocution and Literature at the Seminary of Western Pennsylvania at Clarion.[204] After serving in this position for two years, she became principal of the graded school in Collins, New York, for one year, and went on to teach two more years at the high school in Clarion, Pennsylvania.[205] In 1887, she came out to Dakota to act as assistant to Professor John Ogden, principal of the new Territorial Normal School at Milnor, which institution lasted but two or three years.[206]

In 1890, Emma Bates ran for Sargent County Superintendent of Schools and was defeated. She also taught school in Sargent County.[207] In 1891, she was asked by John Ogden, who was now state Superintendent of Public Instruction, to write a manual for the county institutes, and in doing so, Miss Bates wrote a new curriculum for reading and physiology.[208]

John Ogden also chose her to conduct county institutes in 1891-92.[209] He chose three men and two women to conduct all of the county institutes. He chose female leaders "since lady teachers form by far the larger part of the teaching force of the state – 72 per cent … and since there are so many things concerning the management of schools that are peculiar to ladies and lady teachers … ."[210]

Emma Bates received her State Professional Certificates (valid for life) in November 1892.[211] This was the highest grade certificate given out by the state in 1892.

In 1891-94, Miss Bates served on the faculty of the Normal School at Valley City and lived in Barnes County.[212] She was the first staff member hired by the normal school, where she taught algebra, botany, pedagogy and reading to the 35 students enrolled in classes.[213] In April 1892, the president of the college resigned and Emma Bates was named interim president.[214] She served in that capacity until August, when a new president, Mr. George McFarland, was hired.

For seven months (December 1895 through July 1896), while in office as state Superintendent of Public Instruction, Emma Bates was editor in chief of *Western Womanhood*.[215] At this time, the monthly magazine was the official voice of the North Dakota Equal Suffrage Association and the North Dakota Women's Christian Temperance Union. Miss Bates wrote articles for the magazine on such varied topics as free schools,[216] the new woman[217] and the value of work.[218] Miss Bates was one of the leaders of the women's suffrage movement in North Dakota from 1894-96.

She was very active in several organizations when she lived in North Dakota. She was a national and state volunteer with the Women's Christian Temperance Union,[219] a leader in the Order of the King's Daughters and Sons (an interdenominational Christian service organization, which is still active today),[220] the North Dakota Women's Suffrage Association[221] and vice president of the National Educational Association.[222]

The Election of 1894

The Republican Party convention was held in Grand Forks, July 18-20, 1894. The Dakotah Hotel in Grand Forks was the scene of much political talk during the convention. People were there from all over the state greeting each other and discussing the candidates. Miss Emma Bates was there as a known candidate for state Superintendent of Public Instruction.

On July 18, Emma Bates was introduced and spoke briefly to the convention delegates. The *Fargo Forum* reported, "At the conclusion of her remarks a vote of thanks was tendered Miss Bates, after which she was given three cheers. The convention then adjourned."[223] Although she was not yet formally nominated, this must have been a very exciting moment for Bates.

J.M. Devine, LaMoure County Superintendent of Schools, was also very interested in being the candidate for state Superintendent. Miss Bates knew she had good support, but she did not take her nomination for granted. The *Fargo Forum* on July 20 noted, "Miss Bates, during the exciting scenes at the Dacotah, got down in the lobby and button holed the delegates. She's as good as any of the boys at it."[224] Later, Mr. Devine withdrew as a candidate,[225] so Miss Bates was the "unanimous choice of the republican convention."[226] The paper that day also mentioned that "Miss Bates address to the convention was simply captivating."[227]

Now she was ready to campaign against incumbent Superintendent of Public Instruction Laura Eisenhuth. Mrs. Eisenhuth was again nominated by the Independent and Democrat parties in the summer of 1894, and thus was known as a "Fusion" candidate.

Miss Bates was also endorsed by the Prohibition Party in 1894. Mr. Kiff, who wrote often for the Prohibitionist Party during the campaign, explained why they chose her instead of Superintendent Eisenhuth:

> "Mr. Douglas says Mrs. Eisenhuth is objectionable to me because she stands upon a resubmission platform; let me say to Mr. Douglas that I worked hard to help elect Mrs. Eisenhuth to her present position. I have not one word to say against her official conduct or capacity, but do say I think she has done well and has done much to build up our educational institutions and have never questioned her temperance principles or her sympathy for the prohibition cause.
>
> "There were two candidates to select from; both were ladies and I simply preferred Miss Bates for our candidate, and my reason for so doing was because she has been actively engaged for several years in the temperance work in our state; her voice has been heard; her labor has been seen all over our state almost, and believe if she is elected she will fill the office with ability and honor to our state."[228]

Miss Bates was working hard to win the election. The July 1894 issue of *Western Womanhood* included an article by Bates, which shared some of her thoughts on education.

> "True Education
>
> Cramming the mind with inapplicable facts is far from educating. Educating is leading out the mental faculties so that they become capable of

> getting results beneficial to themselves and their co-ordinate natures, the physical and spiritual …
>
> The average age of leaving school is about fifteen. Most pupils of fifteen, as well as many above that age, cannot read to enjoy, or get profit for themselves or others out of an ordinary newspaper, book or magazine.
>
> The principal education of the masses, the hope for their advancement in thinking out the living issues of the time, must come from reading."[229]

By October 12, the *Bismarck Weekly Tribune* reported, "So far she (Miss Bates) has made more speeches than any candidate on the ticket."[230] The same issue of the paper included two letters from women writing in support of Miss Bates.[231]

Two events that Emma Bates addressed were "an immense audience at the Minnesota State Fair on Suffrage Day,"[232] and the North Dakota state convention of the Women's Christian Temperance Union, where she spoke on "Motherhood." In that speech, she urged the women "to be wise, as well as loving, in the care of children, as they were the mothers of the nation, and her brilliant plea for suffrage was full of good things."[233] Also, after speaking to many groups in the eastern part of the state, she spoke to the public at the Athenium in Bismarck on November 3.[234]

Things heated up near the end of the campaign. The *Fargo Forum and Daily Republican* ran the following letter on November 5, the day before the election, on Page 1:

> "To: W. A. Douglas, Fargo, North Dakota.
>
> Dear Sir, In answer to your letter of Aug.25, [whether] Miss Emma Bates held a first grade certificate in this county (Sargent) but I have been informed by ex Superintendent Donferd that he gave her a certificate and did not require her to write.
>
> There are letters on file in the office of the county superintendent of this county from Miss Bates to Supt. Donferd that go to corroborate Donferd's statement. As to the popularity which Miss Bates had gained at Milnor, where she had taught for two years. The vote which she received for county superintendent in Milnor during the year 1890 speaks distinctly. Of the 166 votes cast, Miss Bates received 22.
>
> I do not like to say very much on this subject, for the reason that during 1890, I defeated Miss Bates in this county for the office of county superintendent, and were it not that I see by the papers that she is making great pretentions to popularity in Sargent County, where she taught, and tries to convey the idea that she is a great favorite with her pupils, while the fact is that in Sargent County I do not believe that one-fourth of her pupils who have votes will vote for her.

> I am strongly of the opinion that Miss Bates will run behind her party in Sargent County. I know she will if any considerable number of women go to the polls on Election Day. My vote will be against Miss Bates, because I am acquainted with her, and know her to be a person with one idea, a hobbyist, and a very unscrupulous woman in politics. Miss Bates has one great object in life, and that is the elevation of her own self, even if it is brought about by the ruin of others. I do not know whether you are a friend or a foe to Miss Bates, but if you are a true friend of education, vote and work for the present state superintendent.
>
> Yours Very Truly,
> D.J. McKenzie
> Ex. Co. Supt. Sargent Co."[235]

Emma Bates won the election on November 6, 1894: Bates – 26,089; Eisenhuth – 20,268.[236] The Republicans won every state office.

A few days later, The *Fargo Forum*, again on the front page, ran the following analysis of Cass County voting for State Superintendent of Public Instruction:

> "The total vote for public instruction is 4,114, while the total on governor is 3,787. This indicates that 327 ladies voted in Cass County. Miss Bates majority is 792 … .This looks as though Miss Bates had polled the ladies vote in Cass almost solid."[237]

Apparently the negative letter on the front page the day before the election did Miss Bates no harm. Now it was Emma Bates' turn to serve as State Superintendent of Public Instruction.

Gossip from Bismarck: Rumpus Among the Ladies – *Fargo Forum*, January 9, 1895

Capitol gossips were busy the day Miss Bates came to take over the Superintendent of Public Instruction office at the state Capitol. A *Fargo Forum* correspondent filed the following report, which he titled, "Rumpus Among the Ladies."

> "Several stories are in circulation about the transfer of the state superintendent's office, and Octopus has been asked to give both sides of the affair. One is to the effect that Mrs. Eisenhuth was showing some ladies through the capitol and on starting to enter Secretary of State Dahl's office saw Miss Bates and immediately turned the other way – refusing to be in the same room as her successor. This is said to have hurt Miss Bates and made her friends indignant.

> "The other side of the affair is told Octopus something like this: Mrs. Eisenhuth had worked hard all day arranging the affairs of the office preparatory to Miss Bates' taking charge and late in the afternoon was awaiting the arrival of the new officials when Secretary Dahl came in the office, and prefacing his remarks by saying he wished to apologize for what he was about to do, told Mrs. E. that Miss Bates requested that the office should be vacated at once.

"This was done, and the first lady superintendent has passed from public to private life, and the second one has done the opposite, but between the two hard feelings have been engendered more than by all the men who have held office before them."[238]

Description of Official Duties of Superintendent of Public Instruction

Two-year term. Preserve in the office miscellaneous documents (books, maps, school reports, etc.); general supervision of the public schools of the state; prepare and furnish school supplies; responsible for teacher examinations and issuing or revoking state certificates; prescribe a course of study for public and Normal Schools in the state; prescribe rules for teacher institutes in the state; advise county superintendents; keep a record of all official acts; print the school laws; hold a conference with the county superintendents; assist at teacher institutes, prepare a biennial report and print and distribute 1,000 copies;, apportion school funds to the counties.

Member: Board of University and School Lands; Normal School Board; High School Board.[239]

Getting Started

Superintendent Emma Bates walked into a brand new office when she took office on January 7, 1895. A south wing had just been added to the 1883 state Capitol building. It featured a "handsome porte-cochere[240] of ample size for three or four carriages to enter at a time." A large corridor, 18 by 50 feet, paved with encaustic tile, approached a "fine, broad stairway in polished oak," which led to the second floor.[241]

Throughout 1894, Governor Shortridge had been supervising the construction of the new wing of the Capitol, which provided a new Senate chamber and offices for several state officials. Miss Bates had one of the "spacious, well lighted offices," which was "finished in Georgia Pine and tinted adamant, and maple floors."[242] Each office also had a fire-proof vault and cloak room. She must have been delighted.

Superintendent Bates let the press know about her appointments. W.C. Baker of the Grand Forks Herald would

In 1895, when Superintendent Bates took office, her office was located in the "new" front addition to the 1883 Capitol building. (SHSND BO716-35)

serve as her deputy. She noted that he will have "charge of the office work and general business" of the office "while she will look after the purely educational, doing the field work and institute work." She also appointed F.W. Cathro, deputy superintendent under two previous Republican state school superintendents, to help "organize the work of the office and remain during the legislative session." Miss Maggie Davidson was appointed stenographer.[243]

Working With the 1895 Legislature

Governor Roger Allin and his fellow Republicans were again in control of state government.

Miss Bates performed her work as Secretary of the Board of University and School Lands, participated in the work of the Normal School Board, took care of the State Library, wrote examination questions for teaching certificates, planned teacher institutes and performed other duties connected with her office.[244]

Although Miss Bates was a novice in legislative politics, the new Superintendent plunged into writing legislation and reviewing proposed bills in her first days in office. The Legislature met during winter 1895 and passed bills that affected each student across the state.

Health and Decency

She continued former Superintendent Laura Eisenhuth's work to put into law requirements that boys and girls have separate, clean and well-built school outhouses, which was called the Health and Decency Law. Superintendent Bates wrote,

> "At the legislative session of 1895 I drafted a bill called the Health and Decency Law, and by the aid of champions of it, members in each house, it passed and went into immediate effect."[245]

Free Text Books

She also worked on free text book legislation, which was another priority of her predecessor and educators around the state. Superintendent Bates later recalled,

> "Strenuous effort was made in the last legislature by a committee from the Superintendents' department of the State Teacher's Association, to secure the passage of a free and uniform text book bill. The effort was comparatively futile, but a very much modified bill passed."[246]

The final bill passed did not allow a district to place the issue of providing free text books on the ballot unless a *majority* of the qualified electors had signed a petition saying they wanted the matter brought to a vote.[247]

High Schools

Superintendent Bates was pleased when the High School Law was enacted, which established a new board called the "high school board." The bill stated, "The Governor, the Superintendent of Public Instruction and the President of the State University, ex-officio, are hereby constituted a board of commissioners on preparatory schools for the encouragement of higher education in the State."[248] The legislation went on to detail requirements for state high schools, including a yearly inspection visit.

Superintendent Bates reported on the progress made as a result of the law in her Biennial Report to the Governor:

> "The State Superintendent, secretary of that board, is pleased to state that all schools except two of any advancement in the State are working to classify themselves in as high a class as possible and taking examinations to that end … . It will be doubly valuable to the State. First, because the schools themselves are bettered; second, because since many district school teachers have only a high school preparation, the better the high school the better will be this class of teachers."[249]

U.S. Flags

This 1895 law required every school district to purchase U.S. flags and to display them on flagstaffs on the school grounds or on the school itself during school hours. Superintendent Bates noted more flags on display as she travelled around the state visiting schools:

> "It is gratifying, as one rides across the country, to see the flag, loved at home and honored abroad, floating from the rural school house. In this state where we have so large a proportion of foreign population, it is eminently proper to keep, as an object lesson, the emblem of our national honor ... before the eyes of the children and the future citizens of our beloved commonwealth."[250]

Cando School, built in 1894, with flag flying. The 1895 Legislature passed a law requiring all schools in North Dakota to fly the U.S. flag. Superintendent Bates wrote, "It is gratifying, as one rides across the country, to see our flag, loved at home and honored abroad, floating from the rural school house." (SHSND Shemorry Photo Collection 1-23B-1)

Veto of Educational Appropriations Bills

In 1895, Governor Roger Allin vetoed appropriations to several state educational institutions. The state was in a desperate financial situation and had to fight to meet its obligations. The legislative assembly generally appropriated more money than taxation was likely to yield, and in 1895, Governor Allin vetoed $122,640 in spending.[251] The universities had to raise their own funds to stay open.[252] Later Superintendent Bates commented:

> "The University, as well as the other special institutions of higher education, has had an increased attendance and unusual vigor among its student body, notwithstanding the adverse conditions of this biennial period, due to the veto of its appropriation. It is a cause for congratulation that the people of our State gave so liberally to keep open the institutions of higher learning."[253]

Appropriations for Clerk Hire in State Superintendent's Office

Superintendent Bates originally had a major increase in appropriation for staff hire in 1895. The 1895 Legislature approved $3,000 for clerk hire in her office for the biennium, which included pay for her assistant superintendent and other clerks needed.[254] The increase was partly the result of the Legislature moving some clerk positions from the Land Department to the Superintendent of Public Instruction office to take care of the detailed bond record work she needed to perform as secretary for the Board of University and School Lands.[255]

However, due to state budget constraints, Superintendent Bates noted the budget for clerk hire in her office was reduced by $1,200 in 1896.[256] Along with causing other problems in her office administration, she had to close the State Educational Library since "no one employed could be spared to devote time to handling the books and keeping the library records."[257] However, as Miss Bates noted, the books did not sit unused:

> "The matron at the penitentiary conceived the idea that the convicts would enjoy and be profited by reading. Arrangements were made whereby they could have the use of the books. They have read extensively and of the very best class of books."[258]

Putting Her Stamp on Her Administration

As the new state Superintendent of Public Instruction, Emma Bates immediately set to work communicating her new ideas with county superintendents, legislators and school district personnel. Her term was for only two years, and she was eager to make an impact on the state's schools. One communication tool she used was sending out "circulars."

In 1895 and '96, she sent out 18 circulars on topics such as procedures for earning a state certificate, educational legislation passed in the 1895 session, Arbor Day, free text books and Parents Day. In addition, she prepared and distributed a new curriculum for the teachers' institutes for 1895 and 1896. She even printed one circular in German and distributed it in McIntosh, Emmons, Morton and Stark counties.[259]

It took time and effort to prepare these circulars. They had to be written, typed, sent to the printer to be typeset and then proofread. Then over a thousand copies had to be mailed to school districts all over the state.

Teachers Institutes – Circular #4, March 1895

Circular #4 was directed to the county superintendents. For one week each year, every teacher in the state was required to attend a week of training, the *Institute*, at the county level. Some institutes in the counties with high student population enrolled over 100 teachers for the training. The training was very important because many teachers in the state had only completed the common school and did not have a good understanding of successful teaching methods.[260] As Superintendent Bates noted,

> "Our teachers are of excellent spirit and purpose. Their work is not inferior in successful results to the work of teachers in other states, but there is room for improvement. Many of our teachers are from the common schools themselves and are not thoroughly proficient in the branches they are to teach, and have received but very little, if any, professional training."[261]

This circular stated her goals for the institutes:

1. To create a professional spirit
2. To promote advanced methods of teaching organization and management
3. To inspire the teacher with the holiness of his work and fill his soul with enthusiasm for his calling
4. To widen his professional acquaintance and thereby create a community of interests and enlarged ideas[262]

Then Miss Bates went on to address practical arrangements that would affect the success of the institute. Some of her recommendations related to the place where the institute would be held:

> "Have a commodious room for the institute. A school house if *possible*, on account of blackboards, and *see that the room is clean*. See that a janitor is provided to give careful attention to the room during the week … . I speak emphatically and in detail upon these points, because by experience

> I know that too often the institute room is utterly neglected, seldom kept properly aired, warmed and ventilated … ."

She added, "The Superintendent of Public Instruction expects to be present in each institute one or two days and will deliver an address to teachers and citizens during her attendance … ."[263]

Institute Manual and Note Book – April 1895

Superintendent Bates set out a very practical curriculum for the 1895 institutes. She started out her institute booklet with an inspirational message to the teachers, which included the statement, "It is not the higher education of the few, but the right education of the masses that determines the safety, strength and prosperity of a nation." The curriculum included sessions on how to teach physiology and hygiene (which was required to be taught in all grades), arithmetic, civil government (a new required subject which we call "civics" today), reading and history. The 30-minute session on intermediate arithmetic proposed the following problem for discussion:

> "My father has a quarter section of land and one-half of it was sowed to wheat. It took a bushel and a quarter to the acre and it cost him eighty cents a bushel. He got 12 bushels an acre and sold it for sixty-two cents a bushel. The threshing cost $28.80, and hired help $40.50. How much did he make over expenses, and how much was that an acre?"[264]

Parents Day Circular #7, June 1896

Superintendent Bates decided to dedicate one day each school year as "Parents Day." She issued a three-page circular in June 1896 promoting the idea. As Superintendent Bates wrote in the circular, "Sixty-eight thousand children and youths of school age in our young state ought to compel the most thoughtful attention of all the adults … . The coming together of parents, children, officers and teachers in the schools on a given day which shall be devoted to exercises in honor and praise of the home and family, and the inculcation of personal virtues, seems to me eminently fitting … .To this end I designate June 26 as Parents' Day in the schools of North Dakota."[265]

Over 26,000 Miles in Two Years

Superintendent Bates made visiting the teacher institutes a priority. She loved visiting the schools and wanted to be with school personnel, encouraging them and giving practical counsel.

> "During the biennial period, the State Superintendent traveled by rail and stage twenty-six thousand, nine hundred and ninety-three miles, vis-

ited sixty-seven institutes held in thirty-four different counties. She gave from one to six lessons in each institute, and gave a public address at nearly every one. The subject of the address in 1895 was 'The Rural School House, Within and Without.' In 1896, 'The Educational Outlook of North Dakota.'"[266]

Trains crossed the state in 1897 and were popular and well-used. In 1894, a reporter gave this account of travelling by train from Fargo to Bismarck:

> "Not only every sleeper was full but every seat, when we started for Bismarck Wednesday on No.1. After standing around we got a seat at Valley City and spent the balance of the night in fitful dozes.
>
> "The breakfast on the diner was a golconda – an oasis in a dreary desert. They served us two bills of fare – either of which should satisfy the most epicurean of epicures. The conductor was – handsome – and the 'colored gemmen,' who served our table, was good natured, jolly, and attentive. Go where you may, there is no better dining car service than furnished by the old pioneer transcontinental line.
>
> "The Northern Pacific track is smooth and the cars luxurious; and with an obliging conductor and clever crew, a trip than cannot but be enjoyed over the N.P." [267]

Stage coach travel started where the rail lines ended. Superintendent Bates lived in Bismarck. She could hop onto the Northern Pacific to travel east or west. Here is how she may have travelled to attend the institutes and other meetings she attended in autumn 1895.[268]

Sept. 28 - Fargo: Train - Bismarck to Fargo (185 miles)

Oct. 1 - Milton: Train – Fargo to Ardoch, switch, Ardoch to Milton (170 miles)

Oct. 2 - Cando: Stage coach - Milton to Cando (73 miles)

Oct. 8 - Minot: Train - Bismarck to Jamestown, switch, Jamestown to Carrington, switch, Carrington to Minot (280 miles)

Oct. 10 - Bottineau: Train - Minot to Rugby, switch, Rugby to Bottineau (95 miles)

Oct. 14 - Wahpeton: Train – Bismarck to Casselton, switch, Casselton to Wahpeton (200 miles)[269]

Her efforts to visit schools in October 1895 were noted in the *Bismarck Weekly Tribune*: Miss Bates "is an experienced practical educator, familiar with all the requirements of the school room and the teacher … . She does not sit in her office and give theoretical directions but is out in the different parts of the state encouraging by her presence and giving practical counsel and instruction."[270]

Superintendent Bates' Special Projects

Courses of Study

Emma Bates continued the "courses of study" work started by her friend and former state Superintendent John Ogden.[271] Her goal was to coordinate university, normal school (two-year teacher college) and common school (generally grades one through eight) curricula with high school curriculum. She "reduced the State Course of Study to a systematic diagram, a copy of which could be easily displayed on the schoolroom walls. She emphasized the need for a systematic organization of subject matter."[272] In her biennial report, she described the process she used to make these changes:

> "The high school board first prepared a course of study for the high schools. A committee appointed by the normal boards outlined a course of study for the normal schools, which correlates with the high school course. Both these in turn correlate with the university course, and the agricultural college adapted its literary and scientific course to these. The county superintendents put their ideas of needs of the rural school on paper and basing it on this, the State Superintendent issued a course of study for the rural schools. Now the entire course is systematized, each grade correlating as nearly as possible with the next higher grade." [273]

Coordinating the Courses of Study[274] was a big project to complete in just two years, and she must have been a skilled leader to accomplish this.

Scientific Temperance

Superintendent Bates had definite ideas about drug and alcohol education that are still pertinent today. *"The child may be taught scientific facts about alcohol and narcotics and be no more helped thereby in the conduct in life than by the knowledge he has of scientific facts in geology. The aim should be to so teach him that he will desire to refrain from all injurious habits. Next, having the right desire he must have the properly disciplined will-power to execute his desires."*[275]

Special Institutions

Miss Bates encouraged more spending and attention to special-needs students. "*Special mention should be given for the School for the Deaf and Dumb. Its peculiar value is very little understood. A visit to the classes and observation of the work done and the condition of these children, deprived of the two most important senses (hearing and speech) shows one the great necessity for providing liberally for the development as far as possible, of these unfortunate little creatures so helpless in the struggle of life."*[276]

The 1896 Campaign

Superintendent Emma Bates was at the "top of her game" in July 1896. In addition to being state Superintendent, Bates was editor in chief of *Western Womanhood*, the monthly magazine that was the official voice of the North Dakota Equal Suffrage Association and the North Dakota Women's Christian Temperance Union. Early in July, she had attended the five-day meeting of the National Educational Association at Buffalo, New York, where she was elected vice president of the association.[277] Now she was in Grand Forks and she anticipated another friendly Republican convention.

However, something went wrong for Superintendent Emma Bates, either at the July 21-23, 1896, Republican convention, or perhaps long before at the 1895 legislative session.[278] The convention, held in Grand Forks, drew between 400 and 500 delegates, plus thousands of onlookers.[279] The *Fargo Forum* reported about the governor's race on the first day, "Grand Forks is in gala attire, with Budge clubs, Budge bands, and Budge badges everywhere. The badges adorn the statesman, the banker, the preacher, the newsboy and the bootblack – all for Budge."[280] William Budge had the same problem as Emma Bates; he was not endorsed for office at the Republican convention.

Several people were vying for her office on the first day of the convention. "Miss Bates, Perkins, Wogan and Halland are all more or less candidates for state superintendent of public instruction."[281]

Republican Party politics was heavy handed in the 1890s. Robinson, in his book *The History of North Dakota*, described how the state slate of candidates was decided.

> "While the McKenzie Machine (the 'Old Gang,' as it was commonly called) regularly controlled the Republican state convention, the slate of nominations was actually made up as a contract among county leaders, who divided the offices in a way to satisfy themselves and voted their delegations as units. Judson LaMoure often ran the convention instead of McKenzie … ."[282]

Then these decisions were announced at a "caucus," which was an informal meeting of delegates before the actual convention took place. At the caucus, leaders told delegates who had been picked to run for each office, and convinced delegates that these people were the best choices.

On July 22, at 1 a.m., after the late trains brought in delegates from the south, the caucus took place. Decisions were made in the middle of the night. Three hundred forty-eight delegates out of 492 delegates came together at the Grand Forks County Courthouse at a meeting which lasted until 2 a.m. By the time the caucus ended, delegates supported a ticket that did not include Miss Bates, and instead endorsed John Halland, Trail County Superintendent of Schools.

The *Fargo Forum* headline that day was, "Robby, Pat, & Jud – They Swing 345 Delegates into Line and Name a State Ticket with Briggs for Governor."[283] Incumbent Republican Governor Roger Allin had been shoved aside. The paper also noted, "It is a mistake to leave off Miss Bates."[284]

The convention approved the caucus slate; Superintendent Emma Bates did not get the Republican endorsement. One political analyst noted,

> "Because she (Bates) would not sacrifice principle to political bribes, schemes and jugglery galore the party soon imagined they an elephant on their hands, and a white one, too .... Political slates were duly written over .... The convention was guided by governmental mathematics instead of governmental morality, and said Trail County must have a representation on the ticket ... ."[285]

And Miss Bates was not happy. Rather than go quietly away and "lick her wounds," she decided to run for office as an independent against the chosen Republican candidate. The Superintendent immediately sat down and wrote a letter to the public. The letter was on the front page of the *Fargo Forum* on July 25, just three days after the close of the convention.

Independent Candidate
Miss Emma F. Bates Announces Herself for
State Superintendent of Public Instruction.
She has Devoted Her Time and Energy to
Education and Women and Refused
To Be Turned Down.

> *Bismarck, N.D., July 25, To the Public: Having discharged my duty to the best of my ability as superintendent of public instruction, and believing that my work is entitled at least to consideration at the hands of the people of the state, if it was not in a political convention, I hereby announce myself as an independent, non-partisan candidate for re-election to the position I now hold. My work has been non-partisan – it has been for the development of the character of the children and youth, for the benefit of the home and for the promotion of good citizenship, and I dislike to have the structure I have builded with so much care, torn down. The policy now well outlined for a successful system in our state educational affairs, must be continued in order to become established and bring good results.*
>
> *I appeal to the fair-minded men of all parties who are not willing to see this high office made a subject of barter. I appeal to the women of the state with*

whom and for whom I have labored for over ten years in our beloved North Dakota – to you voters of North Dakota I appeal for support in this course I am taking.

I have labored under greater difficulties than my predecessors. The veto of the educational appropriation bills, the withholding of proper clerk hire from my office, were the root of some of these difficulties.

I have done my work faithfully and believe I have accomplished good results. There has been no claim that I have not.

For the cause of education and the right I ask for your aid and your votes.

Emma F. Bates
Superintendent of Public Instruction[286]

That November, Emma Bates' name was on the ballot as a Prohibition Party candidate. Her opponents were Laura Eisenhuth, Fusion candidate (Independents and Democrats) and John Halland, Republican. When the final votes were tallied in December, Superintendent Bates received only 3,011 votes, Laura Eisenhuth received 21,427, and John Halland was elected the new state Superintendent of Schools with 26,912 votes.[287]

Afterthoughts

Miss Bates served as Superintendent of Schools until January 4, 1897. After working in education for 10 years in North Dakota, she decided to leave the state and pursue foreign missionary work. Superintendent of Public Instruction Bertha Palmer provided the following information in 1932:

> "After leaving public office, Miss Bates spent a year near Santa Barbara, studying the Japanese language and customs preparatory to becoming a missionary. She spent a year or two in Japan, but her health made it necessary to return to California." [288]

She returned from Japan in 1906.[289] She taught school and lived in Oakland, California, until she died in 1921, when she was 67 years old.[290] There is no evidence that she married or had children.[291]

Superintendent Emma Bates was a leader. She was an excellent teacher and orator, and as she travelled around the state, her speeches inspired teachers and county administrators. She worked with the Legislature to pass several needed pieces of school legislation. As state Superintendent, she reached out to involve other state educational leaders in her projects. For example, when she set out to put her stamp on the state curriculum, she involved members of the state high school board, representatives of the university system and county superintendents. She then coordinated all of their ideas into a coordinated curriculum for primary through college level.

At the 1896 Republican convention, Miss Bates was shocked by the realities of Republican politics dominated by party bosses. Although the Republican Party in the 1890s often did not re-nominate good incumbent state officials to another term, Superintendent Bates rebelled when she did not again receive her party nomination in 1896. She chose to run against the endorsed Republican candidate. Perhaps if she had accepted the convention decision, she may have been hired or appointed to another position in the administration in 1897. The state lost a gifted educational leader when she left the state in 1897.

In May 1895, while she was in office, *The Record* wrote an article about Miss Bates, which included this tribute to her:

> "In her public speeches Miss Bates touches the heart, appeals to conscience, convinces the judgment and leads her pupils to think better of themselves and better of humanity and through her work men and women are striving to reach higher planes politically, socially, morally, religiously. Here is a noble character and the state should be congratulated that she is in position to carry out and on the good work in which she entered with so much heart and soul."[292]

North Dakotans did not elect another woman to statewide office for 22 years.

Challenging Times Attract Strong Leaders

1919-56

THIRTEEN

My Business is Education

Minnie Jean Nielson

State Superintendent of Public Instruction
1919-26

By
Susan Wefald

"My business is education, not politics."

Superintendent Minnie Jean Nielson, January 11, 1919.[293]

Minnie Jean Nielson*

1874-1958

State Superintendent of Public Instruction 1919-26

State Superintendent of Public Instruction Minnie Nielson - 1919
(SHSND D612)

Personal Information

Born 1874 in Jackson, Michigan, and raised in Valley City, North Dakota. In "spare time," enjoyed participating in women's organizations.

Party Affiliation

Elected on No Party Ballot but endorsed by Independent Voters Association (IVA) Republicans

Education

Valley City High School; attended University of North Dakota; attended University of Michigan, Ann Arbor, Michigan, 1903-04 school year; University of Chicago summer school.

Professional Experience Before Taking Office

Stewart Township, Barnes County, teacher one year; Valley City Schools, teacher nine years; Valley City High School, Head of Science Department teaching chemistry and physics, four years; Barnes County Superintendent of Schools, 1906-18.

Memberships Include

As State Superintendent of Public Instruction: National Association of Administrative Women in Education, president three years; National Education Association life member, director and vice president.

Other: North Dakota Education Association; North Dakota Federation of Women's Clubs, president, 1914-18; National Federation of Women's Clubs board member; National Business and Professional Women's Clubs, vice president; Women's Committee for several Liberty Loan Drives, state chair; War Victory Committee of WW I, chair; Congregational Church, American Legion Auxiliary, PEO Sisterhood, Girl Scouts, 1920 Republican convention in Chicago, first woman delegate from North Dakota.

*Bio includes information through 1926

The 1918 fall election was two weeks away, and Miss Minnie Nielson, Lincoln Republican[294] candidate for state Superintendent of Schools, wondered if the election would take place. Deadly influenza had struck the state in October. Schools and churches had closed, and public gatherings were canceled to prevent spread of the flu.[295] Not that these steps seemed to be helping. Almost everyone in the state knew someone who had contracted the flu and died. Miss Nielson's beloved maternal aunt, Isabelle Spurr, had died just the week before from the flu.[296]

Each day, headlines reported World War I news from the battle fronts in Europe. North Dakota men were fighting in the trenches, where high casualties occurred daily. The flu epidemic and the war news made thinking about the November 5 election seem trivial.

But Miss Nielson had concerns about her election race against incumbent Nonpartisan League (NPL) endorsed candidate Neil C. Macdonald. For weeks, he had been sharing information with the public that she was not qualified to run for state Superintendent of Schools. There was an unlikely ally who might help her quell these rumors – NPL official William (Bill) Langer, North Dakota Attorney General. Langer was running for his second term as Attorney General on the Republican ticket, but his election was assured as a known member of the NPL.

So, approximately two weeks before the election, Miss Nielson made a trip to Bismarck to visit Attorney General Bill Langer. She asked him to issue an opinion as to whether or not she was legally qualified to be state Superintendent of Public Instruction. He realized that this meant thousands of votes to her, one way or another. He knew a decision in her favor would not endear him to NPL officials.[297]

The constitution stipulated that to hold the office of state Superintendent of Public Instruction, she must be qualified to vote in state elections, be at least 25 years old on the day of the election and have been a resident of the state for five years preceding the election. She met all of these requirements. On October 29, 1918, Langer broadcast the opinion that she met all constitutional qualifications for state office. Miss Nielson followed up by making copies of the opinion and distributing them all over the state.[298] On Election Day, November 5, Minnie J. Nielson beat her opponent by over 5,500 votes. Governor Lynn Frazier, Bill Langer and other NPL candidates won every other statewide office and a majority of the legislative seats. She was now the only elected state official who was not endorsed by the NPL.

Peace was also on the horizon; the November headlines were full of news about the Armistice that would be signed on November 11, 1918. However, the flu was still taking its toll of lives in North Dakota.

Unfortunately for Miss Nielson, Mr. Neil Macdonald did not consider losing the election the end of his fight to keep his position as state Superintendent of Public Instruction.

Introducing Miss Minnie Jean Nielson

On January 18, 1874,[299] Minnie Jean was born in Jackson, Michigan, to Mr. and Mrs. Wylie Nielson. In 1880, Minnie moved with her parents to Valley City, where her father had purchased a tract of farmland when he visited the area in 1879. Minnie had two younger siblings, James Wylie and Hazel Belle.[300]

The Nielson family spent their summers on their farm until baby Hazel was born and then lived year round in Valley City while Mr. Nielson continued farming.

After graduation from high school, Miss Nielson became a teacher and taught for 13 years in and around Valley City. During that time, she attended the University of North Dakota, spent one school year at the University of Michigan taking science classes and attended summer school at the University of Chicago. She ended her teaching career as head of the Valley City High School Science Department, where she taught chemistry and physics. In 1906, she was elected Barnes County Superintendent of Schools. Through her work as county superintendent, she was an active member of the North Dakota Education Association and was a recognized educational leader in the state.[301]

Already in 1910, County Superintendent Nielson had her own red Maxwell convertible she drove to meetings all over the county, even in severe weather. She enjoyed offering delighted children and adults their first ride in an automobile.[302]

Unlike many young women of their time, both Minnie Jean and her sister, Hazel Belle, did not marry. Miss Nielson was a professional woman throughout her life and an active "clubwoman." By the time she ran for state office, Nielson knew people all over the state through her volunteer work as president of the North Dakota Federation of Women's Clubs. During her career, she was also an active member of the Congregational Church, American Legion Auxiliary, PEO, Girl Scouts, and Business and Professional Women's Club. [303]

Bertha Palmer, State Superintendent of Public Instruction (1927-32), assistant superintendent under Minnie Jean Nielson and also her political opponent, wrote, "Miss Nielson had a strong, aggressive personality, energetic, untiring physique, and a broad far-reaching vision … . Her enthusiasm was contagious … ."[304] Bill Langer admired her "spunk and ability."[305]

The 1918 Campaign

Having served 12 years as Barnes County Superintendent of Schools, Miss Minnie Jean Nielson was ready for a change. Now 44, she was an independent, confident woman who was a known leader as state chair of the World War I Women's Liberty Loan Committee. Her loving family was supportive of her work; her aunt, Isabelle Spurr, had been

Riding in a convertible in parades was part of her political campaigns when Miss Nielson ran for State Superintendent Public Instruction in 1918, 1920, 1922 and 1924.
(SHSND 00117-003)

elected Barnes County Superintendent of Schools in 1887.[306]

County School Superintendent Nielson had a solid 12-year record as a progressive leader in a large school district. Working with her county and local school boards, she encouraged one-room rural school consolidation, replacing 47 one-room schools with 18 consolidated schools. She implemented a county school nurse program and worked to increase the number of books in school libraries from 6,556 to 25,302. High school attendance increased from 167 to 574 pupils, and the average length of school term in her county increased from 7.5 months to 8.4 months. She instituted a county "play day," with sporting events, which attracted national attention, and inaugurated and carried out a system of traveling art galleries for the rural schools of the county.[307]

Amazingly, given the politics of consolidation, she had the absolute support of each president of the Barnes County School Board from 1907 to 1918 by the time she decided to run for state Superintendent in 1918.[308]

On May 2, 1918, Miss Nielson received the endorsement of the Lincoln Republican League at their convention in Minot for state Superintendent of Public Instruction.[309] The vote was unanimous. She also was endorsed by the Democrats in May.[310]

She entered statewide politics at a very interesting time in North Dakota history. In

1918, the NPL was the dominant political party in North Dakota, but it had adopted a different approach to politics. Rather than run candidates under the NPL name, the party chose to run their candidates in the June primary on the Republican ticket since they knew that most people voted for Republican candidates in the November election. Also, most of their candidates had been Republicans in the past, and so in the June Republican primary election, voters had a choice between NPL Republicans and traditional Republicans. Miss Nielson was endorsed in Minot by the "traditional" Republicans, or as the NPL called them, the "Old Gang."[311]

Already the NPL was a very controversial party. Headed by Arthur Townley, farmers across the state had organized into a powerful political machine. Seventy percent of the 600,000 people in the state in 1916 were farmers. The NPL platform emphasized fair prices for farmers and publicly owned farm services such as terminal grain elevators and banks. By 1918, if you wanted to win an election, you had to get the votes of NPL Republicans as well as traditional Republicans.

In 1918, the June primary was held on June 26. Miss Nielson wanted to make a good showing in the primary against her opponent, incumbent NPL state Superintendent Neil Macdonald, who was her same age. She and her supporters got right to work and started writing letters to the newspapers around the state. She hired Pollock's Clipping Service in Minneapolis to clip and send her copies of all news items in the state that referred to her campaign.[312] In the week before the primary, letters of support or endorsements appeared in papers in Williston, Fargo, Parshall, Mandan, Cooperstown, Valley City, Dickinson, St Thomas and others, and a paid quarter-page advertisement with her picture and an extensive biography appeared in the Bismarck Tribune.[313]

Women could still only vote for the position of state Superintendent of Public Instruction, and Miss Nielson courted the woman voters. She was the only woman on the ballot. On June 20, *The Post* carried an article which included the following statements:

> "Minnie J. Nielson will have United Support of Women in Primaries is Prevailing Belief"
>
> "... She has successfully filled the chair of president for four years of the North Dakota Federation of Women's clubs, ... she is a member of the State Board of Education; that she has efficiently served as chairman of the Woman's Liberty Loan committee for North Dakota during the second and third drives ... and THAT MISS NIELSON IS RESPONSIBLE FOR MORE ADVANCEMENT AND ORIGINALITY IN RURAL IMPROVEMENT OF SCHOOLS AND COOPERATION OF PARENTS THAN ANY ONE ELSE IN THE STATE OF NORTH DAKOTA ... EVERY WOMAN SHOULD MAKE SURE SHE IS REGISTERED

FOR VOTING. ASK THE COUNTY AUDITOR IF YOUR NAME IS ON THE LIST."[314]

The *Cooperstown Courier* also noted that Miss Nielson was a speaker at the "Old Settlers Picnic" on June 20.[315]

Despite all of these efforts, NPL-endorsed candidate Neil Macdonald defeated Minnie J. Nielson in the primary, but she polled more votes than any other "traditional" Republican on the ballot. On the "nonpartisan" ballot, both she and Macdonald could move forward as candidates in the November election. People took notice and Miss Nielson kept working.

Pamphlets were popular campaign materials, and Miss Nielson produced at least two campaign pamphlets and a "palm card" to use during the election. One pamphlet was titled, "The Peoples Candidate for the Office of Superintendent of Public Instruction," and is subtitled a "Record of Achievement in Barnes County." This pamphlet does not contain any criticism of her opponent, but instead focuses on her accomplishments and endorsements.[316] Another 19-page pamphlet was printed after October 3, 1918, because it includes an endorsement letter of that date signed by all of the presidents of Barnes County school boards she worked with from 1907 to 1918. This pamphlet, "The Proof of the Pudding," again does not include any criticism of her opponent, but does include 10 pages of short endorsement letters and pictures of new consolidated schools built while she was county superintendent.[317] Miss Nielson used endorsements to tell others about her accomplishments and qualifications, a very good strategy.

However, the "Educators Campaign Committee" letter to "Fellow Teachers," signed by five county superintendents, contained strong attacks on her opponent, including, "He has indulged in and sanctioned most ungallant attacks upon the womanhood of the state. He has proved himself entirely unfit in temperament and personality for leadership in a democracy. He has acted the typical Prussian in his bearing towards fellows. He has acted the part of the slave driver and autocrat."[318]

Macdonald, for his part, produced pamphlets and letters to the editor challenging Miss Nielson's qualifications to hold office.[319] The *North Dakota Leader*, the newspaper owned by the NPL, ran a full-page article stating she did not legitimately hold the teaching certificate required of a state Superintendent of Public Instruction and that she did not have a college degree.[320] Minnie Nielson never claimed to have a college degree, but she had attended UND, the University of Michigan and the University of Chicago, and she had a valid life-time professional certificate issued in 1902.

When Bill Langer issued his opinion on October 29, declaring Miss Nielson was indeed qualified to serve as state Superintendent of Public Instruction, she must have breathed a sigh of relief.

Description of Official Duties as Superintendent of Public Instruction

Two-year term. Preserve in the office miscellaneous documents (books, maps, school reports, etc.); general supervision of the public schools of the state; prepare and furnish school supplies; responsible for teacher examinations and issuing or revoking state certificates; prescribe a course of study for common schools in the state; prescribe rules for and assist at teacher institutes in the state; advise county superintendents; keep a record of all official acts; print the school laws; hold a conference with the county superintendents; publish the proceedings of North Dakota Educational Association and distribute throughout the state; prepare a biennial report and print and distribute 3,000 copies; may establish and direct public evening schools available to all persons over 16 years of age; inspect school building plans; employ school inspectors to examine schools; apportion school funds to the counties. (Note: From June 1919 to November 1920, many of these duties were under the supervision of the Board of Administration.)

Member: Board of Administration (supervises state educational, penal and charitable institutions), Educational Commission, Board of University and School Lands, Board of Canvassers of General Elections, Teachers Insurance and Retirement Fund, State Historical Society Board.[323]

On November 2, *The Fargo Forum* reported on Nielson's campaign:

> "In Fargo a thorough organization has been perfected to bring out the greatest possible women's vote. Not only this city, but in every town and city in the state, the same step has been taken, while appeals also have been made to the rural women to go to the polls and cast their ballots against permitting the continuation of the present condition. The response in every instance has been a promise to vote – and in light of the reports available, the supporters of Miss Minnie J. Nielson of Valley City are confident that she will be elected."[321]

The vote totals for the election were Minnie J. Nielson: 58,324, Neil Macdonald: 52,777.[322]

Miss Nielson's First Week "In Office"

Events seemed to be moving along smoothly in December, as Miss Nielson made plans to move to Bismarck. On December 9, 1918, Governor Frazier signed her certificate of election, which stated that she was entitled to serve as Superintendent of Public Instruction for two years commencing on the first Monday in January 1919.[324] She recruited well-respected men and women to work with her in the Superintendent's office come January: Dr. George McFarland, who had served for more than 25 years as President of Valley City Normal; J.W. Riley, former Cass County Superintendent of Schools; H.G. Arnsdorf of Valley City; and Miss Bertha Palmer, an art and music education expert.[325]

On Monday, January 6, Miss Nielson filed her bond with the Secretary of State's office and prepared to take her oath of office at the swearing-in ceremony in the legislative chambers that afternoon. She must have been excited at the thought of starting her new duties. But then the day turned sour. As *The Fargo Forum* reported:

> "When Miss Nielson and her deputy, H.G. Arnsdorf, entered the office this morning, Macdonald immediately informed her that he would not surrender the office. Miss Nielson responded that she was relying upon Attorney General Langer's opinion that she was entitled to the office under her qualifications to which Macdonald replied that the 'attorney general's opinion did not cut any ice with him.' At this stage Mrs. Macdonald entered into the conversation and when her interview of recent date ... to the effect that no contest of Miss Nielson's claim to the office would be made, was called to her attention, she replied that it had only been decided last night to make the fight to retain office."[326]

The Bismarck Tribune shared a few more details:

> "Miss Nielson, after becoming convinced that Mr. and Mrs. Macdonald intended to hold the office until ousted by legal action, withdrew to the offices of Attorney General Langer, where she received Mr. Langer's assurances of support and a promise that application would be made to the supreme court this afternoon for a writ of mandamus compelling the retiring state superintendent to relinquish the office of public instruction to his successor."[327]

Later, Miss Nielson said she was "wholly relying upon Mr. Langer's opinion and judgment in the matter."[328] There is no evidence she gave any other public statements on her thoughts that day. We can only imagine her feelings of frustration and disappointment.

On Thursday afternoon, January 9, the Supreme Court heard the case regarding the writ of mandamus and determined that the certificate of election held by Miss Nielson was prima facie evidence of her right to that office and that Mr. Macdonald had no grounds for declining to turn over the office to her.[329] On Friday afternoon around 4 p.m., the Burleigh County Sheriff served the order to vacate the office on Neil C. Macdonald.

> "Miss Nielson went into the office a few minutes after the sheriff had served the order. She was accompanied by her deputy H.G. Arnsdorf, and by Geo. H. McFarland. There was a brief conference, Mr. Macdonald demanding that Miss Nielson surrender title of the office to him. 'I certainly do not intend to do so,' replied Miss Nielson."[330]

Mr. Macdonald stepped out of the office at 4:15 p.m., escorted by Governor Lynn Frazier and Mrs. Macdonald, his wife and deputy.[331]

As if being denied her office wasn't enough, another issue came up the first week of January. Governor Lynn Frazier proposed to remove the administration of the school system from the Superintendent of Public Instruction to an official he appointed. When asked about this development on January 10, Miss Nielson gave a short statement: "My business is education, not politics. I do not care to discuss the situation at this time."[332]

Starting Her Work as State Superintendent

With legislative proposals to remove responsibilities from her office to other NPL officials constantly swirling around her, State Superintendent Nielson decided to get right to business and call a conference of county superintendents. She scheduled the conference for January 23 and 24 in Bismarck, and her office noted that now more than 50 percent of the elected county superintendents were women.[333]

Governor Frazier and famous Monday luncheon club of state officials and assistants in 1919. Miss Nielson is seated at right front. (NDIRS, NDSU, MSS 220. 9. 15)

A few days later, state Superintendent Nielson announced the program for the conference and speakers. Bertha Palmer, her assistant superintendent (and future state Superintendent of Public Instruction), would lead singing on the first day and give a speech on "Spring House Cleaning and the School Director's Responsibility." Attorney General Bill Langer was on the program speaking on "Enforcement of School Laws." John McFarland was on the program on day two discussing "Americanization." Friday afternoon, state Superintendent Nielson would lead a round-table discussion on "School Problems." Other speakers were also scheduled.[334]

Miss Nielson included the results of this conference in her 1920 Biennial Report to the Governor:

"In January, 1919, when the present State Superintendent of Public Instruction took office, a conference of the County Superintendents was immediately called in Bismarck. Every county but one was represented.

At this meeting a state program of education looking toward a systematic advancement in things educational throughout the whole state was outlined to be promoted in all counties. It was agreed that the following seven definite points would be emphasized and pushed:

1. *AMERICANIZATION including the enforcement of the compulsory attendance law, the establishment of public evening schools for the elimination of illiteracy among adults and the organization of Parent-Teachers Associations for closer cooperation between homes and school. The slogan 'No illiteracy in North Dakota in 1924' was adopted.*
2. *HEALTH WORK including the employment of a school nurse in every county of the state, the establishment in every county of the state of the county wide Play Day to develop community spirit as well as physical education, and the introduction of the Hot School Lunch into all schools not having same.*
3. *CONSOLIDATION of schools wherever possible.*
4. *STANDARDIZATION of high schools, consolidated, graded and rural schools for which state aid may be given.*
5. *The Teaching of the Principles of GRAIN GRADING and CREAM TESTING in consolidated schools and all other schools where the pupils are advanced enough to receive such instruction.*
6. *The Teaching of the Principles of GOOD ROAD MAKING.*
7. *Campaign for BETTER SALARIES FOR BETTER TEACHERS."*[335]

However, the evening before the conference was held, state Superintendent Nielson was served with more legal papers. Former state Superintendent Neil Macdonald had instituted a summons and complaint in a quo warranto proceeding in district court to test her qualifications to hold office. *The Bismarck Daily Tribune* wrote, "he's North Dakota's only and original state superintendent of public instruction, because, Miss Nielson doesn't possess the qualifications that he possesses and therefore cannot qualify for the job that is his."[336] You can imagine the side talk the next day at the superintendents meeting on this new development.

Miss Nielson would again rely on help from Attorney General Bill Langer. Earlier in the month he had stated, "Miss Nielson is the legally elected superintendent of public instruction of this state, and I'll fight her battles in every court of the state if necessary."[337] And he did.

Rough Going With the Legislature and Administration in 1919

These were heady days for the NPL, when they had a majority in both houses of the Legislature and a mandate to put their agenda through the Legislature.

The 1919 Legislature was busy passing legislation that, as Agnes Geelan noted in her book *Dakota Maverick,* "future league candidates would point with pride. The Bank of North Dakota, the State Mill and Elevator, the Industrial Commission to manage those institutions, the Workmen's Compensation Bureau, the 8-hour day and the minimum wage law were established and have all stood the test of time. It was when the League went overboard to enact punitive and blatantly partisan legislation that the organization ran into serious difficulty."[338]

One of those pieces of blatantly partisan legislation was the Board of Administration bill. The NPL-dominated Legislature and Governor Frazier were not happy that Miss Nielson was now Superintendent of Public Instruction. They wanted NPL officials to determine the course of education in North Dakota, and so they passed legislation establishing a Board of Administration that would enable NPL control.

Feelings ran high in the public about what was happening in the state. Traditional Republicans joined with traditional Democrats and formed an organization called the Independent Voters Association (IVA). These folks viewed the NPL as socialists and anarchists. NPL members viewed the IVA members as out-of-touch tycoons who did not care about the welfare of the farmers.

In June 1920, Bill Langer published his first and only book, *The Non-Partisan League.*[339] Chapter 13 of the book contains a detailed account of state Superintendent of Public Instruction Minnie Nielson and the NPL actions in 1919 that affected her office. Nielson changed a few words, but basically quoted whole sections of Chapter 13 in Langer's book when she gave two speeches in Minnesota in September 1920, explaining the NPL grab for power over educational matters. Here are excerpts from her speech:

"Under the former system, there were three boards – the State Board of Edu-

cation, the State Board of Regents and the State Board of Control. The State Board of Education had charge of the Common and High schools, and the State Superintendent was chairman of this Board. The State Board of Regents had charge of the higher educational institutions; the State Board of Control had charge of the penal and charitable institutions.

... But Senate Bill No 134 did away with all three Boards and established one Board known as the Board of Administration.

The Board of Administration[340] – which in reality is the Governor – has power to reach down into every local locality; IT CAN DICTATE THE POLICIES TO BE FOLLOWED IN THE SCHOOL SYSTEM, THE COURSES TO BE STUDIED, THE TEXT BOOKS TO BE USED, ETC.

Even the Presidents, or heads of the state educational[341] institutions, AND THE STATE SUPERINTENDENT OF PUBLIC INSTRUCTION ARE PLACED UNDER CONTROL OF AND MADE RESPONSIBLE TO THIS BOARD.

Senate Bill No. 134, as first introduced, made no provision for the State Superintendent being a member of the Board of Administration. There arose great opposition to this bill, especially from those engaged in educational work all over the state. The League leaders feared they would lose control of some of the members of the legislature, and at last realized that this bill could not pass; it was then changed so that the State Board of Administration should consist of five members – three members to be appointed by the Governor, and two ex-officio members – the Commissioner of Agriculture and Labor and the State Superintendent of Schools.[342]

The three members of this Board appointed by the Governor may be removed for cause by the Governor, which simply means that the majority of the Board is always in control of the Governor – who is under the control of Townley and Lemke.

This bill provides that this Board shall take over absolute control of all the penal, charitable and educational institutions of the state, and have general supervision over the public schools. Note especially that charitable and penal institutions are included – there is a reason. The leaders knew that this bill would be referred to the people so that, by including matters other than school affairs, THE WOMEN of the state WOULD BE UNABLE TO VOTE ON IT. This of course, was done deliberately, and when the bill was referred, the women who voted for me[343] *were unable to vote for me to retain the duties for which they had elected me. YET THESE LEADERS CLAIM THAT THEY ARE IN FAVOR OF WOMEN SUFFRAGE ... .*

One of the first acts of this new Board was to create a new official expert called 'Educational Advisor to the Board and General School Inspector.' They appointed Neil C. Macdonald, the defeated Nonpartisan League candidate for State Superintendent to this new position, at the same salary he had as State Superintendent.

An Educational Commission was provided for in the new law, to consist of five members, one being the State Superintendent as ex-officio member and chairman, and four others appointed by the Board of Administration. Whom did they appoint? Four supporters and friends of Macdonald's the defeated candidate.

At the first meeting of the Educational Commission, the office of Secretary of the Commission and Supervisor of Certification was created and E.P. Crain was appointed to this position. This man had been in charge for a short time of certification in the State Superintendent's office when Macdonald was State Superintendent. New office rooms were arranged for this new department of certification in the Capitol building and furnished by taking funds from the high school and rural aid funds. They removed from the State Superintendent's office nine cart loads of records, books and other material pertaining to certification which had been a part of that office since statehood.

Under the old law, the State Superintendent was Secretary and the work of certification of teachers was done by and through the office of State Superintendent.[344]

Now the State Superintendent does not have anything to do with certification of teachers, does not see the examination papers and is not even permitted to sign the teachers' certificates. These are signed by George A. Totten, Chairman of the Board of Administration and E.P. Crain.

E.P. Crain is only nominal head of the certification department for he is Secretary of the State Motor Vehicle Registration Department, and draws a salary as such. He has an office down town in the Bank of North Dakota building and does not office at the Capitol. In reality, Mrs. Neil C. Macdonald has charge of the certification department and uses E.P. Crain's rubber stamp to sign all letters, hence the public is deceived.

The Macdonalds, therefore, although ejected from the control of the schools by the vote of the majority of the people of the state, ARE BACK IN THE SADDLE IN SPITE OF THE VOTERS.

Why? Because they are good spreaders of the Socialist propaganda. It is well, the League leaders believe, to have in charge of certificating the teachers those persons who are sympathetic with the doctrine the Socialists want taught in the schools … ."[345]

The Board of Administration took away other major responsibilities of the state Superintendent of Public Instruction's office as well. Therefore, by August 1919, Miss Nielson no longer was responsible for the supervision and certification of teachers, standardization of schools and uniformity of textbooks, examinations for eighth-grade and high school pupils and preparation of courses of study for the several classes of public schools. The board organized on July 26, 1919, and as each change was proposed by the Board of Administration, Superintendent Nielson voted no, but she had only one vote out of five on the board.[346]

To make matters worse, starting in late August 1919, Superintendent Nielson was not notified of and did not receive minutes of meetings of the Board of Administration.

North Dakota Supreme Court Cases Involving Miss Nielson in 1919

Two important Supreme Court cases involving Superintendent Nielson were decided in October 1919.

Since the 1918 campaign, Neil Macdonald had been raising issues that Miss Nielson was not qualified to hold office. Although the Supreme Court determined in January 1919 that she held a valid certificate of election to the office of Superintendent of Public Instruction, Mr. Macdonald was not satisfied. He filed another lawsuit in late January 1919, stating Minnie J. Nielson is not "the holder of a teacher's certificate of the highest grade issued in this state, and hence is not eligible to the office of superintendent of public instruction." [347]

On October 10, 1919, the North Dakota Supreme Court determined that "a professional certificate issued under the provisions of section 737, Rev. Codes 1899, is a teacher's certificate of the highest grade issued in this state … ."[348] This was good news, as this was what Miss Nielson had claimed all along.

Questions had also been raised that she had not "properly" received the certificate – i.e., that she had never taken an examination to prove she was worthy of the certificate. The order went on to refute those claims by explaining how her certificate was issued.

From 1897 to 1905, two types of certificates were valid throughout the whole state. One was a normal certificate and one was a professional certificate, valid for life, unless revoked.

> *"The statute provided that a (professional) certificate should be issued only to persons of good moral character, who passed a thorough examination in all the branches included in the courses of study prescribed for the common and high schools of the state … . It further provided that such certificate should in no case be granted unless the applicant had had at least five years experience as a teacher, and could satisfy the superintendent of his ability to instruct and properly manage any high school of the state.*
>
> *It appears from the record in this case that the defendant, Minnie J. Nielson, on November 27, 1900, received from the then superintendent of public instruction a normal certificate under the provisions of section 738, supra. The result of the examination taken by her is indorsed on the certificate. It appears there from that she was examined in 24 different subjects, including methods of teaching, history of education, pedagogy, and psychology. It also appears that in the subjects enumerated she received very favorable marks. The record also discloses that on December 8, 1902 the then superintendent of public instruction issued a professional certificate to the defendant. The certificate refers to the previous normal certificate issued to the defendant and recites that she has spent two years in study at the state university, and performed twelve years of successful work as a teacher … . This latter certificate was concededly the highest certificate issued in this state at the time it was issued … .*
>
> *The defendant acted under the certificate for more than 16 years before she was elected to the office of superintendent of public instruction, and during this time the validity of the certificate has not been questioned … . If the plaintiff in good faith believed that the certificate held by the defendant was invalid and properly subject to revocation, why did he fail to institute proceedings for revocation while he was at the head of the educational department of the state?"*[349]

This ruling was very good news for Superintendent Nielson, but the next Supreme Court ruling on October 20, 1919, was not.

Superintendent Nielson and Attorney General Langer wanted the court to clarify whether the Legislature could take away powers the state Superintendent of Public Instruction had held since statehood, especially the right to prescribe and prepare the courses of study for the common schools of the state. When the North Dakota Supreme Court issued a ruling on this matter, it determined that the:

"Legislature, pursuant to constitutional authority, and excepting as restricted by constitutional limitations, possesses the power to regulate the educational system and public schools of this state and to prescribe the courses of study in such schools."

The court noted that "the Constitution provides for the election of a superintendent of public instruction … . It further provides that the power and duties of such superintendent shall be as prescribed by law."[350]

Superintendent Nielson's office duties were subject to the will of the Legislature, and so for the time being, she needed to work within the powers her office retained.

Superintendent Nielson Testifies Before the December 1919 Legislative Investigating Committee

The Legislature held a special session in late November through early December 1919. The first item on their agenda was state ratification of the women's suffrage amendment.[351] However, the *First Annual Report of the Board of Administration* was issued on November 30 and immediately recommendations in that report captured the attention of legislators. It called for abolition of the elected office of state Superintendent of Public Instruction[352] and it presented a highly critical report of the collection of books and magazines in the State Library. [353]

Both issues were controversial, but the latter caused an uproar, especially once Representative Olger Burtness reported the shocking books he had found ready to be distributed to schools in the travelling library. In addition, State Auditor Kosizky received an invoice for a shipment of books that he noted contained "titles about bolshevism and authors with muckraking and/or socialist reputation," and he placed a copy of the invoice on the desk of each legislator.[354]

The Legislature appointed a Book and Library Investigating Committee in early December. As a member of the Board of Administration that supervised the State Library, Superintendent Nielson was called to testify under oath about magazines in the State Library that were in question during the investigation. Mr. Johnson was a member of the committee:

"Mr. Johnson: Miss Nielson, my idea of the magazines and Mr. Totten's idea of the magazines as to which were radical are different and yet honest.

Miss Nielson: I presume that is true.

Mr. J: Is there any one magazine here that you would consider harmful?

Miss Nielson: I consider any magazine that stirs up trouble and helps to make more apparent the feeling of unrest in this world is harmful at this time; we are in a period of reconstruction after a great world struggle and instead of dividing classes, it seems to me we should have more brotherly love in this world and I would not put anything about the I W.W.'s and anarchism for the public to read.

Mr. J: And you think some of them are harmful?

Miss N: I do. Typical journals of the various non-conformist groups, etc., as given in the report."[355]

Superintendent Nielson's comments were "mild" compared with the comments of others at this time. One of the books in question in the library was Ellen Key's *Love and Ethics*. As Agnes Geelan noted in her book *The Dakota Maverick*, "'Free Love' became an

Political Cartoon from the RED FLAME, September 1920 depicting Superintendent Of Public Instruction Nielson's problems with the Board of Administration in 1919. (SHSND)

issue that was to haunt the League for years and was one of the hottest issues, no pun intended, in the campaigns of 1920."[356]

Legislators were also interested in finding out what was happening or not happening at the Board of Administration meetings. A committee member, Mr. O'Connor, asked Superintendent Nielson about her attendance at Board of Administration meetings.

"Mr. O'Connor: You as a member of this Board of Administration have the supervision of the Library Commission?

Miss Nielson: The Board of Administration has supervision of the Library Commission.

Q: Do you know anything about the ordering of the books referred to by Mr. Burtness?

A: I do not except the conversation that I had with Mr. Totten last Tuesday afternoon when I came into the gathering.[357] *Mr. Totten said it was not a meeting; four members were there and the secretary also.*

Q: With reference to the meetings, you have been notified, have you, of all meetings?

A: I imagine not. I do not know when the board is meeting always. I was out of town attending the teachers' institute in October. I asked my deputy if any message was left at the office. He said there was not. I was where I could have been summoned if any important questions came up, or were going to be.

Q: Now, if you should miss a meeting, when you are out of town, Miss Nielson, you have access to the minutes of the meetings?

A: I have had no minutes since the 7th of August. I sent in a written request that all members be furnished copies of all the minutes, also that a definite date be set so that I could meet with the board, but, as Mr. Totten explained, it is owning to Mr. Liessman's rush of work.

Q: That you have not seen, or had furnished to you copies of these minutes since August 7th?

A: Yes."[358]

Now it was public knowledge that the Board of Administration had been playing "hard ball" politics: not notifying the Superintendent of Public Instruction of meetings and not providing her with minutes. Nothing came of the Board of Administration's recommendation to do away with the election of the Superintendent of Public Instruction. Instead, the IVA started making plans for an initiated measure to restore the powers of her office.

The Election Year of 1920

Superintendent Nielson's first year in office was so dramatic politically that it is easy to ignore the educational work that was progressing through her office. By 1920, several projects were well under way.

Miss Nielson encouraged the "professional spirit" among teachers of the state by emphasizing attendance at summer schools. In later years, when reviewing some of her accomplishments as state Superintendent, Miss Nielson considered her early directives on summer school important for teachers and students:

> "In the past rural teachers attended summer schools, but only reviewed elementary subjects which did not count toward graduation or an advance diploma. When the direction of this work came under Miss Nielson's supervision, she urged the state institutions to offer only courses in the summer schools for which credit would be given toward a diploma. As a result, hundreds of teachers have gone on with their normal and college work and have received diplomas from the advanced courses … . North Dakota ranks high in the percentage of teachers who do work toward advancement." [359]

Superintendent Nielson also attended an emergency Federal Conference of Education in Washington, D.C., in May 1920, which included discussions on attracting and retaining qualified teachers across the country. Eight delegates from North Dakota who attended the national conference were sent home to "sell education." *Better Salaries for Better Teachers* became a slogan to get teacher salaries raised during the 1921 legislative session. The Superintendent's 1920 Biennial Report to the Governor stated, " It has been a shame that men digging in the ditch who cannot read nor write have been receiving better wages than the teachers, whose duty it is to mold the minds and characters of our future American Citizens. … Not only must salaries be raised but teachers' qualifications must advance accordingly."[360]

Through the efforts of the State Teachers Association, the 1921 Legislature enacted a bill that provided for minimum training and salaries for teachers. Minimum training included a diploma from a four-year high school course and minimum salary for a teacher so qualified was set at $810 per school year. Teachers whose training included a degree from an approved standard college, in addition to a four-year high school course, would receive a minimum salary of $1,300 per school year.[361]

Miss Nielson was very concerned about the needs of children, and on September 1, 1920, she chaired what became the organizing meeting of the North Dakota Conference of Social Welfare (NDCSW). Child welfare specialists from around the state gathered in Bismarck. Twenty-five years later, she sent greetings to the NDCSW on their 25th anniversary and recalled:

"The urge which prompted the call for the formation of this organization came through interest in promoting better conditions physically, educationally, socially, and spiritually, for the children of North Dakota. The county superintendents of schools formed a large part of the organizing body. The need for a Children's Code Commission was eminent."[362]

Superintendent Nielson was working hard campaigning as the November 1920 election approached. This was a milestone election for women because, with the passage of the 19th Amendment and ratification by the states in August 1920, North Dakota women could vote for the first time on all positions and all issues on the ballot. She was running against NPL candidate Ruth M. Johnson. Her former nemesis, Neil Macdonald, and his wife had left the state in spring 1920 to pursue other opportunities.[363]

Her campaign featured innovative approaches, such as holding a "Minnie Nielson Night" at Bismarck movie theaters. Each theater in Bismarck set aside time between the first and second shows for the use of her local campaign committee, who brought in a speaker about state Superintendent Nielson.[364]

In speeches, Nielson was talking about her accomplishments while mentioning the upheaval in state education administration over the past two years. When she spoke on October 30 at a meeting of the Cass County Women's Campaign Committee, she made a point of answering recent NPL attacks. *The Fargo Forum* ran a front-page article with highlights of her remarks:

> *"Counties in North Dakota that she has visited in the last month will go over for the independent candidates with good majorities, Miss Nielson said … . The statement attributed to her by the Non-partisan press, that she had told a Minneapolis audience that the farmers of North Dakota were degenerate, was branded as absolutely false by Miss Nielson.*[365] *'My father has been a farmer in this state since 1880, he has farmed land in Barnes County for 40 years and I certainly have the highest respect for the farmers of this state,' said Miss Nielson.*
>
> *The word 'free love' was never mentioned in her Minneapolis speech, Miss Nielson declared. 'The Non partisan press, in an attempt to distort my meaning, has credited to me many things which I did not say. What I did say was true. They know it is true, and that is why they are squirming so. It is the truth that hurts.'*
>
> *'I told my Minneapolis audience that I had no fight with the rank and file of the Non-partisan league, that I believed most of them were honest and sincere. But I have a fight with the Socialist leaders of the League … (they) are determined to take over the school system of North Dakota and make it an agency for Socialist propaganda.'*

The attempt of the League to prove she was not educationally qualified to fill office was ridiculous, Miss Nielson said. Her qualifications to hold office ... have twice been passed upon by the supreme court ... ."[366]

She was also hoping an IVA-sponsored initiated measure would pass, which would restore powers to the state Superintendent's office which had been removed by the Board of Administration.

On November 2, 1920, Minnie J. Nielson had a good day. She won the election with 119,684 votes; Ruth Johnson received 105,330 votes. The initiated measure also passed.[367]

Miss Nielson's supporter, NPL Attorney General Bill Langer, was not so lucky in 1920. Having burned his bridges with the NPL, Langer ran for governor as an IVA candidate against incumbent Governor Lynn Frazier and lost in the Republican June primary. Bill Langer would return to private law practice in January.[368]

"No Illiteracy in North Dakota in 1924"

Superintendent Minnie Nielson had a real commitment to stamp out illiteracy. She worked on this project in North Dakota throughout the time she was in office, and after she left office, she directed the National Illiteracy Crusade from 1929 to 1931.

In 1917, the Legislature appropriated $7,000 and provided for the establishment of evening schools. Several night schools were started during Macdonald's term of office (1917-18), but in January 1919, Superintendent Nielson's number one goal was:

> *"AMERICANIZATION including the enforcement of the compulsory attendance law, the establishment of public evening schools for the elimination of illiteracy among adults and the organization of Parent-Teachers Associations for closer cooperation between homes and school. The slogan 'No illiteracy in North Dakota in 1924' was adopted."*[369]

Two years later, substantial progress had been made. By June 30, 1920, 42 Evening Public Schools were reported in 22 counties, with a total enrollment of 924. The department was also aware of six more schools which were not reported by the counties. Students ranged from 12 years to 65 years of age and represented at least 14 different nationalities. Comments from the teachers included in the biennial report evidenced the interest and appreciation by teachers and pupils and are an inspiration to read:

> "On the opening night of our school we enrolled nine pupils, consisting mostly of Russians and Germans, and later we enrolled four more, making a membership of thirteen. Two of our pupils were members of the school board. They were both Russians and their object in coming was to

learn to read and understand what they read so, as they said, 'the other members can't put it over on us'."[370]

In 1920, the federal census was taken; it showed that North Dakota had 9,937 persons over 10 years of age who could not read or write in any language. Soon people in North Dakota wanted to know, "Where are the Illiterates?" and "How can we secure their names and locate them?"[371] Miss Nielson took this challenge to heart. She personally wrote to Washington, seeking ways to get detailed information from the national census about who was illiterate in North Dakota. Secretary of Commerce Herbert Hoover answered her letters in January 1922, informing her that federal money was not available to copy the census lists.[372]

This did not deter Nielson. She encouraged each county superintendent to find a way to obtain funds to get copies of the census lists. Private individuals and local organizations donated the money needed, and as each county received its list, volunteers assisted the county superintendent in checking the accuracy of information on the lists. A national speaker on stamping our illiteracy, Mrs. Cora Wilson Stewart, was brought to the state, and she spoke to the North Dakota Education Association, the State Press Association, the Annual Conference of County Superintendents, teacher institutes in 27 counties and the annual meeting of the State Federation of Women's Clubs.[373]

The State Board of Administration passed a resolution requiring all illiterates at the State Penitentiary to attend night school.[374]

The 1926 Biennial Report included the following results of the campaign to stamp out illiteracy:

> "Although the goal 'No illiteracy in North Dakota in 1924' was not reached by June 30, 1924, ... great progress had been made. The percentage had been reduced from 2.1% in 1920 to .7% on June 30, 1924. It was noted that ten counties had not yet made the survey and check. Golden Valley had the distinction of being the first county in the state to stamp out illiteracy ... The last illiterate person left in the county was taught by the county superintendent."

Night schools continued in 1925-26, serving 771 pupils. The Biennial report noted:

> "Our state problem is different from many states in that our illiterates are scattered over a wide area. This means more individual service, for it is more difficult to conduct evening schools for a very small group covering several miles than in a large city .... Each citizen should do his share in this campaign to guard against future illiteracy by enforcing the compulsory attendance law and by teaching every one capable of learning to read and write the English language."[375]

Afterthoughts

While state Superintendent of Public Instruction, Minnie Nielson was extremely active in professional organizations on the national level and held offices in many of these organizations. She was director and vice president of the National Education Association; national vice president of the Business and Professional Women's Club; president of the National Council of Administrative Women in Education; and delegate to the First World Conference in Education (San Francisco).[376]

Superintendent Nielson was also the first woman delegate from North Dakota to a national Republican convention (Chicago, 1920).[377]

Miss Nielson won two more elections in 1922 and 1924. In 1922, she beat her opponent, Martha T. Fulton, 107,684 to 80,986. In 1924, she beat her opponent, Bertha Palmer, 97,631 to 93,476. In 1926, she decided not to run again for office, and moved to Washington, D.C., where she was field secretary for the National Illiteracy Crusade from 1929 to 1931. She continued working nationwide with state departments of education to eliminate illiteracy from 1931 to 1938, speaking in 42 states.[378]

Upon the request of the Board of Trustees of the North Dakota Teacher's Insurance and Retirement Fund, Miss Nielson returned home to North Dakota in 1938 at age 64 to become executive secretary. She served in that role for 12 years, retiring in 1950 to her childhood home in Valley City.

One of Miss Nielson's personal interests was music and singing. As Barnes County Superintendent, she arranged for a Victrola with records to travel between schools.[379] As state Superintendent, she encouraged songs to be written about and sung during the illiteracy campaign.[380] She also asked North Dakota poet laureate Mr. James Foley to write words for a song about North Dakota, which became the North Dakota hymn.

In 1926, James Foley attended an educational meeting in Watford City. That night at the Park Hotel (The Travelers Home), he sat down and wrote the words for *North Dakota* on the hotel stationary:

"North Dakota, North Dakota
With thy prairies wide and free
All thy sons and daughters love thee
Fairest State from sea to sea
North Dakota, North Dakota
Here we pledge ourselves to thee."

Foley wrote four verses for his song that night and signed the original manuscript, "For Miss Minnie J. Nielson – State Superintendent of Public Instruction, James W. Foley, Watford City, Oct. 18, 1926."[381]

Minnie Jean Nielson died in Valley City on February 27, 1958, at the age of 83.[382]

FOURTEEN

Improving Education in Challenging Times

Bertha Rachel Palmer

State Superintendent of Public Instruction
1927-32

By
Susan Wefald

"Teaching in rural schools has taken on professional dignity and respect and the children are receiving the benefit."

Superintendent Bertha Palmer, October 1932[383]

Bertha Palmer*

1881-1959

State Superintendent of Public Instruction 1927-32

State Superintendent of Public Instruction Bertha Palmer - 1920
(SHSND 361-19)

Personal Information

Born 1880 at Worthington, Minnesota, and raised on farm near Devils Lake, North Dakota. In "spare time," wrote travel articles and her book Beauty Spots of North Dakota (1928).

Party Affiliation

Elected on No-Party Ballot but endorsed by Independent Voters Association (IVA) Republicans

Education

Devils Lake High School; graduate of Mayville Normal School, Mayville, North Dakota; University of Minnesota summer school sessions.

Professional Experience Before Taking Office

Teacher in rural schools near Devils Lake, three years (1898-1901); teacher of music and art in Larimore, Dickinson, Rugby, Cando, Williston and Bismarck, 1903-15; Field Deputy to the Superintendent of Williams County Schools, 1915-17; Children's Division Superintendent and Field Worker for the State Sunday School Association, 1918; Assistant State Superintendent of Public Instruction, 1919-24; Field Worker, North Dakota Council of Religious Education, 1925-26.

Memberships Include

As State Superintendent of Schools: National Congress of Parents and Teachers, director of rural demonstration in North Dakota, 1928; National Association of State School Superintendents; National Educational Education.

Other: North Dakota Federation of Women's Clubs, state art chairman, 1918-24; National Council of Religious Education, committee member, 1928; Sully Hill Chapter of Daughters of the American Revolution (D.A.R.); Current Events Club and the Delphian Study Chapter, Bismarck; PEO Sisterhood of Bismarck; First Presbyterian Church, Bismarck, member and director of religious education, where she started the first Bible School in North Dakota, 1919-24.[384]

*Bio includes information through 1932

Radio was new technology in 1926. People were amazed that a person speaking at the WDAY studio in Fargo could be heard by North Dakotans hundreds of miles away. Earl Reineke established Fargo commercial radio station WDAY in May 1922 before any commercial radio station was on the air in the Twin Cities, and just two years after the first commercial radio station started broadcasting in Pittsburgh, Pennsylvania. Other stations in North Dakota were soon established, including KDLR in Devils Lake.[385]

Bertha Palmer, age 46, the newly elected Superintendent of Public Instruction, was interested in radio. Already in 1919, soon after she had started working as Assistant Superintendent in the North Dakota Department of Public Instruction, she contributed the article "Use of the Talking Machine in Schools" to *School Education*.[386] Now, just a few days after her election to public office, she decided to use this new technology to reach out to the people of North Dakota. Two newspapers ran articles about her broadcast, which hints that using this new medium was not "business as usual" for state officials.[387]

Miss Palmer stepped up to the microphone at KDLR in Devils Lake shortly after noon in early November 1926 and gave the following remarks:

> "To my unseen audience: Ladies and gentlemen, greetings: It is not possible for me to meet personally the hundreds in Ramsey county and the thousands in the state who voted for me on November 2. Many of you, besides putting a cross after my name on the ballot, gave many hours of work in behalf of my candidacy for the office of superintendent of public instruction. To all of those in this great audience which I can not see, I take this opportunity to say for that work which you did and for that cross which you made, ladies and gentlemen, I thank you."[388]

Bringing Art and Music to North Dakota's School Children

Bertha's name was not Bertha Palmer, but Bertha Paramore, when she was born on August 31, 1880, in Worthington, Minnesota.[389] Her parents, Lafayette Paramore and his wife, Eliza, changed their name to Palmer when the family moved to Devils Lake, North Dakota, in 1882.[390] She grew up on a farm, which was called Woodbine Farm, on the shores of Devils Lake in Lake Township and attended a one-room school house four miles from her home. Bertha was the oldest of four children.

In 1898, at the age of 17, after graduating from high school in Devils Lake, Miss Palmer started teaching school. For the next three years, she taught in country schools near Devils Lake, and then she attended the State Normal School at Mayville, graduating in 1903.

While continuing her education at summer terms at the University of Minnesota and special schools in Chicago, she taught for 11 years in schools in Larimore, Dickinson, Bismarck, Rugby, Cando and Williston. She was a trained music and art specialist in these public schools. From 1915 to 1917, she served for three years as deputy superintendent of Williams County Schools.[391] After her parents both died in 1917, she worked in 1918 as Children's Division superintendent and field worker for the State Sunday School Association.[392]

In 1919, she was recruited by state Superintendent of Public Instruction Minnie Nielson to serve on her staff. Miss Palmer was on Miss Nielson's small staff from the very beginning and served as assistant superintendent. Her new job enabled her to act as a consultant on music and art activities to the schools around the state while she took care of other duties in the office as well.

She watched as Miss Nielson made decisions and often thought about what her own approach would be. For many years, Miss Nielson and Miss Palmer were friends. When Miss Nielson's parents celebrated their 50th wedding anniversary in April 1923, Miss Nielson invited Miss Palmer to the celebration at their home in Valley City. Bertha Palmer was chosen to "assist" serving food in the dining room to the many friends and relatives who attended the special reception.[393]

Assistant State Superintendent Bertha Palmer with girls and boys from the Bismarck Indian School at the state Capitol. (1920 - SHSND MSS 10098 Photo Album)

The 1924 Election – Running Against Superintendent Minnie Nielson

Miss Palmer was quite well-known in the state when she ran for Superintendent of Public Instruction in 1924. She was a noted writer and she had served as Assistant Superintendent of Public Instruction for five years. Her first run for the office of state Superintendent of Public Instruction in 1924 was an unusual campaign.

Miss Palmer, who loved writing newspaper articles about North Dakota, wrote 16 one-half page feature articles for the *Fargo Forum* on "Art in North Dakota," which appeared in the *Fargo Forum* in 1923 and January and February 1924.[394] She authored these articles as part of her volunteer work as chairman of the fine arts section of the North Dakota Federation of Women's Clubs from 1919 to 1925. She was a popular public speaker on "Art in North Dakota." This volunteer role complemented her work as a school art and music consultant, which was part of her responsibilities as Assistant Superintendent of Public Instruction.

Soon there were news articles praising her, such as "Miss Palmer is a splendid speaker. Not only was she a delight to listen to, but the talk she gave was of inestimable value." Also, one from Wahpeton; "Miss Bertha Palmer, is a most charming woman … . She has the charm of personality that comes from culture, sympathy, sincerity and understanding."[395] From Jamestown, announcing the parent-teachers meeting that evening, "The main speaker will be Miss Bertha Palmer … . Miss Palmer has written many interesting articles and has entertained audiences over the entire state with her talks on North Dakota."[396]

By mid-April 1924, work relations between Superintendent Minnie Nielson and Miss Palmer were no longer congenial. Palmer decided to quit and, on April 21, announced to the press that she was resigning. She presented to the press a copy of her resignation letter, which included the following statement, "Because of the differences of opinion which make harmonious work impossible, I ask to be released not later than May 1, 1924, from my connection with the department of public instruction."[397] The press also reported:

> "Miss Palmer's resignation had been rumored for some time in capitol circles … . Miss Palmer's name has been suggested as candidate for state superintendent in the coming election, but she denied that her resignation was for this intention. 'I am not resigning to become a candidate,' she said. 'Whether I am or not depends upon what my friends do and other developments in the next few weeks.' Miss Palmer said she was making arrangements to go to Glasgow, Scotland, as delegate to the World Sunday School conference in June, the month of the state primary. Miss Nielson declined to comment on the resignation." [398]

However, on May 2, one day after she left the office, she held another press conference where she announced,

> "Some 10 days ago when announcement was made of my resignation from the department of public instruction, I stated I did not know whether or not I would be a candidate for the office of superintendent of public instruction … . Since that time letters from all parts of the state and personal interviews have led me to decide to be a candidate for that office."[399]

The article went on to share Bertha Palmer's views on how she believed the office of Public Instruction should be conducted, which included:

> "I believe that the state superintendent of public instruction should be a leader in education and should counsel, but not dictate state and county policies.
>
> "I believe that the department of public instruction should be so organized that the public may receive efficient service from the office and the field with the least possible waste of time and expense … .
>
> "I believe that the cost of teachers' institutes may be greatly reduced and their value increased by (1) having a definite program, (2) limiting the number of outside speakers, (3) economically planned itineraries for conductors and speakers … .
>
> "I believe that where there is but one dollar to spend, but one dollar should be spent.
>
> "I believe in courtesy, appreciation, and co-operation in all personal and professional relations."[400]

Although these press conferences were part of any normal campaign for office, Miss Palmer's activities during the rest of the campaign were not. On June 7, she sailed to Europe on the SS Doric, attended the Sunday School Conference in Scotland June 18-26, and continued travelling throughout Europe, arriving in New York in late August.[401] Meanwhile, on June 25, the state primary election took place and the two nonpartisan candidates who moved forward to the general election were Superintendent Minnie Nielson and Miss Bertha Palmer, both previously associated with the Independent Voters Association (IVA).

She obviously had made contact with the *Fargo Forum* because between August 28 and November 13, 1924, 17 one-half page feature articles on her trip to Europe, written by Palmer, were published in the paper. These articles described sites that she had seen, countries visited and thoughts about world peace. [402] However, in the same paper, there is almost no coverage of her election campaign.

She ran two campaign ads in the Bismarck Tribune before the election. The ads, which included her picture, stated, "Endorsed by Many Leading Educators of the State – A Vote for Miss Palmer is a vote for Efficiency, Economy, and Courtesy."[403] On November 4, Minnie Nielson won the election. The election results were Minnie Nielson, 97,631 votes; Bertha Palmer, 93,176 votes.[404] Bertha Palmer made an excellent showing in her first election. She probably started thinking about the 1926 election.

The 1926 Election Against John Bjorlie

After the 1924 election, Bertha Palmer was soon hired to be a field worker for the North Dakota Council of Religious Education. In this job, she travelled the state, speaking to religious, community, service and women's groups about religious education. She also continued to write feature articles for the *Fargo Forum*, which published 12, one-half page articles in 1925 on "Beauty Spots of North Dakota." In May 1925, she commented about why she had written these articles.

> "If the stories even in a small way lead the people of the state who have come since the pioneer days to realize that we have something here to talk about besides crop failures and blizzards, and to see the beauty in our level plains, rolling prairies, and precipitous Badlands, our summer skies and fields, and our winter sunshine and landscapes, I shall be more than repaid for the time and energy expended."[405]

Miss Palmer received more speaking invitations around the state to talk about these "Beauty Spots." In 1928, Gorham Press published a collection of these articles and others she had written about North Dakota under the title *Beauty Spots of North Dakota.*[406]

By 1926, Miss Palmer was ready for a serious race for the office of Superintendent of Public Instruction. State Superintendent Nielson had decided not to run for another term of office, and there were several people interested in being her successor. On May 22, Miss Palmer filed her petitions with the Secretary of State to be on the June 30 primary ballot.[407] Five candidates, four men and Miss Palmer, were on the nonpartisan ballot for state Superintendent.

After the primary, her opponent was John Bjorli, who was a state high school inspector in the state Superintendent's office. Retiring Superintendent Minnie Nielson, apparently not happy that Bertha Palmer had run against her in 1924, threw her full support behind John Bjorlie and worked hard for him during the campaign.[408]

Bertha Palmer enlisted Mrs. Alfred Zuger, Bismarck, as her campaign manager and together they sent out a letter to "Friends" of Bertha Palmer on July 30, 1926. The following excerpts show that Miss Palmer was closely calculating votes needed in the 1926 election.

"We have waited to send you this letter till we knew the results of June 30th, which are: Barnes 18,420; Bjorlie 29,965; Crain 16,569; Lokken 11,687; Palmer 69,481; Total 146,122. We lost but four counties, Bottineau, McIntosh, Richland, and Sargent, unless the final count shows some grave errors. We lack 3,581 of having a majority of votes cast which is necessary to elect.

This means we must change an average of two votes in each precinct in the state. At the last general election there were almost 200,000 votes, so there will be about 50,000 more votes in November … .

The opposition is promoting their campaign through School Officers' Meetings in every county, and the Summer Institutes at each State School, all of which are held at state expense. The tax money is paying for this travel for this purpose … .

There are all sorts of detrimental and uncomplimentary stories regarding education and qualifications going about. It is unfortunate that in America such things spring up like weeds about the name of any person who dares to seek public office … .

By public addresses and in private interviews we shall continue to meet as many people as possible during the summer and fall … .Be constructive. Work for a change."[409]

Money for the campaign apparently was tight since Miss Palmer wrote this note on a slip of paper from an anonymous donor: "This note came to me in answer to prayer, attached to a $100.00 bill – with which I paid the newspaper advertising for my 1926 campaign."[410]

On October 15, 1926, the *Fargo Forum* reported that although there was not much public interest in the November 2 election, "considerable interest attaches to the result of the contest for Superintendent of public instruction… ."[411] On November 1, a *Fargo Forum* article mentioned, "The campaign for state superintendent of public instruction … has taken on added intensity during the last 10 days … . The Bjorlie forces have organized an intensive campaign that has been carried to all sections of the state, with the result that the Palmer forces, too, have exerted themselves to the utmost."[412]

Election Day dawned with freezing rain, wind and snow, and thus there was a light voter turn-out.[413] National women's organizations estimated that 200 women were candidates in 1926 for federal, state and municipal offices throughout the country.[414] Miss Palmer was one of these women candidates. When the votes were counted, she won the election – Bertha Palmer 84,093; John Bjorlie 78,862.[415]

Description of Official Duties of Superintendent of Public Instruction

Two-year term. Preserve in the office miscellaneous documents (books, maps, school reports, etc.); general supervision of the public schools of the state; prepare and furnish school supplies; responsible for certification of teachers; prescribe courses of study for the several classes of the public schools; prescribe rules for and assist at teacher institutes in the state; advise county superintendents; keep a record of all official acts; print the school laws; hold a conference with the county superintendents; prepare a biennial report and print and distribute 3,000 copies; may establish and direct public evening schools available to all persons over 16 years of age; employ school inspectors to examine schools; inspect school building plans, apportion school funds to the counties.[416]
Member: Board of Administration (supervises state educational, penal and charitable institutions), Board of University and School Lands, Board of Canvassers of General Elections, Teachers Insurance and Retirement Fund, State Historical Society Board.

Taking Office in January 1927

When Superintendent Bertha Rachel Palmer walked into her office on January 3, 1927, the office space and work of the department were not new to her. Unlike the women Superintendents of Public Instruction who had preceded her, Palmer had worked as an assistant superintendent in this very office for Superintendent Minnie Nielson for five years, from 1919 to 1924. The suite of offices for the Department of Public Instruction was located on the west side of the first floor of the 1883 state Capitol building in Bismarck. This Capitol building was now proving inadequate, and re-elected Governor Sorlie, in his message to the state Legislature, would speak the next day about the need for a new Capitol building.[417]

Palmer had been making plans for her work with the Department of Public Instruction since right after the November election. On November 20, she wrote a short letter to her election opponent, John Bjorlie, an employee of the department, and asked him to stay on as inspector. She wrote, "You and I both have the welfare of the schools of the state at heart. Certainly it will not be the best thing for the High Schools to change Inspectors in the middle of the year."[418] Mr. Bjorlie wrote a gracious reply on December 4, which he concluded by saying, "Your letter of November 20 was greatly appreciated, but I believe it is for the best interest of all concerned that my resignation become effective at the date before mentioned and I am sending in my formal resignation to Miss Minnie J. Nielson to-day and am asking her kindly to accept same."[419]

On January 4, 1927, soon after her swearing-in ceremony, Superintendent Palmer held a press conference on her plans for reorganization. "Miss Palmer Reorganizes Department – W.E Parsons to be Deputy – E.P Crain to be Director of Certification," announced the headline on the front page of the *Bismarck Tribune*. The new Superintendent was tapping educational leaders who had been involved in state education in prior administrations. W.E. Parsons had been deputy superintendent from 1911 to 1916, and E.P. Crain was a favorite state school inspector of former Nonpartisan League (NPL) leaders from 1917 to 1920. She also announced several other appointments in her office, clearly signaling a new direction in the department.

That night she stood in the Governor's office with other elected officials greeting the 6,000 guests that attended the inaugural reception from 8 to 11 p.m. in the Capitol building. The reception was an elaborate affair, with Alabama pine, northern spruce and ropes of laurel adorning the main corridor and reception hall. Fresh pink and red roses, palms, ferns and the large punch bowl and candlesticks which were part of the USS North Dakota silver service were also used for the "unusually lovely" reception. Entertainment included a musical program in the House chamber, and dancing after 10 p.m. on the third floor.[420] Superintendent Bertha Palmer wore a "pretty frock of cinnamon colored canton."[421]

It must have been an exciting day. Now the new Superintendent was ready to tackle a special project that needed attention: the rural one-room schools that more than 50 percent of North Dakota students attended across the state. Students in these schools were not getting the education they disserved, and Palmer's mission was to effect changes to help those rural students.

Religious Issues in the 1927 Legislative Session

New Superintendent Bertha Palmer got off to a rocky start with the Legislature and with the county superintendents in 1927. For the past two years, she had been working as field representative for the North Dakota Council for Religious Education and she was dedicated to the work of the council. Brought up Presbyterian in a religious family, Miss Palmer did not have any qualms about asking the public schools to allow release time for religious education during the school day. And so, when a bill was proposed in the Legislature in early 1927 called the weekly religious education bill, the new state Superintendent came out strongly in favor of the bill at a legislative hearing on January 18.

However, the next day, the Senate committee asked to know the opinion of the county superintendents, who were meeting in Bismarck. In a vote of 43 to 6, the county superintendents passed a resolution "requesting the senate committee on education to take no action on the matter."[422] General comments among the educators, reported the *Bismarck Tribune*, were "to the effect that they felt the bill would make an unnecessary encroachment on school time. Several declared they believed the instruction could be given after school and felt that excusing part of a class, as would probably be the case, would disrupt the whole teaching routine."[423] The Senate committee paid attention to the resolution, and the bill failed in the Senate.

Also, in 1927, Senator Bakken, Williams County, introduced a bill which required that "school boards appropriate funds to have placards with the (Ten) commandments printed on them, posted in every class room."[424] The law passed on March 3 as follows:

> "Section 1. It shall be the duty of the School Board, Board of Trustees, or Board of Education of every school district, and the President of each and every institution of higher education in the state, which is supported by appropriations or by tax levies in this state, to display a placard containing the Ten Commandments of the Christian religion in a conspicuous place in every school room, class room or other place in said school where classes convene for instruction.
>
> Section 2. The Department of Public Instruction shall have authority to print such placards and shall be permitted to charge for them such an amount as will cover the cost of printing and distribution."[425]

Superintendent Palmer "arranged with the Art Department at the State Agricultural College in an effort to get an artistically designed placard ... which would attract the eyes of the children."[426] A copy of the original placard in her scrapbook shows a beautifully lettered placard, which includes John 3:13, "That ye love one another as I have loved you," as well as the Ten Commandments.[427] Superintendent Palmer had the blue and orange lettered copies ready for schools by September 2, 1927. Although there were efforts to repeal, the law stayed in place until 1999.[428]

A Program for Better Rural Schools

Superintendent Bertha Palmer knew the problems facing one-room schools. She attended a one-room school as a child and she taught at several one-room schools right after high school. While assistant state superintendent from 1919 to 1924, she visited rural schools on a regular basis. In 1927, working with the county superintendents, Superintendent Palmer set three goals to improve the teaching in one-room schools, and she worked on these goals for the six years that she was state Superintendent. In 1930, Superintendent Palmer wrote about the progress made in the program for improving classroom teaching in rural schools.

> "While we have always had rural schools, the fact that there are teacher problems peculiar to rural schools is only now being recognized. The farmer pays his share for the support of the higher institutions of learning in his state including those devoted to training teachers. That the country does

not get its proportionate return for this support is apparent, for in every state the unprepared gravitate to rural teacher positions. In rural schools employing teachers with some normal training, it is found that the work she has taken has not fitted her for the one-teacher situation.

North Dakota holds second place in rurality. Sixty-one percent of its people live on farms, 56% of its boys and girls attend schools in the open country most of them in one-teacher schools, 58% of all its teachers teach in country schools, and 67% of these have less than one year of training above high school graduation.

In January 1927, the Department of Public Instruction entered upon a definite program for improving class room teaching which has been advanced and developed under the following projects:

1. A NEW COURSE OF STUDY FOR THE ELEMENTARY SCHOOLS: A volume of 400 pages accompanied by handbooks for literature, picture study, physical education, and information about North Dakota has been prepared and is now in use. The main volume contains a suggested Daily Program for the one-teacher school indicating the grouping of classes for certain recitations, and the alternation by years of certain subjects. By giving special consideration to these problems, it makes available to the children in rural schools the same benefits from a scientific Course of Study as are enjoyed by children in large city systems. The North Dakota course is listed by the Federal Office of Education as one of the five best courses for elementary schools.
2. IMPROVEMENT OF RURAL TEACHERS IN SERVICE: Our minimum requirement for certification is twelve weeks of Normal Training after high school graduation. Teachers with so little training need much professional help. Therefore, in September, October and November a corps of Demonstration Teachers is employed to help solve problems where the problems are encountered. For one week, group meetings of the teachers are held in each county. A definite program of classes, with the regular pupils of the school, is taught by the Demonstration Teacher during the forenoon, the afternoon is devoted to conference [with the teachers about methods.]… .
3. SPECIAL TRAINING FOR TEACHERS IN RURAL SCHOOLS: In 1927 only one of our five institutions for training elementary teachers was offering courses for teaching in rural schools. The need has been placed before the presidents of these Institutions each spring and courses

in rural methods and management ... are now included in the regular course of those institutions ... .

4. PROFESSIONAL TRAINING FOR RURAL SCHOOLS: ... All schools in North Dakota have children from the country. The children profit when the teacher understands conditions which surround them. In the one-teacher school there are at least one hundred duties, activities, and relationships which are not met by the grade teacher who works with superintendent, principal, other teachers, supervisors and janitors. The State Board of Administration has this spring (1930) authorized all teacher training institutions to offer a one year course to include the subjects necessary for the one-teacher school. This course will be accepted with full credit as the first year of the two year standard course. ...[429]

Superintendent Palmer and her staff worked tirelessly on these goals. In 1927, she was proud of saying regarding the new *Course of Study*, "sixty persons accepted invitations to work without salary on thirteen course of study committees. In ten months from the time of the first committee meeting the Course of Study was written, printed, and in use in the schools ... . Our course is furnished <u>without cost</u> to every school."

Palmer went to the Legislature in 1929 for money for two state supervisors to follow up the work of the demonstration teachers at the fall conferences. The supervisors would communicate with the one-room teachers about special problems they encountered with students and about new methods for teaching lessons. The Legislature provided funds to hire the two state supervisors, who started working with teachers that fall.[430]

Also in 1929, Superintendent Palmer decided it was time to have an outside expert come to the state to review the "Training of Teachers in North Dakota." Knowing that this study related to courses of study at all of the teaching schools in the state, as well as to the work of her department, she convinced the Board of Administration to authorize the study of "certain aspects of the program of teacher training as supported by the State of North Dakota."[431]

The complete report by W.E. Peik of Minnesota was filled with fascinating and jarring facts about the teachers in one-room schools:

"North Dakota is second among the states in the per cent of its population which lives in the open country and in towns of less than 2500. Eighty-seven and four-tenths per cent of its people, approximately seven-eighths of them, are rural in life interests, according to the definition of rural population which is employed by Federal departments. **This signifies that the teacher training program ... must be one which fits the open country and the smaller town.**

> North Dakota has made a substantial effort to support its educational system."
>
> A chart showed that North Dakota schools employed 4,361 one-room rural teachers (51.1 percent of all), 2,603 grade teachers in schools employing more than one teacher (30.5 percent of all) and 1,570 full-time or part-time teachers of high school subjects (18.4 percent of all).
>
> **"A Vital Problem.** It is tragic that almost two of three North Dakota rural schools have a new teacher each year, when the job is so difficult because it covers all grades, when supervision has to be inadequate at best, and when the teacher herself is so young.
>
> **Rural Teachers.** As long as the state allows this entirely inadequate certification of young girls with only twelve weeks of training, just so long will many schools hire them at low salaries and keep down the efficiency of rural schools. The supply of the one, two, and four year elementary people should be increased and the oversupply of the "twelve-week" teacher reduced quickly for the best interests of education, particularly rural education in the state.
>
> **The Training Status of Teachers Now in Positions:** Comparable with only 60 town teachers who have less than one year of professional training there are 3277 rural teachers, or two-thirds of them, who have no more professional training than that, and there are 78 who have not completed a high school.
>
> While two-thirds of North Dakota's rural teachers have less than one year of professional training, Kansas has only 5%, Minnesota only 3.5%, Montana 40%."[432]

Superintendent Palmer and the Board of Administration used these statistics to convince the 1931 Legislature to upgrade requirements for teacher certificates. Although the state continued to allow applicants to take examinations to qualify for elementary certificates, a "first grade" elementary certificate now required either 18 months experience and an examination or a high school diploma and a one-year normal course. Applicants had to be at least 18 years of age. Also, now "professional" certificates required a diploma from a two-year normal school or four-year teachers college.[433]

In 1932, one year after the law had taken effect, Palmer commented, "Teaching in rural schools has taken on professional dignity and respect and the children are receiving the benefit."[434]

Experimenting With Radio as an Educational Medium

Miss Palmer took to radio like a duck to water. As a person who enjoyed writing and public speaking, she was soon in demand to give 15-minute talks over the air on various topics. North Dakotans also loved the radio. By 1930, 40 percent of North Dakota farm families owned receiving sets, a percentage nearly double that of the farm families in the nation.[435]

Miss Palmer fortunately kept a file with many of the scripts of her different broadcasts from 1927 to 1932.[436] Many of these radio talks had nothing to do with her work as Superintendent of Public Instruction, but even today people in politics often go onto the radio and talk about topics that do not relate to their office. Some of the topics she discussed included "Dakota Missionaries," KFYR, May 1927; "I Breathed a Song into the Air," KFJM, April 1928; "Word Pictures of Beauty Spots," KFYR, December-March 1929-30; "Through the Poet's Eye," KFYR, January-April 1931.

However, in January 1930, officials in Washington, D.C., appointed an *Advisory Committee on Education by Radio*. In early February, a representative of the committee

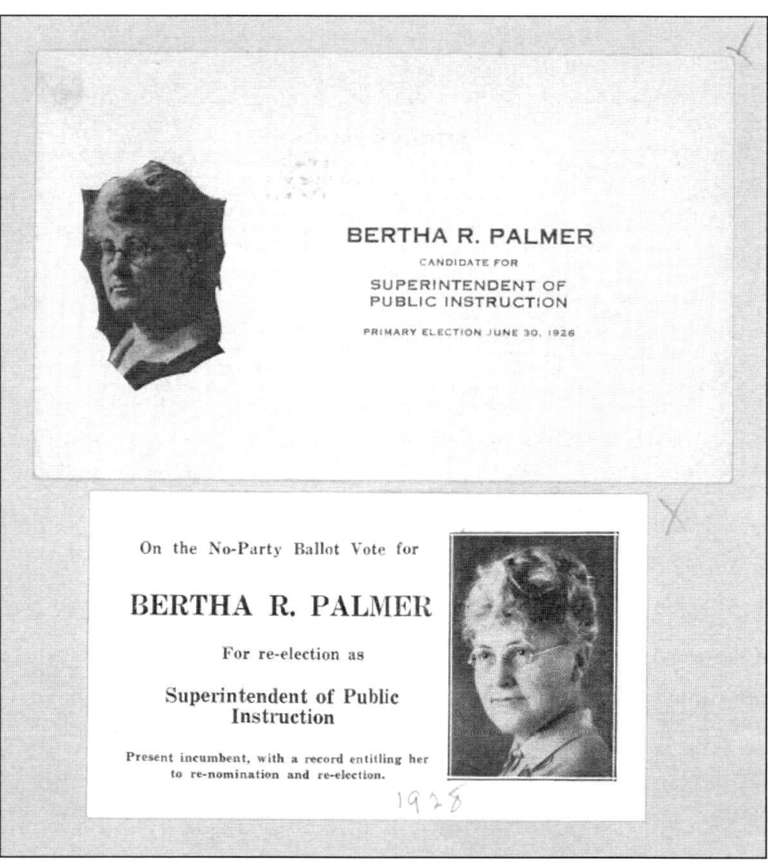

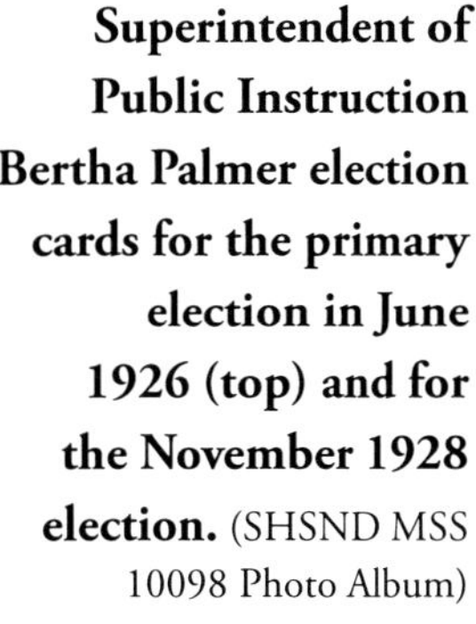
Superintendent of Public Instruction Bertha Palmer election cards for the primary election in June 1926 (top) and for the November 1928 election. (SHSND MSS 10098 Photo Album)

visited Bismarck. On February 12, 1930, Superintendent Palmer gave a radio address over KFYR about some new initiatives:

> "Last evening, between the hours of 5:00 and 8:00, you heard from the radio stations in North Dakota[437] the first program, I believe, in the state ever put on the air for the boys and girls in the grades, and particularly for those in the rural schools. We chose Lincoln's Address at Gettysburg, which they study, but seldom do they hear it suitably read, and the Battle Hymn of the Republic, which they sing, but with little understanding … . On Friday evening, February 21 a similar program will be given in honor of George Washington's Birthday. …
>
> Radio is coming into the school room, but this will never mean that when the loud speaker comes in, the teacher goes out. It means that the teacher can have for a few minutes a day the help of a specialist in some subject … .
>
> We know in a general way that few schools in North Dakota have receiving sets, and we do not want school boards to buy radios before worth while programs are available … . It is estimated that there are 75,000 receiving sets in the state, most of which are in country homes. This would make it possible to reach thousands of pupils and teachers on a Saturday hour; say at 12:30 or at 1:00 immediately after the noon meal. The parents would be able to 'visit' for this period without taking the time to go to the school house … .
>
> … First, that our greatest need as a nation of self governed citizens is more and better education; second, that radio is the greatest modern invention in the science of communication; third, that if radio and education can be geared into effective partnership on a sound basis and with skilled guidance, the good that can come out of that partnership may be beyond all reckoning … ."[438]

Superintendent Palmer pursued her idea of Saturday family radio programs, and WDAY, now broadcasting with a 1,000-watt transmitter, offered 30 minutes a day for an educational program for elementary schools. By May, she had four weekly 30-minute Saturday programs planned; 10 minutes she would do herself sharing poetry, the Fargo librarian would provide a 10-minute talk on books, and the Extension Service would provide a 10-minute segment on home economics for boys and girls.

She called these broadcasts "The North Dakota Saturday School of the Air." They were a great success, but unfortunately, as Miss Palmer wrote later, "the responsibility was too great to be met with our present limit of personnel and travel funds,"[439] and the programs could not be continued.

Miss Palmer personally travelled to Fargo each Saturday to read her part of the script. One week, the roads were muddy after spring rains, and she was 300 miles away from Fargo. She had to "take an airplane in order to catch the train to keep the appointment with Saturday School of the Air … . The aviator took keen interest in seeing that we made that train. This trip gave the program some valuable newspaper publicity."[440] For Superintendent Palmer, this adventure was all in a day's work!

Fire Destroys the North Dakota Capitol Building – December 28, 1930

In November 1930, Miss Palmer won the election for state Superintendent against her opponent, Arthur E. Thompson. When the votes were tallied, Palmer had 106,501 votes and Thompson had 81,829. After the election, she must have relaxed a little and pondered how to convince the 1931 Legislature to end certification of teachers with only 12 weeks of training. Then suddenly, everything changed.

On Sunday morning, December 28, 1930, the Capitol building went up in flames. The whole building was on fire in a short time, and within hours, the Capitol was demolished. "Smoke and flame could be seen in distant parts of the city and brought thousands of persons in hundreds of cars to the scene."[441] Only the brick walls were left standing. No one was injured because the fire was on a Sunday.

Although people were shocked by the fire, by the next day, Governor George Shafer had put plans in place for state government to keep operating. The *Fargo Forum* noted on Monday, December 29, that the Department of Public Instruction will be "in offices on the top floor of the Quain and Ramstad Clinic building, offered free for use during the emergency."[442]

Although Superintendent Palmer had office space, she lost virtually all of her department records. The fire ravaged the record vaults in her office and "only one vault in her office seemed in good condition."[443] Also, she had no equipment for her employees. Months later, she would still be writing to people to try to recover information that had been lost in the fire.[444]

Miss Palmer started her third two-year term as Superintendent of Public Instruction in January 1931, and the Legislature met as scheduled in the new World War Memorial Building in Bismarck. Superintendent Palmer's temporary offices were only two short blocks away from the Memorial Building. The new Capitol building would not be ready for use until 1935.

1932 – Campaign, Drought and Despair

Agnes Geelan, in her book *The Dakota Maverick,* described the issues that faced North Dakota candidates for office in the 1932 election:

> "The issues were everywhere. Deserted farms. Unpainted and deteriorating farm buildings of the depression times. Emaciated cattle trying to find a few spears of grass in drought burned pastures. Dust and tumbleweeds in the ditches and along fence rows. Patches of white alkali where there had once been sloughs. And depressed and worried people. The farmers of North Dakota were experiencing the most prolonged and most cruel depression in the history of the state. The 1930 census showed North Dakota's farm population to be 83.4 percent of the total population, leaving only 16.6 percent urban." [445]

The 1920s had been a series of economic "ups and downs" for North Dakota. Elwyn Robinson's *History of North Dakota* gives a good description of conditions in the state in 1932. Although low prices for commodities and falling land values hurt farmers, by 1930, "North Dakotans owned 183,000 automobiles, one for every 3.7 persons, and 87 per cent of the farmers were car owners. In the United States as a whole, there was only one automobile for every 5.3 persons."[446] Banks started failing in North Dakota in 1923, when 99 banks closed their doors, and "dozens more went under each year until 573 of the 898 banks in business in 1920 had closed by 1933."[447] North Dakotans lost $50 million dollars in deposits through these bank failures, and they also lost confidence in banks.[448]

Some crop years in the 1920s were good, but:

> "June, 1929, was one of the driest Junes on record; in 1930 hot winds cut down the crops; spring rains were light in 1931, and in July searing heat withered the vegetation. By fall more than half the farmers in the hardest hit northwestern counties needed relief. The next year 1932 had normal moisture."[449] As if bad crops conditions were not enough, crops prices were at record low levels. "At the bottom in 1932, North Dakota farmers sold wheat for 36 cents a bushel, oats for 9 cents, barley for 14 cents, potatoes for 23 cents … and beef cattle for $3.30 per hundredweight."[450]

It had to be a real challenge for Palmer to be Superintendent of Public Instruction during these hard years. She cared for rural schools and the children who attended them, and she saw the unpainted farms and deteriorating farm buildings caused by the drought and low prices for farm commodities. Ironically, her book "Beauty Spots of North Dakota" was published in 1928, just before drought and depression scoured the state.

Little federal assistance was available yet, and so people just had to work together to take care of each other. Money was very tight in state and local government units, and cuts had to be made in services and salaries. Schools were impacted.

In November 1931, the state Department of Public Instruction, the state Health Department and the Extension Division of the North Dakota Agricultural College promoted a program called "Hot Lunch Made Easy." The program was prompted by a study by a county school nurse in North Dakota who had found that farm children weighed less for their age and height than those living in towns. Suggestions to make hot lunch easy at rural schools included these items which would be *brought from home*:

- Pint Jar Lunch: soup, macaroni, creamed vegetables, vegetables in gravy, etc. brought from home in pint jars and heated at school;
- Baked Potato, carrot, squash, etc. cooked at school served with butter and salt;
- Boiled oatmeal, rice, whole wheat or cereal served with butter and brown sugar or honey (cooked at school at lunch time)

The guidelines went on to say that the teacher and PTA may arrange for different families to supply fresh food for the lunches each day.[451]

In February 1932, 44 counties reported reductions in teacher salaries from 2 to 30 percent. Records from 44 of 53 counties showed that 22 schools had closed during the 1931-32 school year. Superintendent Palmer noted that all of the children impacted by the closed schools are being transported to other schools. She also stated, "County and school officials have employed good business methods to bring about economy without denying children an education."[452]

In the middle of all this, Superintendent Palmer was researching and writing a history of the state Department of Public Instruction. Having lost all pictures and records of the former superintendents in the fire, she took on the project of finding new pictures and writing histories of each superintendent from 1860 to 1932. This information was published in the fall of 1932 as a small booklet and was also included in her *1932 Biennial Report of the Department of Public Instruction.*[453]

With all of these issues facing the state, 1932 was not a good year to run for re-election. Miss Palmer was endorsed in 1932 by the IVA. In June, before the primary, Mrs. Alfred Zuger, who was still her campaign chair, sent out a letter to supporters which included the following information about Palmer:

> "The voters are entitled to know <u>her</u> record as superintendent of public instruction:
>
> <u>She</u> has revised the Course of Study for elementary grades with special consideration for conditions in one-teacher schools.
>
> <u>She</u> has organized demonstration conferences for teachers in service, to

> improve methods in teaching, and the arrangement and management of small schoolrooms.
>
> She has secured courses in rural education in all normal departments with observation and teaching in rural schools.
>
> She has outlined practical plans for hot lunches with no expense for supplies and special equipment.
>
> She has organized units of play equipment for physical education with little or no expense for materials.
>
> She has revised and rewritten the Course of Study for high schools.
>
> She has arranged a combined system of modern tests and examinations for eighth grade and high school, satisfying to teachers and pupils."[454]

Miss Palmer's opponent in the election, after the June primary, was Nonpartisan League (NPL) candidate Arthur Thompson, whom she had beaten in the 1930 election. However, most public attention was on the top of the ticket, where Franklin D. Roosevelt was running for president against Herbert Hoover. In North Dakota politics, NPL-endorsed candidate William (Bill) Langer was running on the Republican ticket for governor, having beaten incumbent Governor Shafer in the June primary.

Superintendent Palmer worked hard in 1932 to spread the word of her accomplishments. Just before Election Day, the Women's State Headquarters of the IVA sent out a letter in her behalf, which asked women "to get in touch with every thinking woman in your district and ask her to actively support Miss Palmer." It also noted that "Miss Palmer will broadcast from the Bismarck Station KFYR on Friday, November 4th at 8 P.M. I hope you will be listening in and ask others to listen also." The letter went to 2,500 people at 3 cents each.[455]

Superintendent Palmer gave her radio address on November 4 and started it by saying, "It is the season for political addresses, but this is not a political talk. The office of Superintendent of Public Instruction for which office I am a candidate is not and never should be in politics. You will find my name, Bertha R. Palmer, on the *No-Party ballot* with the Judges, *NOT* on the guide cards."[456]

On Election Day, Palmer lost the election: Bertha Palmer 112,314 votes; Arthur Thompson 132,524 votes.[457] Superintendent Palmer was swept out of office, in a year that did not favor incumbents, by a major NPL victory. NPL candidates won both U.S. House seats, all state offices and control of the Legislature – the NPL's most successful year since 1919.[458]

Although the state and its people were facing very serious personal, economic and environmental challenges in 1932, things progressively got worse for the people of the state during the terrible '30s.

It would be 80 years until another woman was elected Superintendent of Public Instruction in North Dakota.

Afterthoughts

In mid-December 1932, Miss Palmer announced that after living in the state for 52 years, she would be leaving the state to take a job in Boston on the editorial staff of the *Scientific Temperance Journal.*[459]

At a luncheon in honor of her 33 years of service to education in the state, she received a "handsome leather travelling case."[460] She needed that suitcase. Palmer started working for the Women's Christian Temperance Union (WCTU) in 1933. She travelled all over the country giving speeches for the WTCU during her 12 years with the organization. Upon her retirement in 1944, she worked as head of Scientific Research for the WCTU and made her home in Wheaton, Illinois. She lived there until her death on December 15, 1959, at the age of 79.[461]

Miss Palmer was gracious in defeat. In December 1932, she wrote a letter to George McFarland, who she had worked with on Superintendent Nielson's staff, and who now was serving as President of the State Teacher's College in Minot.

> "... Your words of praise and expressions of gratitude are balm to the bruises dealt by the public. When I have turned to you for help, your responses have been kind and generous and I have been cheered and encouraged ... .
>
> The past six years have been wonderfully rich in opportunities for public and personal service, and have afforded me not only personal growth and development but the inestimable values which come from contacts with fine personalities. These things become personal possessions and are eternal; they are not at the disposal of the voters. I am humble that I have been privileged to enjoy them ... ."[462]

FIFTEEN

An Honest and Efficient Public Servant

Elberta (Berta) E. Baker

State Treasurer 1929-32
State Auditor 1933-56

By
Susan Wefald

"In all official matters coming before me, I have endeavored to make such decisions as in my best judgment are right, without fear or favor or political consideration."[463]

State Auditor Berta Baker, 1942

Berta Baker nee Colcord*

1876-1964

North Dakota State Treasurer 1929-32 and
North Dakota State Auditor 1933-56

State Auditor Berta Baker - 1940
(SHSND 00751)

First Woman in North Dakota to Serve as State Treasurer and State Auditor
Longest Serving Woman State Official in North Dakota
First Woman to Hold Two Elected Statewide Offices in North Dakota

Personal Information
Born 1876 and raised in Sterling, Illinois. Married to Bert (deceased), four children. In "spare time," enjoyed spending time with her grandchildren.

Party Affiliation
Nonpartisan League (NPL) Republican

Education
Public schools near Sterling, Illinois

Professional Experience before taking office
Teacher in Chadwick and Coleta, Illinois, 1890-95; Clerk and Head of Farm Loan Department, state Treasurer's office, 1925-28.

Memberships Include
As State Auditor: National Association of State Auditors Treasurers and Comptrollers, vice president, secretary and treasurer.

Other: Member of Business and Professional Woman's Club, Zonta International, the Eastern Star, McCabe Methodist Church.

*Bio contains information through 1956

Berta Baker's life changed completely the Saturday afternoon her husband, Bert, died in a car accident. Mrs. Baker was 48 years old. For 17 years, she had been a North Dakota farm wife, raising their four children, and serving several years as treasurer of the Prescott School District near Glenburn, about 20 miles northeast of Minot. Now three of the children were grown; Don, her oldest, age 27, lived in Mandan; Mildred, 25, and Helen, 19, both taught school near Glenburn. Robert was 8. [464]

On May 3, 1924, her husband, Bert, age 57, was campaigning for State Agriculture and Labor Commissioner as an endorsed Nonpartisan League (NPL) Republican. The important June primary election was less than two months away.

Arthur G. Sorlie, NPL candidate for governor, and Bert Baker were travelling together. They attended a political meeting on Saturday afternoon in Steele and then started their 70-mile drive to Carrington, where they expected to attend another meeting that evening. They left Steele at about 4 p.m., with Roy Frazier, a member of the NPL state executive committee, driving the car. The *Fargo Forum* reported these details of the accident:

> "It is thought that the accident probably happened about 4:45 pm. Mr. Frazier was known as a driver who liked to get over the roads at a good gait, and the party was trying to make Carrington for a night political meeting … . The car turned over at least twice, throwing all occupants clear of it, but perhaps crushing them as it rolled over … . Two young men reached the scene of accident very few minutes after it occurred, although they did not see it. Mr. Baker was alive, but dying. When they returned from a farmhouse, from which they telephoned for help, he was dead." [465]

Sorlie and Frazier both suffered fractures of the skull and other injuries and were brought the next day, in serious condition, by train to Bismarck, where they were hospitalized at the Bismarck Evangelical Hospital. The body of Bert Baker was taken by train from Steele to Minot, by way of Fargo, for burial.[466]

In 1924, there was no widow's Social Security to help pay the bills. Without her husband, the work of the farm was an arduous task. Within a few months of the accident, Mrs. Baker knew she needed to find a good-paying job. Fortunately, she had NPL friends in Bismarck.

Mrs. Baker's First 50 Years

Berta, born November 27, 1876,[467] grew up near Sterling, Illinois, the daughter of Mr. and Mrs. William H. Colcord. She was one of 10 children, and like many young women of that time, she started teaching school when she was 14, after completing her own education in the public schools. She had already been teaching school for five years in Chadwick and Coleta, Illinois, when she met Bert Baker, the handsome new principal of her school in Coleta. She and Bert were married in Coleta on June 27, 1895, when she was 18½ years old. Marriage ended her teaching career. While teaching, she took a correspondence course in education, but beyond that course, Mrs. Baker had no formal higher education.[468]

The next few years were eventful ones for the young couple. Mr. Baker served as Superintendent of Schools for five years at Chadwick, Illinois, and the young family then moved to Warren, Illinois, where he also served as Superintendent of Schools. Meanwhile Mr. and Mrs. Baker's first child, Don, was born in June 1896 and Mildred was born in 1898. By the time Mrs. Baker was 22, she had two children and was a busy homemaker.[469] Baby Helen was born in 1905.

Around the time Helen was born, Bert and Berta started talking about moving to North Dakota. Berta's two brothers, Clayton and Glenn, had already moved to a farm near Glenburn, North Dakota. A *Berta E. Baker 1928 campaign flier* described what happened next.

> "In 1906, Bert Baker heard the call to the open prairies of the northwest and 'took up' a homestead in what is now Renville county. The following year he brought his little wife and family out to North Dakota to live on the claim."[470]

It was not easy for Mr. Baker to make the transition from a career in education to a career in farming. Mrs. Baker, in addition to taking care of the children and home, had new challenges as well. In 1955, she wrote these recollections of their first Christmas on the farm:

> "We had come to a new home in a new state in the year 1907, when our little family consisted of three small children. We had been here nearly nine months and now we were to spend our first Christmas on the prairies.
>
> On an adjoining farm, my brother C.E. Colcord, with his wife and two small daughters, had homesteaded. Weeks before the holiday, we were determined that the children should have a Christmas tree. Now, the snow was piled in deep drifts around the farmstead, framing it in hard-packed corridors that covered the fields and trails. The plans made earlier had at last materialized.
>
> A branch of a box elder tree from our small grove, planted by the former owner, was taken for a Christmas tree. We did not dare to take the whole tree, and anyway, there was room only for a branch in the shack. There it stood, bedecked with strands of popcorn and cranberries in fes-

toons covering the naked branches. A star, formed of in foil from a package of tea, shone from the tree top. A few candles on the tree shed a soft glow over the room and completed the decorations.

Suddenly we heard chimes at the door and with a great fanfare of "Ho-Ho" and "Merry Christmas" in came Santa Claus, straight from the North Pole. My brother was a typical Santa Claus with a disguise that made the children's eyes open wide. They were especially interested in the bag of gifts Santa was carrying.

We had some nice little stores in our small town and we were able to buy materials and our gifts were planned and had been fashioned with love, and each of us had been remembered. That far away Christmas is long past, but etched in my memory. Christmas time has always meant much to our family.

Many holiday seasons have come and gone since our first Christmas in North Dakota. Our state grew rather rapidly from a pioneer state to a developed one. In a few years we were able to purchase the real Christmas trees, but I am sure that we did not enjoy them any more than our little box elder branch."[471]

In 1916, when Mrs. Baker was 40, baby Robert joined the family. However, soon the Baker home was filled with lots of "political" talk as well as baby talk. Bert was very involved in NPL politics and, in 1920, was elected to the state Senate as an NPL Republican from Renville County.

North Dakota politics was lively in 1921. The Independent Voters Association (IVA), the opponents of the NPL Party, circulated petitions to recall all three NPL members of the Industrial Commission: Governor Lynn Frazier, Attorney General William Lemke, and Commissioner of Agriculture and Labor John Hagan. The petitions also nominated three men to take their positions: Ragnavold Nestos for Governor, Sveinbjorn Johnson for Attorney General, and Joseph Kitchen for Commissioner of Agriculture and Labor. At the recall election, all three NPL officials were voted out of office, and the three new IVA officials took office in fall 1921.[472]

When state Senator Bert Baker was nominated by the NPL to run for Governor in 1922, he was running against Governor Nestos, who had just been elected in the recall election; thus a difficult race to win. Nevertheless, his family must have been excited when he received the nomination. His defeat in the Republican primary election in June stopped any thoughts of the Baker family moving to Bismarck to live in the Victorian Governor's home on the corner of Fourth Street and Avenue A in Bismarck. But that defeat did not end Bert's political ambitions. In 1924, he accepted the NPL nomination for Commissioner of Agriculture and Labor and died that May in the tragic car accident near Steele.

Berta Baker, a 48-year-old widow with an 8-year-old son, suddenly needed to change her life. She had not worked outside of the home since she was 19 years old, but she had acquired many skills and learned a great deal while married to Bert for 29 years. She also had contacts in Bismarck. Arthur Sorlie, who had fractured his skull in the same accident that killed Bert Baker, was elected Governor in November 1924. The new State Treasurer, A.E. Fisher, was a member of the NPL.

With these NPL contacts and others, in 1925, she landed a job as clerk and eventually as head of the Farm Loan Department in the State Treasurer's office.[473] Mrs. Baker moved to Bismarck with her son Robert and started working at the state Capitol. Throughout her career in state government, she continued to own and operate the farm at Glenburn and listed Glenburn as her legal residence.

Mrs. Baker Runs for State Office

In 1928, a North Dakota State Treasurer could only be State Treasurer for four years, and then a new person had to be elected to the position. This provision helped to ensure that a new person looked at the state's books every four years and helped to prevent fraud.

It is difficult to know when Mrs. Berta Baker was first approached about running for state Treasurer. From comments she made later on, it sounds as if she was approached when she was at the state NPL convention in February 1928. This certainly may have been the case because the *Bismarck Tribune* reported on February 7, "Alfred S. Dale, state manager for the NPL and deputy state treasurer was being mentioned as the leading candidate for that nomination. Although some delegates were openly opposed to Dale, no other name was being mentioned as a rival for the convention's favor."[474]

Things changed dramatically on February 9, when the state Treasurer endorsement was before the delegates.

> "What looked like a fight turned into a rout when the state treasureship was considered. The first nominee was Alfred S. Dale, present deputy state treasurer.
>
> "Dale Withdraws
>
> "The next nominee was Mrs. Bert F. Baker, a clerk in the treasurer's office and widow of Bert F. Baker, one-time Nonpartisan leader. Seconding speeches for Mrs. Baker became so numerous that Dale asked permission to withdraw and the nomination was unanimous. As a clerk in the treasurer's office Mrs. Baker has held a responsible position, has handled her

work well and is fully capable of performing the duties of state treasurer, Dale said. Cheers greeted his withdrawal and Mrs. Baker's nomination was one of the most spontaneous moves of the entire convention."[475]

In a 1956 Minot Daily News interview, Baker recalled what happened at the 1928 convention:

> "They told me I was going to be endorsed for the office, and I said I didn't want to be … . They told me to quit worrying – I was going to be endorsed, and that was it."[476]

Berta Baker started campaigning. She needed to find her own style. Soon she was known as a "woman of few words while on the platform where she appeared with other candidates from her party. But she had a vast acquaintanceship among the state's voters and was at her best in quiet conversations with her constituents."[477]

An NPL campaign flier from the 1928 campaign elicited support for Mrs. Baker before the June primary. After Mr. Baker died,

> "He left a little woman back on the farm, with a brood of children to be taken care of. Like all farmers, he also had a mortgage on the farm. But the little woman back on the farm rose to the occasion. She has continued the fight. She ob-

BERTA E. BAKER

Republican Candidate for Re-Election to the Office of

State Auditor

BERTA E. BAKER

Berta E. Baker has been a resident of North Dakota for thirty-three years, of which eighteen years were spent on the farm which she still owns and operates.

She has endeavored as a public official to give to the state honest and efficient service. She has stood squarely and consistently for economy in state government and if re-elected will continue to perform the duties of the office for the best interests of the citizens and taxpayers of North Dakota.

—32—

Campaign card from one of State Auditor Berta Baker's many elections.

(*Bismarck Tribune* Berta Baker file)

tained a position as farm loan clerk in the treasurer's office. She has helped her girls continue their education. She has fought bravely on. She has used part of her salary to keep the farm going. Today she is bravely working to keep that farm and to give all her children an education. That woman has been endorsed by your organization for the high office of state treasurer – A FARMER'S WIFE IN OFFICE. It is up to every live and red-blooded Leaguer to see that she is nominated in June. She has done her part. Now do your's, and see that she wins in the June election."[478]

Mrs. Baker won the June primary and went on to win the election for state Treasurer in November 1928. She was 52 years old.

1928 was the first year that the North Dakota voters elected two women to statewide office: state Treasurer Berta Baker and state Superintendent of Public Instruction Bertha Palmer. Both would be re-elected in 1930.

Description of Official Duties as State Treasurer

Two-year term (limited to four years of service). Acts as custodian of all state funds and securities belonging to the state of North Dakota; pays on demand and presentment all warrants properly drawn on the various state funds or trusts in his custody; approves and takes charge of all bonds and securities deposited by insurance, title and trust companies as required under the laws of this state; collects cigarette and snuff tax.

Member: Equalization Board, Teachers' Insurance and Retirement Fund; Board of Canvassers - General Election; Auditing Board.[479]

Berta Baker on the Job as State Treasurer

On Saturday, January 5, 1929, The *Fargo Forum* reported new Governor George Shafer was ill with influenza but was on the mend and hoped to be able to deliver his State of the State message the next week. Treasurer Baker was also in the news that day, announcing that she would appoint C.A. Fisher, the former state Treasurer, to be her chief deputy. Mr. Fisher stayed with Berta, as her deputy, for the four years she served as state Treasurer.[480]

On Monday, January 7, the new Treasurer, on her first day in office, filed her oath of office. On Wednesday at 2:30 p.m., when the Governor was feeling better, Berta and the other state officials were sworn in before a joint session of the Legislature. This was the last swearing-in ceremony in the "old" state Capitol building, which was destroyed by fire in December 1930.

It is interesting to note that both the state Treasurer and the state Auditor filed almost exactly the same reports on state finances during the years that Baker was Treasurer and then Auditor. However, the reports often contain different numbers for the same time periods. For example, when Mrs. Baker was Treasurer in 1932, her office showed the balance in the general fund on June 30, 1932, just one fund of hundreds, as $688,692.[481] The State auditor showed the general fund balance on July 1, 1932, as $510,443.90.[482] It must have been tricky for the state Legislature to know how much was available to spend!

Prior to computers, the state probably thought it wise to have two state offices keeping track of state assets and expenses.

On March 31, 1930, Mrs. Baker's oldest daughter died in childbirth. She died "in a Minot hospital at 5:10 pm ... six hours after she gave birth to a son. Her mother and other near relatives were at her bedside when the end came."[483] Mildred Ruby Baker Redington was 32 years old. Her marriage the previous summer on June 27 (the anniversary of her parents' wedding) must have been a very happy time for the family.[484] Her infant son was reported in good health after her death.

Treasurer Baker must have had a heavy heart as she made plans in 1930 for another two-year term in office as state Treasurer. Her son Robert was now 14 years old and a student in high school. She won the election that fall. In future election years, the NPL would state, "In 1930, voters of North Dakota accorded her the largest majority of any candidate in either of two parties."[485]

Running for State Auditor and the 1933 Inauguration

In November 1932, Mrs. Baker was on the NPL Republican ticket running for state Auditor. In the June primary election, she had beaten John Steen, who had been state Treasurer from 1921 to 1924 and then state Auditor from 1925 to 1932, a 12-year incumbent. William Langer, candidate for Governor, was at the top of the ticket. One resolution adopted at the 1932 NPL convention was:

> "Candidates indorsed by the convention 'pledge themselves not to hire married women whose husbands are able to work, or who are working, but to hire women for office work who are dependent upon themselves for a livelihood.'"[486]

Now Mrs. Baker was running against Democrat Grace Hoopes. On election night, the NPL Republicans won every office in state government. North Dakota voters, several years into the Depression, sought change and new ways to address the issues of unemployment, low farm prices and general unrest. It was the biggest win for the NPL since 1919.

State Auditor Berta Baker took her oath of office, with other state officials, on January 3, 1933. The afternoon ceremony was held in the Bismarck City Auditorium (now the Belle Mehus Auditorium) since the new Capitol building was still under construction.[487]

Although the state was in a desperate situation economically, socially and environmentally, crowds of NPL supporters poured into Bismarck on January 3, 1933, to celebrate the Langer win and the NPL win at the inaugural celebration. The World War Memorial Building in downtown Bismarck was the site of the celebration. As the *Bismarck Tribune* reported the next day:

> "It was demonstrated that the capacity of the World War Memorial Building was inadequate for a state occasion Wednesday night ... as the largest crowd which has assembled in the building to date thronged the halls, galleries and bleachers and spread over almost the entire floor space ... . Nearly every section of the state was represented ... . What made the event out of the ordinary was the enthusiasm and good humor of the train-loads of visitors from New Rockford and intermediate points and from Dickinson and western North Dakota. Auto caravans from the central and eastern part of the state brought hundreds here during the afternoon. It was a gala evening, with everyone finding opportunity to extend felicitations to incoming state officials ... ."[488]

State Auditor Berta Baker must have had a wonderful time, and she may have visited with the new Speaker of the House, Minnie D. Craig. Governor Langer was in the hospital and missed all of the festivities.

Lorena Hickok Reports on the Situation in North Dakota, October 30, 1933

Lorena Hickok travelled throughout North Dakota in late October 1933 as chief investigator for Harry Hopkins, the director of the Federal Emergency Relief Administration.[489] Franklin Roosevelt had been sworn in as president that spring, and now seven months later, federal relief dollars were starting to flow into North Dakota. North Dakotans needed every bit of help available. "In 1933, the low year, the per capita personal income in the United States was $375, but in North Dakota it was only $145."[490] Professor Elwyn Robinson, in *History of North Dakota*, discussed the financial picture in the state during 1933:

> "By the end of 1932 the counties and private charity could no longer carry the relief burden. In January, 1933, Governor Langer appointed a

> state emergency relief committee with Supreme Court Judge A.M. Christianson as chairman. The 1933 legislature appropriated no money for relief, but Christianson's committee, working feverishly in the crisis, borrowed $492,000 from the Reconstruction Finance Corporation and organized county relief committees to distribute the funds. On June 1, 1933, the committee began to receive its money from the Federal Emergency Relief Administration (F.E.R.A.), headed by Harry L. Hopkins."[491]

Miss Hickok was visiting the state to see if the FERA funds were being fairly distributed. On October 30, 1933, she visited Morton County:

> "Farmers, these, 'hailed out' last summer, their crops destroyed by two hail storms that came within three weeks of each other in June and July, now applying for relief.
>
> Most of them a few years ago were considered well-to-do. They have land – lots of land. Most of them have 640 acres or so. You think of a farmer with 640 acres of land as being rich. These fellows are 'land poor.' A 640-acre farm at $10 an acre – which is about what land is worth hereabouts these days – means only $6,400 worth of land … their hens are not laying. Much of their livestock will die this winter. And their livestock and their land are in most cases mortgaged up to the very limit. They are all way behind on taxes, of course. Some of them five years!
>
> … For themselves and their families they need everything. Especially clothing … . The women and children are even worse off than the men. Where there has been any money at all, it has gone for shoes for the children and work clothes for the men. The women can stay inside and keep warm, and the children can stay home from school.
>
> In the county I visited this afternoon the Federal Relief Administration, through the North Dakota State Relief Committee, is doing a 100 percent job.[492] The county's financial resources are exhausted, and nobody will take their tax warrants. The job, as I wired you tonight, is shamefully inadequate.
>
> I don't know exactly what is wrong. I'm going to try to find out when I return to Bismarck Friday. But what is actually happening, I was told is this:
>
> In the country [county][493] there are now 1,000 families – a third of the population – on relief. Mostly farmers. To handle the job the County Commissioners are given $6,000 a month. That means $6 per family. And most of the families are huge – eight or ten children. The set-up in this

county is different from that in most counties in the state. The relief here is being handled by the County Commissioners. Bismarck apparently suspects them of using relief for political purposes. They are constantly after the commissioners, I was told, to cut down the load. Whether there's any politics in the show in that county I don't know. But this I do know – those people at that church applying for relief today certainly looked as though they needed relief." [494]

By spring 1934, the federal government was disbursing all federal relief funds in North Dakota and the state emergency relief committee no longer handled these funds. That change came quite suddenly. "On March 1, 1934, by long distance telephone, Harry Hopkins took control of federal relief in North Dakota away from the state emergency relief committee. Early in 1935 the legislature created the Public Welfare Board and passed a sales tax to provide money for its work. The relief program was then reorganized."[495] The following statistics tell the story of relief assistance:

"From February, 1933, to the end of December, 1935, relief in North Dakota cost over $36,000,000. The federal government furnished more than $32,000,000, the counties $3,500,000, and the state only $139,000 (all of it in December, 1935)."[496]

An August 1934 article in the weekly *Bismarck Capital*, which reviewed all federal expenditures in North Dakota since February 1, 1933, stated the federal relief dollars included money for:

"direct and work relief, livestock feed relief, civil works administration projects, transient relief, and the various services such as public nursing, visiting housekeepers, sewing service (CWS), emergency educational relief, educational rehabilitation, student aid, and community gardening. It does not include such relief activities as the surplus commodity distributions … (which included) 10,800 cotton blankets."[497]

The State of North Dakota's Own Financial Crisis

As state Treasurer and then as state Auditor, Berta Baker was an expert on the state's finances. In her reports as state Treasurer, she saw the total cash assets of the state fall from $13,497,903 on June 30, 1929, to $10,699,904 on June 30, 1932.[499] The state's cash assets did increase in the mid-1930s, but by 1939, the total cash assets of the state had dropped to $7,322,295[500] and the general fund held only $279,794.[501]

As the new state Auditor, she was the one to report on June 30, 1933, that the general fund, which paid expenses for state agencies, the Legislature and other legislative appropriations, was **overdrawn** by $59,545.[502] Just one year before, as Treasurer, she had reported the balance was $688,692.[503]

Description of Official Duties as State Auditor

Two-year term. Superintends fiscal affairs of the state; keeps segregated accounts of appropriations, funds, revenues, expenditures, disbursements, investments, etc.; directs and superintends collections of money due to the state, including gasoline tax; audits all claims of persons against the state and issues warrants upon the state Treasurer for the same; keeps account between state and state Treasurer and charges state Treasurer with balance in the treasury and all moneys received by him when he assumed office and credits him with all warrants paid by him.

Member: Auditing Board; Board of University and School Lands; State Board of Auditors; Tax Equalization; Budget Board; State Board of Canvassers, General Election; and Historical Society.[498]

The public, as well as the Legislature and Governor, knew that expenses needed to be cut. In the November 1932 election, when Berta Baker was elected state Auditor, the public passed a large number of initiated measures. In addition to repealing Prohibition, they passed several that addressed state expenses. These initiated measures reduced the fees paid to newspapers for legal notices; repealed the requirement to publish public notice of sale of real estate for delinquent taxes; reduced the salaries of district judges from $4,000 to $3,500 per year; reduced the salaries of Supreme Court Judges from $5,500 to $5,000 per year; reduced the salaries of elected and appointed state officials by 20 percent; and abolished the office of District Tax Supervisor created in 1919.[504]

Auditor Baker's salary was cut from $3,000 per year to $2,400 per year. Other expenses in her office were cut as well, such as gas tax law enforcement, which went from $3,000 per biennium to $500 per biennium.[505]

Mrs. Baker was also a member of the state budget board, which was composed of five members: the Governor, the chairman of the Appropriations Committee of the Senate of the preceding legislative assembly, the chairman of the Appropriations Committee of the House of Representatives, the state Auditor and the Attorney General. The Governor was chairman of the board and the state Auditor was secretary.

This was a very important state board, and Mrs. Baker was the first woman to serve on this board. The 1930s, with state income low and needs high, were especially challenging years for the people planning the state budget.

Her office was an important part of the budgeting process. By August 1 of each year proceeding a legislative session, the state Auditor had to send each department in state government a budget form. This form needed to be completed by the head of the department, with an itemized statement of the amount of money necessary for the running of that department for the next biennium. The form had to be returned to the state Auditor's office by October 1. The state budget board then met on the second Tuesday of November of that year and prepared estimates of a state budget of the amounts required to be appropriated by the state Legislature in the coming session.[506]

Auditor Baker's biennial reports from 1933 to 1956 included the biennial budgets of many departments in state government and provide an interesting record of how appropriations and expenses changed from year to year.

1934 – New Capitol is Completed, National Guard is Called Up to Protect State Capitol Building During Riots, North Dakota Supreme Court Orders Governor to Leave Office, Berta Baker Wins Again

One huge new state government project brought hope and pride to the people of North Dakota from 1932 to 1935. A spectacular new Capitol building was rising up over the prairies on the north side of Bismarck. The bold design of the building had Art Deco roots, but its simplicity linked it to the International Style of architecture popular after World War II.[507]

Contrast in your mind this new palace on the prairie with the unpainted, poorly repaired homes many North Dakotans were living in during the Depression. It is no wonder that although Governor George Shafer held a groundbreaking for the new building in 1932, no official dedication of the new building ever took place. State government just moved in, as spaces were finished, in 1934-35.

The 1931 Legislature passed legislation which established a three-member Capitol Commission, which would "select an architect, a design and construction materials, and hire laborers to complete the replacement structure." [508] They also mandated that the completed structure cost no more than $2,000,000. "By employing local draftsmen, labor and materials they hoped to keep state tax dollars at home."[509] However, although the huge cornerstone came from near St. Anthony in Morton County, most of the materials for the state Capitol building came from outside the state.

The Legislature used its new chambers for an emergency session in mid-July 1934, even though desks and woodwork in the new legislative chambers were not yet installed. On July 17, Burleigh County Sheriff J.L. Kelley called for aid from the National Guard. His letter stated:

> "... Whereas, apparently the same persons of about two hundred in number had a few days ago caused destruction of the property of the Capitol Building, and as a certain person of such mob had thrown a missile

The Depression years were hard times for many North Dakota families, including this family of 12 from Williams County in front of their home in 1937.
(Library of Congress, Farm Security Administration Photos of ND, 8b19854)

> through the plate glass window of the capitol building, causing damage to said building, and apparently the same mob forcibly removed one John A. Williams, who was then connected as an officer of the Federal Relief Administration, … from his office … ."[510]

Today, in more settled times, it is difficult to comprehend that Auditor Berta Baker needed to work with four different governors in seven months in 1934-35. The State Supreme Court, on July 17, 1934, ordered Governor Langer to leave office because he had been convicted of a felony.[511] Lieutenant Governor Ole H. Olson moved into the new Governor's office a few days later. Democrat candidate Thomas Moodie won the election for Governor that November. Moodie, who took office in January, served only until February 2, 1935, when the State Supreme Court determined that he was disqualified due to living out of state for a while. Lieutenant Governor Walter Welford then became Governor.[512]

State Auditor Baker's offices were located on the third floor in the "tower" of the new Capitol. Her spacious office was located in the southeast corner of the building, where four large windows provided a view of the grounds and lots of morning sun. She must have been thrilled to move into this space where once again state officials were gathered together to be more easily accessible to the public and to more easily meet with each other.

Meanwhile, while all of this was going on, Mrs. Baker was again on the ballot for state Auditor as an NPL Republican in 1934 and she won another two-year term in November.

1934-1939 – Berta Baker and the North Dakota Supreme Court

By 1934, Mrs. Baker was confident enough in her role as state Auditor to challenge the system. She trusted her knowledge of state law and the North Dakota Constitution. If she was not convinced that she was following both, she refused to "sign and issue warrants," i.e., sign and issue checks for questionable state expenses. And when she refused to sign and issue a warrant, the case went before the North Dakota Supreme Court.

It is important to understand how little authority the state Auditor possessed, on her own, to act as Auditor. Her office did not conduct any audits of state departments, institutions or county offices; the state examiner, with a staff larger than that of the state Auditor, was responsible for all of these audits.[513] The state examiner was the chief officer of the Department of Banking.

She also could not authorize any payments on her own. Auditor Baker was secretary of the State Auditing Board, which was composed of the Governor, state Auditor, state Treasurer and the state Examiner. The duty of this board, in a meeting of at least three of its members, was to look at each and every claim, account, bill or demand against the state and give their approval before the state Auditor could "sign and issue a warrant." The group had to meet at least monthly.[514]

In 1934-42, state Auditor Baker was a party in 11 Supreme Court cases. Many state officials are never a party in a Supreme Court case.

State v. Baker – October 1934[515]

Secretary of State Byrne brought an action against State Auditor Baker asking the Supreme Court to compel Auditor Baker to draw a warrant that had been approved by the State Auditing Board. Byrne had incurred expenses for printing and distributing a publicity (information) pamphlet on the initiated measures which would be voted on in the November general election. Mrs. Baker refused to pay the bill because although the Legislature had appropriated money for such expenses, almost all of the money had already been expended on the costs of printing and mailing similar needed pamphlets earlier in the biennium. The total cost of the pamphlet was $3,500, $3,000 in excess of the unexpended appropriation.

Auditor Baker represented herself in the case before the North Dakota Supreme Court. In the brief, which she signed, she stated,

> "Admits that she refuses and will continue to refuse, unless otherwise directed by order of this court to sign and issue any warrant withdrawing any state funds in excess of the said unexpended balance of the 1933 legislative appropriation for the publicity pamphlet, for the purpose of defraying the expenses of publication and distribution of the said publicity pamphlet for the November, 1934 general election … ."[516]

The Supreme Court determined that Auditor Baker should draw the warrant because the state constitution mandated that the publicity pamphlets be issued. They noted:

> "Upon the oral argument the state auditor stated, in open court, that it was her desire to perform her duty as prescribed by law; and that if this court determined that it was her duty to draw warrants in payment of the bills audited and allowed for the printing and mailing of the publicity pamphlet, she would comply with such determination. This being so, no formal writ will issue. No costs will be awarded to either party."[517]

Stray v. Baker – August 1938[518]

This case involved a state legislator who was appointed Commissioner of University and School Lands and who wanted his salary paid. However, since his appointment, a constitutional amendment was passed by the voters which stated no state official could appoint a legislator to any office, or give him or her any employment whatsoever. On August 18, 1938, the Supreme Court affirmed the ruling of the district court that the amendment was passed after Stray's appointment, and so he deserved to be paid.

Not all of the Supreme Court cases were a result of Auditor Baker refusing to make payment. Two in 1939 involved other issues.

King v. Baker – October 1939[519]

Auditor Baker's office was responsible for collecting the state's motor vehicle tax, which was approved by the voters in an initiated measure in 1926. King wanted to stop collection of the tax on the grounds that the tax was unconstitutional. The Court determined on October 9, 1939, that the plaintiff was a user of motor vehicle fuel and not a dealer of motor vehicle fuel, and thus he was not entitled to bring the case to court.

State v. Baker – October 1939[520]

This case was brought by the state to restrain the State Auditor and State Treasurer from disbursing any of the $35,000 provided for by the Legislature to employ a Code

Revision Commission. The commission, under supervision of the Supreme Court, would prepare, annotate and index a complete set of rules of practice and procedure for all courts of the state. The question was whether the law mandating such a commission was constitutional. The court determined on October 25, 1939, that the law was constitutional and the funds could be disbursed.

The 1940s - North Dakota Recovers From the Depression, and State Auditor Berta Baker Takes on Many Controversial Issues

State government finances were improving. Auditor Baker reported that on June 30, 1941, the state general fund had $1,765,355,[521] almost $1 million more than one year before. Total state cash assets were up over $2 million from the year before, at $9,336,841.[522]

Meanwhile, World War II had started in Europe and by December 1941, the United States was fully involved in the war effort. The new decade brought almost immediate changes in the climate and the economy of the state:

> "With plenty of rain and with good prices for farm produce, the state enjoyed greater prosperity than it had ever known. Sober in good fortune, the farmers paid off their debts, bought land at low prices, and put aside savings for future hard times. The state government reduced its debt and built up its reserves … . Depression scarred North Dakota farmers reacted slowly to their new prosperity. They needed many things. In 1940 most of their homes lacked electricity, running water, indoor bathrooms, mechanical refrigeration, and central heating; a third of their homes needed major repairs. But they spent cautiously, buying mostly farm machinery, automobiles, and trucks."[523]

Election years seemed to come along very quickly when most state officials had to run for office every two years. In 1940, Baker described herself in a campaign ad, which included a good picture of the 64-year-old candidate.

> "Berta E. Baker has been a resident of North Dakota for thirty-three years, of which eighteen years were spent on the farm which she still owns and operates.
>
> She has endeavored as a public official to give the state honest and efficient service. She has stood squarely and consistently for economy in state government and if re-elected will continue to perform the duties of the office for the best interests of the citizens and taxpayers of North Dakota."[524]

Mrs. Baker won the 1940 November election.

In October 1942, The *Bismarck Tribune* asked State Auditor Baker to write a short article on why she should be the people's choice in the election that fall.

> "I appreciate the opportunity you have given me to present a statement to the readers of the *Bismarck Tribune.*
>
> I was endorsed for the office State Auditor at a statewide convention held in Bismarck in March. This convention was composed of delegates from every county in the state. I was nominated on the Republican ticket by a vote of the people of the state at the primary election in June.
>
> The office of state auditor is an important one, and its many and varied duties require accuracy and detailed attention. In addition to the regular duties, the state auditor is a member of several important boards and commissions which require personal attention.
>
> During the time that I have held the office of state auditor I have endeavored to discharge the duties of the office honestly, efficiently, and to the best of my ability. In all official matters coming before me, I have endeavored to make such decisions as in my best judgment are right, without fear or favor or political consideration. If re-elected, at the November election, I shall endeavor to discharge the duties of the office fairly and impartially and to the best of my ability, and upon this pledge I seek re-election."[525]

Baker won the 1942 November election as the NPL Republican candidate.

North Dakota Supreme Court Cases 1940-1945

In the early 1940s, feisty Auditor Berta Baker took on the Highway Department, the Governor, the Legislature, Ford Motor Co. and others in seven more cases before the Supreme Court. She could have just issued the warrants. But obviously she wanted to act in accordance with state law and the state constitution, and took her responsibilities very seriously.

Department of State Highways v. Baker – January, 1940[526]

In 1939, the Legislature raised the motor vehicle fuel tax by 1 cent and provided that the revenues from this new gas tax would go into the state highway fund. Baker was advised by the Attorney General that the new tax was unconstitutional, and so although she collected the new tax dollars, she refused to disburse almost $400,000 to the state Highway Department.[527]

The Highway Department brought a lawsuit against Auditor Baker to compel her to issue warrants. One important issue in this case was whether the "state auditor may question the constitutionality of the statute upon which the proceedings are based."[528]

On January 16, 1940, the Supreme Court ruled:

> "Passing now to the right of the state auditor to raise a question of the constitutionality of an act and under the terms of which it is her ministerial duty to make disbursement, we find the weight of authority to be in favor of such right."[529]

However, the court also ruled the Legislature had acted in accordance with the state constitution, and Auditor Baker was ordered to issue the warrants.[530]

Eighteen months later, the North Dakota Supreme Court issued *three orders within two weeks* that involved compelling Auditor Baker to draw warrants.

King v. Baker – July 1941[531]

Attorney General Strutz again represented the Auditor, arguing that drawing the warrant to make the payment was not constitutional. The state Highway Department had caused damages to the land of four Stark County landowners when constructing a highway. However, the 1939 Legislature did not make any specific appropriation to pay the judgment which was due to them. Thus, the Attorney General argued that Auditor Baker should not draw the warrant because Section 186 of the constitution forbid the payment. On July 14, 1941, the Supreme Court disagreed and ordered the state Auditor to issue the warrants totaling $5,979.[532]

Moses v. Baker – July 1941[533]

One week later, on July 21, 1941, the Supreme Court issued another order where Auditor Berta Baker was the defendant. Governor John Moses asked the court to compel Auditor Baker to issue warrants in payments of bonds bought by the Board of University and School Lands (BUSL). Attorney General Strutz again represented Auditor Baker. She refused to issue the warrants to purchase the bonds because the price for the bonds was above par. Also, she refused to draw a warrant for the accrued interest.

The Supreme Court directed the state Auditor to draw a warrant to purchase the bonds because they found the BUSL had done nothing wrong in purchasing the bonds above par. However, they agreed with Auditor Baker that she should not draw a warrant for the accrued interest.

State v. Baker – July 1941[534]

Four days later, on July 25, the Supreme Court issued a decision relating to the motor vehicle fuel tax. In 1926, the public, through an initiated measure, put in place a motor vehicle fuel tax and had designated the office of the state Auditor to be in charge of enforcing and collecting the tax. In 1941, the Legislature passed legislation, by a majority vote, and not by a two-thirds vote, which moved the enforcement and collection of the tax to the state Tax Department. Auditor Baker transferred equipment and records to the state Tax Commissioner, anticipating the law would take effect on July 1.

Attorney General Strutz sought to have the law passed by the Legislature declared null and void because two-thirds of all the members of each house did not vote for the change, as required by the state constitution when dealing with subject matter of an initiated measure. The Supreme Court agreed that the law passed by the Legislature should be null and void, and the Auditor's office remained in charge of enforcement and collection of the state motor vehicles tax.[535]

As soon as the decision was made, Tax Commissioner Gray said he would be returning equipment and records to the Auditor's office. Auditor Baker announced "she was making arrangements with the printers to get out the new forms for dealers tax exempt licenses, and said she expected to have them in the mails as soon as possible."[536]

Ford Motor Co. v. Baker – October 1941[537]

There was no question the state of North Dakota owed Ford Motor Co. $55,580 in back taxes. This particular case arose because the Legislature did not specifically appropriate any money to pay the judgment. Auditor Baker contended that Section 186 of the state constitution required a specific legislative appropriation to issue the warrant. Ford Motor Co. argued that a constitutional amendment, passed by the public in 1938, allowed money to be disbursed from certain funds (such as the State Hail Insurance Fund) without legislative authorization.

The Supreme Court had previously decided in a case on this amendment (Langer v. State[538]) the state funds in question needed specific appropriations for administrative purposes and thus the funds had to file statements required by the State Budget Law. On October 22, 1941, the Supreme Court found that it was constitutional to pay the claim, but that the state could not be held to pay interest on the claim.

State v. Baker – May 1942[539]

In 1939, state finances were tight. Retail sales tax collections did not bring in as much money as was needed to pay out school funds, through the State Equalization Fund. Auditor Baker did not know whether she should issue the warrants from other moneys in the state treasury not otherwise appropriated, and so refused to issue the warrants. This case also posed the question of whether the legislative appropriation approved for financing the public schools from June 1, 1939, to June 30, 1941, could continue to be used to pay school bills submitted until October 1, 1941. Former Governor George F. Shafer argued the case for the state to compel payment. Attorney General Strutz presented the case of Auditor Baker. On May 6, 1942, the Supreme Court answered both questions in the affirmative. Auditor Baker issued the warrants.

The most famous case involving State Auditor Berta E. Baker – State v. Baker – May 1945[540]

The pages in the North West Reporter, at the North Dakota State Law Library, that record the case of *State v. Baker* are worn and well-used. This is the most cited case involving State Auditor Berta E. Baker. It involved a very controversial issue in North Dakota in the mid-1940s.

The North Dakota constitution stated that each member of the legislative assembly shall receive $5 per day for his services for each session, and $10 cents per mile for necessary travel. In 1941, the Legislature voted to increase its pay. Governor Moses vetoed the measure, the veto was sustained, and the legislative assembly proposed a constitutional amendment to change their pay, which the voters rejected in the primary election. In 1943, the legislative assembly again voted to increase its pay by allowing each legislator $300 in living expenses in addition to the payments stated in the constitution. Governor Moses again vetoed the bill and stated:

> "In the public mind there is some question about the constitutionality of this Bill. The Attorney General[541] has indicated to me that it is the opinion of his office that this Bill is constitutional … . That the compensation for the members of the Legislature is too low there is no question. I urge you to pass a concurrent Resolution providing for a Constitutional Amendment and sincerely hope that the people will approve it … ."[542]

The Legislature overrode the Governor's veto and passed the bill and approved an appropriation of $50,000 to cover the expenses.

State Auditor Baker refused to draw the warrants to pay the legislators and justified her action due to her grave doubt as to the constitutionality of House Bill 84. She worried that if she issued "the warrants and the statute is unconstitutional she will have violated her duty under her oath of office and become liable on her official bond."[543] In short, Baker was worried if she issued the funds and the law was later declared unconstitutional, she would not be able to compel the legislators to return the funds to the state, and she would be liable.

Rather than determine if the law was constitutional, the Supreme Court's decision centered on whether the state Auditor should bring a constitutional question to the court. In this case, the Supreme Court stated that Auditor Baker should not bring a constitutional question to the Supreme Court. In their May 26, 1945, opinion they stated:

> "Presumptively the statute was constitutional. It was the law until the court declared to the contrary. The respondent's duty was to act in compliance with the law; not to pass upon its propriety. If she doubted its validity her duty was to consult and advise with the attorney general, the chief law

officer of the state, and to act in accordance with such opinion as he might give her. She did not do this but, contrary to the opinion which she knew he would give her, took it upon herself to say that the statute was unconstitutional."[544]

After this decision, Auditor Baker was not involved in any more Supreme Court cases.

The 1950s – Berta Baker Visits President Eisenhower and Retires as State Auditor at Age 80

The war was over, and after the prosperous 1940s, the state was in a much more stable financial position. On July 1, 1951, Auditor Baker reported $14,135,358 in the state general fund[545] and that the state had total cash assets of $63,307,480.[546]

However, the state's population had dropped from 642,000 in 1940 to 620,000 in 1950. Through the 1940s, farm life in much of North Dakota was very difficult, and different from town life. While people in town had electricity and telephones, most farm families were without these services. Farmers used wind chargers or generators and batteries to power a radio or lights in the home, but this was no substitute for electrification of their farmsteads. However, by 1954, due to Rural Electrification Administration loans, and farm families joining rural electric cooperatives, 90 percent of North Dakota's farms had electricity and joined the modern world.[547]

Mrs. Baker's farm near Glenburn received electricity around 1948.[548]

In 1955, Auditor Baker was 79 years old. She was in good health and enjoyed her work. Eisenhower was President, and he invited 18 women leaders in public and professional affairs from 12 states to join him in Washington, D.C., for breakfast.[549] Mrs. Baker was invited. When she arrived home, she commented on the exciting experience:

> "I was wondering if we'd have to sit up and be prim, but the President puts you so at ease you just can't be nervous … . (I) wasn't one bit nervous at meeting and talking with the President and I don't think the others were either … . We visited like any other social gathering."[550]

When she arrived home, she received a personal letter from the President congratulating her on serving in public office since 1928. She was thrilled with the whole experience.

Now in 1956, a whole new era in North Dakota politics was beginning. Democrats decided that they wanted to incorporate the objectives of the NPL in their party platform, and the Democrats held their first convention in Bismarck in March. This was a major change because, since the NPL's inception, the main political battles were fought in the Republican June primary elections.[551]

People at the Democrat NPL convention that spring, who had previously been endorsed by the NPL, were called the "Old Guard." Some new and some old faces appeared on the ticket when the convention was adjourned. However, "Six incumbent state office holders, some of whom have been re-elected with League endorsement since the 1930's were abandoned along with Rep. Burdick. These included State Auditor Berta Baker, Secretary of Agriculture and Labor Math Dahl, Insurance Commissioner A.J. Jensen, State Treasurer Albert Jacobson, Secretary of State Ben Meier, and Atty. Gen. Leslie R. Burgum."[552] All except Berta Baker joined the ticket of the Republican Organizing Committee (ROC) ticket and were elected in the November election.

Mrs. Baker had announced her decision to retire before either convention.[553] She attended the Republican convention in Valley City the following week, and appeared before the convention to thank "the many voters in North Dakota who have placed me in office so many years."[554]

She had won many of her 14 elections by the largest margins of any candidate on the ballot.

Afterthoughts

For a few years after she retired, Mrs. Baker worked in the state Auditor's Department. When her health failed, she moved to Minot to be closer to her daughter Helen (Mrs. Carl Knonaas). Her son Donald had died in 1943, and her son Robert was a doctor in Maryland. Baker had 10 grandchildren and 25 great-grandchildren.

After Berta E. Baker announced her retirement, the Minot Daily News wrote an editorial praising her work as a state official. The editorial concluded with these words:

> "In office, or out of office, Mrs. Baker will be long remembered as a courageous woman who proved that widowhood, brought about by the tragic accidental death of her husband in 1924, need not be a deterrent to assuming responsibilities to her family, and the public. Her life, and her achievements, might well afford inspiration to others."[555]

Mrs. Baker died in Minot on May 4, 1964.[556] She was 87 years old.

Serving the Greater Good

1969-87

SIXTEEN

You Either Like Figures or You Better Step Out

Bernice Muriel Asbridge

State Treasurer
1969-72

By
Susan Wefald

"I'm still human even if I have been in politics."

Bernice Asbridge, 1979[557]

Bernice Muriel Asbridge nee Wenaas*

1919-2004

State Treasurer 1969-72

State Treasurer Bernice Asbridge
(LaFave Family Files)

Personal Information

Born 1919 in Arena, North Dakota, and raised in Arena and Bismarck, North Dakota. Married to Donald (deceased), two children. In "spare time," enjoyed doing needlepoint, painting and gardening.

Party Affiliation

Republican

Education

Bismarck High School.

Professional Experience before taking office

Bookkeeper, AW Lucas Store, Bismarck, 1937-42; U.S. Army bases, clerk typist, 1942-45; Burleigh County auditor's office, clerk typist, 1945-48, machine bookkeeper, 1948-55, second deputy auditor, 1955-59; Burleigh County auditor, 1959-68.

Memberships Include

As Treasurer: National Association of State Auditors, Treasurer and Comptrollers; National Association of State Liquor Administrators.

Other: County Auditor's Association of North Dakota, president; Governor's Advisory Committee to Government Received Federal Funds; National Federation of Republican Women; Bismarck Elkettes, president; Bismarck Cancer Society, eight years as secretary; Bismarck Business and Professional Women, president; Sons of Norway; Bismarck American Legion Auxiliary; Trinity Lutheran Church.[558]

*Bio contains information through 1972

New state Treasurer Bernice Asbridge, age 50, was smiling as she visited with a constituent at the inaugural ball in the Bismarck War Memorial Building in 1969. A photograph taken that evening shows her tall, 18-year-old son, Darold, standing by her side.[559] Ignoring her aching feet and tender hands, she, along with all of the other elected state officials, greeted more than 2,000 people who proceeded slowly through the receiving line. The receiving line lasted 3½ hours.[560] Then the dancing started, and Bernice loved to dance. The dancing ran past midnight.[561] She looked lovely in her long gown, with a draped fur collar.

Not only was she delighted to be state Treasurer, but she was also thrilled that she had been invited, and was going to attend, the inauguration of President Richard Nixon in Washington, D.C., in a few weeks.[562]

These events were the culmination of years of hard work raising her children, caring for her disabled husband, Don, working 14 years in the Burleigh County auditor's office, then serving 10 years as Burleigh County auditor, and running her successful Republican campaign for state Treasurer. It is no wonder Treasurer Asbridge was smiling in the photograph.

Getting Started

Bernice, the daughter of Sigurd and Nellie Wenaas, was born in Arena, North Dakota, on September 7, 1919.[563] She had three sisters, Mildred, Irene and Adeline. When she was 5 years old, her family moved to Bismarck, and except for a few years during World War II, she lived in Bismarck for the rest of her life.

Bernice visited the Burleigh County Courthouse when she was 11 years old. As reporter Janelle Cole later wrote for the *Bismarck Tribune*:

> "On a sweltering July day in 1931, Sigurd and Nellie Wenaas brought their 11-year-old daughter Bernice along as they watched an old chum from Arena take part in the dedication of the new Burleigh County Courthouse.
>
> The chum was County Auditor A. C. Isaminger.
>
> No one, of course, knew that little Bernice would grow up to be the only other Arena native to be Burleigh County auditor. Or that she would be our auditor longer than all except one."[564]

Or that she would grow up to serve as Treasurer of the state of North Dakota.

Right after graduating from Bismarck High School in 1937, while North Dakota was still in the midst of the Depression, Miss Bernice Wenaas was lucky to be hired at the locally owned department store, A.W. Lucas, as a bookkeeper. She worked at A.W. Lucas until she married her Bismarck sweetheart, Donald Asbridge, in March 1942.[565]

As a war bride, she decided not to stay in Bismarck. She accompanied Don to various U.S. Army bases while he trained with the 9th Infantry Division and served in Germany. Mrs. Asbridge applied for jobs at the bases and worked as a clerk-typist at each new place Don was stationed. Baby Donna was born in 1943. It was not easy to have a new baby at an Army base, and so Donna stayed with her maternal grandparents, Sigurd and Nellie Wenaas, in Bismarck while her mom worked at an Army base in Texas. [566]

Now World War II was over. Mr. and Mrs. Asbridge and their little daughter, Donna, were home together in Bismarck, and it was time to find new jobs. Mrs. Asbridge decided to apply for a job at the Burleigh County Courthouse.

When County Auditor Adolph Schlenker offered Bernice Asbridge the clerk-typist job in 1945,[567] she was just glad to be hired at a good, steady job in an office near her

In January 1969, State Treasurer Bernice Asbridge greets visitors with her son, Darold (on her right), in the Inaugural Ball receiving line. (LaFave Family Files)

home. As she settled in at the county auditor's office, she liked working for the public. Soon she would be the sole breadwinner for her young family. For now, she was learning new skills that would prepare her to be county auditor and state Treasurer.

New Challenges

In 1950, only 12 percent of mothers with children under age 6 were working outside of the home.[568] Bernice Asbridge was one of those mothers. Baby Darold was born in 1950 when daughter Donna was 7 years old. Family members such as aunts and grandma cared for the children while Mrs. Asbridge was working during the day. When Bernice and Don had any "spare time," the young couple loved to dance together.[569] Life was good. Mrs. Asbridge had been promoted to machine bookkeeper in 1948.

Then in August 1952, the "unthinkable" happened. Her husband, Donald, suffered a cerebral hemorrhage, which left him paralyzed on the right side and without speech. Slowly he regained his ability to speak, but even after years, he could only walk in the house by leaning on and pushing a kitchen chair. He could no longer work. It was a very challenging time for the young family.

Mrs. Asbridge was now the sole "breadwinner" for the family. It helped that County Auditor Adolph Schlenker recognized her hard work and potential by promoting her to second deputy auditor in 1955.[570]

When the *Bismarck Tribune* interviewed Burleigh County Auditor Asbridge in 1966, she talked about her decision to run for county auditor.

> " 'There was no one finer than Mr. Schlenker to have trained under,' she maintains. And it was at his urging that she decided to run for the auditor's office later on.
>
> 'I started training without realizing that someday I would run for the office,' she recalls, and very soon found the work very much to her liking.
>
> Mrs. Asbridge had had no formal bookkeeping or accounting training – 'just the usual secretarial training, and that wasn't much help in this kind of work.'
>
> In 1956, two years before he retired, Mr. Schlenker asked her if she would be interested in running for the office.
>
> The suggestion was a complete surprise to Mrs. Asbridge. 'I told him I didn't think Burleigh County would support a woman for the job,' she said.
>
> Then Mr. Schlenker decided to take on another two-year term and she had a chance to think it over. By the time he was ready to announce his

> retirement in 1958, Mrs. Asbridge was receptive to the idea of making a run for the office.
>
> She was second deputy auditor at that time and her opponent was Allen C. Pfenning, the first deputy auditor. Contrary to her earlier view, Burleigh County did support a woman for auditor … . She was the 13th woman auditor in the state and only the first in Burleigh County … .
>
> Mrs. Asbridge obviously feels the county auditor's job is one of the finest in the world. But she remarks, 'you either like figures or you had better step out.' "[571]

Asbridge had no political experience when she ran for county auditor in 1958, but Mr. Schlenker, her boss, was a wonderful mentor. Her father helped her raise money, and Mrs. Asbridge hit the road, knocking on doors and handing out campaign "palm cards." A campaign poster from her first campaign featured a head-and-shoulders picture of Bernice Asbridge with the following text:

ELECT
BERNICE (MRS. DON)
ASBRIDGE
NEE: BERNICE WENAAS
BURLEIGH COUNTY AUDITOR
Your Vote and Support Appreciated Spons. & Paid for by Bernice Asbridge

As her daughter, Donna, recalled, campaign work was difficult for her because "she wasn't into politics. As it turned out, it was the beginning of her political career." [572]

Mrs. Asbridge was elected to be Burleigh County auditor when she was 39 years old. She was elected first to a two-year term and then ran unopposed for two more four-year terms.

1959-1968 – Serving as Burleigh County Auditor

Burleigh County Auditor Asbridge soon found herself in the midst of all parts of the county's business. She soon found that in addition to bookkeeping, she needed to be "a part-time lawyer and engineer to understand some of the documents you deal with."[573] As county auditor, Mrs. Asbridge was "secretary to all county boards as well as unofficial adviser to the whole courthouse … . 'We attempt to keep abreast of all new laws and amended laws in order to help others who are not so familiar with them.' "[574] It was a special challenge to serve as secretary to the all-male Burleigh County Commission. She sometimes left the room when tempers flared. "The language wasn't really so bad. I just dislike arguments. If tempers start to flare, I leave, if it is not part of the minutes."

Mrs. Asbridge was serving as county auditor in November 1963 when President John F. Kennedy was shot and killed in Dallas. Although a staunch Republican, Asbridge was deeply affected by his death, and sat down and wrote the following letter to Mrs. Kennedy, enclosing a poem[575] she wrote:

"Dear Mrs. Kennedy,

I have written these few lines especially to John, Mrs. Kennedy. I am not a poet, as you can readily see. But the happenings of these past few days have affected the world so deeply that I felt I must put down on paper what was in my heart.

As you and the children hold your feelings with you, we, the nation cried outright. We cried for you as a family first and for our loss secondly.

I am speaking for the whole of Burleigh County when I say, please accept these few words with our profound sympathy to you and the children, for your great loss of a husband and father.

With deep affection and respect, I remain,

Sincerely yours,

Bernice Asbridge
Burleigh County Auditor
State of North Dakota[576]

Looking Forward to the Future

In spring 1968, Mrs. Asbridge was 49 years old and she had served as county auditor for 10 years. Her daughter, Donna, was now married to Joe Lafave and living in Bismarck. Her son, Darold, was 18 and would graduate from Bismarck High School in June. Home life was different now because not only were her children grown, but her husband, Don, had died in March 1964.[577] In December 1963, she had written this poem to him:

"My Darling
T'was on an August morning, so many years ago,
Our faith and love was tested, by God, with such a blow.
He spared you Dear, and we have lived, with happiness and bliss,
To watch and guide our children's growth, and receive their loving kiss.
Our days and years together have been undaunted by our love.
Our lives received fulfillment from the Dear Lord up above.
When this is read, my Darling, one of us has been called to rest.

The one remaining, shall continue to do his very best.
One day we'll be together Dear, and I will lean on thee,
We'll both walk straight and tall, my Dear, thru all eternity."[578]

Now Bernice Asbridge was ready for new challenges. She decided to run for state Treasurer.

June 1968

The Republican convention was scheduled for mid-June 1968 and Mrs. Asbridge was ready. In early May, she had announced her decision to become a candidate "after being contacted by a number of legislators and also members of the Republican Women's Federation."[579] So far, no other Republicans had announced that they were running for state Treasurer. If she received the party nomination, she would be running against Democrat Walter Christensen, a four-year incumbent.

Other state races were getting far more attention. Democrat Governor Guy had already served eight[580] years, and he had not yet said whether he would seek another term as Governor or run for the Senate against incumbent Milton Young. Five men were vying for the Republican nomination for Governor; since Guy had already served eight years, they thought that he was vulnerable.[581]

The nation was in turmoil. At 12:15 a.m. on June 5, Senator Robert F. (Bobby) Kennedy had been shot after winning the California primary, his biggest win so far as he sought the Democratic nomination for President. One day later, he was dead, and his assailant, Sirhan Sirhan, was in custody. His assassination, just two months after the assassination of Dr. Martin Luther King Jr. and just 4½ years after the assassination of President John F. Kennedy, had everyone wondering just what was going wrong in the United States of America. Congress was discussing gun control legislation.

On the Republican presidential ticket, Nelson Rockefeller was campaigning against Richard Nixon. Rockefeller planned to make an appearance at the North Dakota Republican convention in Fargo.

The North Dakotan Republican convention took place without incident. Delegates met in Fargo and the June 15 *Bismarck Tribune* announced "Doherty Gets the Nod."[582] Ed Doherty was a newspaper publisher from New Rockford who was keeping an eye on Robert McCarney, who said he would run against Doherty in the September primary. Bernice Asbridge received the Republican nod for state Treasurer. "Her son and daughter were at the GOP convention in Fargo, and watched as their mother received the endorsement by acclamation."[583] She was the only woman on the Republican state ticket.

Incumbent Democrat Governor Guy decided later in June to run for another term as

Governor. A new name was on the Democrat ticket; Byron Dorgan was making his first run for state Tax Commissioner.

The 1968 Campaign

For most of the public, Bernice Asbridge's campaign for state Treasurer was completely overshadowed by events happening on the national political stage. She campaigned hard, while arranging her schedule "so as not be away from her work as Burleigh County auditor." [584]

In early August, while she may have been arranging fundraising parties, Richard Nixon was endorsed at the Republican national convention for President with far more delegate votes than his opponents. In late August, when Mrs. Asbridge may have been passing out palm cards around the state, Democrats held their infamous national convention in Chicago, where anti-war rioters protested the Vietnam War and the nomination of Vice President Hubert Humphrey to run for President.

Closer to home, in September, while Mrs. Asbridge may have been distributing posters around the state, Robert McCarney beat Ed Doherty in the North Dakota Republican primary and became the Republican candidate for Governor.

1968 Campaign Poster of State Treasurer Candidate Bernice Asbridge. (LaFave Family Files)

In spite of all of the "noise" of national and state politics, Mrs. Asbridge was busy. She recruited Gene Weekes to be treasurer and Ruth Robinson to be finance chair of her campaign. One palm card she used had a penny attached to a recipe card:

My recipe for NORTH DAKOTA
HERE'S A COIN – GUARD IT WELL
Stir up support and cast your vote for
BERNICE ASBRIDGE
For State Treasurer
Seasoned and prepared to serve
Our STATE well.
Sponsored by Ruth Robinson, Finance Chairman[585]

Her campaign posters featured a head-and-shoulders picture of Mrs. Asbridge and read:

MEET
BERNICE ASBRIDGE
REPUBLICAN
CANDIDATE FOR
STATE TREASURER
YOUR VOTE AND SUPPORT WILL BE APPRECIATED[586]

One flier, illustrated with an elephant and coffee mugs, sent out over the name of Ruth Robinson, was directed to presidents of Republican Women's Clubs:

> Dear Club President:
>
> Help is wanted and needed!! Our Republican Party is fortunate to have a qualified Woman Candidate running for a State Office in the coming General Election - - November 5th … .
>
> Now is the Time for all good Women to come to the Aid of Their Party … . The Women of this State can elect Bernice if we all give her our Support and Vote - - Remember: State Treasurer. After your "Coffee Party" please mail donations to: Ruth Robinson, Fin. Chrm … . "Support Bernice A. All The Way"[587]

The election was held on November 5. Bernice Asbridge won the election: Asbridge 112,692; Walter Christensen 107,953.[588] State Republican candidates won every race except Governor and Tax Commissioner. Richard Nixon was elected President, and Governor William "Bill" Guy would serve for four more years in North Dakota. Mrs. Asbridge and her children left town right after the election night party for an out-of-town family wedding. She did not know for sure that she was elected state Treasurer for several days.[589]

Thoughts on Being a Woman State Official

Shortly after Mrs. Asbridge was elected to office, the *Bismarck Tribune* interviewed her and asked "if being a woman among so many men in what is generally conceded to be a man's world bothered her. Asbridge replied only, 'I'm very proud.'"[590] In another interview, she commented, "I just felt that women should further themselves if the opportunity arose. I'm hopeful other women will feel the same way."[591]

State Treasurer Asbridge was a popular public speaker and tried to be a mentor to other women. One night in 1970, she spoke to Farm Bureau women and their guests from the Association of University Women and Business and Professional Women's Clubs. She talked on the "importance of women in all areas of education, business and politics. She urged women to use their influential abilities in these areas but their influence in the home should be predominant."[592]

Description of Official Duties as State Treasurer

Four-year term. Custodian of all state moneys and securities; accountable for all money received and disbursed; treasurer's office collects the estate tax, oil and gas production tax, beer and liquor tax, airline, express and carline tax, and the tax on performing rights; issue licenses to all beer and liquor whole-sale dealers; file an annual report to the Governor on the condition of this office as to receipts and disbursements during the fiscal year and balances in the various funds at the beginning and ending of the fiscal year. This report also includes the place where the funds are deposited.
Member: State Laboratories Commission, State Equalization Board, Board of Canvassers, Board of Trustees of Teacher's Insurance and Retirement Fund, Investment Board, State Historical Society Board.[593]

Getting Started as State Treasurer

Treasurer Asbridge had a trusted employee from the Burleigh County auditor's office at her side as she tackled the duties of state Treasurer. Clarence Mathys served as her deputy when she was county auditor, and he agreed to move with her to be her deputy treasurer at the state Capitol.

Important issues demanded her attention her first week in office. She asked for an attorney general's opinion within a few days of taking office. It involved a controversial issue involving her duties as state liquor administrator. In 1969, the state Treasurer was responsible for collecting both the state excise tax and the wholesale liquor transaction tax and for enforcing the collection of both taxes.[594]

Treasurer Asbridge had received correspondence from a commanding officer of an Air Force base in North Dakota. Mrs. Asbridge then wrote a letter to Attorney General Helge Johanneson asking "whether or not beer and liquor sold to officers' clubs are subject to the North Dakota taxes." The section in the North Dakota Century Code (NDCC) that referred to the collection of liquor taxes had been amended by the 1967 Legislature and now included the following statement, "Sales of beer and liquor to instrumentalities of the federal government on military reservations shall be tax exempt."[595]

On January 7, 1969, the Attorney General, in his opinion, addressed the question of whether or not officers' and noncommissioned officers' clubs on military reservations were "instrumentalities of the federal government."[596] Attorney General Helge Johanneson determined that such clubs were instrumentalities of the federal government, but that in order to qualify for the exemption, each club or mess had to provide required paperwork to the state Treasurer.

His opinion stirred legislative interest in the issue. The Bismarck Tribune reported on January 20, 1969, that a bill was introduced in the Senate that would "plug a tax loophole regarding sales of alcoholic beverages to federal military establishments in North Dakota."[597] The article went on to state that the "loophole would cost the state about $140,000 every two years unless changed."[598] The bill passed and was signed into law by the Governor.[599]

On March 5, 1969, Treasurer Asbridge attended her first meeting of the North Dakota State Investment Board. At this meeting, she was elected chair and served in that capacity through 1972. She described the duties of this board in 1971:

> "I have the privilege of serving as Chairman of the State Investment Board – the other members of the Board are the Governor, State Land Commissioner, Chairman of the Workman's Compensation Bureau and the State Insurance Commissioner. We are charged with the investments of the State Bonding Fund, Teacher's Insurance and Retirement Fund, State Fire & Tornado Fund, Workmen's Compensation Fund and the Highway Patrol Retirement Fund. The President of the Bank of North Dakota is the Investment Director. The Board approves general types of securities for investment, and it sets policies and procedures regulating securities transactions on behalf of the various funds. The types of legal investments are specified in our North Dakota Code."[600]

She may have been surprised to see former state treasurer Walter Christensen at the first meeting. He had been hired to serve in the Governor's office and would attend almost all of the Investment Board meetings as a representative of the Governor's office. Before the first meeting ended, Chair Asbridge directed that "in the future, before any investments are approved by this Board, a financial statement and complete list of stockholders from the applicant, shall accompany the request."[601] The board met four or five times each year.

In April 1969, the National Republican Women's Conference invited Treasurer Asbridge to "sit at the head table with the wife and daughters of President Richard Nixon at the banquet to be given in their honor."[602] The *Bismarck Tribune* reported:

> "Realizing that this was a rare honor, Mrs. Asbridge was torn with indecision. She had been in Washington to attend the inaugural ceremonies. It would be an unofficial visit and she considered the expense. Also, it was a busy time at the State Treasurer's office.
>
> 'You just don't turn down an invitation like that,' she was told by one prominent Republican official.
>
> So she planned to accept.
>
> But then came the death and funeral of President Eisenhower. Mrs. Asbridge, an ardent admirer of the late president, decided to attend the funeral instead of the Republican Women's festivities.
>
> She doesn't regret her decision. But it isn't strange that her mind strays now and then toward Washington and the important part she could be playing at the conference as one of the elected women officials of the Republican party."[603]

Her Work Continues

As county auditor and as state Treasurer, Bernice Asbridge practiced an "open door" policy, encouraging people to call her or come in to visit about their concerns. She enjoyed this part of her job as county auditor. However, soon she noted constituents did not contact her as often in the office of the state Treasurer. "Comparing county and state positions, I've found at the county level people see government as more accessible to them … . They're not afraid to come in and discuss their problems and visit with you. At the state level they were more reluctant to go into a state office just to visit."[604]

State Treasurer Asbridge was custodian of all state moneys and securities. She was held accountable for all money received and disbursed. While she was Treasurer, interest rates rose and the state was able to receive higher rates on investments placed in certificates of deposit, or CDs. For example, the average rate of a three-month CD in 1967 was 5.5 percent; by December 1969, the rate on a three-month CD had risen to 7.7 percent. By 1972, Asbridge was able to say:

> "The investments made by me as state treasurer in certificates of deposit have earned a total of $6,086,545.17 during the years of 1969 to 1972 … . Under the administration of the preceding state treasurer, the interest

from 1965 to 1969 amounted to $4,917,395.73."[605]

With interest rates rising, the state invested in CDs, as well as other investments, securities in custody of the state Treasurer increased from $119,056,288[606] on June 30, 1969 to $141,165,455[607] on June 30, 1972.

Another responsibility of the state Treasurer was to serve on the state canvassing board. This board met after each state primary and general election to certify the vote totals. Some of these meetings were very brief, such as the one after the September 1970 primary. Robert McCarney and Richard Elkin were vying to be the Republican candidate for Congress. The state canvassing board declared McCarney the winner by three votes over Elkin.[608] Elkin did not contest the results because, at that time, he would have had to pay for the recount himself. McCarney won the primary but not the November general election. Democrat Art Link went to Washington to serve one term in Congress.

Other Interests Inside and Outside the Office

State Treasurer Asbridge loved having her family nearby and thoroughly enjoyed spending time with her two grandchildren.

However, Bernice Asbridge enjoyed being with people and spent much of her "spare time" participating in community organizations. Throughout her career, she took on leadership positions in many civic groups, including the North Dakota Federation of Republican Women, American Legion Auxiliary, the Elkettes, the Burleigh County Cancer Society, and Bismarck Business and Professional Women. She attended Trinity Lutheran Church and was a member of the Sons of Norway.

The Constitutional Convention of 1972

Treasurer Asbridge loved to visit with people, and so it is no surprise to find a photo of her in the *Bismarck Tribune*, in January 1972, talking with visitors at the Constitutional Convention.[609] The convention, held in the legislative chambers of the Capitol building, was a historic event since this was only the second time a constitutional convention had been held in North Dakota. Mrs. Asbridge, as well as other state officials, had a particular interest in the "executive" section of the constitution. Delegates were seriously considering having only seven elected state officials, rather than 14. The state Treasurer position was one that would no longer be an elected state official.

All of this had started when the 1969 Legislature passed a concurrent resolution, signed by Governor Guy, which provided that the people would vote in September 1970 on calling for a constitutional convention. The 1969 Legislature also passed a law which established how delegates would be selected.

At the September 1970 primary election, the electorate voted to hold a constitutional convention, and in the November general election, they elected 98 convention delegates, including 12 women. The 1971 session of the Legislature appropriated $600,000 for the convention and also passed laws establishing the timing of the election to vote on the new constitution, providing regulation for lobbyists and directing state agencies to assist the convention.

Two volumes, *Debates of the North Dakota Constitutional Convention of 1972,* edited by Dean Bard, record all of the debates of the convention and provide a concise history of the convention.[610] A three-day organizational session of all the delegates was held in April 1971, and committee meetings were held during the summer and fall to allow time to study all of the issues and come up with recommendations before the actual convention started in January 1972. The convention itself could last only 30 working days but also included a 10-day break for drafting the actual wording of the document.

State officials were mainly on the sidelines during the actual convention, but on August 11, 1971, they had been called to give their input to the Executive Functions Committee.

First Governor Guy shared his thoughts with the committee. He advocated that the Secretary of State, Attorney General, state Treasurer, Commissioners of Agriculture, Labor, Tax and Insurance all be appointed by himself. He advocated that the state Auditor be appointed by the Legislature. This would address problems he had experienced such as when the "attorney general and secretary [sic. commissioner] of agriculture, both elective and currently of an opposing political party, blocked his attempt to initiate new policies for the Bank of North Dakota."[611] The only offices he suggested be elected were Governor, Lieutenant Governor, the three Public Service Commissioners and the Superintendent of Public Instruction.

Next the committee called on all of the other elected state officials. Testimony broke on party lines. All of the Republican state elected officials, including Treasurer Bernice Asbridge, "made it clear … they wanted no change in their status as elected officials." They "all presented a united front opposing any move towards changes in their offices." Attorney General Helge Johanneson "summed up the feelings of the state officials when he told the committee that officials should 'be independent to act as they think best and not be beholden to any one man. No person has a strong enough character not to be biased toward the person who appointed him.' "[612] State Auditor Curtis Olson promised to campaign against the proposed new constitution if elected offices were eliminated.

However, state Tax Commissioner Byron Dorgan and Public Service Commissioner Bruce Hagen, both Democrats, supported making their positions appointed positions.

"Dorgan said a tax commissioner should not be faced with trying to enforce tax laws and still win elections. He said his letters indicated that a tax commissioner doing a good job 'is building a launching pad for a political nose dive.' "[613]

The League of Women Voters supported changing many elective offices to appointed positions for three reasons: "1) A long ballot discourages informed voting. 2) A short ballot would make it easier to pinpoint credit or blame. 3) Some offices require persons with highly specialized qualification and would thus be better appointed than elected."[614]

At the end of the hearings, the committee decided to draft a proposal to "limit North Dakota's elected officials to a governor and lieutenant governor elected jointly, secretary of state, auditor, and three public service commissioners … ."[615] The other seven state elected officials would be appointed by the Governor with the consent of the Senate.

However, the delegates at the Constitutional Convention approved the following language in the proposed constitution: "The elected state officials shall be the governor, lieutenant governor, secretary of state, attorney general and three public service commissioners. The governor and lieutenant governor shall be elected on a joint ballot. Each vote cast for a candidate for governor shall be deemed cast also for the candidate for lieutenant governor nominated jointly with him."[616] The remaining seven state officials would be appointed by the governor and serve at his pleasure. They would be confirmed or rejected by the Senate.

The people voted on the proposed new constitution on April 28, 1972, and rejected it. The vote was 64,073 in favor; 107,643 opposed.[617] Over time, many parts of the rejected constitution were accepted as amendments to the existing constitution. However, as of 2013, North Dakotans still elect 13 state executive branch officials. Only the state Labor Commissioner has become a position appointed by the Governor.

1972 Campaign for Treasurer

Bernice Asbridge didn't wait for the people to vote on the new constitution to find out if she would have a chance to run again for office. She had already formally announced that she would be seeking re-election on January 18 at a North Dakota Federation of Republican Women's meeting.[618] She received a unanimous endorsement from the Republican Party convention held in Bismarck in early July. The Democrats again nominated Walter Christianson.

The Republican candidate for Governor was former Lieutenant Governor Richard Larson. The Democrats nominated Congressman Arthur Link. Both Art Link and Larson were discussing needed coal mining regulations, since on May 2, 1972, the North American Coal Corp. and Michigan Wisconsin Pipe Line Co. of Detroit had signed an option agreement to set aside 1.5 billion tons of lignite reserves for Michigan Wisconsin's conversion into gas.[619]

Nationally, anti-war activists were also making news. On May 12, the headline on the front page of the *Bismarck Tribune* read, "Over 1000 Arrests Reported – Protests Hit 23 States." The article went on to report that William Kunstler, supporter of the protests, declared, "Now is the time to get to the streets. We are in the grip of a dictator. We should disrupt every public function."[620] On May 19, 1972, a bomb exploded in a restroom of the Pentagon and anti-war groups claimed responsibility.[621]

As State Treasurer Bernice Asbridge campaigned around the state, she mentioned increased earnings on investments while she was state Treasurer. She was proud of the job she had done as state Treasurer and wanted to continue.

However, the voters decided otherwise. Walter Christensen received 130,211 votes; Bernice Asbridge, 125,856.[622] It must have been a difficult loss because all other incumbents who ran stayed in office. Arthur Link was elected Governor and Richard Nixon was re-elected President. Mrs. Asbridge, age 53, needed to find a new job.

Moving On

Mrs. Asbridge had plenty of political contacts in state government, and so in 1973, she found work as an investment adviser at the state Land Department. While working there, she also worked part time as public relations coordinator for the Bank of North Dakota.[623]

She still had the "bug" to run for state Treasurer. In 1976, she challenged Walter Christensen for the position, but again lost the election. So, in 1978, she decided to run for her former position as Burleigh county auditor. She won the county race, and she served as county auditor for eight more years. When elected, The *Bismarck Tribune* interviewed Mrs. Asbridge, "Party politics does not belong in county government, she said, and will never enter as a part of her office. 'Besides,' said Grandma Asbridge, 'I'm still human even if I have been in politics.' "[624]

Mrs. Asbridge served the public until 1986, when she was defeated when running for re-election as Burleigh County auditor. She had worked in county and state offices for 41 years when she retired at age 67.

Bernice Asbridge had many traits that endeared her to people over the years. A Bismarck Tribune article in 1967 noted about the Burleigh County auditor, "Mrs. Asbridge hasn't lost her faith in human nature and manages to maintain an unruffled aplomb in all official duties. She smiles disarmingly, and it must help a lot."[625]

Bernice Muriel Asbridge died on June 13, 2004, in Bismarck.

SEVENTEEN

A Lively Interest in Politics

Ruth Lenore Meiers

Lieutenant Governor
1985–87

By
Susan Wefald

"Women in public life are already making a difference. Why do you think that such issues as day care facilities, nursing home care, battered wives programs, displaced homemakers programs, and others are finally surging forward in the nation's consciousness – because women's groups are addressing these problems – because women are lobbying for change – because women care."[626]

Lieutenant Governor Ruth Meiers, 1986

Lieutenant Governor Ruth Meiers

Ruth Lenore Meiers nee Olson*

1925-87

Lieutenant Governor 1985-87

First Woman to Serve as North Dakota Lieutenant Governor

Personal Information

Born 1925 and raised on farm near Parshall, North Dakota. Married to Glenn, four children. In "spare time," enjoyed boating on Lake Sakakawea.

Party Affiliation

Democratic - Nonpartisan League

Education

Parshall High School; received degree in social work from University of North Dakota.

Professional Experience Before Taking Office

Mountrail County Welfare Board, executive secretary (director), 1947-51; Mountrail County Welfare Board, caseworker and child welfare worker, 1955-58 and 1962-66; Mountrail County Welfare Board, member; North Dakota House of Representatives, representing District 4, 1975-84.

Memberships Include

As Lieutenant Governor: Governor's Commission on Children and Adolescents at Risk, chair; State Child Support Enforcement Commission, chair; Legislative Audit and Fiscal Review, chair; Community Development Block Grant Advisory Board, chair; Capitol Grounds and Planning Commission, chair; member of Women Executives in State Government, Order of Women Legislators, National Conference of Lieutenant Governors.

Other: Upper Missouri District Health Unit, board member, 1956-84; Silver-Haired Legislature Steering Committee, 1980-81; Judicial Nominating Committee, 1979-80; Economic Development Commission, 1979-80; State Adoption Council, 1980-83; North Dakota Public Health Association; Disciplinary Board of the Supreme Court, 1981-85; Judicial Standards Committee of the Supreme Court, 1981-85; Mountrail County Cancer Society; Mountrail County Historical Society, president, 1984-85; Sew and So Homemakers Club; American Lutheran Church.[627]

*Bio contains information through 1987

Lieutenant Governor Ruth Meiers looked over her schedule for the week of June 23-27, 1986. She could see that it was going to be another week of the varied duties that kept her job interesting, and also "kept her on her toes." Monday, she would be in Williston giving a speech at the American Legion state convention and participating in a parade. Tuesday, she would be concentrating on the state's financial matters, chairing a meeting of the Legislative Audit and Fiscal Review Committee and attending a meeting of the State Board of Tax Equalization.

Wednesday, she would be working on the report to the Governor for the Commission on Children and Adolescents at Risk, attending meetings about the State Laboratory and visiting with Governor Sinner. Thursday, she would be chairing the Capitol Grounds Planning Commission and consulting with an expert on child abuse cases. Friday, she would hold a meeting to explore issues relating to children of alcoholics. In addition, she would be attending a breakfast and two dinners this week.[628]

At age 61, Ruth Meiers loved her work as Lieutenant Governor.

Growing Up in Mountrail County

In 1912, Ruth's father, Axel Olson, filed a homestead claim near Parshall, North Dakota, in Mountrail County, when Fort Berthold Reservation land was made available for homesteading. Then in 1913, Axel brought his wife, Grace, and their three sons to join him on the claim. The Olson family was a member of the group of homesteaders who continued to flock into the state to obtain land in the second decade of the 20th century.[629] In the "teens," grain prices were good and there was adequate moisture to grow good crops.

When Ruth was born on November 6, 1925, Axel and Grace had nine children, six boys and three girls.[630] Ruth, or Ruthie, as she was known, was the baby of the family. By the time she was 4 years old, the Depression, which would last a decade in North Dakota, made life much tougher on the farm. Ruth later recalled,

> "As the youngest of nine children I grew up in the thirties and I know the heartaches and the hardships my mother endured. She was the first one up in the morning and the last one in bed at night. Nearly all of the food on our table was the result of endless hours of canning from a garden that had to be watered constantly to produce. And yet, she found the time to nurture her family and instill in them the love of beauty, literature and the arts."[631]

As a child, Ruth loved to read. She talked about her love of reading in a speech at the Young Author's Conference in 1985:

> "As a youngster I lived on a farm – we had no television in those days and very little entertainment except that which we developed ourselves. Books became one of my best friends – I loved to read and literally devoured every book I could get my hands on. I still love to read. I travel to foreign lands with my reading – I became a tolerable cook through reading – I have laughed and cried while reading. It extended my horizons, my friendships, and my imagination and it can do the same for each of you."[632]

Her parents, Axel and Grace Olson, took a lively interest in politics in North Dakota. Axel was a charter member of the Nonpartisan League (NPL) and the Farmers Union. He also served on several local boards in the community. Ruth took part in political discussions around the lunch and supper table from an early age. In 1934, when she was 9 years old, Axel ran for the state legislature and won a seat in the House. He served there for one session, and then ran and was elected to the state Senate from 1936 to 1958.[633]

> "Personally, my involvement [in politics] began as a very young child. My parents stressed three things in life to which we were to be committed – the Lord, our family, and our country. To some that may sound trite – like believing in Mom and apple pie - but it never seemed so to me. In fact, I confess to being fond of Mom and apple pie. Actually, politics and public affairs were served like bread and butter at our supper table and I was exposed to that dialogue at an early age. In addition, my father 'put his money where his mouth was' by serving in the legislature for 22 years, as well as being active in community affairs. My mother was an activist at a time when that wasn't considered a women's role – so it was almost inevitable that I follow in their footsteps. They were excellent role models."[634]

Attending the University of North Dakota

Ruth graduated from Parshall High School in 1942 and decided that she wanted to attend college. However, first she had to convince her father that she should attend the University of North Dakota (UND). He wasn't so sure girls should attend the university, but her older brothers convinced him that she and her older sister should have the chance.[635] At UND, she was a member of the Sigma Alpha Epsilon social sorority, worked two jobs to pay her expenses and graduated with a BA in social work in 1946.[636]

Sometime in 1946 she met a 24-year-old World War II veteran, Dallace E. Pariseau, often referred to as Dallas, who had grown up in Pembina County, North Dakota. Dallas had been released from the Army in December 1945 after having served in the parachute infantry in Europe, where he was detained in a German prisoner of war camp from June

1944 to June 1945.[637]

On September 28, 1946, Ruth and Dallas were married in Parshall at the Evangelical Lutheran Church. The *Mountrail County Record* featured nice coverage of Ruth and Dallas' wedding on Page 1, describing the beautiful fall flowers on the altar, Ruth's dress and stated, "A coronet of orange blossoms held her finger tip veil and she carried a bouquet of American Beauty Roses." The article went on to report that a reception with a three-tiered wedding cake followed the ceremony at the bride's home and that the couple planned to make their home in Grand Forks while the groom completed his education at UND.[638]

However, those plans did not come to fruition. The young bride worked in Stanley, 36 miles from home, for the Mountrail County Welfare Board from October to December 1946. In 1947, she and her husband, Dallace Pariseau, had a baby boy they named David, and Mrs. Pariseau started working for Mountrail County again that October.[639]

This first marriage did not go well. The young couple divorced on June 4, 1948.[640] At the time of the divorce, Ruth was 22 years old with a 1-year-old baby and executive secretary (director) of the Mountrail Country Welfare Board in Stanley.

1947–1973: Juggling a Career in Social Work, Marriage and Four Boys

The years 1947 to 1973 were busy years for Ruth, juggling working for the Mountrail County Welfare Board, raising four boys with her husband, Glenn Meiers (who she married in June 1950), and taking care of her home and farm responsibilities.

When Ruth Olson Pariseau returned to work in October 1947, the year after she graduated from UND, she was hired to be the executive secretary (director) of the Mountrail County Welfare Board. She entered the field of social work at a time when social work professionals were desperately needed all across the state. County social service offices were established in North Dakota in 1935 to provide direct services to those in need in the county, and to administer and distribute the funds available from the county, state and federal government. In the 1940s, even though farm prices had improved and crops were good, the state continued to lose population, and by 1950, there were only 620,000 people living in the state.[641]

The exodus, to work in jobs needed by the war effort, took many college graduates from the state, including those qualified to work as social workers. By 1950, North Dakota had only 10 people in the state employed as child welfare workers, far fewer than were needed. Of course, there were people who worked for the counties who delivered other social service programs, but many of these people did not have the specialized training needed.[642]

So Ruth Olson Pariseau, with a degree in social work from UND, was needed in her home county. She served as executive secretary (director) from October 1947 to October 1951 and directed the work of the small office staff. In October 1948, the caseload for Mountrail County was 171 people receiving Old Age Assistance, 28 families receiving Aid to Dependent Children funds, zero receiving Aid to the Blind and 19 families receiving any type of general assistance.[643]

In the meantime, her family was expanding. After her divorce, Ruth married Glenn E. Meiers on June 28, 1950, and they had three more babies, Michael, Monte and Scott, between 1952 and 1955.[644] In 1955, they built a new home on the farm. With four children under 8 years old in 1955, Mrs. Meiers, age 30, was a busy mom and Ross farm wife. She returned to work as a county caseworker from March 1956 to August 1957, and as a child welfare worker from 1961 to 1963 and from 1965 to 1969.[645] She also served as a member of the Mountrail County Welfare Board from 1958 to 1960.[646] In an interview in 1987, Ruth Meiers recalled working for the county. "They came to ask if I would come to work for a year, until they got someone. Usually, two or three years later I would say, 'Well, I think I'm going to go home for a couple of years.' And that's literally what happened."[647]

Later, a neighbor remembered her as a person dedicated to her work. "She was very concerned about kids. I knew she'd take kids home and give them baths before they were placed in foster homes."[648]

Joanne Yocum, who was Ruth's immediate supervisor when she was a child welfare worker, spoke of Ruth as a "generous, sensitive and caring individual who frequently took children into her own home when an emergency called for an immediate placement. Meiers was very knowledgeable and understanding of the people and resources in her own county, which includes the Ft. Berthold Indian Reservation." [649]

Ruth's husband, Glenn, a farmer-rancher, was active in community affairs and Democratic politics. Ten years her senior, he was very supportive of his wife. "As long as she enjoys it, I don't mind," he told the Bismarck Tribune in 1985, when Ruth was Lieutenant Governor. The same article stated, "He's mild mannered and she's easy to get along with, so they don't fight much."[650]

Glenn was a World War II veteran who served in the Middle East. His community service included serving as secretary of the Ross Farmers Elevator for 20 years, serving on the Ross and Stanley school boards for 20 years and as a board member of the Mental Health Center. When Ruth died in 1987, she and Glenn had been married for almost 37 years.[651]

They both attended the Bethlehem Lutheran Church in Ross, where Mrs. Meiers taught Sunday School for 20 years and was active in American Lutheran Church Women.[652]

Running for the State House of Representatives

By 1974, Ruth Meiers, age 49, was ready for a new challenge. Her children were grown – her youngest son Scott was 18 years old, and now that she no longer was working for the county, she became involved in party politics. When she was attending the Democratic-NPL district convention in New Town in 1974, several young people approached her and asked her to become a candidate. She said "Yes," and was nominated that night to run for the state House seat.[653]

Ruth Olson Meiers had watched her father run for the state Legislature and win 11 elections, so she knew what running for a district office entailed. She needed to raise money, visit face to face with people all over the county and run ads in county newspapers. Most importantly, she had to convince people that she could be a good legislator.

She recognized that in order to win, she had to conform to unwritten rules about the role of a woman in her community. Years later, in June 1985, Lieutenant Governor Meiers gave a speech about "Feminism in Rural America" to the National Woman's Political Caucus and described her approach:

> "As a woman who has always been an activist I found I had to learn to work within the 'limits or rules' of my locality to be elected as a legislator and later to understand the mood of my state to be elected Lieutenant Governor.
>
> To give you some examples:
>
> In social groups, women gathered in one area and discussed recipes and kids – the men discussed the more weighty topics such as taxes and crops. You did not join the men, but on a "one to one" basis men would accept your input. Women generally accepted this arrangement – if you didn't you were considered pushy and you lost credibility.
>
> Women did not speak at public meetings to effect change – that would be too dominating, etc. It frequently had to be done more subtly prior to the meeting or afterwards – again on a one to one basis.
>
> If I had had school age children, I very likely would not have been elected the first time – 'woman's place is in the home' thinking." [654]

Ruth Meiers as a farmwife, homemaker and partner felt herself "somewhat knowledgeable about how rural women view themselves."[655] She found women in the age group 40 to 65 not as accepting of her running for office.

> "Most farm women believe they are people of value but largely within the context of their role as wife and mother. They look somewhat askance at a woman who thinks she can affect change in the community or in government because the majority do not view themselves as assuming that

> role. Their attitude: 'How can this farm wife presume to think she can perform that function?'
>
> On the other hand the women who are feminists are truly activists, but they have to develop techniques that will work to accomplish their goals. To simplify the techniques I use the three I's – be interested, be informed, be involved. Attend the right functions – be a source of reliable information – let them know you are willing to help in any way possible.
>
> And in a rural community, employment that establishes your expertise in a particular field adds to your acceptance – particularly if that is in a traditional 'women's field.' "[656]

It is obvious that Ruth Meiers gave a great deal of thought to how she should run her campaign in Mountrail County and following her own rules, she went on to win the election in the fall, becoming the first woman from District 4 to be elected to the House of Representatives.[657] She won her first election by only 75 votes.

Things did not go so smoothly in 1976. In her second bid for her House seat, she did not get the nomination at the party convention and had to run in the primary against the endorsed candidate. She won the primary and later commented, "I didn't get the (party) nomination and had to run against the nominee. You have to get your ducks in line is a lesson I learned."[658]

Representative Ruth Meiers went on to win four more terms in the House of Representatives. While a member of the Legislature, she chaired the Social Service and Veterans Affairs Committee and was a member of the Appropriations and Judiciary committees.[659]

The 1984 State Democratic-NPL Convention in Minot

The party nomination for Governor was the main event at the state Democratic-NPL convention in Minot in 1984. George Sinner, a former legislator and Cass County farmer, was competing for the nomination with former Governor Arthur Link, who had lost to Attorney General Allen Olson in 1980. Although there were other candidates for Governor, these two had the most committed delegates. However, there were many delegates who would not commit their vote to any candidate until they arrived at the convention. Sinner ended up winning the nomination, and rather than hand-pick his choice for Lieutenant Governor, he allowed the convention to pick his running mate.[660]

Richard "Dick" Backes, who was a longtime member of the state House, "came to the convention as the only announced candidate for lieutenant governor and was a Sinner supporter."[661] However, an organized group of women at the convention, known as the women's caucus, had other ideas. They wanted a woman to run for Lieutenant Governor. Even before the convention, Ruth Meiers later recalled, "a number of people called her, and asked if she would consider running for the Democratic nomination" [for lieutenant governor].[662]

But Meiers didn't want to run just as "a woman." She wanted people to want Ruth Meiers as the candidate and so she asked her friends to informally poll Democrats at the convention to see if they wanted her as Lieutenant Governor. It turned out that people at the Democrat – NPL convention were excited about Ruth Meiers running, and so Meiers consented to have her name placed in nomination, running against Backes at the convention for a spot on the ticket as Lieutenant Governor.[663]

The delegates voted and Meiers won the nomination by a vote of 697 to 465½. Backes then made a motion to cast a unanimous ballot for Meiers.[664] The Bismarck Tribune reported:

> "In accepting the endorsement for lieutenant governor, Meiers told delegates that she was nominated for her qualifications, but that she was proud 'that the Democratic-NPL Party has given viable consideration to the population of 50 percent of this state (women).' "[665]

Now Ruth Meiers needed to campaign around the state, advocating the Sinner-Meiers ticket, but George Sinner had the main responsibility for running the campaign. As Sinner planned his campaign, his campaign manager, Chuck Fleming, made a list of Sinner's assets and liabilities. One of his assets was "a woman on my ticket as a running mate," but Fleming also listed "a woman on the ticket" as a liability. They really didn't know how North Dakotans would react to Representative Ruth Meiers.

She worked hard the summer and fall of 1984 on the campaign trail. Meiers campaigned in large and small towns all over the state, often travelling with state Auditor candidate Heidi Heitkamp, who was running for office for the first time.[666]

By the end of August, Meiers was holding her own press conferences, and they continued about every other week for the remainder of the campaign. Topics included talking about doing more for displaced homemakers,[667] accusing the GOP of false statements,[668] blaming Governor Olson's administration for not correcting problems at the State Hospital,[669] challenging Olson on an ad about the Air Force bases[670] and attacking Olson's tax increase proposal in the 1983 session.[671]

On Tuesday, November 6, George Sinner and Ruth Meiers won the election against Allen Olson and Ernest Sands: 173,922 to 140,460.[672] It was Ruth's birthday. The *Bismarck Tribune* reported:

> "Just after midnight, Rep. Ruth Meiers, Sinner's running mate, prepared to address a live television audience from the Ramada Inn banquet room … . Then in a spontaneous celebration, the entire room sang "Happy Birthday" to Meiers who turned 59 on Tuesday.

'It is an exciting day,' Meiers said, 'and I think I'm going to have the biggest birthday I've ever had.' "

Taking Office

Taking office was not "business as usual" for the Sinner-Meiers team. Two state Supreme Court appointments were pending, and Sinner wanted to be able to make those appointments. If he took office on January 8, when he took his oath of office in a traditional ceremony before the Legislature, outgoing Governor Allen Olson would be able to make the two court appointments.

Sinner and Meiers took their oaths of office on Monday, December 31, 1984, before Secretary of State Ben Meier and made plans to move into the Governor's office immediately. Governor Olson said that he would not stop being Governor without a decision from the Supreme Court and did not move out of the Governor's office. And so on Friday, January 4, the Supreme Court held a hearing on the matter, pondered the case and issued their decision, deciding that Sinner had been Governor since January 1.[673]

A few weeks later, on January 17, Governor Sinner appointed Herb Meschke and Beryl Levine to the Supreme Court. Justice Levine was the first woman to serve on the North Dakota Supreme Court.

Lieutenant Governor Meiers could not move into her new office at the state Capital

Former Governor Art Link (left) and Governor George Sinner congratulate Lieutenant Governor Meiers at the Ruth Meiers Appreciation Day Dinner on March 14, 1985.
(SHSND 31811-007)

until the dispute about who was Governor was settled. The Lieutenant Governor's small, wood-paneled office, facing the Capitol mall, is located adjacent to the Governor's reception area. The floors and ceiling of the office are covered with Burman teak wood.

Historically, Meiers' office was the Governor's office. This office had been occupied by every Governor since the new Capitol was built, except Governor Allen Olson. When the Legislature made the Lieutenant Governor position full time in 1981, Governor Olson moved the Governor's office down the hall to the larger Governor's conference room, and Lieutenant Governor Sands occupied the smaller "historic" office. This arrangement has suited all Governors and Lieutenant Governors since that time.

It took a while to get her office running "smoothly." In a January 31 letter to constituents who had written her congratulatory messages, she wrote:

> "I apologize for the long delay in responding to your expression of support but frankly I have not had secretarial help[674] available until recently … . We do have an excellent staff on board now and everything is beginning to run smoothly.
>
> It is truly an honor and a privilege to serve as your Lt. Governor and I hope to fulfill the responsibilities of that office to the best of my ability. I have even reached the point that I recognize it's me people mean when I'm addressed as 'Lt. Governor.' "[675]

Description of Official Duties as Lieutenant Governor

Four-year term (elected with the Governor). The Lieutenant Governor acts as chief executive in case of the Governor's death, resignation or on other occasions when the Governor is unable to fulfill his responsibilities; serves as President of the Senate and in the event of a tie may cast the decisive vote; assumes other board chairmanships and functions as prescribed by the Governor.[676]

President of the Senate

Although Lieutenant Governor Meiers had 10 years of experience in the state House of Representatives, as Lieutenant Governor, she acted as president of the Senate and thus presided over the state Senate. This constitutional responsibility started on January 8 and kept her busy every day the Legislature was in session until their work was finished in April 1985. In late January, she noted, "Presiding over the Senate is a new experience and a challenging one. Once I feel entirely comfortable with the parliamentary procedure I believe I will actually enjoy it."[677]

The *Williston Daily Herald* interviewed her in mid-February 1985 and reported:

"With her husky voice and no-nonsense manner, she runs the legislators through the first, second and third orders of business: the opening prayer; roll call; and referring to the journal.

Those formalities completed, the Senate is on its way. Meiers guides the process with apparent ease, keeping the flow steady … . Occasionally, Meiers will ask the advice of Sen. Frank Wenstrom, R-Williston, the lieutenant governor in 1963 and 1964. Meiers is doing a good job, Wenstrom said.

'When I first started I was somewhat nervous,' admitted Meiers. She wishes she would have spent a term in the Senate, she said, since that would have made her more familiar with the Senate protocol."[678]

Lieutenant Governor Ruth Meiers' Favorite Project

With her strong background in social work, Ruth Meiers enthusiastically took on the role of chair of the Governor's Commission on Children and Adolescents at Risk (CAAR). It became the centerpiece of her work as Lieutenant Governor.

Advocates for children and youth from the Mental Health Association, the Department of Human Services, the Supreme Court and the North Dakota Association of Counties proposed the study in December 1984. They were "aware of the gaps in effective delivery of service and shortfalls of the present system,"[679] and they met several times with the Governor and Lieutenant Governor-elect and legislators from both parties to share their concerns about services available to children and adolescents at risk.

Those at risk included children and adolescents who were emotionally and behaviorally disturbed, victims of abuse and neglect, suicidal, chemically dependent or abusing, runaway and homeless, status offenders, delinquent or children of alcoholic or chemically dependent parents.[680]

On January 31, 1985, Governor Sinner issued an executive order to create a commission to study and make recommendations on these issues, and made Lieutenant Governor Meiers chair of the commission. A resolution also was passed by the Legislature which directed that findings be reported to the Legislative Council by March 1, 1986, and on to the 1987 legislative assembly.

However, no money was available for the study. Therefore, shortly after the Governor appointed members to CAAR on May 19, 1985, funding applications were prepared to request $58,000 to fund the work of the group. This amount included the funds to pay a coordinator and a clerical assistant, who would be under the supervision of the chair of the committee, Lieutenant Governor Meiers.[681] Soon funding was received from the Bremer Foundation and the North Dakota Community Foundation, and the North Dakota Mental Health Association acted as receiver and payee of the funds.

Lieutenant Governor Meiers was totally involved with CAAR from its inception. She met with commission members and wrote updates about the progress of the work. She was a cheerleader for the work of the commission when she gave speeches. One letter to over 90 commission subcommittee members stated:

> "I would like to assure you that the level of your personal effort and commitment to the project will directly affect the outcome of the Commission. This may well be a once-in-a-generation opportunity for all of us to impact a positive change in the delivery system to children and adolescents."[682]

In May 1986, she addressed a legislative budget committee on CAAR progress and talked about how long it had been since the state had made a major study on these issues.

> "Sixty-four years have passed since the last comprehensive report on troubled children and the resources available to them has been given to the Legislature. Sixty-four years – two generations – of changes and yet a surprising amount of things remain the same.
>
> The current Commission did not have to worry about almshouses, orphan trains, or baby farming as the 1922 Commission did. However, the current Commission and the 1922 Commission had to deal with problems of services in rural areas, the question of home care versus institutional care, and the lack of a continuum of services."[683]

Presentations were made to the commission by over 40 agencies and public hearings were held all over the state.[684] The five CAAR subcommittees made recommendations after digesting all of this public input, and these were delivered in a report on July 1, 1986, to Governor Sinner. Unfortunately, this was four months later than requested by the Legislature and, by the time the report was digested by the Governor and legislators, it was too late to incorporate the recommendations into the budgets of the state agencies that could implement the recommendations.[685]

However, in April 1987, after the death of Lieutenant Governor Ruth Meiers, the Legislature appropriated $1 million that went to fund child welfare programs at the Department of Human Services that carried out CAAR recommendations. Other recommendations in the report were funded by leveraging other funds. For example, the Ruth Meiers Adolescent Center in Grand Forks and Manchester House in Bismarck, treatment centers for emotionally disturbed teenagers, were both built with other sources of money.[686]

On the Job as Lieutenant Governor

In addition to serving as presiding officer of the Senate during the legislative session, Meiers took on a number of other duties to assist Governor Sinner with his work. She gave several speeches a week and wrote them herself. Her speaking engagements included talks to agriculture groups, youth groups, industry groups and service clubs. She was asked to speak to many women's groups, and she obliged, encouraging women to run for office and challenging them to make the most of their lives. In a speech titled, "The Women's Role in Politics," she stated:

> "Whether or not there is a future in politics for women depends upon the women themselves. If we have sufficient desire and determination to work and elect qualified women candidates, then there is most definitely a future. Perhaps some of you in this room might consider running for public office. I would urge you to do so."[687]

In March 1985, the Lieutenant Governor gave a speech to the state members of the National Organization for Women (NOW), a group which encouraged women to be political activists.

> "When I speak of 'involvement' I don't limit that to political activity but I do think that is a vital element to the success of women in leadership in this country. Political activity is essential if we are to affect change. Many of the problems which plague women today must be resolved politically and we all must participate. Is there one of the so called 'women's issues,' that does not require political action – ERA – Day care; Reproductive Rights; Pay Equity; Comparable Worth; Child Support; Spouse Abuse, etc. We simply must become more involved in the political process."[688]

In a speech to teenage girls at Girls State in June 1986, she encouraged them to run for school boards and serve as county commissioners, legislators and state elected officials. She noted:

> "Women in public life are already making a difference. Why do you think that such issues as day care facilities, nursing home care, battered wives programs, displaced homemakers programs, and others are finally surging forward in the nation's consciousness – because women's groups are addressing these problems – because women are lobbying for change – because women care."[689]

Lieutenant Governor Meiers in her office autographing a picture to give to Jody Fossen, North Dakota Junior Miss Charm. (May 27, 1986 - SHSND 31811-006)

Governor Sinner determined which projects his Lieutenant Governor would chair. Although Lieutenant Governor Meiers stated at the beginning of her term, "George Sinner wants to keep in touch and chair committees,"[690] she ended up chairing quite a few committees. In 1985, in addition to chairing CAAR, she was chair of the State Child Support Enforcement Commission, Legislative Audit and Fiscal Review Committee, Community Development Block Grant Advisory Board, and Capitol Grounds and Planning Commission. In 1985, she was also a member of the Disciplinary Board of the Supreme Court and a member of the Judicial Standards Committee of the Supreme Court.[691] In 1986, her "bio" shows that she also served as chair of the Investment Board and the Heritage Foundation.[692]

She was an active member of the National Conference of Lieutenant Governors. In 1985, she was one of only five women lieutenant governors in the nation.[693] This sometimes caused some confusion. The *Bismarck Tribune* related this story:

"She grins as she tells of going to Washington, D.C., for a lieutenant governors' conference. She checked in and was asked, 'Where is he?' 'I said, I'm she.'"[694]

Lieutenant Governor Meiers also took time to write "thank you" notes. Her records reveal copies of hundreds of thank you notes that she wrote to people who came to see her at her office, gave her small courtesies or helped the state in some way. She obviously thought saying "thank you" was an important part of her job.[695]

Visiting Russia

Lieutenant Governor Ruth Meiers' comments about Russian women "raised some eyebrows" after she attended a "Women in Leadership" tour to the Union of Soviet Socialist Republics (USSR) in May 1986. The three-week trip with 51 other women to Russia was "designed to match women in leadership positions in the US with their counterparts in the USSR."[696] Ruth paid her own way on this trip, and she was matched with a deputy premier in Russia. The trip was approved by the State Department and sponsored by the U.S. – U.S.S.R. Initiatives, an American organization.[697]

It must have been a wonderful trip, and given the fact that she died less than a year later, it was particularly meaningful that she had the opportunity to go abroad to make that visit. On the trip, she was able to visit homes, schools, churches and shops, and the Soviet Women's Committee set up formal meetings in Leningrad, Moscow and Minsk. The Lieutenant Governor was not able to travel to Minsk because it was too close to Chernobyl, where the nuclear plant incident had just exploded and released a great deal of radiation.

When she returned home, the Lieutenant Governor held a news conference to talk about her experiences and what she had learned. One of the topics of the news conference was the Chernobyl nuclear plant disaster, which occurred on April 26, and which the Soviet government did not disclose to the West for almost three days. By then, Ruth Meiers was in Finland for an orientation session before her trip to Russia. "I had all kinds of people (here at home) ask me if I glowed," she remarked.[698]

The *Bismarck Tribune* reported:

"Meiers said the American press sensationalized the accident. Soviet people were upset that the U.S. media didn't seem to focus on the human effect of the accident."[699]

The North Dakota Associated Press also covered her remarks about her trip and focused on her remarks about the "freedom" of Soviet women.

" 'Soviet women probably have more freedom … than in almost any

> country in the world,' said Meiers. 'It depended on how you interpret freedom, but they do have a considerable amount of power.'
>
> 'They state very strongly that there are more opportunities for women than in any country in the world. I don't know if that's true or not, but it appears that it's true,' she said.
>
> However, personal freedom is obviously very limited there, and the standard of living was much lower in the Soviet Union than in the United States, she said."[700]

At a speech to the National Association of Social Workers on May 29, 1986, the Lieutenant Governor shared thoughts about the role of women in Russia.

> "Only recently I returned from the Soviet Union where women have really made their influence felt. The government women's committee maintains that women are in a more favorable position there than anywhere on the face of the globe. There is no pay inequity in their country – any woman who wishes to work may do so and may obtain any level of education her abilities allow. Child care is provided for everyone. There are more women physicians and lawyers than in any other country. Women hold many non-traditional jobs. One third of the membership of the Supreme Soviet are women. We may not agree with their political philosophy but we have to be impressed with their accomplishments."[701]

Frederick Smith, a conservative columnist for the *Bismarck Tribune,* could not resist writing a column on her remarks. Titled, "Gullible Ruth swallowed 'silly' Soviet stories," he lambasted her finding that the American media had "sensationalized" the Chernobyl accident and her remarks about the "freedom" of Soviet women.

A flurry of letters to the editor around the state commented about her remarks. In October 1986, Elizabeth Hampsten wrote a sharp rebuttal article titled "Ruth Meiers travels to Russia" in the *Plainswoman*. In that article, she stated "Ruth Meiers admits that in the North American context she probably should not have used the word **freedom** to describe Soviet women's status."[702]

Lieutenant Governor Ruth Meiers was known for speaking her mind, and it is no wonder that every once in a while her remarks resulted in public comment.

Making Time for Her Family

While serving in state office, Meiers lived in Bismarck and commuted home to the farm in Ross on weekends. Her husband, Glenn, lived on the farm. In 1985, she was interviewed by the *Bismarck Tribune* for a feature article and she talked about her marriage to Glenn.

> " 'The hardest thing (for him) is not having me there to share things.' Sometimes he drives the 175 miles to Bismarck, but more often she goes home on Fridays and returns on Sundays. 'We've sort of got one of those "commuter marriages," ' she says. 'I hibernate when I get home.'
>
> Meiers likes to sleep until nine or 10 on Saturday mornings. Then she cooks and stocks the freezer because Glenn isn't much of a cook and he loves desserts – eggs and soups are his culinary specialties.
>
> Her idea of fun is to go to Lake Sakakawea to boat and hunt for arrowheads. Someday she would like to write more poetry, maybe even a book, and make a quilt for each of her seven grandchildren.
>
> Time is at a premium. 'It's hard to find time to get a haircut, exercise, shop and walk (daily).' "[703]

The article also included a recipe for cookies that the Lieutenant Governor had baked the previous weekend. Glenn told the *Bismarck Tribune,* "They're real tasty."

In a letter to a young woman on August 22, 1986, Ruth Meiers wrote, "I am a woman, a homemaker, a mother, a grandmother, a social worker – in addition to being Lieutenant Governor. As is true of most women, I wear many hats." The letter went on to mention her husband Glenn, her four children, one foster son and seven grandchildren. It continued:

> "I feel one of Glenn's and my greatest accomplishments was raising four children who are productive citizens. I had a desire to complete graduate work or law school and never accomplished that goal and consider it my greatest failure.
>
> At present I intend to do a capable job as Lieutenant Governor. My future prospects will depend on my continued good health and my family's needs. I really do not dwell on the future but there are many things I would like to do. I simply have not been able to devote any time to other projects. I will never live long enough to be bored. Specifically, I would like to do some writing in the future."[704]

Cancer

Just 21 months into her term, Lieutenant Governor Meiers was diagnosed with advanced cancer.[705] A staff member found her at her desk struggling to talk and breathe on the morning of September 9, 1986, and she was rushed to the hospital in an ambulance. Three days later, her doctors and the Lieutenant Governor held a press conference at the hospital and announced that she had lung cancer, which had spread to her brain. Everyone knew that it was a very serious situation. She said, "I believe in prayer. I believe in miracles. I also believe in reality, and I believe I can deal with that."[706]

Meiers smoked an average of 1½ packs of cigarettes a day for 30 years, but quit when her cancer was diagnosed.[707] That fall, she received 25 radiation treatments,[708] had gall stone surgery, spent two weeks in the hospital with pneumonia, but also performed some duties as her health permitted. For example, on September 17, she travelled to Devils Lake to give a speech. In mid-October, she was at her office for a few hours each day.[709] In early December, she presided over a special five-day session of the Legislature.

In mid-December, her doctors decided to operate on one of her brain tumors, and the surgery went well. She recuperated from the surgery quickly, feeling much better, and she was able to preside over the Senate from January 6 until January 22, 1987, when she needed to re-enter the hospital. A few days later, she learned that the cancer had spread to her liver, and she made her last appearance in the Senate on February 17.[710]

On March 10, 1987, over 500 people attend a banquet in her honor, and Lieutenant Governor Meiers was able to stand to receive the North Dakota Hall of Fame's Citizen Award. She re-entered the hospital on March 11 and died on March 19, 1987.[711]

After her death, her casket was placed in the Great Hall of the Capitol building for public visiting and two funerals were held – one at Trinity Lutheran Church in Bismarck and one at her Lutheran Church in Ross. North Dakotans knew that they had lost a very special and caring state leader.

Remembering Ruth Meiers

Governor Sinner, in his book *Turning Points,* remembered the eulogy he delivered for Meiers at her home church in Ross.

> "I talked about how much Ruth loved life, and how we would miss her hearty laugh in the office. I remembered the delight that showed on her face in the photos taken when she entered a milking contest and lost to another woman, Mandan's mayor. Both of them beat the only male contestant.
>
> I also recalled the time when she rode a circus elephant for which Ringling Brothers presented her with a certificate of achievement."[712]

Sinner also commented on his Lieutenant Governor's legacy.

> "Ruth Meiers left a legacy for North Dakota people and took the role of women and the role of service to new heights … . She was a terrific woman who had a strong background. She came from the farm and she

> didn't mind doing the things that get your hands dirty and was matter of fact about dealing with lots of problems. She cared about taking care of people. She knew better than most that government is about protecting the rights of people and the rest of us better serve that end or you are badly mistaken about government."[713]

In October 1985, Lieutenant Governor Meiers testified before the Centennial Planning Commission, asking the commission to celebrate the women who contributed so much in the first 100 years of our state.[714] She inspired women at the University of North Dakota to establish a Committee for the North Dakota History of Women Project, which decided to sponsor publication of a special book about North Dakota women. Ruth Meiers was chair of this project and received progress reports on it until she died. In 1988, the Book *Day In and Day Out -Women's Lives in North Dakota* was dedicated to Ruth Olson Meiers.[715]

CONCLUSION

By
Kjersten Nelson

The previous chapters included the stories of some of North Dakota's inspiring women of politics. What can these interesting narratives tell us about some of the bigger questions of female representation in politics? As I mentioned in the Foreword, women are significantly underrepresented in the politics of the state. However, this is not a problem unique to North Dakota. Political scientists have spent decades trying to figure out why the percentage of women in elected office did not track the upward trend in other professions, like law, business, education leadership and other venues for political activism. What do these perspectives tell us about some of these more general theories and conclusions?

Given the historic nature of this volume, the earliest eras bear out beliefs that women would not be elected even if they ran because elected office was not an acceptable role for women to fill.[716] In other words, the voters would not stand for it. While women earned the right to vote and run for offices besides the Superintendent of Public Instruction in 1919, Berta Baker was the only woman elected to a statewide position *besides* Superintendent of Public Instruction until 1968, when Bernice Asbridge was elected state treasurer.

In fact, the Superintendent of Public Instruction is the statewide elected office that has most frequently been filled by a woman. If anywhere, it might be acceptable for a woman to fulfill a role devoted to children and their educations, an issue that, to this day, voters presume women will be more competent to handle.[717] These traditionally "female" issue areas provide common motivation for women even thinking about running for office.[718] Lieutenant Governor Rosemarie Myrdal pursued this type of path in politics, as she moved from a teaching and school business management career to the school board, to the Legislature, to statewide executive office (Chapter 2).

At some point, however, voters became less skeptical of female candidates – at least to the point where, when women run, they stand an equal chance of winning as compared to male candidates.[719] And yet, even with this encouraging factor, women did not start entering electoral politics, at least as candidates, in the numbers that were initially hoped.

More subtle factors may influence women's decisions to run or not. The first, perhaps most obvious, suspect was family obligations. To this day, while men's share of housework and childcare has increased, women continue to do more than half of these responsibilities.[720]

Throughout the time period covered by this book, women's participation in the paid labor force also increased. Adding a campaign to employment, household, and childcare responsibilities is no small undertaking. Moreover, for many candidates, a successful campaign means moving to Bismarck either with their families – potentially disrupting children's social networks and a spouse's career – or moving away from their families. Justice Maring's narrative particularly notes the difficulty of a split-family arrangement.

It is not surprising, then, that, in keeping with national-level findings, many of the women here either did not have children or waited to run until their children were in school (or older). This appears to be true throughout the time span of the book: the first four officials chronologically did not have children, an uncommon phenomenon for the time period.

Perhaps even more notably, five out of the first six state officials were single or widowed at the time of their statewide campaigns; in an era where children weren't the only household members that needed caretaking, husbands may have been more detriment than support in political careers (at least in this sample here). Even in the later years, Public Service Commissioner Wefald notes the fine line she walked of campaigning with her husband because she was worried about looking like his "helpmate" (Chapter 6).

Later on, though many women had children and participated in politics, most waited until their children were at least in their teens to run for higher office. The one exception was Heidi Heitkamp, who first ran for office with small children. She does note that, by the time she ran for the U.S. Senate in 2012, her "children were grown," among other reasons that her focus and loyalties weren't as split as before (Chapter 1).[721] Supreme Court Justice Carol Kapsner also had grown children by the time she was appointed to and ran for a position on the Supreme Court; but her chapter is particularly interesting in describing the flexibility and creativity that was required to balance professional and personal obligations (Chapter 10).

Family obligations can't be the whole story, though. Another established contributing factor to low female representation in elected offices is that women don't get asked to run as much as similarly-situated men do. This is well-documented for many of the professions that typically lead to elected office; when men and women look basically equivalent on paper – in terms of experience, education and qualifications – significantly more men than women report having been asked to run.[722] State Treasurer Kelly Schmidt reflects on the state party chair asking her to run; it appears to be a conversation that served as a tipping point for her decision to run. Similar urging was fundamental in Heitkamp's initial decision to run, as well as Public Service Commissioner Wefald's.

Much of this recruitment can come from formal party leaders, but it doesn't have to. Lieutenant Governor Meiers, Heitkamp and Secretary of Agriculture Sarah Vogel all refer to strong recruitment efforts from a group of women from within the party who were not necessarily public figures themselves. State Treasurer Kathi Gilmore (Chapter 3) got her start in politics because she liked the neighbors who approached her to run for the state Legislature. From this perspective, a mindful dedication to cultivating young women as they show interest in politics, paired with focused recruiting of those women, appears to be a vital tool in the effort to increase women's representation.

Perhaps one of the harder aspects of women's hesitance to run for office is the finding that women generally are less confident in their abilities or doubt that they have thick enough skin to withstand the rigors of a campaign.[723] Unfortunately, this corroborates decades of studies in all sorts of fields; one of the effects of second-class status is systematically lower levels of confidence and self-esteem.[724] Of course, the stories we read here are stories from the women who were able to overcome that discrepancy.

But the years of experience, high levels of education and hard work are notable in this sample. Even with a post-graduate degree (i.e., her law degree), Agriculture Commissioner Sarah Vogel needed to reassure voters on the campaign trail that just because she wasn't a farmer didn't mean she didn't understand agricultural issues. Treasurer Bernice Asbridge had almost 25 years of experience working in the Burleigh County Auditor's Office – 13 years of it as a deputy or head auditor – before she ran for her statewide office. Every single Superintendent of Public Instruction had decades of teaching and education administrative experience before her run for this office. And Public Service Commissioner Susan Wefald discusses how she worked to demonstrate her competence; she didn't want to have to refer journalists to her staff on hard questions, even though her contemporary Public Service Commissioners (both men) did so without a second thought (Chapter 6).

To be sure, the narratives we see here come from women who did have the confidence to assert themselves into this male-dominated arena. It would be fascinating to ask further questions, specifically to this issue, to identify specific processes, people or institutions that helped instill that confidence.

In sum, I hope you take a few things from these incredible stories. First, perhaps, is inspiration and an appreciation for the accomplishments of those who came before us. Second is the charge to recognize the abilities, in ourselves and others, that would make us similarly inspiring elected leaders. This collection should only be the beginning volume in a story of women in elected leadership that is still unfolding.

ENDNOTES

1 Center for American Women and Politics. 2014. "Did You Know?" Accessed at http://www.cawp.rutgers.edu/fast_facts/resources/Didyouknow.php#congress.

2 Center for American Women and Politics. 2014. "Women in State Legislatures." Accessed at http://www.cawp.rutgers.edu/fast_facts/levels_of_office/documents/stleg.pdf.

3 U.S. Census Bureau. N.D. "Census Regions and Divisions of the United States." Accessed at http://www.census.gov/geo/maps-data/maps/pdfs/reference/us_regdiv.pdf.

4 The raw numbers may be helpful here, given that the denominator is so different from state to state. As of 2014, four out of North Dakota's 16 statewide elected offices were held by women. This compares with two out of 13 for South Dakota, four out of 11 for Montana, and four out of seven for Minnesota. These figures were computed from individual "State Fact Sheets" for each state, available from the Center for American Women and Politics at http://www.cawp.rutgers.edu/fast_facts/resources/state_fact_sheet.php. North Dakota, by statewide vote, elects 13 executive branch officials, three members of Congress and five Supreme Court Justices. The number and percentage for North Dakota in the Rutgers data does not include the two women justices on the North Dakota Supreme Court who are also elected by a statewide vote. When they are added into the mix, 29 percent of North Dakota's statewide elected offices were held by women in 2014. As of summer 2014, two of these six women, Public Service Commissioner Julie Fedorchak and Supreme Court Justice Lisa McEvers, were appointed by the Governor and had not yet run for election.

5 Handy-Marchello, Barbara. 2009. "Woman Suffrage at Statehood – Introduction." *North Dakota Studies Program.* Bismarck, North Dakota: State Historical Society of North Dakota. Accessed at http://history.nd.gov/textbook/unit4_1_suffrage_intro.html.

6 Gerrity, Jessica C., Tracy Osborn and Jeanette Morehouse. 2007. "Women and Representation: A Different View of the District?" *Politics & Gender,* 3: 179-200. Swers, Michele. 2002. *The Difference Women Make.* Chicago: University of Chicago Press.

7 Pearson, Kathryn, and Logan Dancey. 2011. "Speaking for the Underrepresented in the House of Representatives: Voicing Women's Interests in a Partisan Era." *Politics & Gender* 7: 493-519.

8 See, e.g., Michael, Jenny. "Legislation seeks to help victims of sex trafficking." *Bismarck Tribune,* February 2, 2014. Accessed at http://bismarcktribune.com/news/local/crime-and-courts/legislation-seeks-to-help-victims-of-sex-trafficking/article_b4b5f24e-8bcf-11e3-aff6-0019bb2963f4.html.

9 Bratton, Kathleen A., and Kerry L. Haynie. 1999. "Agenda Setting and Legislative Success in State Legislatures: The Effects of Gender and Race." *Journal of Politics* 61: 658-679; Caizza, Amy. 2004. "Does Women's Representation in Elected Office Lead to Women-Friendly Policy? Analysis of State-Level Data." *Women and Politics* 26: 35-70; Dolan, Kathleen, and Lynne Ford. 1995. "Women in the State Legislatures: Feminist Identity and Legislative Behaviors." *American Politics Quarterly* 23: 96-108.

10 Critical mass is the idea, originally stated by Moss Kanter, that different behavior by women (and

other minorities) may only emerge as they move from token status to actual substantive proportions of representation. This is a general theory, applied to all sorts of organizations and institutions. See Moss Kanter, Rosabeth. 1977. *Men and Women of the Corporation.* New York: Basic Books.

11 U.S. Bureau of Labor Statistics. January 2014. "Highlights of Women's Earnings, Region VIII: Denver." Accessed at http://www.dol.gov/equalpay/regions/2014/denver.pdf.

12 See, for example, Jewell, Malcolm, and Marcia Lynn Whicker. 1993. "The Feminization of Leadership in State Legislatures." *PS: Political Science and Politics* 26: 705-712. Jewell, Malcolm, and Marcia Lynn Whicker. 1994. *Legislative Leadership in the American States.* Ann Arbor, MI: University of Michigan Press; Kathlene, Lynn. 1994. "Power and Influence in State Legislative Policymaking: The Interaction of Gender and Position in Committee Hearing Debates." *American Political Science Review* 88: 560-576; Simon Rosenthal, Cindy. 1997. "A View of Their Own: Women's Committee Leadership Styles and State Legislatures." *Policy Studies Journal* 25: 585-600.

13 Kenny, Sally. 2013 *Gender and Justice: Why Women in the Judiciary Really Matter.* New York: Routledge; For citations on the pervasiveness of women's lower self-confidence, see Chapter 6 of Lawless, Jennifer L., and Richard L. Fox. 2005. *It Takes a Candidate: Why Women Don't Run for Office.* New York: Cambridge University Press.

14 *North Dakota Blue Book 1995* (Bismarck: North Dakota Secretary of State Al Jaeger) 145.

15 *North Dakota Centennial Blue Book – 1889-1989* (Bismarck: Secretary of State Ben Meier, 1989) 147.

16 *North Dakota Blue Book – 1995-97* (Bismarck: Secretary of State Al Jaeger, 1995) 158-160.

17 *North Dakota Centennial Blue Book, 1889-1989* (Bismarck: Secretary of State Ben Meier, 1989) 143.

18 Editor's Note: Lieutenant Governor Myrdal's husband, John, died in 2000, shortly before she retired from state office.

19 *1999-01 North Dakota Blue Book*, (Bismarck: Secretary of State Al Jaeger, 1999) 255 and *1993-95 North Dakota Blue Book*, (Bismarck: Secretary of State Al Jaeger, 1993) 144

20 *North Dakota Blue Book 1997-99*, (Bismarck: Secretary of State Al Jaeger, 1997) 311

21 *North Dakota Blue Book 2005-2007* (Bismarck: Secretary of State Al Jaeger, 2005) 256.

22 *North Dakota Blue Book 2011-2013* (Bismarck: Secretary of State Al Jaeger, 2011) 248.

23 *North Dakota Blue Book 1995* (Bismarck: Secretary of State Al Jaeger 1995) 147.

24 There are many books and articles about the League, its philosophy and accomplishments. See, e.g., *Political Prairie Fire: The Nonpartisan League, 1915-1922*, Robert Morlan, Minnesota Historical Society Press, 1985, with an introduction by Larry Remele (Reprint of the book, first published in 1955). One can also watch the 1978 movie Northern Lights, produced and directed by North Dakota native John Hanson for a dramatic story about the founding of the League.

25 As the years passed and my research deepened, I realized that I had learned only about the virtues of these legendary leaders, not their flaws or intra-party battles.

26 The Farmers' Holiday Association was a Midwestern movement of farmers fighting foreclosures and repossessions that was active between 1932 and 1934. For more information on the Farmers Holiday Association, the Langer Moratorium, the Langer Grain Embargo and the otherwise wild times in North Dakota in this period, see "The Law of Hard Times: Debtor and Farmer Relief Actions of the 1933 North Dakota Legislative Session" by Sarah Vogel. Originally published in 60 North Dakota Law Review 489 (1984); available at www.NationalAgLawCenter.org.

27 See "Going Under: North Dakota Lawyer Sarah Vogel Fights to Save Family Farmers," *Life Magazine*, November 1982.

28 The national class covered 45 states, excluding five states with copycat class actions.

29 Heidi later became Attorney General of North Dakota and we served together on the Industrial Commission for four years, from 1992 to 1996. She is now a U.S. Senator from North Dakota.

30 Because of Civil Service, an elected official generally inherits all of the existing agency staff but has the right to appoint an administrative assistant and a deputy. My selection of Jeff as Deputy was a great choice. Jeff was Deputy Commissioner of Agriculture for my two terms, and then continued working in the same capacity for Roger Johnson from 1997 to 2009. He won the National Association of Departments of Agriculture Excellence in Administration Award in 2006. He typically stayed in the background, but he was critical to every successful program I had during my two terms.

31 The vote (in a four-way race) was 132,959 (Sarah Vogel, Dem/NPL) to 115,817 (Keith Bjerke, endorsed Republican candidate) to 41,386 (Kent Jones, the incumbent Commissioner who had not been endorsed by the Republican Party) to 4,229 (Harley McLean, Independent). Some observers felt that the Republican vote had been split between Bjerke and Jones, and I would have lost but for Jones' candidacy. While it was then and still is irrelevant, I disagreed. Mr. Bjerke's vote total was more than the "base" votes for several other Republican candidates in two-way races, so the difference was in how the independents voted, not the Republicans. Indeed, I felt that Jones and McLean had pulled independent voters from me, and Jones may even have pulled some Democratic votes. Regardless of the "what ifs," I felt it was a decisive win. One odd aspect of this race was that I won with rather large margins in the rural areas of the state, while Mr. Bjerke (a farmer) had better results than me in cities such as Fargo and Bismarck. I was proud of my support in the rural areas. On the other hand, being a woman seemed to be a wash: Some people favored me because I was a woman, and likely an equal amount did not.

32 All states but Arkansas have a Commissioner or Director of Agriculture. There are 12 states that elect Commissioners (North Dakota, Iowa and 10 Southern states, including Texas and Louisiana.) The remainder of the states typically have a governor-appointee (analogous to a cabinet-level position) or the appointment is made by a board of agricultural leaders (e.g., Wisconsin). I am not sure if I can lay claim to being the first woman to serve as Agriculture Commissioner/Director to serve in the U.S. because I have heard that there were two women who had been acting or interim Commissioners prior to 1988. However, I think that if one considers permanent positions (not acting or interim), I may have been the first woman Agriculture Commissioner in U.S. history. It is a topic I have never researched.

33 The vote in this race was 170,237 (me) to 114,892 (Republican) to 12,708 (Independent.)

34 *North Dakota Blue Book 1995* (Bismarck: Secretary of State Al Jaeger, 1995)158-160.

35 2009 was the year in which Roger Johnson left North Dakota to head the National Farmers Union, and the year that Senate Budget Committee duties precluded Kent's continuing co-sponsorship.

36 MarketPlace for Kids was held in 10 locations and over 10,000 kids participated in 2013. Readers who wish to be supportive of a bright future for North Dakota can make a tax-deductible donation for the "kids"!

37 See Project Safe Send, 2011 Annual Report, available at the North Dakota Agriculture Department's website. This report has year-by-year totals of pounds received and participants. I believe the department also keeps a running tally of the pounds of specific chemicals received over the years, but it is not available online.

38 Predicted Further Economic Impacts of Biological Control of Leafy Spurge in the Upper Midwest (Ag. Econ. Report No. 382).

39 See "The Interactive Mill" at www.ndmill.com to place an order.

40 "ND State Mill Grinds Out Profits," *Grand Forks Herald,* August 7, 2013.

41 In sharp contrast, compare how the American Crystal Sugar cooperative recently treated its union workers by locking them out for two years. Though I always try to buy North Dakota products, I won't now buy Crystal Sugar. The farmer members of the cooperative should have hired Lloyd Omdahl to work out a better solution.

42 The current list of the communities in each quintile is available at http://banknd.nd.gov. Search for PACE Program.

43 See http://banknd.nd.gov. Search for AG-PACE Program.

44 At the time this chapter was written, a court had dismissed one case without prejudice, in order to require exhaustion of administrative remedies at the Industrial Commission. The other case had not been decided.

45 I now am a solo practitioner in what I call a "consulting law practice." See www.sarahvogellaw.com for my legal biography and key cases.

46 PSC Commissioners are elected to a six-year term. However, when I was appointed, only four years remained in the six-year term since Commissioner Dale Sandstrom had served two years of his term before being elected to the North Dakota Supreme Court. I needed to run in 1994, in the first general election after my appointment, and then again in 1996 for a full six-year term on the Commission.

47 *North Dakota Public Service Commission Biennial Report for the period ending June 30, 1995*, 4, State Archives, State Historical Society of North Dakota.

48 Superintendents Page on NDDPI Website, accessed 01/29/14. www.dpi.state.nd.us/dept/supt.shtm

49 *North Dakota Blue Book 2011-2013* (Bismarck: Secretary of State Al Jaeger, 2011) 255

50 Application of Beryl Levine (1984) to the Supreme Court (Bismarck Tribune Files)

51 Beryl Levine interviewed by author, August 21, 2008, Bismarck, North Dakota (recording deposited at North Dakota State University Archives).

52 Ibid.

53 Ibid.

54 Ibid.

55 Ibid.

56 Ibid.

57 Ibid.

58 Ibid.

59 Ibid.

60 Ibid.

61 Ibid.

62 Ibid.

63 Randy Bradbury, "Fargoan and Minot Man Named ND Justices," *Fargo Forum*, January 18, 1985, A1&A10.

64 Beryl Levine interviewed by author, August 21, 2008, Bismarck, North Dakota (recording deposited at North Dakota State University Archives); Randy Bradbury, "Fargoan and Minot Man Named ND Justices," *Fargo Forum*, January 18, 1985, A1&A10.

65 George Sinner interviewed by author, October 1, 2008, Fargo, North Dakota (recording deposited at North Dakota State University Archives).

66 Ibid; United States of America United States Declaration of Independence

67 George Sinner interviewed by author, October 1, 2008, Fargo, North Dakota (recording deposited at North Dakota State University Archives).

68 David K. Levine, "Justice Beryl Joyce Levine: Behind the Scenes," *North Dakota Law Review* 72 (1996): 1053.

69 *North Dakota Blue Book 1995-97* (Bismarck: Secretary of State Al Jaeger, 1995) 357.

70 *Gravning v. Gravning* 389 N.W.2d 621(N.D. 1986); William A. Neumann and Vigness Kolb, "A Woman's Touch," *North Dakota Law Review* 72 (1996): 961-65.

71 *Gravning v. Gravning* 389 N.W.2d 621(N.D. 1986); Neumann and Kolb, "A Woman's Touch" 961-65.

72 Ibid.

73 *Gravning v. Gravning* 389 N.W.2d 621(N.D. 1986).

74 Ibid.

75 Ibid.

76 Ibid.

77 Beryl Levine interviewed by author, August 21, 2008, Bismarck, North Dakota (recording deposited at North Dakota State University Archives).

78 Ibid.

79 *Dick v. Dick*, 414 N.W.2d 288 (N.D.1987).

80 Ibid.

81 Ibid.

82 Ibid.

83 Beryl Levine interviewed by author, August 21, 2008, Bismarck, North Dakota (recording deposited at North Dakota State University Archives).

84 Ibid.; Sarah Andrews Herman interviewed by author, February 11, 2009, Fargo, North Dakota (recording deposited at North Dakota State University Archives); Janell Cole, "N.D. intends to weed out sexism in legal community," *The Bismarck Tribune*, March 13, 1994, A1,A12.

85 Beryl Levine interviewed by author, August 21, 2008, Bismarck, North Dakota (recording deposited at North Dakota State University Archives).

86 Sarah Andrews Herman interviewed by author, February 11, 2009, Fargo, North Dakota (recording deposited at North Dakota State University Archives).

87 Ibid.

88 "A Difference in Perception: The Final Report of the North Dakota Commission on Gender Fairness in the Courts," *North Dakota Law Review* 72 (1996), 1140, 1142, 1150.

89 *Swenson v. Northern Crop Insurance, Inc., and John Krabseth,* 498 N.W.2d 174 (N.D. 1993).

90 Ibid.

91 Ibid.

92 Ibid.

93 Ibid.

94 Ibid.

95 Ibid.; Erickstad and Hagburg, "In Justice Beryl Levine's View," 944-50.

96 "In Re Application of Beryl J. Levine," 1984, Beryl Levine File, Bismarck Tribune Files.

97 *North Dakota Blue Book 2011-2013* (Bismarck: Secretary of State Al Jaeger, 2011) 211.

98 *North Dakota Blue Book, 2011-13* (Bismarck: Secretary of State Al Jaeger, 2011) 214.

99 83 N.D.L.Rev. 1 (2007).

100 *North Dakota Blue Book 2011-2013* (Bismarck: Secretary of State Al Jaeger, 2011) 212

101 Ibid, 214.

102 *Third Biennial Report of the Superintendent of Public Instruction to the Governor of North Dakota*, (Jamestown: Alert, State Printers and Binders, 1894), 22. In 2013, North Dakota had 181 school districts. Twelve districts did not have women serving on their school boards. Don Martinson (North Dakota School Boards Association) in discussion with the author, January 2013.

103 "State Fact Sheet – North Dakota," Center for American Women and Politics, Rutgers University, last modified January 2013, http://www.cawp.rutgers.edu/fast_facts/resources/state_fact_sheets/ND.php

104 William Mitchell served from November 1889 to March 1890, when he died unexpectedly. W.J. Clapp was appointed to fill the position in April 1890 and served through December 1891. John Ogden was elected in November 1890 and served in 1891-92.

105 *Superintendent of Public Instruction Administration Superintendents Record 1887-1897,* Series 1172, State Historical Society of North Dakota, State Archives, 191

106 "Autobiography of Laura J. Eisenhuth Alming," Historical Data Project, Pioneer Biography Files (Series 30529), State Archives, State Historical Society of North Dakota.

107 Ibid. Ancestry.Com and The Church of Jesus Christ of Latter-day Saints, *1880 United States Census*[database on-line], accessed February 6, 2013, http://search.ancestrylibrary.com ; also, "Women of the State, "*Western Womanhood*, September, 1894, 6.

108 "Mrs. Laura Eisenhuth," *The Record* (Fargo, North Dakota) June 1895, 8.

109 "Autobiography of Laura J. Eisenhuth Alming."

110 "Eisenhuth Dead," *The Fargo Forum and Daily Republican* (Fargo, North Dakota), May 15, 1902, evening edition, 10, and "Mrs. Laura Eisenhuth returns from Eastern Trip," *Bismarck Weekly Tribune*, November 3, 1893, 8.

111 "City News," *Jamestown Alert*, January 6, 1887, 8.

112 "Autobiography of Laura J. Eisenhuth Alming."

113 "Autobiography of Laura J. Eisenhuth Alming."

114 "Honor the Better Sex," *Carrington News*, June 7, 1888, 8; "Minnewaukan Siftings," *Jamestown Weekly Alert*, July 5, 1888, 8.

115 "Mrs. Laura Eisenhuth," *The Record* (Fargo, North Dakota), June 1895, 8.

116 Bertha Grant, "Wives and Daughters of the Administration," *Western Womanhood* (Buffalo, North Dakota), July 1894, 1.

117 *North Dakota History*, Unit 4: Set 1 – Woman's Suffrage at Statehood-Debates of the Constitutional Convention, (Bismarck; State Historical Society of North Dakota, 2013)

118 *Third Biennial Report of the Superintendent of Public Instruction to the Governor of North Dakota* (Jamestown: Alert, State Printers and Binders, 1894), 29-30.

119 *The North Dakota Blue Book*, (Bismarck: Tribune, State Printers and Binders, 1897) 25.

120 Robinson, *History of North Dakota*, 221.

121 "Mrs. Laura Eisenhuth," *The Record* (Fargo, North Dakota), June 1895, 8.

122 "Temperance Work," *Jamestown Weekly Alert*, October 2, 1890, 2.

123 Ibid., 8

124 Robinson, *History of North Dakota*, 221.

125 *Second Biennial Report of the Superintendent of Public Instruction to the Governor of North Dakota*, (Bismarck: Tribune, State Printers and Binders, 1892), 325-326

126 Ibid., 313

127 Ibid.

128 "Judge has Rendered Decision in Foster County," *Bismarck Weekly Tribune*, September 2, 1892, 4.

129 "Will Name a Full Ticket," *Bismarck Daily Tribune*, June 18, 1892, 3; Robinson, *History of North Dakota*, 223.

130 "Ticket." *Bismarck Weekly Tribune*, October 21, 1892, 2. Her name appeared on the ballot twice, as both an Independent and Democrat.

131 *Second Biennial Report*, 125.

132 Ibid., 257

133 "Educational Column," *The Citizen*, August 12, 1892, 8.

134 "Educational Column," *The Citizen*, November 4, 1892, 8.

135 Robinson, *History of North Dakota*, 223.

136 "Abstract of Votes Cast in the State of North Dakota, at the General Election, November 8th, 1892," *The Bismarck Daily Tribune*, December 16, 1894, 4.

137 *The General School Laws of the State of North Dakota* (Bismarck: Tribune, State Printers and Binders, 1890) 19-22.

138 United States Senator Lyman Casey was from Carrington and served from 1889-93.

139 *Superintendents Record*, 191-95

140 "And Nothing Crooked," *Bismarck Weekly Tribune*, February 17, 1893, 3.

141 *First Biennial Report of the Secretary of the Board of University and School Lands and Report of the Land Commissioner for the Period Ending June 30, 1894* (Jamestown, Alert, State Printers and Binders 1894) 4.

142 Robinson, *History of North Dakota*, 299. Each section is one square mile. There are 36 square miles in a township.

143 Ibid., 214.

144 *Third Biennial Report*, 10-11.

145 "And Nothing Crooked," *Bismarck Weekly Tribune*, February 17, 1893, 3.

146 *First Biennial Report of the Secretary of the Board of University and School Lands and Report of the Land Commissioner*, 4.

147 Ibid., 8.

148 Robinson, *History of North Dakota*, 324.

149 *Third Biennial Report*, 31.

150 Superintendents Laura Eisenhuth, John Ogden and Emma Bates all advocated for free text books for all students in the state, paid for by district or state funds.

151 *Ibid.,* 13-15.

152 *Fourth Biennial Report of the Superintendent of Public Instruction to the Governor of North Dakota,* (Jamestown: Alert, State Printers and Binders, 1896), 59

153 An apportionment was a distribution of funds to each school district.

154 George F. Bird and Edwin Taylor, Jr., *History of the City of Bismarck North Dakota, The First 100 Years, 1872-1972,* (Bismarck: Bismarck Centennial Association, 1972), 80.

155 Superintendent Eisenhuth made her own staff decisions as a state official. The governor did not have the power to endorse or nix these decisions.

156 *Superintendents Record,193*

157 Miss Emma Bates, a Republican who succeeded Mrs. Eisenhuth, did this also.

158 *Superintendents Record,* 204

159 *Ibid.*, 213-217

160 *Ibid.*, 195

161 "Notes and Comments," *Jamestown Weekly Alert*, February 9, 1893, 7.

162 "Mrs. Laura Eisenhuth's husband was in Ellendale," *Bismarck Weekly Tribune*, September 14, 1894, 4.

163 "Opposes Such Politics," *Fargo Forum*, September 22, 1894, 1.

164 *Superintendents Record,* 195

165 *Ibid.*, 195-96

166 *Third Biennial Report,* 39.

167 Bertha Grant, "Wives and Daughters of the Administration," *Western Womanhood* (Buffalo, North Dakota), July, 1894, 1.

168 "Off to Spiritwood," *Bismarck Weekly Tribune*, August 4, 1893, 3.

169 *North Dakota at the World's Columbian Exposition*, (Chicago: Authority, 1893) 83.

170 *Third Biennial Report,9,*10

171 *Ibid.,* 15-16.

172 *Ibid.*, 17-18. There was an increase of 19,611 children of school age during 1893 and 1894, and 202 new school houses built to accommodate the increase. *Third Biennial Report*, 9.

173 In 2013, North Dakota has 181 school districts. In 2012-13 school year, full-day kindergarten was provided in 173 districts, half-day kindergarten in three districts. Sherry Sayler (Management Information Systems, State of North Dakota Department of Public Instruction), in memo to the author, January 2013.

174 There was one free, publicly funded kindergarten in Fargo in 1894. *Third Biennial Report,* 405.

175 *Third Biennial Report,* 19-20.

176 *Ibid.*, 20, 22.

177 "Miss Emma Bates," *Western Womanhood* (Buffalo, North Dakota), September, 1894,2.

178 Fourth Biennial Report of the Superintendent of Public Instruction to the Governor of North Dakota (Jamestown: Alert, State Printers and Binders, 1896), 164.

179 "Women of the State," *Western Womenhood* (Buffalo, North Dakota), October 1894, 5.

180 "Women's Christian Temperance Union, The State Convention," *Western Womanhood,* October 1894, 6-7.

181 "Abstract of Votes by Counties, Cast at the General Election held November 6th, 1894, for the various State Officers, as returned by the several County Auditors," *Bismarck Daily Tribune* (Bismarck, North Dakota), December 20, 1894, 1.

182 Ibid.

183 "At Hillsboro," *Bismarck Weekly Tribune*, January 4, 1895, 8.

184 "Mrs. Laura J. Eisenhuth," *The Record* (Fargo, North Dakota), June, 1895, 8.

185 "Official Canvas of the Votes Cast at the General Election in North Dakota November 3, 1896," *Bismarck Daily Tribune*, (Bismarck, North Dakota), December 18, 1896, 2.

186 "Vote of North Dakota by Counties 1900, Returned to Secretary of State," *Bismarck Daily Tribune*, December 24, 1900, 4.

187 "Eisenhuth Dead," *The Fargo Forum and Daily Republican* (Fargo, North Dakota), May 15, 1902, evening edition, 10.

188 "Mrs Laura Eisenhuth is Assistant Principal," The Bismarck Weekly Tribune, September 28, 1903, 3.

189 "Early-Day Head of N.D. Schools Dies in Oregon," *The Fargo Forum*, (Fargo, North Dakota), October 1, 1937, morning edition, 1.

190 *Third Biennial Report,* 166.

191 *Ibid,* 27.

192 *Ibid,* 417.

193 *First Biennial Report of the Secretary of the Board of University and School Lands*, 8.

194 *Third Biennial Report*, 41-42.

195 *Fourth Biennial Report of the Superintendent of Public Instruction to the Governor of North Dakota* (Jamestown: Alert, State Printers and Binders, 1896) 38.

196 Republican Estelle Reel was also elected Wyoming State Superintendent of Public Instruction on November 6, 1894. "State Fact Sheet – North Dakota," Center for American Women and Politics, Rutgers University, last modified January 2013, www.cawp.rutgers.edu/fast_facts/resources/state_fact_sheet.

197 J.M. Devine was LaMoure County superintendent of schools and had run as the Republican candidate against Laura Eisenhuth in 1892.

198 "The Republicans Nominate," *Jamestown Weekly Alert*, 26 July, 1894, 1.

199 Ibid.

200 The 1860 census indicates that she lived in Otto, New York, in Cattaraugus County when she was 6 years old. Ancestry .com 1860 United States Federal Census [data base on line]. Accessed December 10, 2013.

201 "Emma F. Bates," *Bismarck Weekly Tribune*, January 11, 1895, 3. In 1870, Emma F. Bates lived in Forestville, New York, with her parents. Forestville is near Otto, New York, where Emma lived in 1860. Ancestry.com 1870 United States Federal Census [data base on line]. Accessed December 10, 2013.

202 Email to the author on December 10, 2013, from Ruth Andel, Archivist, Peltier Library, Allegheny College. Emma F. Bates was signed up for classes in Latin, German and Math during the fall of 1878, winter 1879 and spring 1879. There is no indication that she graduated.

203 *Twenty Second Biennial Report of the Superintendent of Public Instruction for the Period Ending June 30, 1932* (Fargo, Knight Printing Co., 1932), 40.

204 The Seminary of Western Pennsylvania is now Clarion University.

205 "Emma F. Bates," *Bismarck Weekly Tribune*, January 11, 1895, 3.

206 *Twenty Second Biennial Report of the Superintendent of Public Instruction*, 40.

207 "Sargent County ex. Rel to Miss Bates," *Fargo Forum*, November 5, 1894, 1.

208 *Second Biennial Report of the Superintendent of Public Instruction to the Governor of North Dakota* (Bismarck: Tribune, State Printers and Binders, 1892) 271-282.

209 Ibid., 263.

210 *Second Biennial Report of the Superintendent of Public Instruction,* 263.

211 *Fourth Biennial Report of the Superintendent of Public Instruction to the Governor of North Dakota* (Jamestown: Alert, State Printers and Binders, 1896), 164.

212 "Are Sworn In," *Fargo Forum and Daily Republican*, January 7, 1895, 1.

213 Donald H. Welsh, *Cornerstones,* (Valley City Times Record, Valley City, 1990) 18.

214 Ibid, 21.

215 "Salutatory," *Western Womanhood*, December 1895, 6; Western Womanhood, July 1896, 6.

216 "We boast of our free schools," *Western Womanhood*, December 1895, 6.

217 "The New Woman, *Western Womanhood*, February 1896, 6-7.

218 "New Year Greeting," *Western Womanhood*, January 1896, 6.

219 "Miss Emma F. Bates," *Western Womanhood*, September 1894, 2.

220 Ibid.

221 "Suffrage," *Western Womanhood*, January 1896, 2.

222 "North Dakota Kernals," *Fargo Forum*, July 14, 1896, 4. Emma was elected Vice President of the National Education Association when she attended their national meeting in Buffalo, New York, in July, 1896.

223 "Governor Miller Chairman," *Fargo Forum*, July 18, 1894, 1.

224 Ticket Echoes," *Fargo Forum*, July 20, 1894, 1.

225 "Baker Gets It," *Jamestown Weekly Alert*, January 3, 1895, 7.

226 "Are Sworn In," *Fargo Forum and Daily Republican*, January 7, 1895, 1.

227 Ibid., 1.

228 "Kiff on Prohibition," *Fargo Forum*, August 22, 1894, 1.

229 Emma Bates, "True Education," *Western Womanhood*, July, 1894, 2.

230 "She's All Right," *Bismarck Weekly Tribune*, October 12, 1894, 6.

231 "Miss Bates," *Bismarck Weekly Tribune*, October 12, 1894, 5, 6.

232 "Women of the State," *Western Womanhood*, October 1894, 5.

233 "Women's Christian Temperance Union, The State Convention," *Western Womanhood*, October 1894, 6-7.

234 "Emma F. Bates," *Bismarck Weekly Tribune*, October 26, 1894, 1.

235 "Sargent Co ex Rel to Miss Bates," *Fargo Forum and Republican*, November 5, 1894, 1.

236 "Abstract of Votes by Counties, Cast at the General Election held November 6, 1894, for the Various State Officers, as returned by the Several County Auditors," *Bismarck Daily Tribune*, December 20, 1894, 1.

237 "State Ticket Cass County," *Fargo Forum and Daily Republican*, November 8, 1894, 1.

238 "Rumpus Among the Ladies," *Fargo Forum and Daily Republican*, January 8, 1895, 1.

239 *The General School Laws of the State of North Dakota*, (Grand Forks, North Dakota: Herald, State Printers and Binders, 1896) 23-25, 46.

240 A covered carriage entrance.

241 "The State Capitol," *Fargo Forum*, September 8, 1894, 1.

242 Ibid.

243 "Baker Gets It," *Jamestown Weekly Alert*, January 3, 1895, 7.

244 The Superintendents Record – 1887-1897, 247-298. Series 1172, Superintendent of Public Instruction Administration, State Archives, State Historical Society of North Dakota.

245 *Fourth Biennial Report*, 15.

246 Ibid., 18.

247 Ibid., 57.

248 Ibid., 58.

249 Ibid., 12.

250 Ibid., 16.

251 Robinson, *History of North Dakota*, 226.

252 William Budge led the campaign to raise $26,000 to save the University of North Dakota. Robinson, *History of North Dakota*, 309. In 1896, people wanted Budge to be the Republican candidate for governor. "Heads of Messes," *Fargo Forum*, July 21, 1896, 1.

253 *Fourth Biennial Report*, 20.

254 "Clerk Hire," *Bismarck Tribune*, February 22, 1895, 1.

255 *Biennial Report of the Secretary of the Board of University and School Lands for the Period Ending June 30, 1896* (Jamestown: Alert State Printers and Binders, 1896) 3.

256 *Fourth Biennial Report of the Superintendent of Public Instruction*, 19

257 Ibid., 19.

258 Ibid., 19.

259 *Superintendents Record 1887-97*, 279.

260 "Common Schools" was the term used for one-room schools where one teacher taught the subjects needed for grades 1-8.

261 *Fourth Biennial Report of the Superintendent of Public Instruction*, 11.

262 Ibid., 34.

263 Ibid., 35.

264 Ibid., 47.

265 Ibid., 147.

266 Ibid., 10.

267 "The State Capitol," *Fargo Forum*, September 8, 1894, 1

268 *Superintendent of Public Instruction Administration Superintendents Record 1887-1897*, Series 1172, State Historical Society of North Dakota, State Archives, 268-269.

269 Jon Mielke, Associate Research Fellow, (Upper Great Plains Transportation Institute), in discussion with the author, February 4, 2013.

270 "The Jamestown Capital," Bismarck Weekly Tribune, October 18, 1895, 4.

271 *Second Biennial Report of the Superintendent of Public Instruction*, 141-218.

272 *Twenty Second Biennial Report of the Superintendent of Public Instruction*, 41.

273 *Fourth Biennial Report of the Superintendent of Public Instruction*, 20.

274 Ibid., 165-189.

275 Ibid., 18.

276 Ibid., 21.

277 "North Dakota Kernals," *Fargo Forum*, July 14, 1896, 4.

278 "The electrical disturbances of politics," *Western Womanhood*, November 1896, 6-7. This article gives a recap of the campaign between Bates and Eisenhuth from a suffrage perspective.

279 "Heads of Messes," *Fargo Forum*, (Fargo, North Dakota), July 21, 1896, 1.

280 Ibid. The buttons are for William Budge. See note 252.

281 Ibid.

282 Elwyn B. Robinson, *The History of North Dakota*, (Lincoln: University of Nebraska Press, 1966) 230-31. However, Robinson goes on to say that Frank Briggs, who the Republicans endorsed for Governor in 1896, was the choice of the McKenzie machine. Ibid., 231.

283 "Robby, Pat, & Jud," *Fargo Forum*, (Fargo, North Dakota), July 22, 1896, 1.

284 Ibid.

285 "The electrical disturbances of politics," *Western Womanhood*, November 1896, 6-7.

286 "Independent Candidate," *Fargo Forum*, July 25, 1896, 1.

287 "Official Canvas of the Votes Cast at the General Election in North Dakota November 3, 1896," *Bismarck Daily Tribune,* December 18, 1896, 2.

288 *Twenty Second Biennial Report of the Superintendent of Public Instruction*, 42.

289 Ancestry.com.*California Passenger and Crew Lists, 1882-57* [database online], accessed February 6, 2013, http://search.ancestrylibrary.com.

290 *Twenty Second Biennial Report of the Superintendent of Public Instruction,* 40.

291 Ancestry.com. *1920 United States Federal Census* [database on- line], accessed February 6, 2013, http://search.ancestrylibrary.com. Ancestry.com. *US City Directories for 1821-1989 – Oakland City Directory: 1913,14, 15, 16, 17[database online],*accessed February 6, 2013, http://search.ancestrylibrary.com.

292 "Emma F. Bates, Superintendent Public Instruction," *The Record*, May 1895, 40.

293 "My Business is Education, Not Politics, Says Miss M. Nielson," *Fargo Forum and Daily Republican*, January 11, 1919, 1.

294 Miss Nielson was endorsed by the "Lincoln Republican League," in a split with the Nonpartisan League (NPL) Republicans.

295 "Spanish Influenza," *Bismarck Tribune*, October 10, 1918, 4. See also "Some Influenza Information," *Ward County Independent*, October 24, 1918, 1.

296 "Pioneer Teachers of Barnes County – a biography of Isabell Stewart-Sampson-Spurr," Nielson Papers, Barnes County Historical Society.

297 William Langer, *The Nonpartisan League – Its Birth, Activities and Leaders*, (Mandan: Morton County Farmers Press, 1920) 197-98.

298 "Langer's Opinion – Attorney General Declares Miss Minnie J. Nielson Qualified to be State Superintendent of Public Instruction,"1918, Series 10107, (A107/3/14) Nielson Family Papers, State Archives, State Historical Society of North Dakota (SHSND).

299 "Minnie Jean Nielson," Series 10107, Box 4, Nielson Family Papers, State Archives, SHSND.

300 "Pioneer Couple Celebrates Golden Wedding Last Night," *Daily Times Record*, April 10, 1923, 1.

301 "Complete Program for Meeting of State Educational Association," Bismarck Daily Tribune, September 27, 1910, 6.

302 "The Proof of the Pudding - 1918 Campaign Pamphlet," Series 10107, A/107/3/14, Nielson Family Papers, State Archives, SHSND, 18. Also, "Do You Remember When," Nielson Papers, Barnes County Historical Society.

303 Draft Resume for Minnie Jean Nielson, Series 10107, A107/1/25 Nielson Family Papers, State Archives, SHSND.

304 *Twenty-Second Biennial Report of the Superintendent of Public Instruction For the Period Ending June 30, 1932,* (1932), 51.

305 Geelan, *Dakota Maverick*, 132.

306 "Pioneer Teachers of Barnes County," Nielson Papers, Barnes County Historical Society.

307 "The Proof of the Pudding – 1918 Campaign Pamphlet," Series 10107, Nielson Family Papers, State Archives, SHSND, 3, 4, 6.

308 Ibid, 18.

309 "GOP Ticket headed by John Steen is picked at Minot Meet," *Fargo Forum and Daily Republican*, May 2, 1918, 1.

310 "The Fargo Post," *Weekly Times Record*, May 23, 1918, 2.

311 Robert Morlan, *Political Prairie Fire – The Non-Partisan League, 1915-1922*, (Minneapolis: University of Minnesota Press, 1955), 5.

312 "Miscellaneous clippings by the Pollock Clipping Bureau of Minnie Jean Nielson, 1918," Series 10107, Nielson Family Papers, State Archives, SHSND.

313 Ibid.

314 "Minnie J. Nielson will have United Support of Women in Primaries is Prevailing Belief-June 20, 1918," Miscellaneous clippings by the Pollock Clipping Bureau, Series 10107, Nielson Family Papers, State Archives, SHSND.

315 "Miscellaneous clippings by the Pollock Clipping Bureau," Nielson Family Papers.

316 "The Peoples Candidate for the Office of Superintendent of Public Instruction," Series, 10107, Nielson Family Papers, State Archives, SHSND.

317 "The Proof of the Pudding," Series 10107, Nielson Family Papers, State Archives, SHSND.

318 "Office of Educators Campaign Committee,"1918, Series 10107, Nielson Family Papers, State Archives, SHSND.

319 "Let the Truth Become Known," *Valley City Weekly Times Record*, October 24, 1918, 8.

320 "False Claims of False Friends as Compared to Real Facts," *The North Dakota Leader*, October 26, 1918, 2.

321 "State to Ballot Next Tuesday on Socialism; Both Sides Confident," *Fargo Forum and Daily Republican*, November 2, 1918, 1.

322 North Dakota Secretary of State Website, March 18, 2013.

323 George McFarland, *State of North Dakota General School Laws*, (Bismarck: Bismarck Tribune, 1919) 15-17, 129, 190, 209. Also, *1919 Legislative Manual* (Bismarck: Secretary of State Thomas Hall, 1919) 10-20.

324 "1918 Certificate of Election," Series 10107, Nielson Family Papers, State Archives, SHSND.

325 "Miss Palmer on State Supt. Staff," *Williston Graphic*, December 19, 1918, 1.

326 Macdonald will not Quit Office until Ousted by Order of Court," *Fargo Forum and Daily Republican*, January 6, 1919, 1.

327 "Incumbents in State Job are Loath to Quit," *Bismarck Daily Tribune*, January 6, 1919, 1.

328 "Macdonald will not Quit Office until Ousted by Order of Court," *Fargo Forum and Daily Republican*, January 6, 1919, 1.

329 "Supreme Court Hears Petition to Oust Mac's," *Bismarck Daily Tribune*, January 9, 1919, 2. Also, "Macdonald Loses Office Grab Case," *Fargo Forum and Daily Republican*, January 10, 1919, 1.

330 "My Business is Education, not Politics, Says Miss M. Nielson," *Fargo Forum and Daily Republican*, January 11, 1919, 1.

331 Ibid.

332 Ibid.

333 "County School Superintendents Will Meet Here," *Bismarck Daily Tribune*, January 14, 1919, 2.

334 "Program for County School Heads' Meeting," *Bismarck Daily Tribune*, January 22, 1919, 5.

335 *Sixteenth Biennial Report of the Superintendent of Public Instruction to the Governor of North Dakota for the two years ending June 30th, 1920*, (Bismarck: Bismarck Tribune, 1920) 119

336 "Macdonald is Again Seeking to Oust Rival," *Bismarck Daily Tribune*, January 23, 1919, 1.

337 "My Business is Education, Not Politics, Says Miss M. Nielson," *Fargo Forum and Daily Republican*, January 11, 1919, 1.

338 Agnes Geelan, *The Dakota Maverick*, (Fargo: Kaye's Printing Company, 1975), 41.

339 Ibid, 50. Bill Langer in 1920 was running for governor on the IVA ticket and distributed his book during his campaign.

340 William Langer, *The Nonpartisan League – Its Birth, Activities and Leaders,* (Mandan: Morton County Farmers Press, 1920), 201. Langer's text was as follows: "Senate Bill 134 gives the State Board of Education, which is the Governor, power to reach down in every local community …"

341 Ibid. 201. Langer's text did not include the word "educational" before Institutions.

342 This paragraph was written by Nielson.

343 In her speech, Miss Nielson refers to herself as "me" rather than referring to herself in the third person as Langer did in his book.

344 Langer, *The Non-Partisan League*, 202. Nielson wrote this sentence. Langer's text read, "Under the old law the State Superintendent was President of the Board of Education, and the Deputy Superintendent was Secretary."

345 Ibid. 199-203. See also "A Message to Minnesota Womanhood (Pamphlet), Reprinted from Minnesota Issues by the Minnesota Sound Government Association, St. Paul, MN, 1920," Masonic Collection, Institute for Regional Studies Archives, North Dakota State University.

346 "A Message to Minnesota Womanhood", 8. See also Langer, "*The Non-Partisan League*," 206.

347 McDonald v. Nielson, 175 N.W. 361, (1919), 362.

348 Ibid., 361.

349 Ibid., 364.

350 State ex el Langer v. Totten, 175 NW 563 (1919), 564.

351 Geelan, *The Dakota Maverick*, 45.

352 *First Annual Report of the (North Dakota) Board of Administration to the Governor*, (Bismarck, 1919), 34.

353 Ibid., 113-140.

354 Larry Remele, "The North Dakota State Library Scandal of 1919," *North Dakota History, Journal of the Northern Plains*, Volume 44, Winter 1977, No. 1, 23.

355 "Report of the Book and Library Investigating Committee, December 10, 1919," *Journal of the House*, Sixteenth Legislative Assembly, 339.

356 Geelan, *The Dakota Maverick*, 45.

357 The "gathering" Miss Nielson is referring to is a gathering of members of the Board of Administration. Since the Board was composed of five members, any "gathering" of over three members establishes a quorum of the board, and hence should be an official meeting of the Board of Administration.

358 "Report of the Book and Library Investigating Committee, December 10, 1919," 337-8.

359 "Resume of Minnie Jean Nielson," Series 10107, Folder A107/1/25, SHSND, 2.

360 *Sixteenth Biennial Report*, 148.

361 *Biennial Report of the Superintendent of Public Instruction for the Period Ending June 30, 1922,* (Grand Forks: Normanden Publishing Co, 1922), 173-74.

362 "Chairman of Conference Organizing Committee Sends Cordial Greetings," *North Dakota Welfare News and Views*, Public Welfare Board of North Dakota (Bismarck, North Dakota) Volume 4, Number 11, September 1948, 15.

363 Jim McMillan, "The Macdonald-Nielson Imbroglio: The Politics of Education in North Dakota, 1918-1921," *North Dakota History, Journal of the Northern Plains*, Volume 52, Number 4, Fall 1985, 9. Macdonald died in 1923 at the age of 47.

364 "Minnie Nielson Night in local movie theatres," *Bismarck Tribune*, October 22, 1920, 2.

365 This charge and others in this article refer to the speeches Miss Nielson gave in September as noted in "A Message to Minnesota Womanhood."

366 "Minnie Nielson Confident that League will be Defeated Nov. 2," *Fargo Forum*, October 30, 1920, 1.

367 *Laws passed at the Seventeenth Session of Legislative Assembly of the State of North Dakota*, (Grand Forks: Normanden Publishing Co, 1921), 256.

368 Geelan, *Dakota Maverick*, 47-52.

369 *Sixteenth Biennial Report* , 119

370 Ibid., 122-26.

371 *Biennial Report of the Superintendent of Public Instruction for the Periods Ending June 30, 1924 and June 30, 1926,* (Fargo: Knight Printing Co, 1926), 44-45.

372 "January 1922 Letters from Congressman Young and Secretary of Commerce Herbert Hoover," Nielson Family Papers, Series 10107, A107/2/10, State Archives, SHSND.

373 *Biennial Report Ending 1924 and 1926*, 44-45.

374 Ibid., 46.

375 Ibid., 50.

376 Draft Resume for Minnie Jean Nielson, Nielson Family Papers, Series 10107, A107/1/25 State Archives, SHSND.

377 Ibid.

378 "Miss Minnie Nielson Dies Thursday Afternoon," *Valley City Times-Record*, February 28, 1958, 1.

379 "The Proof of the Pudding," Nielson Family Papers, Series 10107, State Archives, SHSND, 8.

380 *Biennial Report Ending 1924 and 1926*, 45.

381 "The original manuscript for the state hymn given to Miss Nielson, 1926," Series, 10107, Box 4, Nielson Family Papers, State Archives, SHSND.

382 "Miss Minnie Nielson Dies Thursday Afternoon," *Valley City Times-Record*, February 28, 1958, 1.

383 "November 4, 1932, KFYR Radio Broadcast," *Bertha Rachel Palmer Papers*, Collection 10098, Box 8, A98/8/3, State Archives, State Historical Society of North Dakota (SHSND).

384 "Bertha Rachel Palmer," Bertha Palmer Vertical File, State Archives, North Dakota State Historical Society.

385 Elwyn B. Robinson, *History of North Dakota*, (Lincoln: University of Nebraska Press, 1966), 534.

386 "Bertha Rachel Palmer," *Bertha Rachel Palmer General Information File*, SHSND Reference.

387 *Bertha Rachel Palmer Papers*, Collection 10098, Book 1, (1926), State Archives, SHSND.

388 Ibid.

389 "Bertha Palmer Funeral Friday," *Bertha Rachel Palmer General Information File*, State Archives, SHSND.

390 "Bertha Rachel Palmer," *Bertha Rachel Palmer General Information File.*

391 Ibid.

392 Ibid.

393 "Pioneer Couple Celebrates Golden Wedding Last Night," *Daily Times Record*, April 10, 1923, 1.

394 "Art Series includes Fargo," *Fargo Forum*, February 2, 1924, 5.

395 *Bertha Rachel Palmer Papers*, Collection 10098, Book 1, (1923), State Archives, SHSND.

396 Ibid.

397 *Bertha Rachel Palmer Papers*, Collection 10098, Box 8, A98/8/11, State Archives, SHSND.

398 "Differences of Opinion cause Bertha Palmer to Quit Office," *Bertha Rachel Palmer Papers*, Collection 10098, Book 1, (1924), State Archives, SHSND.

399 "Bertha Palmer gives views on Office of State Superintendent," *Fargo Forum*, May 2, 1924, 3.

400 Ibid.

401 *Bertha Rachel Palmer Papers*, Collection 10098, Book 1 (1924), State Archives, SHSND.

402 Ibid.

403 "Bertha Palmer Campaign Ad," *Bismarck Tribune*, November 1, 1924, 2; November 3, 1924, 3.

404 "Oldness Leads Candidates in Official Vote," *Bismarck Tribune*, December 4, 1924, 3

405 "Appreciation of North Dakota," May 24, 1925, *Bertha Rachel Palmer Papers*, Collection 10098, Book 1.

406 I encourage readers to obtain this delightful book from the North Dakota State Library. It is a wonderful travelogue of the state from the 1920s, and these spots are still well worth a visit today.

407 "Bertha Palmer Files Petition," *Bertha Rachel Palmer Papers*, Collection 10098, Book 1 (1926), State Archives, SHSND.

408 "North Dakota Fails to Get Excited Over Nov. 2 Election," *Fargo Forum*, October 15, 1926, 1,2.

409 *Bertha Rachel Palmer Papers*, Collection 10098, Box 8, A98/8/10, State Archives, SHSND.

410 *Bertha Rachel Palmer Papers*, Collection 10098, Box 8, A98/8/11, State Archives, SHSND.

411 "North Dakota Fails to Get Excited Over Nov. 2 Election," *Fargo Forum*, October 15, 1926, 1, 2.

412 "Senate Control is Coveted Election Prize," *Fargo Forum*, November 1, 1926, 1, 3.

413 "Exceptionally Light Vote is Seen in All Parts of ND," *Fargo Forum*, November 2, 1926, 1.

414 "Women in Politics, From the New York Times," *Fargo Forum*, October 18, 1926, 4.

415 "Official Abstract of Votes Cast at the General Election Held on Nov.2, 1926," *Bismarck Tribune*, December 13, 1926, 5.

416 *State of North Dakota General School Laws*, (Fargo: Knight Printing Co., 1927) 23-25, 50,107,131.

417 "Governor A.G. Sorlie's Message to the 20th Legislative Assembly," *Bismarck Tribune*, January 4, 1927, 2.

418 *Bertha Rachel Palmer Papers*, Collection 10098, Box 3, A98/7/18, State Archives, SHSND.

419 Ibid.

420 "North Dakotans Greet Governor Sorlie and other State Officials at Inaugural Reception," *Bismarck Tribune*, January 5, 1927, 1.

421 "Beautiful Gowns Worn at Inaugural Reception Tuesday," *Bismarck Tribune*, January 5, 1927, 5.

422 "County Superintendents Disapprove Religious Education Bill, 43 to 6," *Bismarck Tribune*, January 19, 1926, 8.

423 Ibid.

424 "Bakken Wants Commandments in All Schools," *Bismarck Tribune*, January 15, 1927, 8.

425 *Laws Passed at the Twentieth Session of the Legislative Assembly of the State of North Dakota*, (Fargo: Knight Printing Co., 1927) 411.

426 Bertha Rachel Palmer Papers, Collection 10098, Book 1 (1927), State Archives, SHSND.

427 Ibid.

428 Kylah Aull, (North Dakota Legislative Council, Research Librarian), in memo to the author, May 10, 2013.

429 *Twenty First Biennial Report of the Superintendent of Public Instruction for the Period Ending June 30, 1930*, 5.

430 Ibid.

431 Ibid., 22.

432 Ibid, 22-37.

433 *Laws Passed at the 22nd Session of the Legislative Assembly of the State of North Dakota*, (Bismarck: Bismarck Tribune, 1931) 416.

434 "November 4, 1932, KFYR Radio Broadcast," *Bertha Rachel Palmer Papers*, Collection 10098, Box 8, A98/8/3, State Archives, SHSND.

435 Robinson, *History of North Dakota,*) 564.

436 *Bertha Rachel Palmer Papers*, Collection # 10098, Box 8, A98/8/3, State Archives, SHSND.

437 Six radio stations around the state broadcast the programs simultaneously. The state Department of Public Instruction prepared the material and the county superintendents in each area arranged the "talent" to read and sing. "The North Dakota Saturday School of the Air," *Bertha Rachel Palmer Papers*, Collection 10098, Box 8, A98/8/3, State Archives, SHSND.

438 "Education by Radio," *Bertha Rachel Palmer Papers*, Collection 10098, Box 8, A98/8/3, State Archives, SHSND.

439 *Twenty-first Biennial Report of the Superintendent of Public Instruction*, 12.

440 "The North Dakota Saturday School of the Air," *Bertha Rachel Palmer Papers*, Collection 10098, Box 8, A98/8/3, State Archives, SHSND.

441 "Conflagration Guts Capitol," *Fargo Forum*, December 29, 1930, 6.

442 "State Offices Get Quarters," *Fargo Forum*, December 29, 1930, 6.

443 "State Records in Chaos as Fire Destroys ND Capitol," *Fargo Forum*, December 29, 1930, 1.

444 *Bertha Rachel Palmer Papers*, Collection 10098, Box 8, A98/8/5, State Archives, SHSND.

445 Agnes Geelan, *The Dakota Maverick*, (Fargo: Kaye's Printing Company, 1975) 59.

446 Robinson, *History of North Dakota*, 379.

447 Ibid., 377.

448 Ibid.

449 Ibid., 398.

450 Ibid., 399.

451 *Bertha Rachel Palmer Papers*, Collection 10098, Book 1 (1931), State Archives, SHSND.

452 Ibid. (1932)

453 *Twenty-second Biennial Report of the Superintendent of Public Instruction for the period ending June 30, 1932,* 15-55.

454 *Bertha Rachel Palmer Papers*, Collection 10098, Box 3, A98/7/23, State Archives, SHSND.

455 Ibid.

456 *Bertha Rachel Palmer Papers*, Collection 10098, Box 8, A98/8/3, State Archives, SHSND.

457 "Official Abstract of Votes Cast at the General Election Held November 8, 1932," *Bismarck Tribune*, December 17, 1932, 2.

458 Robinson, History of North Dakota, 404.

459 "Bertha Palmer to Leave State," *Bertha Rachel Palmer Papers*, Collection 10098, Book 1 (1931) State Archives, SHSND.

460 "Farewell Luncheon is Given for Miss Palmer," *Bismarck Tribune*, December 23, 1932, *Bertha Rachel Palmer Papers*, Collection 10098, Book 1, State Archives, SHSND.

461 *Twenty-second Biennial Report of the Superintendent of Public Instruction*, 53.

462 *Bertha Rachel Palmer Papers*, Collection 10098, Box 3, A98/7/23, State Archives, SHSND.

463 "Berta E. Baker, Republican Candidate for Re-Election to the Office of State Auditor, 1940, *Bismarck Tribune* Files.

464 "Skulls Are Fractured; Bert Baker is Killed," *Fargo Forum*, May 5, 1924, 1.

465 Ibid.

466 Ibid.

467 Ancestry.com *Social Security Death Index* [database on-line], Provo, Utah, USA: Ancestry.com Operations Inc, 2011.

468 "Mrs. Berta Baker, State Auditor 24 Years, Dies," *Minot Daily News*, May 4, 1964, 1.

469 "Skulls Are Fractured; Bert Baker is Killed," *Fargo Forum*, May 5, 1924, 1.

470 "Berta E. Baker," 1928, *Bismarck Tribune* Files.

471 "Christmas Brings Back Memories," *The Bismarck Tribune*, December 12, 1955, 1.

472 Elwyn Robinson, *History of North Dakota*, (Lincoln, University of Nebraska Press, 1966), 349.

473 *1954 North Dakota Blue Book* (Bismarck: Bismarck Tribune, 1954), 49.

474 "Maddock, Richardson, Scott foremost in Governorship Gossip," *Bismarck Tribune*, February 7, 1928, 1.

475 "T.H. Thoresen is candidate for Governor," *Bismarck Tribune*, February 10, 1928, 1.

476 "Mrs. Berta Baker Plans Retirement From Public Office At End Of Year," *Minot Daily News*, March 27, 1956, 1.

477 "Mrs. Berta Baker, State Auditor 24 Years, Dies," *Minot Daily News*, May 4, 1964, 1.

478 "Berta E. Baker," 1928, *Bismarck Tribune* Files.

479 Charles Liessman, ed, *Manual for the State of North Dakota – 1932* (Bismarck: Bismarck Tribune, 1932) 33,34.

480 "Governor Shafer Better Today," *Fargo Forum*, January 5, 1929, 1.

481 1932 Annual State Treasurer Report, 4, *North Dakota Treasurer 20th-45th Annual Reports, 1922-1947* (Grand Forks: Normanden Publishing Co., 1948).

482 *23rd Biennial Report of the State Auditor to the Governor of North Dakota*, 33.

483 "Mrs. Redington, Velva Woman, Dies in Minot," *Minot Daily News*, April 1, 1930, 1.

484 Ibid.

485 "State Auditor," June 6, 1938, *Bismarck Tribune* Files.

486 "Ranks Shaken as Progressive Affiliation is Out of the Picture," *Fargo Forum* evening edition, March 4, 1932, 8.

487 "Tremendous Crowd Packs Auditorium at War Memorial," *Bismarck Tribune*, January 5, 1933, 5.

488 Ibid.

489 Richard Lowitt and Maurine Beasley, ed, *One Third of a Nation – Lorena Hickok Reports on the Great Depression*, (Urbana: University of Illinois Press, 1983) xiii.

490 Robinson, 400.

491 Ibid., 406.

492 "100 percent job" means 100 percent of the relief comes from federal funds.

493 Hickok is referring here to rural people in the *county* – just Morton County.

494 Lowitt and Beasley, 56, 57, 58.

495 Robinson, 408.

496 Ibid., 407.

497 "Federal Relief In State Is $1,500,000 Monthly," *The Bismarck Capital*, August 7, 1934, 3.

498 *North Dakota Blue Book 1942* (Bismarck: Secretary of State Herman Thorson, 1942) 14.

499 *North Dakota Treasurer 20th -45th Annual Reports, 1922-1947.*

500 *26th Biennial Report of the State Auditor to the Governor of North Dakota*, 33.

501 Ibid., 33.

502 *23rd Biennial Report of the State Auditor to the Governor of ND*, 33. Eighty years later, the North Dakota Office of Management and Budget estimated that the general fund surplus would be more than $1.66 billion on June 30, 2013. "Surplus estimate keeps growing," Bismarck Tribune, June 19, 2013, 1.

503 1932 Annual State Treasurer's Report, 4.

504 *North Dakota Centennial Blue Book, 1889-1989*, (n.p: 1989) 439.

505 *23rd Biennial Report of the State Auditor to the Governor of ND*, 41.

506 *Chapter 8, State Budget*, Supplement to the 1913 compiled laws of North Dakota, 1913-1925, (Rochester, N.Y.: The Lawyers' Co-operative Publishing Co., 1926) 312, 313.

507 Larry Remele, ed, *The North Dakota State Capitol: Architecture and History*, (n.p.: The State Historical Society of North Dakota, 1989)51.

508 Ibid., 45.

509 Ibid., 46.

510 "Kelly Asks Aid of State Troops," *Bismarck Capitol*, July 19, 1934, 5.

511 William Langer, cleared of the charges, was elected governor again in 1936.

512 Robinson, 410, 411.

513 *Manual for State of North Dakota-1932*, 59.

514 Article 8, Section 375. State Auditing Board; Duties; *Supplement to the 1913 Compiled Laws of North Dakota, 1913-1925* (Rochester, N.Y.: The Lawyers' Co-operative Publishing Co., 1926)209.

515 State v. Baker, 262 NW, 183.

516 *Return and Answer to Petition for Writ of Mandamus, Ibid.*

517 State v. Baker, 262 NW, 184.

518 Stray v. Baker, 281 NW, 86.

519 King v. Baker, 288 NW, 565.

520 State v. Baker, 288 NW, 202.

521 *27th Biennial Report of the State Auditor*, 37.

522 Ibid., 39.

523 Robinson, 421, 427.

524 "Berta E. Baker, Republican Candidate for Re-Election to the Office of State Auditor, 1940, *Bismarck Tribune* Files.

525 "Why Should You Be the People's Choice," October 8, 1942, *Bismarck Tribune* Files.

526 Department of State Highways v. Baker, 290 N.W. 257.

527 "Court Upholds Additional Gasoline Tax," *Bismarck Tribune*, June 17, 1940, 1.

528 Department of State Highways v. Baker, 290 N.W. 257.

529 Ibid., 260.

530 Ibid.

531 King v.Baker, 299 N.W. 247.

532 "Court Holds ND Must Pay $5,979 to Stark People," *Bismarck Tribune*, July 15, 1941, 3.

533 Moses v. Baker, 299 N.W. 315.

534 State v. Baker, 299 N.W. 574.

535 The motor vehicle fuel tax remained part of her office responsibilities all the time Baker was Auditor.

536 "Enforcement Act to Suffer Same Fate as HB 44," *Bismarck Tribune*, July 26, 1941, 8.

537 Ford Motor Co. v. Baker, 300 N.W. 435.

538 Langer v. State, 284 N.W. 238.

539 State v. Baker, 3 N.W. 2nd, 802.

540 State v. Baker, 21 N.W. 2nd, 355.

541 The new attorney general was Nels G. Johnson.

542 State v. Baker, 21 N.W. 2nd, 368.

543 Ibid., 358.

544 Ibid., 364.

545 *32nd Biennial Report of the State Auditor to the Governor of ND*, 73.

546 Ibid., 76.

547 Robinson, 447.

548 Phone conversation with Tom Rafferty, Verendrye Electric Cooperative, June 14, 2013.

549 "No Nervousness at Breakfast With Ike, Mrs. Baker Says," *Bismarck Tribune*, June 10, 1955, 8.

550 Ibid.

551 "Editorials – Political Forces Redeployed," *Bismarck Tribune*, March 24, 1956, 4.

552 "New Names Dominate NPL Primary Ticket," *Bismarck Tribune*, March 30, 1956, 1.

553 "Mrs. Berta Baker Plans Retirement From Public Office at End of Year," *Minot Daily News*, March 27, 1956, 1.

554 "Duffy gets No 2 Spot on GOP State Ticket; Seven Incumbents Endorsed," *Fargo Forum*, April 6, 1956, 6.

555 "Mrs. Berta E. Baker," *Minot Daily News*, March 28, 1956, 4.

556 "Mrs. Berta Baker, State Auditor 24 Years, Dies," *Minot Daily News*, May 4, 1964, 1.

557 "New Auditor Really 'Going Back Home,' " *Bismarck Tribune*, April 2, 1979, 17.

558 *Resume of Bernice Muriel Asbridge*, Grand Forks Herald Collection, Biographical Clippings File, Series III, Box 5, Folder 29, UND Archives.

559 Photograph of Bernice at 1969 inaugural Ball, records of Donna Lafave.

560 "2,000 Greet Guys at Relaxed Inaugural Ball," *Bismarck Tribune*, January 1969, records of Donna Lafave.

561 Ibid.

562 Interview with Donna Lafave, daughter of Bernice Asbridge, June 2013.

563 Ibid.

564 "Burleigh auditor is set to stop taxing, start relaxing," *Bismarck Tribune*, January 8, 1987, 8A.

565 Resume of Bernice Muriel Asbridge, *Grand Forks Herald* Collection OGLH864, Series III, Box 5, University of North Dakota Archives.

566 Interview with Donna Lafave, daughter of Bernice Asbridge, June 2013.

567 Resume of Bernice Muriel Asbridge, *Grand Forks Herald* Collection OGLH864, Series III, Box 5, University of North Dakota Archives.

568 Theodore Caplow, Louis Hicks, Ben J. Wattenberg, *The First Measured Century – An Illustrated Guide to the Trends in America, 1900-2000*, (Washington, D.C., The AEI Press, 2001) 38.

569 Interview with Donna Lafave, June 2013.

570 Resume of Bernice Muriel Asbridge, *Grand Forks Herald* Collection OGLH864, Series III, Box 5, University of North Dakota Archives.

571 "Auditor's World of Figures Dull? Not at All, Says Bernice Asbridge," *The Bismarck Tribune*, January 7, 1966, 7.

572 Interview with Donna Lafave, June 2013.

573 "Auditor's World of Figures Dull? Not at All, Says Bernice Asbridge," *Bismarck Tribune*, January 7, 1966, 7.

574 Ibid.

575 Note: This is the poem attached to the letter:

LITTLE JOHN
DEAR LITTLE JOHN, YOU ARE ONLY THREE,
BUT WHAT A MAN YOU'LL GROW UP TO BE.
THE WHOLE WORLD MOURNED YOUR FATHER'S DEATH,
OUR HEARTS WENT OUT TO THOSE HE LEFT.
YOU GRASPED THE HAND OF YOUR SAINT-LIKE MOTHER,
CONTINUE, JOHN, SHE IS LIKE NONE OTHER.
YOUR LITTLE HAND SLIPPED FROM ITS USUSAL PLACE
AND SALUTED THE DEAD WITH SUCH EASE AND GRACE.
YOU NOW ARE THE HEAD OF YOUR FAMILY, JOHN.
YOUR FATHER'S WORK, YOU MUST CARRY ON.
WITH GOD'S GUIDING HAND AND LOVE TO ALL,
THE WORLD OF TODAY WITH SURVIVE HIS FALL.
YOU WILL GROW, LITTLE JOHN, BIG AND STRONG
WITH LOVE IN YOUR HEART TO RIGHT THIS WRONG.
WE'LL WAIT, LITTLE JOHN, WE'LL WAIT AND SEE
WHAT A MAN, GROWN-UP, YOU ARE DESTINED TO BE.

576 Letter to Mrs. Kennedy, November 1963, records of Donna Lafave.

577 "Donald Asbridge, 47, Is Dead Here; Funeral Friday," March 3, 1964, Bernice Asbridge *Bismarck Tribune* Files.

578 "My Darling," December 1963, records of Donna Lafave.

579 "Burleigh Auditor Enters the Race for State Office," May 5, 1968, *Bismarck Tribune Files*.

580 Governor Guy had already been elected to two-year terms in 1960 and1962, and a four-year term in 1964.

581 "Doherty Gets Nod," *Bismarck Tribune*, Junel 5, 1968, 1.

582 Ibid.

583 "Biographical Sketch, Mrs. Bernice Asbridge," November 1968, *Bismarck Tribune* File.

584 Ibid.

585 Penny Palm Card, 1968, records of Donna LaFave.

586 1968 Bernice Asbridge Campaign Poster, records of Donna LaFave.

587 Victory Help flier, 1968, records of Donna LaFave.

588 Official Abstract of Votes Cast at the General Election Held November 5, 1968, North Dakota Secretary of State Website accessed July 2013.

589 Interview with Donna Lafave, June 2013.

590 "State Job is 'Just Bigger' to Mrs. Asbridge," December 11, 1968, *Bismarck Tribune* File.

591 "Bernice Asbridge Moves Up," *Bismarck Tribune*, November 9, 1968, 3.

592 "FB Women Hosts At Dinner Meeting," May 8, 1970, *Devils Lake Journal*, records of Donna La-Fave.

593 *Letter from Bernice Asbridge to Agnes Geelan*, File 11078, State Archives, North Dakota State Historical Society.

594 1975 North Dakota Century Code, Chapter 5-03 Sale and Taxation of Liquor.

595 January 7, 1969, Attorney General Opinion to Honorable Bernice Asbridge, State Treasurer re: Taxation – Alcoholic Beverages – Federal Instrumentalities Exempt.

596 Ibid.

597 "Plug for Loophole in Liquor Sales Asked in Senate," *Bismarck Tribune*, January 20, 1969, 6.

598 Ibid.

599 *Laws at the Forty First Session of the Legislative Assembly of the State of North Dakota*, (State of North Dakota, 1969) 180.

600 Letter from Bernice Asbridge, State Treasurer to Agnes Geelan, Chairman of Workmen's Compensation, April 19, 1971, Archives SHSND, File 11078, File 2/17.

601 "North Dakota State Investment Board Minutes," Wednesday, March 5, 1969, File 30187, Folder 13, Archives SHSND.

602 "She Could Be Chatting With the Nixon Family," April 15, 1969, records of Donna LaFave.

603 Ibid.

604 "New Auditor Really 'Going Back Home,' " 1978, *Bismarck Tribune*, records of Donna LaFave.

605 "Asbridge," Bismarck Tribune, November 3, 1972, 15.

606 *Sixty-eighth Annual Report of the State Treasurer of North Dakota* (Bismarck, *Bismarck Tribune*, 1970) 23.

607 *Seventieth Annual Report of the State Treasurer of North Dakota* (1972) 25.

608 "State Canvassing Board Meeting was Brief," September 1970, records of Donna LaFave.

609 "Delegate, Treasurer Meet Citizens," *Bismarck Tribune*, January, 1972, records of Donna Lafave.

610 Dean Bard, Editor, *Debates of the North Dakota Constitutional Convention, Vol. 1*, (Bismarck, Quality Printing Service, 1972) XIV.

611 *North Dakota Constitutional Convention, A Newspaper Account*, Vol I, (Bismarck: State Library Com mission, 1974) 364.

612 Ibid., 367.

613 Ibid.

614 Ibid.

615 Ibid., 375.

616 *North Dakota Constitutional Convention, A Newspaper Account*, Vol. 4, (Bismarck, State Library Commission, 1974) 1948.

617 Dean Bard, Editor, *North Dakota Constitutional Convention,* Vol. 1, XV.

618 "NDFRW Support Mrs. Asbridge," January 18, 1972, *Bismarck Tribune* Files.

619 "Lignite Gas Plant Planned," *Bismarck Tribune*, May 2, 1972, 1.

620 "Over 1000 Arrests Reported – Protests Hit 23 States," *Bismarck Tribune*, May 12, 1972, 1.

621 "Pentagon Restroom Damaged by Bomb," *Bismarck Tribune*, May 19, 1972, 1.

622 Official Abstract of Votes Cast at the General Election Held November 7, 1972, North Dakota Secretary of State Website accessed July 2013.

623 Resume of Bernice Muriel Asbridge, *Grand Forks Herald* Collection OGLH864, Series III, Box 5, University of North Dakota Archives.

624 "New Auditor Really 'Going Back Home'," *Bismarck Tribune*, April 2, 1979, 17.

625 "She Doesn't have to Be Handy, But It Helps," December 9, 1967, *Bismarck Tribune* Bernice Asbridge Files.

626 Speech to Girls State, June 2, 1986, Ruth Meiers Collection, Box 6, Series 31811, Archives State Historical Society of North Dakota.

627 Ruth Meiers Biographical Information, Box 1, Series 31811, State Archives, North Dakota State Historical Society.

628 Schedule for Lieutenant Governor, June 23-27, 1986, Ruth Meiers Collection, Box 3, Series 31811.

629 Elwyn B. Robinson, *History of North Dakota* (Lincoln: University of Nebraska Press, 1966) 244.

630 "Meiers services today and Monday," *Minot Daily News*, March 21, 1987, A4.

631 Speech to Centennial Planning Commission, October 25, 1985, Ruth Meiers Collection, Box 6, Series 31811.

632 Speech to Young Author's Conference , 1985, Ruth Meiers Collection, Box 6, Series 31811.

633 Axel Olson, Ruth Meiers Collection, Box 9, Series 31811.

634 Speech to Lincoln Women of Today and Jaycees, June 16, 1986, Ruth Meiers Collection, Box 6, Series 31811.

635 "Last Interview," *Bismarck Tribune*, 22 March 1987, 1D.

636 Biographical Information, Ruth Meiers Collection, Box 1, Series 31811.

637 National Archives and Records Administration, WWII, Prisoners of War, 1941-46 [database on-line] Provo, Utah. USA: Ancestry.Com Operations Inc., 2005.

638 "Miss Ruth Olson Bride of Dallas Pariseau," *Mountrail County Record*, October 3, 1946, 1.

639 Ruth Meier and Ruth Pariseau Payroll Records, Mountrail County Auditor's Office, Provided by County Auditor Joan Hollekim, to the author, November 26, 2013.

640 Divorce date provided to the author by Helen Grant, Clerk of Court Office, Mountrail County, December 4, 2013.

641 Elwyn B. Robinson, *History of North Dakota,* 443.

642 "Education for Social Work in North Dakota," *North Dakota Welfare News and Views,* April 1948, Vol. 4, Number 6, (Bismarck, ND) 11.

643 "Public Assistance Cases," *Ibid,* 15.

644 "Meiers services today and Monday," *Minot Daily News*, March 21, 1987, A4.

645 Ruth Meier and Ruth Pariseau Payroll Records, Mountrail County Auditor's Office.

646 *12th Biennial Report of the Public Welfare Board of ND for the Period Ending June 30, 1958, and 13th Biennial Report of the Public Welfare Board of ND for the Period Ending June 30, 1960* (Bismarck: Capitol) 8.

647 "Last Interview," *Bismarck Tribune*, March 22, 1987, 1D.

648 *Bismarck Tribune*, March 24, 1987, 41, Bismarck Tribune Archives

649 T. N. Tangedahl, *From Vision to Legacy, Social Services in North Dakota*, (Bismarck: North Department of Human Services, 1989) 33-34.

650 "Who's Lt. Gov? 'I'm she,'" *Bismarck Tribune*, Ruth Meiers Collection, Box 9, Series 31811.

651 Glenn and Ruth Meiers, Ruth Meiers Collection Box 9, Series 31811.

652 1977 ND Legislature Biographical Sketches, Ruth Meiers 1925-1987 File, Archives of the State Historical Society of North Dakota.

653 "Lt. Gov. Meiers is very visible in state Senate," *The Williston Daily Herald*, February 12, 1985, 1.

654 Feminism in Rural America, Speech to the National Women's Political Caucus, June 28, 1985, Ruth Meiers Collection, Box 6, Series 31811.

655 Ibid.

656 Ibid.

657 Glenn and Ruth Meiers, Ruth Meiers Collection, Box 9, Series 31811.

658 "Who's Lt. Gov? 'I'm she,'" *Bismarck Tribune*, Box 9, Series 31811

659 Biographical Information, Ruth Meiers Collection, Box 1, Series, 31811.

660 George Sinner and Bob Jansen, *Turning Points*, (Washburn: The Dakota Institute Press of the Lewis & Clark Fort Mandan Foundation, 2011) 100.

661 "Democrats turn to woman for Lieutenant Gov.," *Bismarck Tribune*, April 15, 1984, 1.

662 "Lt. Gov. Meiers is very visible in state Senate," *Williston Daily Herald*, February 12, 1985, 7A.

663 Ibid.

664 "Democrats turn to a woman for Lieutenant Gov.," *Bismarck Tribune*, April 15, 1984, 1.

665 Ibid.

666 US Senator Heidi Heitkamp, Interview by the author, Bismarck, ND, June 29, 2013.

667 "Meiers: Do more for displaced homemakers," August 27, 1984, Bismarck Tribune Archives.

668 "Meiers: GOP circulating false letter," August 28, 1984, Bismarck Tribune Archives.

669 "Management comes in for criticism," September 18, 1984, Bismarck Tribune Archives.

670 "Meiers: Olson's ads wrong; cancel them," October 11, 1984, Bismarck Tribune Archives.

671 "Parties continue to trade tax charges," October 24, 1984, Bismarck Tribune Archives.

672 "Official Abstract of Votes Cast at the General Election Held November 6, 1984," North Dakota Secretary of State Website, accessed November 20, 2013.

673 George Sinner and Bob Jansen, *Turning Points*, 104-06.

674 Newly elected Governor Sinner hired almost all new staff for the governor's office. When staff decisions were finalized, Lieutenant Governor Meiers had one administrative assistant to help her with her work and access to other staff in the governor's office.

675 Letter from Ruth Meiers to Constituents January 31, 1985, Ruth Meiers Collection, Box 4, Series 31811.

676 *North Dakota Centennial Blue Book, 1889-1989* (Bismarck: Secretary of State Ben Meier, 1989) 143.

677 Ibid.

678 "Lt. Gov. Meiers is very visible in state Senate, *Williston Daily Herald*, February 12, 1985, 7A.

679 *Governor's Commission on Children and Adolescents at Risk* (Bismarck: Office of the Lieutenant Governor, 1986) 110.

680 Governor Sinners remarks when he signed the executive order establishing the Commission on Services for Children and Adolescents at Risk, January 31, 1985, Ruth Meiers Collection, Box 4, Series 31811

681 The coordinator was Elllen Glood, an employee of the North Dakota Mental Health Association.

682 Draft Letter to CAAR Commission Subcommittee Members, August 30, 1985, Ruth Meiers Collection, Box 4, Series 31811.

683 Speech to Budget Committee on Human Services, May 20, 1986, Ruth Meiers Collection, Box 6, Series 31811.

684 *Governor's Commission on Children and Adolescents at Risk*, 112.

685 Don Schmid, Assistant Chair of CAAR, Interview by the author, November 9, 2013.

686 Ibid. The Ruth Meiers Adolescent Center in Grand Forks was dedicated on June 15, 1989.

687 The Women's Role in Politics, Ruth Meiers Collection, Box 6, Series 31811.

688 Speech to NOW Convention, March 2, 1985, Ruth Meiers Collection, Box 6, Series 31811.

689 Speech to Girls State, June 2, 1986, Ruth Meiers Collection, Box 6, Series 31811.

690 "Meiers to tackle top job in Senate," *Bismarck Tribune*, January 6, 1985, 20L.

691 Biographical Information, Ruth Meiers Collection, Box 1, Series 31811.

692 1986 Biographical Sketchbook for National Conference of Lieutenant Governors, Ruth Meiers Collection, Box 1, Series 31811.

693 Letter from Rutgers Center for the American Woman and Politics to Ruth Meiers, April 9, 1985, Ruth Meiers Collection, Box 9, Series 31811.

694 "Who's Lt. Gov? 'I'm she'," *Bismarck Tribune*, Ruth Meiers Collection, Box 9, Series 31811.

695 Ruth Meiers Collection, Box 4, Series 31811.

696 Elizabeth Hampsted, "Ruth Meiers Travels to Russia," *Plainswoman*, October 1986, Vol. 10, Number 2, 10.

697 "Meiers on three-week Soviet 'mission," *Bismarck Tribune*, April 28, 1986, 18.

698 "Meiers says Soviets deserve more facts," *Bismarck Tribune*, May 19, 1986, Bismarck Tribune Archives.

699 Ibid.

700 "Meiers calls women in Soviet Union free," *Fargo Forum*, May 20, 1986, A6.

701 Women Make a Difference, Speech to National Association of Social Workers, May 29, 1986, Ruth Meiers Collection, Box 6, Series 31811.

702 Elizabeth Hampsten, "Ruth Meiers travels to Russia," *The Plainswomen*, October 1986, Vol. 10, Number 2, 10.

703 "Who's Lt. Gov? 'I'm she'," *Bismarck Tribune*, Ruth Meiers Collection, Box 9, Series 31811.

704 Letter to Jerzy Bala, August 22, 1986, Ruth Meiers Collection, Box 9, Series 31811.

705 In 1981, Ruth had a previous bout with cancer when a tumor was removed from her thyroid. "Meiers' cancer inoperable," *The Forum*, September 13, 1986, 1.

706 "Last Interview," *Bismarck Tribune*, March 22, 1987, 1D.

707 "Meiers televises cancer story, *Bismarck Tribune*, October 22, 1986, 24.

708 "Meiers doctors to operate," *Bismarck Tribune*, December 17, 1986, 28.

709 "Meiers refuses to surrender to cancer," *Bismarck Tribune*, October 16, 1986, 25.

710 "Last Interview," *Bismarck Tribune*, March 22, 1987, 1D.

711 Ibid.

712 George Sinner and Bob Jansen, *Turning Points*, 250.

713 Ibid.

714 "Centennial Planning Session – October 25, 1985," Speech, Ruth Meiers Collection, Box 6, Series 31811.

715 Bjorn Benson, Elizabeth Hampsten and Kathryn Sweney, Editors, *Day In, Day Out – Women's Lives in North Dakota,* (Grand Forks, University of North Dakota 1988)

716 See, e.g., Witt, Linda, Karen Paget and Glenna Matthews. 1994. *Running as a Woman.* New York: Free Press.

717 Sanbonmatsu, Kira, and Kathleen Dolan. 2009. "Do Gender Stereotypes Transcend Party?" *Political Research Quarterly,* 62: 485-494; Dolan, Kathleen. 2012. "Political Gender Stereotypes and Voting for Women Candidates in 2010." Paper presented at the annual meeting of the Southern Political Science Association.

718 For example, potential female candidates are more likely than male potential candidates to name the school board as a position they would consider pursuing (Lawless and Fox 2005, 49) and there is a correlation between prioritizing "women's issues" and the intent to run for office (*ibid.,* page 83). Moreover, women who have been elected to state legislatures tend to come from education and health occupations more than male state legislators (Sanbonmatsu, Kira, Susan J. Carroll and Debbie Walsh. 2009. "Poised to Run: Women's Pathways to the State Legislatures." New Brunswick, N.J.: Center for American Women and Politics. Accessed at http://www.cawp.rutgers.edu/research/reports/PoisedtoRun.pdf, page 20).

719 For a list of studies that have concluded this, see page 67 of Lawless, Jennifer, and Kathryn Pearson. 2008. "The Primary Reason for Women's Underrepresentation? Reevaluating the Conventional Wisdom." *Journal of Politics* 70: 67-82.

720 Krantz-Kent, Rachel. 2009. "Measuring time spent in unpaid household work: results from the American Time Use Survey." *Monthly Labor Review*, July. Accessed at http://www.bls.gov/opub/mlr/2009/07/art3full.pdf.

721 Heitkamp's discussion in Chapter 1 of coming to the realization that she couldn't do *everything* – campaigning, working, parenting – and do it perfectly is a refreshingly frank discussion of the pressures of such a position. It is, I would argue, to our detriment that we don't have more women with young children in positions of power, given the particular constraints and concerns these citizens face. And yet, it is entirely understandable that these are the very people who don't have the

time or energy for such endeavors. What is the answer? How can we make space for these voices and concerns at a crowded table? What of men with small children? I sometimes think the discussion shouldn't *always* be about how women can have what men have, but also discuss how men could have what women have – the desire to, when necessary, make the difficult decision to put home and family above professional or political concerns.

722 Lawless and Fox. 2005, 88.

723 Lawless and Fox. 2005; Lawless, Jennifer L., and Richard L. Fox. 2012. "Men Rule: The Continued Underrepresentation of Women in U.S. Politics." Washington, D.C.: Women & Politics Institute. Accessed at https://www.american.edu/spa/wpi/upload/2012-Men-Rule-Report-web.pdf.

724 For citations on the pervasiveness of this phenomenon, see Chapter 6 of Lawless and Fox. 2005.

INDEX

Page numbers in *italics* indicate the full profile of the woman, which includes an official photograph.
Page numbers in **bold** indicate photographs and/or captions.
Endnotes indicated as "n" with the number of the note.